Religion and Contemporary Liberalism

Notes on Contributors

Paul J. Weithman
Assistant Professor of Philosophy
University of Notre Dame

Robert Audi
Charles J. Mach Distinguished Service Professor of Philosophy
University of Nebraska

Sanford Levinson
W. St. John Garwood and W. St. John Garwood, Jr., Centennial Chair in Law
University of Texas Law School

Martha Nussbaum
Ernst Freund Professor of Law and Ethics
The Law School and The Divinity School
The University of Chicago

Philip L. Quinn
John A. O'Brien Chair in Philosophy
University of Notre Dame

Nicholas Wolterstorff
Noah Porter Professor of Philosophical Theology
Yale Divinity School

Timothy Jackson
Assistant Professor of Christian Ethics
Candler School of Theology
Emory University

Jorge Garcia
Professor of Philosophy
Rutgers University.

Jean Bethke Elshtain
Laura Spelman Rockefeller Professor of Social and Political Ethics
The Divinity School
The University of Chicago

John Coleman, S.J.
Charles Cassasa Chair in Social Values
Loyola Marymount University

David Hollenbach, S.J.
Margaret O'Brien Flatley Professor of Catholic Theology
Boston College

Religion and Contemporary Liberalism

Edited by Paul J. Weithman

University of Notre Dame Press
1997

Library of Congress Cataloging-in-Publication Data

Religion and contemporary liberalism / edited by Paul J. Weithman.
   p. cm.
  Includes bibliographical references and index.
  ISBN 0-268-01658-5 (cloth : alk. paper). — ISBN 0-268-01659-3 (pbk. : alk.
paper)
  1. Christianity and politics. 2. Liberalism. I. Weithman, Paul J., 1959- .
BR115.P7R4338 1997
261.7—dc21   97-1806
                                                 CIP

Contents

Acknowledgments   *vii*

Introduction: Religion and the Liberalism of Reasoned Respect
    Paul J. Weithman   *1*

The State, the Church, and the Citizen
    Robert Audi   *38*

Abstinence and Exclusion: What Does Liberalism Demand of the
    Religiously Oriented (Would Be) Judge?
    Sanford Levinson   *76*

Religion and Women's Human Rights
    Martha C. Nussbaum   *93*

Political Liberalisms and Their Exclusions of the Religious
    Philip L. Quinn   *138*

Why We Should Reject What Liberalism Tells Us about Speaking
    and Acting in Public for Religious Reasons
    Nicholas Wolterstorff   *162*

The Return of the Prodigal? Liberal Theory and Religious
    Pluralism
    Timothy P. Jackson   *182*

Liberal Theory, Human Freedom, and the Politics of Sexual
    Morality
    J. L. A. Garcia   *218*

The Question Concerning Authority
    Jean Elshtain   *253*

Deprivatizing Religion and Revitalizing Citizenship
    John A. Coleman S.J.   *264*

Politically Active Churches: Some Empirical Prolegomena to a
    Normative Approach
    David Hollenbach, S.J.   *291*

Index   *307*

Acknowledgments

This volume contains the proceedings of the conference "Religion and Contemporary Liberalism" held at the University of Notre Dame on February 23 and 24, 1995. The conference was made possible by a generous grant from the Paul M. and Barbara Henkels Visiting Scholars Series. I am grateful to the Henkels family for their generous support of this conference and for their continuing support of the series of which it was a part. Henkels grants are administered by the Institute for Scholarship in the Liberal Arts at the University of Notre Dame's College of Arts and Letters, directed by Professor Jennifer Warlick. I am also grateful for financial support from the John A. O'Brien Chair in Philosophy at Notre Dame, held by Philip Quinn, and from the Jacques Maritain Center at the University of Notre Dame, directed by Ralph McInerny, the Michael P. Grace Chair in Philosophy. The Department of Philosophy at the University of Notre Dame bore some of the costs associated with the conference and with the production of this volume. Thanks are therefore due to Professors Gary Gutting and Steve Watson, respectively the former and current chairs of the department.

The conference could not have been held without the staff of the Center for Continuing Education at the University of Notre Dame, whose expertise is surely without equal. Special thanks are due to Peter Lombardo, the Center's director, and to Harriet Baldwin, the Center's conference administrator.

Those who attended the conference contributed their thoughts and their questions and without them the weekend would have been much the poorer. I particularly appreciate the enthusiastic response to the conference from my colleagues on the faculty here at Notre Dame. Of course no conference is possible without speakers. The speakers at this conference displayed a marvelous generosity of spirit throughout the weekend even in the face of deep and enduring disagreements. I am deeply grateful to them for setting so high a tone of collegiality and civility; in so doing they exemplified what is best in academic life. Special thanks are due to Fr. Theodore Hesburgh, President Emeritus of the University of Notre Dame, for opening the conference, and to Todd Whitmore of the Department of Theology at the University of Notre Dame, M. Kathleen Caveny of the Notre Dame Law School, James Davis of the Department of Sociology at the University of Chicago, and David Solomon of the Department of Philosophy at Notre Dame, for chairing conference sessions.

The cover of the paperback edition is based on the poster used to advertise the conference. It reproduces a rare aquatint of a portrait of Thomas Jefferson. The portrait from which the aquatint was executed was drawn by Jefferson's friend the Polish Catholic patriot Tadeus Kosciusko. It seemed appropriate to advertise a conference on religion and politics with a portrait of Jefferson, the great champion of American religious liberty. The aquatint—the Pierpont Morgan Library, New York, MA 6024—appears by the library's kind permission. The conference poster was designed by Diann Nelson and executed by Apollo Printing of South Bend, Indiana. For their help with pre-conference publicity I am grateful to Irfan Khawaja and Coleen Hoover. I am also grateful to the staff at the University of Notre Dame Press for their work on this book and to Rebecca Konyndyk DeYoung for her help at various stages of its production.

The contributors to this book differ in their religious commitments. Several would be reluctant to describe themselves as liberals while others would readily do so. In spite of their doctrinal and philosophical differences, authors of the essays in this book made common cause on a task that religion and liberalism agree has an urgent claim on our resources: that of liberating humanity from the scourges of poverty, famine, and disease. All royalties from this volume are being donated to Oxfam America. Contributors readily agreed to forego them to help the good people of Oxfam in their continuing efforts to feed the hungry, heal the sick, and clothe the naked. For that act of charity, and for the high quality of their work, they richly deserve the reader's commendation.

Paul J. Weithman, Editor
Department of Philosophy
University of Notre Dame

Introduction: Religion and the Liberalism of Reasoned Respect

Paul J. Weithman

I.

It is a shibboleth of contemporary American political analysis that religion and liberalism are mutually antagonistic. This commonplace draws some credence from the fact that the most visible religious political activism currently favors conservative candidates. It draws more from the fact that some of the policies most prominently associated with American liberalism are opposed by religious conservatives. Religion's opposition to liberalism appears to have been reciprocated, at least in the United States, for liberalism seems no kinder to the religious than the religious are supportive of liberalism. A recent best-selling book argued that liberalism has created a public "culture of disbelief" in America, a culture in which liberal politics and jurisprudence trivialize religion.[1] Nor is the United States the only country in which liberalism and religion are at odds. Religious fundamentalism is among the most potent political forces of the contemporary world. Where it is present, it is often directed against liberal ideals and policies.[2] The fact that there is a religious backlash against liberalism in so many parts of the world suggests that an explanation of this backlash should be sought in the nature of the antagonists.

Many find an explanation ready to hand. Liberal politics and culture, they think, instantiate a political philosophy that has been hostile to religion from its infancy. According to one standard version of the history of political thought, liberal philosophy was conceived in reaction to the wars of religion. It was premised on the supposition that religion poses a threat to political stability and so early liberal theorists attempted to isolate common moral principles which could serve as the basis of government. Given religious pluralism, those principles were secular. The only way to avert the threat religion posed to stability was to relegate religious practice to a private sphere of thought and conduct. Latter-day liberal philosophers, it is said, have inherited the assumption that religion poses a threat to the orderly practice of liberal democracy. They find that assumption confirmed by the resurgence of militant fundamentalisms around the world and by the ascendancy of the religious right in the United States. The liberal philosophical tradition there-

---

1   Stephen Carter, *The Culture of Disbelief* (New York: Basic Books, 1993).

2   *Fundamentalisms Observed: The Fundamentalism Project*, vol. I (Chicago: University of Chicago Press, 1991) eds. Marty and Appleby, xiii.

fore retains its founding suspicion of religion as a force which can destabilize politics. Contemporary liberals continue to seek a common ground as the basis of agreement and endorse their tradition's founding strategy of privatizing religion to cope with the threat it poses. For their part, the stock explanation continues, religious citizens think liberals mistrust and marginalize them. They think liberals do so because liberals harbor the suspicions of religion on which liberal theory has long been premised. Thus the tension between religion and liberalism so characteristic of contemporary politics is generated by a tension between religion and the political philosophy liberal politics embodies. The defining and offending feature of liberal political philosophy, the explanation concludes, is its lingering suspicion that political expressions of religion threaten the stability of liberal democracy.

One of the most important conclusions of the present volume is that the standard explanation is doubly mistaken. It misrepresents the way liberal political philosophers treat the political expression of religion. It also misrepresents the reservations that some religious critics of liberalism have about contemporary political philosophy. This volume contains the papers presented at a conference which was held at the University of Notre Dame in February of 1996. The Notre Dame conference brought together a small number of scholars from philosophy, political science, sociology, religious ethics, and the law in order to provide an overview of work on liberal political philosophy and the place of religion within it. The conference was held because some of the most interesting challenges to philosophical liberalism's discussion of religion come from those outside the discipline of philosophy. Unfortunately, disciplinary barriers often prevent sustained and systematic exchange among philosophical liberals and their theological, sociological, and legal critics. The papers, taken together, show the fruitfulness of an interdisciplinary approach to the questions at issue. They show that religious criticisms of liberalism depend upon empirical claims about what social and cultural conditions democracy requires, about the importance of religion in realizing those conditions, and about how citizens can develop the civic virtues. The papers therefore show that philosophical differences between liberalism and religion are tied to political and sociological differences. The result, I shall suggest, is to raise a number of questions that liberals will have to answer, questions that would not have arisen in an exchange among philosophers alone.

The importance of these questions dispels two other misconceptions. It might be thought that questions about religion and liberalism are of marginal philosophical interest, deriving their significance from the salience of religion in contemporary politics. This impression might be sustained by current philosophical literature, which too often treats of religion and politics without rethinking key concepts or questioning fundamental assumptions. On the contrary, this volume shows that to examine liberalism's treatment of religion is to raise some of the most important questions in political philosophy, questions about the nature of citizenship and civic friendship, about the proper role of secondary associations and about how those associations should be conceptualized by political theory. In dispelling this first misconception, however, the volume seems to foster a second. It might be thought that religion's criticisms of liberalism reflect philosophical differences so fundamental that they preclude meaningful exchange. This volume points to the opposite conclusion. It suggests that contemporary liberalism may have difficulty coming to grips with questions its proponents are committed to answering in their own terms.

A formidable obstacle faces attempts to reconceive the standard view that philosophical liberals think religion a threat to political stability. That view has become the standard one in part because so many philosophical liberals seem to endorse it. A cursory reading of contemporary liberal philosophers suggests that many of them are impressed by the disruptive character of religion and the real possibility of religiously inspired political violence. It further suggests that they define themselves and their tradition by a distinctively liberal strategy for averting that threat. Thus Charles Larmore sees sectarian warfare as the alternative to liberalism.[3] Robert Audi, one of the contributors to this volume, harbors similar fears. He concludes one of his articles by remarking, "We are prone to extremes in the service of our holy causes. Conflicting secular ideas, even when firmly held, can often be blended and harmonized in the crucible of free discussion; but a clash of gods is like a meeting of an irresistible force with an immovable object."[4] David Richards thinks the strategy of privatizing and then tolerating religion is central to liberalism, and he argues for its extension to non-religious areas of thought, speech and conduct.[5] John Rawls explicitly locates the origins of liberalism in the aftermath of the wars of religion, takes religious toleration as one of liberalism's defining achievements and famously argues that toleration should be extended to philosophy itself.[6] Richard Rorty writes that a public world "disenchanted" of religion and metaphysics "lie[s] at the end of the road we liberal intellectuals have been travelling since the Enlightenment".[7] The gradual secularization of public life

---

3   Charles Larmore, "Political Liberalism," *Political Theory* 18 (1990): 357.

4   Robert Audi, "The Separation of Church and State and the Obligations of Citizenship," *Philosophy and Public Affairs* 18 (1989): 296. See also his "The Place of Religious Argument in a Free and Democratic Society," *San Diego Law Review* 30 (1993): 691, and his contribution to this volume.

5   David A. J. Richards, *Toleration and the Constitution* (New York: Oxford University Press, 1986), 68, 243–44.

6   John Rawls, *Political Liberalism* (New York: Columbia University Press, 1993) xxiv ff., 10, 154.

7   The road metaphor comes from Richard Rorty, "Thugs and Theorists: A Reply to Bernstein," *Political Theory* 15 (1987): 578 n. 25. Rorty talks of a disenchanted world in "The Priority of Democracy to Philosophy," *The Virginia Statute for*

is, he thinks, the Enlightenment's "central achievement" and the way in which liberal democracies have achieved civic peace.[8]

The truth is not as simple as a quick reading of liberal philosophers suggests, and the path from the Enlightenment to a culture of disbelief was far more tortuous than Rorty's easy historiography indicates. A more accurate map would show that the path had no one trailhead. It would show that, while early liberals were concerned to find a lasting and peaceful settlement to the wars of religion, they were concerned to show the illegitimacy of absolute rule as well. It would show that they were inspired by modern science and what it suggested about the ability of human reason to understand social and political arrangements.[9] A more subtle map of Rorty's path would also mark a number of forks in various states of repair. Some are now overgrown because they were trod by only a pioneering few; others, trod by those who defended religious liberalisms, may now be obscured but they are periodically cleared and traveled anew. Despite its twists, turns, and offshoots, the winding road traveled by liberal theory runs parallel to the tangled history of liberal politics. At important periods of American history, religious political activism favored liberal causes like abolition and civil rights. And American liberalism has a complex history even in this century, with some strands according far less importance to individual rights than what now passes for liberalism in the United States.[10]

In the short space of an introduction I can neither provide a more accurate history of liberal theory nor paint a balanced picture of contemporary political philosophy. The best way to present the issues and conclusions of the conference is to depict one strain of contemporary liberal thought and show where many of conference papers criticized and departed from it. That strain, which I shall refer to as the "liberalism of reasoned respect," is found in the work of John Rawls and was represented at the conference by Robert Audi. The central animating idea of the liberalism of reasoned respect is a vision of an ideal and well- ordered society of civility and mutual respect. To specify this ideal, its proponents attempt to isolate a set of values and principles that reasonable citizens could willingly and publicly endorse as the basis of that society's political arrangements; given the pluralism of the modern world, religious values and principles will not, as such, be members of that set. The ideal of a

---

Religious Freedom, ed. Peterson and Vaughn (New York: Cambridge University Press, 1988), 264.

8   Richard Rorty, "Religion as Conversation-Stopper," *Common Knowledge* 3 (1994): 1.

9   See Jeremy Waldron, "Theoretical Foundations of Liberalism" in his *Liberal Rights* (New York: Cambridge University Press, 1993), 35–62.

10   Here I rely on Alan Brinkley, *The End of Reform* (New York: Alfred A. Knopf, 1995).

well-ordered society helps locate exactly what is wrong with appealing to values outside the set, like religious values, in public political argument. It is not wrong because it leads to social and political instability. Rather, it is said, appealing to those values in public political argument might undermine the conditions necessary for the pursuit of basic justice. Furthermore, according to the liberalism of reasoned respect, when reasonable citizens cooperate on the basis of principles they can publicly endorse before one another, they cooperate on the basis of their common reason. Cooperation on the basis of common reasonability itself engenders distinctive forms of civic friendship and mutual respect. Appeal to values and principles outside the set in public political argument, or cooperation on the basis of such values and principles, threatens the very important political goods that would be found in the well-ordered society. It is because they value these goods and want to realize them in a social world, and not because they fear political instability, that proponents of the liberalism of reasoned respect "privatize" religion to the extent that they do. And it is because they attach lesser value to these distinctive forms of civic friendship and mutual respect that some of the religious thinkers in this volume criticize the liberalism of reasoned respect and its social ideal. Or so I shall argue. Having sketched this form of liberalism in broad outline, I now want to fill in the details. I begin with the conditions of the modern world that, it is thought, make the liberalism of reasoned respect both possible and desirable.

II.

The liberalism of reasoned respect takes the pluralism of modern democracies as its starting point. These societies have, since the Reformation, been characterized by the presence of a plurality of moral and religious conceptions of life. These conceptions are, for practical political purposes, incommensurable. In light of this pluralism, the task of political philosophy is to specify a moral view that can serve as the basis of social cooperation. It must specify a moral view that can serve as a shared and publicly acknowledged foundation of rights and liberties, that can guide government action and that can serve as the basis for its justification. It is important to see why religious views cannot serve in this capacity. When religious pluralism first showed itself on a large scale, there was a real danger that using religion as a basis of social cooperation would lead to civil strife and armed conflict, as in fact it did. Things in the Western democracies are different now. They are different in large part because of the political and philosophical settlement to the religious wars consequent on the Reformation. Now the terms of that settlement, and their wide acceptance, themselves provide reasons for not using religion as the basis of social cooperation. Thus the danger of religious warfare in Western democracies may have been permanently averted. But the way it has been averted has brought about cultural and political changes that tell against using religion as a basis of social cooperation, even when the danger of religious warfare has passed. At the same time, gradual acceptance religious toleration opened new social possibilities. It gives grounds for reasonable faith in the possibility of a society where civility and reasoned respect prevail. To show this, I want to focus on a line of thought central to the liberalism of reasoned respect since its first articulation in the work of Kant and Rousseau.

Political philosophy has the task of locating a moral basis of social cooperation rooted in what citizens have in common. Under conditions of permanent religious pluralism, what citizens have in common is not their religion but their reason. It is their reason, rather than their religion, that citizens have as such. Therefore the task of political philosophy is to locate a basis of cooperation rooted in citizens' reasonable interests and in their common powers of reason. One of their common powers of reason is their ability to adopt and revise projects and goals, including religious goals. The exercise of this ability is importantly affected by the possibilities they are permitted to consider, by what incentives and disincentives are connected with various choices, and by citizens' sense of justice and injustice as it is shaped by the political institutions under which they live. Another of citizens' common powers of reason is their equal (but possibly undeveloped) rational capacity to understand and assess those institutions. Furthermore, every citizen is presumed to have an interest in how social and political institutions shape citizens' choices, their senses of justice and of themselves. They are presumed to have this interest for two reasons. First and most obviously, they have this interest because political institutions have a profound impact on their own life prospects. Second, they have it because they are co- holders of political power and so the political power which shapes citizens' choices is their power, exercised by their institutions on their behalf. They are interested in how their power is exercised because each is presumed to have an interest in making only those demands of others that all others can regard as reasonable.

For the state to base cooperation and exercise power on terms of cooperation that citizens could not reasonably endorse as free equals is to show them a form of disrespect. Relying on such terms disregards the interest all citizens take in assessing the formative consequences of basic institutions or it, in effect, denies that they have the equal rational capacities needed to give their approval. Relying on terms that privilege some disregards the interest they have in making only reasonable demands of all others. Respect for citizens as such requires recognizing and satisfying this interest. Respect therefore requires that social cooperation be based on terms citizens can accept on the basis of their common reason, understood as including these powers and interests. Such terms, it is argued, would guarantee liberty of conscience, the political liberties necessary to avoid despotism, and the expressive liberties necessary for personal freedom. A society in which citizens cooperate on these terms is one in which they treat one another with civility and respect; it is one in which citizens can realize their common nature as such.

This Kantian line of thought is central to the liberalism of reasoned respect. In addressing contemporary democracies, its proponents face four conditions. First, moral and religious pluralism have increased in the last two centuries. Second, Kant's heirs inherit a body of political thought according to which citizens are free, equal, and worthy of respect as reasonable. Third, they address liberal democracies whose political practice is deeply informed by this centuries-old conception of citizenship. They address societies whose governments typically justify their policies by appealing to the moral and philosophical ideas associated with liberalism, including the principles of free faith and religious toleration. Consequently citizens of these democracies have increasingly come to think of themselves and others as liberalism describes them. Contemporary political philosophers addressing liberal democracies therefore address societies whose citizens expect to be accorded respect as free, equal, and reasonable. Finally, the doctrine and practice of many mainline religions have been shaped by the experience of living under liberal democratic institutions. Many of these religions now recognize the impact of liberal thought on citizens' self-conception. They think that this self-conception itself provides an important reason for accepting freedom of conscience as a matter of principle.[11]

Proponents of the liberalism of reasoned respect single out these four conditions as salient features of the contemporary political world. Political philosophers sympathetic to other positions may object that other features are more important or that one or more of these four is unimportant. Those who defend the liberalism of reasoned respect therefore need to defend their political and sociological judgments about the conditions on which their project is premised, but I put this need aside for the moment. For now, note that those who defend this form of liberalism accept the essentials of the Kantian argument I sketched above, but vary it somewhat in light of the four conditions.

Citizens of contemporary liberal democracies, they claim, have come to regard themselves as free equals with an interest in living on terms of which they could approve on the basis of their reason. If the state were to rely on terms which citizens could not endorse, it would show them disrespect by affronting the conception citizens now have of themselves. Those who defend the liberalism of reasoned respect attempt to specify terms all can endorse because those are the only terms consistent with respect for citizens under contemporary conditions. Relying on a religious basis for social cooperation would also exact high opportunity costs. Only the experience of cooperating

---

11   See *Dignitatis Humanae, Vatican Council II* ed. Flannery, O.P. (Collegeville, Minn.: Liturgical Press, 1991), paragraph 1.

with others on terms all involved can accept as reasonable will reinforce citizens' conception of themselves as reasonable, as able and willing to cooperate with others on a footing of equality. This, it is said, lays the basis for self- and mutual respect. That respect is what I have called reasoned respect because it depends upon a conception of oneself and others as reasonable. Given religious pluralism, a religious basis for cooperation is not one that all citizens could accept as reasonable. To rely on it is to forego an opportunity to reinforce the conditions necessary for a social world of reasoned respect. Reasoned self- and mutual respect are good in themselves. They are also necessary to sustain cooperation and the pursuit of justice in the long run. So, the argument concludes, the costs of using religion as a basis of social cooperation under contemporary conditions are too high.

Similar considerations apply to the question of whether religious arguments may be introduced into public political debate or may serve as the basis of voting. Public political argument is argument in the public forum in which citizens try to convince one another to pass legislation or to adopt policies. To offer others an argument that depends on reasons of a sort that they cannot reasonably be expected to accept displays a willingness to coerce them, via the law or policy in question, for reasons they could reasonably reject. This fails to respect their capacity for and interest in affirming the grounds on which they are coerced, and the grounds on which their power is exercised. It therefore fails to respect the capacities and interests others have as citizens. Showing disrespect of this kind is wrong, it is said, because citizens are at least prima facie obligated to respect one another as such. Furthermore, disrespect may not lead to armed civil strife, but it may engender resentment because it evinces a willingness to coerce others for reasons they cannot reasonably endorse. This resentment may impede realization of desirable political ends in the long run. That resentment may be exacerbated, under contemporary conditions, by the fact that citizens believe they are owed reasons of a sort they can be expected reasonably to accept. Finally, there is an opportunity cost to offering public arguments that depend on considerations of a sort others cannot accept. When someone offers such an argument, she foregoes the opportunity to offer one that shows an unwillingness to coerce others illegitimately. This evident unwillingness contributes to a relationship of mutual reasoned respect, a relationship important for future cooperation. Given religious pluralism, religious reasons are reasons of a sort that we cannot reasonably expect all others to accept. Therefore, the liberalism of reasoned respect concludes, citizens should not offer one another arguments, or only arguments, that depend upon religious claims.

This argument seems to depend upon the claim that public political argument is argument addressed to everyone. But why think that? Why not think instead that public political argument is offered to subsets of our fellow citizens? If we know that those in the subset we address share some of our religious views, what could be disrespectful about trying to win them over to our side of a political question by offering them religious arguments?

Here proponents of the liberalism of reasoned respect offer a distinction and two replies. The distinction is between arguments that take place in the public forum and those that do not. Some proponents of this view, like Rawls, are relatively unconcerned with arguments outside the public forum; there the constraints on argument do not apply. If it takes place in the public forum, then there are two reasons why it is not acceptable. First, when citizens argue publicly about how to exercise their political power over one another, they are arguing publicly about what concerns them as citizens. Under these circumstances, there is something valuable about citizens cooperating with one another as such, even if they could cooperate as coreligionists. The value of cooperating as citizens generates at least a prima facie obligation to do so. Second, when citizens use religious arguments to persuade one another to take their side of a political question, they are trying to persuade others to take their side of a question on which others who do not share their religious views may disagree. They are using religious arguments to build a coalition and amass sufficient political power to pass coercive legislation. If the coalition is willing to present itself in the public forum with secular arguments, then it is hard to see why it could not have built itself up in the same way, so the question does not arise. If that coalition presses its case in the public forum by using religious arguments or only religious arguments, then it runs afoul of the same considerations that individuals do when they rely on or only on such arguments.

Proponents of the liberalism of reasoned respect are sometimes said to be squeamish about conflict and to disdain the coalition-building in which so much of ordinary politics consists. It is this squeamishness and disdain, it is said, that really motivate constraints on public political argument.[12] The liberalism of reasoned respect does not deny the importance of building coalitions and majorities. It does imply constraints on how coalition-building can proceed and on how the power of majorities can be used to justify state action. To see this, consider the "pluralistic" view of democracy. According to this view, democratic politics is properly thought of as the competition of individuals and groups who build coalitions in an attempt to satisfy the preferences they bring to the political process. The state justifies its distribution of benefits and burdens by showing how this satisfies the preferences of the majority. The liberalism of reasoned respect rejects this understanding of

---

12   For this charge, see John Langan, S.J., "Overcoming the Divisiveness of Religion," *Journal of Religious Ethics* 22 (1994): 47–51, 50 f. See also John Gray: "What [Gauthier and Dworkin] have in common with Rawls is the deployment of an unhistorical or abstract individualism in the service of a legalistic or jurisprudential paradigm of political philosophy." A bit later, Gray writes that "the theoretical goal of the new liberalism is the supplanting of politics by law[.]" "Against the New Liberalism," *Times Literary Supplement* (July 3, 1992): 14.

democracy on moral grounds,[13] contemporary political practice notwithstanding. The proper relationship among citizens, according to the liberalism of reasoned respect, is one of cooperation rather than competition. The state should treat citizens, and citizens should treat one another, as citizens—as free and equal holders of political power each of whom has a fundamental interest in cooperating on terms she can endorse before all others.

To insure cooperation, proponents of the liberalism of reasoned respect make two important moves. First, they isolate the reasons, or the sort of reasons, that can legitimate the state's exercise of political power. They then argue that the state respects citizens by acting only in ways that can be justified by these reasons. Second, because they think political power is ultimately citizens' power, proponents of this liberalism exploit their account of legitimating reasons to specify the reasons citizens may permissibly offer one another in arguments about how their power should be exercised and their coalitions built. When citizens offer one another reasons of the sort that would legitimate the exercise of power they advocate, or only such reasons, they show respect for one another as citizens, as coholders of political power. Because those reasons are rooted in citizens' common reasonability, that respect is reasoned. These two moves are characteristic of the liberalism of reasoned respect. They are motivated, not by aversion to conflict or by disdain for democratic politics, but by concern for the moral quality of public life in democratic societies.

III.

I have already indicated that the liberalism of reasoned respect has its origins in the work of Kant and Rousseau. The idea that every citizen should treat every other as a free and equal coholder of political power bears obvious affinities to Kant's idea that every person should treat every other as a possible legislator for a realm of ends. The most prominent contemporary proponent of this liberalism is John Rawls, the most prominent contemporary Kantian. The liberalism of reasoned respect is also found, in one form or another, in the work of Charles Larmore,[14] Ronald Dworkin,[15] and Thomas Nagel.[16] It is

13   For a creative attack on pluralism, see David Estlund, "Democracy Without Preference," *The Philosophical Review* 94 (1990): 397–423. For a different line of argument, see Cass Sunstein, "Naked Preferences and the Constitution," *Columbia Law Review* (1984): 1689–732; also his "Beyond the Republican Revival," *The Yale Law Journal* 97 (1988): 1539–90. For Rawls's anti-pluralism, see his remarks on voting in *Political Liberalism*, 219–20, paragraph 4. For a brief defense of pluralism, see Richard A. Epstein, "Modern Republicanism—Or The Flight From Substance," *The Yale Law Journal* 97 (1988): 1633–50. The pluralist view is also found in Robert Dahl, *A Preface to Democratic Theory* (New Haven, Conn.: Yale University Press, 1959).

14   Larmore, "Political Liberalism."

represented in a different way by the Catholic liberalism of the American Jesuit John Courtney Murray.[17] It is also a prominent strain in the view of Robert Audi, as represented by his contribution to this volume. I will discuss that contribution below. Since Rawls's work received a good deal of attention from a number of contributors, I want first to note three features of his view in virtue of which it is a paradigm of this form of liberalism.

First, Rawls gives a central place to the Kantian argument that lies at the heart of the liberalism of reasoned respect. Thus he begins by noting that religious pluralism is an enduring feature of modern life. He proceeds by relying on a normative conception of citizenship. According to that conception, citizens are free equals each of whom has the capacity to form, revise, and pursue a conception of the good, and the capacity for a sense of justice.[18] He stresses that both capacities are shaped by the institutions under which citizens live.[19] This gives citizens a higher-order interest in living under arrangements they can endorse on the basis of what they have in common: their rational capacities. The original position is an intellectual device which represents citizens as reasonable and rational in order to construct terms of cooperation those represented can freely endorse.[20]

Second, the terms citizens can freely endorse depends upon the way the public political culture of the Western democracies has been shaped by the history and practice of liberalism. Liberal thought and practice, including the practice of religious toleration, have nurtured important political ideas in the public culture. These ideas include the conceptions of citizenship and cooperation on which Rawls draws in constructing justice as fairness.[21] Furthermore, justice as fairness is an appropriate conception of justice for contemporary democracies because of the way liberal theory and politics have influenced religious thought. Justice as fairness is fully justified only if it can be the object of an overlapping consensus among diverse religious and moral views. Among the reasons he thinks this a real possibility is that the practice

---

15   Ronald Dworkin "Liberalism" in his *A Matter of Principle* (Cambridge, Mass.: Harvard University Press, 1985), 181–204.

16   Thomas Nagel, "Moral Conflict and Political Legitimacy," *Philosophy and Public Affairs* 16 (1987): 215–40; also his *Equality and Partiality* (New York: Oxford University Press, 1991).

17   John Courtney Murray, S.J., *We Hold These Truths* (Kansas City, Mo.: Sheed and Ward, 1960).

18   Rawls, *Political Liberalism*, 30.

19   Ibid., 312 f., 315 f.

20   Ibid., 24 ff.

21   See Rawls, "The Idea of an Overlapping Consensus," *Oxford Journal of Legal Studies* 7 (1987): 2, paragraph 2. The relevant remarks are not included in the revised version of this essay, which appears in *Political Liberalism*, 133–72.

of toleration has helped to shape religious doctrine over the last several centuries so that toleration is now widely accepted on religious grounds.[22] Those who object, with only slight hyperbole, that Rawls writes as if he were addressing the conditions of religious warfare in the seventeenth century therefore overlook an important nuance in his liberalism of reasoned respect.

Finally, Rawls thinks the ongoing attempt to comply with the principles of justice should be a cooperative enterprise. Central to his account of this cooperation is his account of a *virtue*, the virtue of civility or of good citizenship. Citizens should aim and be seen to aim at promoting the common interest rather than the satisfaction of individual preferences or the imposition of individual choices.[23] And so their political activity and public political argument should satisfy certain requirements. Rawls's "ideal of citizenship" and its associated virtues therefore implies a duty of civility: They should treat and address one another as equal coholders of civil or political power. At minimum, citizens' arguments should not convey the impression that are willing to use that power against one another illegitimately. Violating this duty may not cause armed conflict, but it may well engender resentment and mutual disdain that lead to retrograde political motion. Violating the duty also has opportunity costs, Rawls thinks, since complying with the duty of civility lays the basis of the self- and mutual respect that would characterize a well-ordered society.[24]

Rawls's constraints on public political argument are sometimes criticized for excluding too much. It is therefore worth noting that they are not as exclusionary as they are sometimes taken to be. The constraints apply only to arguments in which what he calls the "constitutional essentials" or matters of basic justice are at stake. He now says citizens may offer what arguments they like, including religious arguments, provided that they are prepared to offer arguments which comply with public reason "in due course". This view, found in the most recent edition of *Political Liberalism*,[25] is not a significant departure from the full-length discussion of public reason in the first edition of that book. Rawls did not say that citizens may not appeal to religious doctrines when constitutional essentials or matters of basic justice are at stake or that appealing to public reason is preferable. A close reading reveals that he said something much weaker. What virtuous citizenship—the virtue of civility—requires is

---

22 See Rawls, *Political Liberalism*, 145 n. 12 and accompanying text.

23 The phrase "common interest" occurs in *Theory of Justice* (Cambridge, Mass.: Harvard University Press, 1971), 213.

24 In this paragraph I draw on Rawls, *Political Liberalism*, 213 f.; the phrase "ideal of citizenship" occurs at 217.

25 I refer to the paperback edition published by Columbia University Press, 1996, li and following.

that citizens be *ready* and *able* to show how their views can be supported by public reason.[26]

Rawls does not say what he means by "ready" and "able"; interpretation must be guided by the reasons he thinks it important that citizens be ready to show how their conclusions can be supported by public reason. It is important because the citizen who evinces readiness to show this thereby evinces her reasonability. She thereby shows her "evident intention" to cooperate with others on terms they can accept as citizens.[27] With this in mind, Rawls's remarks about public reason can be interpreted as saying that citizens may offer one another religious arguments in the public forum provided they are able and willing to provide non-religious arguments for their position if their reasonability, or the reasonability of their position, is called into question. The non-religious argument they must be willing to offer must be one that is cast in terms of public reasons, though these public reasons may themselves have been given a distinctive interpretation by the religious tradition in question. The argument need not be such that no reasonable person could reject any of its premises or inferences. It must, however, be such that "those who oppose [its conclusion] can nevertheless understand how reasonable persons can affirm it."[28]

Virtuous citizenship and compliance with the requirements of public reason lay the basis for foundations of mutual and reasoned respect. These relationships are, Rawls thinks, important to ongoing cooperation in pursuit of justice, and so are "a very great public good, part of society's political capital."[29]

The first paper in this volume is Robert Audi's "The State, The Church and the Citizen." Audi defends constraints on the political activities of religious citizens and groups, and on their use of religion in public political argument, that are interestingly different from Rawls's. Unlike Rawls, he does not attempt to derive them from a theory of liberal democracy. As we have seen, some of his remarks suggest that he defends these constraints because he is worried about the outbreak of civil strife. But elsewhere in his contribution to this volume and in other published work, Audi defends the constraints by appealing to many of the same considerations Rawls does. These arguments bear the greater burden in his argument and it is in virtue of the weight he places on them that Audi's view counts as a liberalism of reasoned respect. I begin with the constraints before turning to the arguments Audi adduces in their support.

Audi's account of the constraints on public political argument, like Rawls's, gives a central place to the virtues of citizenship. Like Rawls, Audi derives the

---

26   See ibid., 217, 218, and 243.

27   For the importance of this "evident intention," see ibid., 163.

28   Ibid., 253. I am grateful to David Solomon and David Estlund for helpful conversation about this matter.

29   Ibid., 157.

virtues from a moral ideal. The virtues with which Audi is concerned are what he calls "civic virtues," the virtues associated with "responsible participation" in political life. The civic virtues can be exhibited by corporate agents like churches, as well as by individual citizens. The centerpiece of Audi's account of civic virtue is the notion of "theo-ethical equilibrium," "a rational integration between religious deliverances and, on the other hand, secular ethical considerations." Very roughly, Audi argues that agents should strive for coherence between the moral implications of their religious views and "seemingly sound moral conclusions"; in cases of conflict, neither religious nor secular beliefs should be immune from reconsideration. The requirement that religious citizens and organizations cultivate civic virtue implies a prima facie obligation to seek theo-ethical equilibrium.

This requirement has motivational consequences. Both individual citizens and churches "should be reluctant or unwilling to support coercive laws or public policies on a basis that cannot be placed in such an equilibrium." What does Audi mean by "unwilling" and "reluctant"? The person of civic virtue, he argues, should act from the *principle of secular rationale* and the *principle of secular motivation*. The former says that "one has a prima facie obligation not to advocate or support any law or public policy that restricts human conduct unless one has and is willing to offer adequate secular reasons for this advocacy or support." The latter "adds to the rationale principle that one also has a (prima facie) obligation to abstain from advocacy or support of a law or public policy that restricts human conduct unless one is sufficiently *motivated* by some (normatively) adequate secular reason." Churches will be virtuous political agents only if they act from the *principle of ecclesiastical political neutrality*. According to this principle "churches committed to being institutional citizens in [a free and democratic society] have a prima facie obligation to abstain from supporting candidates for public office or pressing for laws or public policies that restrict human conduct."

What is important for present purposes are the grounds on which Audi defends these principles of civic virtue, for it is in these grounds that his commitment to the liberalism of reasoned respect lies. Audi opens his defense of the principles at the characteristic starting point of the liberalism of reasoned respect. Liberal democracy, he says, is committed to achieving social cooperation by means of rational persuasion. This entails that social cooperation should be on terms that all can autonomously accept and "identify with," given their common rationality. The moral and religious pluralism of contemporary democracies implies that those terms must be secular. So the state can appeal only to secular reasons in justifying coercive laws and policies. Like Rawls, Audi argues that citizens' ongoing attempts to pass laws and policies, and to persuade others to support them through public political argument, should themselves be cooperative endeavors in pursuit of justice. The public political argument citizens address to one another include arguments offered in terms that others can accept and identify with. The arguments citizens offer one another, like the justifications the state offers its citizens, should therefore include secular arguments which satisfy the principles of secular rationale and motivation. Constraints on the arguments citizens offer one another therefore follow, in Audi's view, from the fact that the liberal democracy of which they are citizens is committed to rational persuasion.

Thus like Rawls, Audi employs the strategy characteristic of the liberalism of reasoned respect. He begins with an account of the sort of reasons that can legitimate state action. Where Rawls derives those ideas from a conception of justice, Audi argues that they must be secular. Audi then exploits that account to specify the sort of reasons citizens may offer one another, consistent with the demands of civic virtue. Where Rawls says that citizens must be prepared to offer one another legitimating reasons in due course, Audi says that they must have and be willing to offer one another reasons of that sort. This, Audi concludes, is what civic virtue requires.

Audi thinks compliance with the demands of civic virtue is necessary to maintain stability and to preserve liberty.[30] He also and more importantly defends compliance as necessary to maintain the moral quality of public life and the conditions necessary for the pursuit of justice. Thus he stresses that offering reasons of the wrong sort can corrupt politics by distracting attention from the public good and produces "deadlock" where a just compromise might have been reached. He argues that citizens should offer reasons which encourage mutual trust; this, he thinks, tells in favor of his two principles and against weaker constraints.[31] He defends his principles by arguing that they establish conditions under which citizens can respect one another "as free and dignified individuals."[32] Audi also offers an argument premised on a claim crucial to the liberalism of reasoned respect, the claim that political philosophy addresses conditions brought about by a history of liberal practice and religious toleration. He argues that violation of his principles risks engendering resentment among those who receive arguments of the wrong sort.[33] This may cause resentment in part because a history of toleration and church-state separation has led citizens to expect that they will not be offered religious arguments for public policy. Audi's arguments for the principles and virtues associated with responsible participation in politics therefore reflect his commitment to the liberalism of reasoned respect.

Much of the conference on Religion and Contemporary Liberalism was spent debating the tenability and desirability of the liberalism of reasoned respect, as represented by Audi and Rawls. Sanford Levinson's paper explores the implications of liberalism for judicial discourse, both at the confirmation

---

30   See also his "The Place of Religious Argument," 691.

31   Audi, "Separation of Church and State," 281–82.

32   Audi, "The Place of Religious Argument," 701.

33   Ibid., 689 ff.

stage and in judges' published opinions. Martha Nussbaum explores its implications for societies in which religion poses a threat to fundamental human rights. Papers by Philip Quinn, Nicholas Wolterstorff, and Timothy Jackson press questions about whether Rawls and Audi attach too much value to civic amity as they understand it. Implicit in the liberalism of reasoned respect is a conception of society in which virtuous citizens respect one another as reasonable and capable of cooperation on terms all can acknowledge. Quinn, Wolterstorff, and Jackson all suggest, though each in different ways, that reasoned respect might come at too high a cost. All, in effect, challenge proponents of this form of liberalism to argue that the cost is worth paying. Jackson goes on to defend a religious liberalism of his own; in this he is joined by Jorge Garcia. Jean Elshtain, John Coleman, and David Hollenbach press a different line of argument against the liberalism of reasoned respect. They query whether this liberalism is capable of sustaining the conditions necessary for its own support.

IV.

Audi's paper is followed by Sanford Levinson's "Abstinence and Exclusion." Levinson has fewer reservations than Rawls or Audi about the introduction of religious claims into public political argument by ordinary citizens. He says, "it seems enough . . . to disagree vigorously with persons presenting theologically-oriented views of politics. To suggest as well that they are estopped even from presenting such arguments seems gratuitously censorial." He then proceeds to ask whether judges and candidates for judgeships should be accorded similar latitude, or whether they are obligated to observe tighter restrictions. Levinson thinks that it is morally permissible for legislators to vote against confirmation of a candidate who says she will draw on her own religious views in reaching her decisions and writing her opinions. He is less sure that legislators are required to do so. His paper is instructively exploratory, drawing on opinions that have actually been written to query what judges may permissibly do. Many of those who take up this question argue that judges, or at least those who interpret the constitution and offer written opinions, occupy a special role. They, it is said, are bound by stricter constraints than citizens, legislators, and executives.[34] Levinson raises the intriguing suggestion that it may prove impossible to draw "bright lines" between those who occupy these different political roles; where some would conclude that judges ought to be accorded more latitude, Levinson wonders whether politicians ought to be allowed less. His gentle probing raises questions about how the liberalism of reasoned respect might work out in one highly structured area of politics—judicial confirmation and practice.

---

34   See Rawls, *Political Liberalism*, 240, 254; also Kent Greenawalt, *Private Consciences and Public Reasons* (New York: Oxford University Press, 1995), 142 ff.

Like Levinson's essay, Martha Nussbaum's paper "Religion and Women's Human Rights" assesses the permissibility of religious political argument by examining actual instances of its use. Levinson draws his examples from judicial opinions issued in American courts. Nussbaum complements this by examining cases of religious political discourse and religiously inspired law from outside the United States. Many of her examples are drawn from the developing world. Nussbaum in effect asks how proponents of the liberalism of reasoned respect should respond to religious political discourse in societies other than the contemporary Western democracies for which that form of liberalism was originally conceived.

Nussbaum argues that attention to the way religious language actually functions outside the Western democracies seems to pose a dilemma for proponents of the liberalism of reasoned respect. Liberals are deeply committed to freedom of conscience and typically claim that this freedom should be abridged only under extreme circumstances. Liberals are also committed, she notes, to a range of other freedoms and rights including freedom of movement, the right to bodily integrity and personal inviolability, and the political and expressive liberties. The dilemma arises because in many parts of the contemporary world, some citizens are denied these latter rights and liberties in the name of religious traditions that freedom of conscience is supposed to protect. "If the government defers to the wishes of the religious group," Nussbaum writes, "a vulnerable group of individuals will lose basic rights; if the government commits itself to respecting equal human rights of all individuals, it will stand accused of indifference to liberty of conscience."

All too often the "vulnerable group of individuals" who lose their basic rights in the name of religious tradition are women. Mustering facts and statistics on women's mortality and morbidity, legal protection of their bodily integrity (including legal protection against spousal rape and genital mutilation), their rights to secure employment outside the home, to speak freely and to participate in politics, to worship freely, to appear in court as full legal persons, to transmit their nationality to their children, to equal treatment in family law, to education, and to contraception, Nussbaum argues that religious discourse is regularly invoked to legitimate practices, laws, and legal codes that deny women fundamental rights in many countries. If forced to choose between according women these fundamental rights on the one hand and the free exercise of religions which deny them on the other, Nussbaum states unequivocally that equal rights have the greater claim. This, she says, implies strict limits on the recognition of religious statutes and legal codes in a constitutional regime. It also implies that religious speech intended to intimidate women who exercise their rights should be illegal. Other religious political discourse, she thinks, should conform to roughly Rawlsian strictures, strictures rooted, as we have seen, in the liberalism of reasoned respect.

Nussbaum recognizes that these norms may seem both imperialistic and utopian. They seem imperialistic because they seem to impose political requirements on societies, cultures, and religions to which liberal values and ideals are foreign. They seem utopian because the possibility that they will be honored seems remote; it seems especially so in light of the evidence that Nussbaum musters to defend the need for these norms in the first place. The answers to both charges, she counters, is at bottom the same. Any religious tradition houses a diversity of views, some of which may be more sympathetic to equality and human rights than others. Those who insist on the norms Nussbaum defends can answer the charge of moral imperialism by pointing out that those norms may find support in alternative strands of the religious traditions in question. One way liberals can promote the observance of these norms is to encourage the development of the strands that support them. They can do this, Nussbaum thinks, by "encouraging pluralistic and comparative religious discourse on these topics, discourse that brings to light and publicizes the plurality of views on all these matters within the religious traditions, and also brings members of the different tradition together for consultation and comparative discussion." Another and related way to do this, she concludes, is to "produce active, unintimidated, educated democratic citizens" capable of critical reflection on the currently dominant interpretation of their own religious traditions.

Philip Quinn's "Political Liberalisms and Their Exclusions of the Religious" was his presidential address to the Central Division of the American Philosophical Association in 1995. Quinn uses the example of public, religiously motivated and argued pro-life advocacy to challenge both the principles that Audi defends and the limits of public reason that Rawls does. Much of Quinn's paper is devoted to the meticulous clarification of Rawls's and Audi's views. He argues that Audi's principles of secular rationale and motivation, once clarified, are too strong to be plausible, and he argues that public reason as Rawls discusses it in *Political Liberalism* is too weak to single out one correct position on abortion. Quinn's arguments are exemplary for their clarity and care, but what is most important for present purposes are his own position and the reasons for which he favors it.

Rawls and Audi, Quinn notes, employ the "strategy of exclusions tempered by exceptions." The strategy is a natural one for liberals who want to bring about a society of mutual and reasoned respect. It stands to reason that they would begin by isolating grounds of political discussion that will foster respect, and then examine what other grounds citizens occasionally may stand on without undermining the respect thus engendered. Quinn argues, however, that this is a not a strategy liberals should adopt. Instead he shows strong sympathy for the view recently endorsed by Michael Perry and defended by Sanford Levinson in a review of Perry's earlier work. Perry argues for an inclusivist ideal according to which religious beliefs should not be excluded as a basis of the ordinary citizens's public political argument and decision making.[35]

Quinn finds the inclusivist ideal attractive because the well-ordered society associated with Rawls's version of the liberalism of reasoned respect presupposes sustained agreement on a conception of justice. It is that conception that serves as a basis of public discussion among citizens in the well-ordered society of justice as fairness. Quinn argues that such a consensus would be impossible to sustain under conditions of free inquiry. So the goods of civility and respect realized by adhering to the restrictions on public discussion would not be realized for long even if the well-ordered society were once realized. Even if following a less inclusive ideal under present circumstances would help bring about a well-ordered society, following the inclusivist ideal would not jeopardize a good citizens could realistically expect to enjoy in the long run. Furthermore, the inclusivist ideal allows citizens to express themselves more fully. It is therefore "apt to mitigate the problem of alienation from the political" that many religious citizens experience. There may be some mutual antagonism as religious debate replaces dialogue. That price is worth paying because the alienation of religious citizens from political life itself has costs. Quinn, himself a liberal and a religious believer, thinks that the current incivility of American politics will not be remedied by more scrupulous adherence to restrictions on argument, but by more open and inclusive discussion. He concludes that a public life more open to religion and less alienating to the religious opens the possibility that American politics will not be split between secular liberals and religious conservatives.

Some of these reservations about the liberalism of reasoned respect are amplified by Nicholas Wolterstorff in the paper that follows Quinn's. In "Why We Should Reject What Liberalism Tells Us about Speaking and Acting in Public for Religious Reasons", Wolterstorff notes that liberalism requires citizens to treat one another as free equals. This requirement commits liberals addressing religiously pluralistic societies to the "independent basis position." According to the independent-basis position, political discourse and decision making should be based on principles yielded by a source which is independent of any and all religious perspectives represented in society. That source must be such that it is fair to insist that everyone base her political discourse and decisions on principles yielded by that source. Wolterstorff carefully distinguishes reasons why different liberals have converged on this requirement. Some have done so because they thought following it would prevent religious warfare and civil strife. Locke defended it on classical-foundationalist grounds. I want to concentrate on his discussion of Rawls who, he says, has still other reasons for holding the independent-basis position. Wolterstorff is therefore careful not to repeat the canard that Rawls supposes religious argument causes political instability.

Wolterstorff reads Rawls as employing what he calls the "consensus populi"

---

35   Perry lays out his current position in *Religion in Politics: Constitutional and Moral Perspectives* (New York: Oxford University Press, 1996).

strategy. Rawls begins with the "consensus populi" or political culture of contemporary liberal democracies as a source independent of religious perspectives. He isolates the fundamental organizing ideas of that consensus and out of those constructs the conception of justice, including the principles of justice, that are to serve as the basis of political discussion and decision making. Wolterstorff criticizes this strategy on a number of grounds, each of which merits more consideration than can be given here. I mention just two that are important because, if sound, they would support Wolterstorff's most damning allegation: that liberalism is unfair to those who want to lead a religiously integrated existence, and that, by being unfair, liberalism tends to undermine itself.

Wolterstorff notes that even if Rawls provides a good argument for the independent-basis position, it does not follow that political discourse and decision making should be based only or exclusively on a public political conception of justice. It implies at most that people who want to base their public political arguments on their religious views should also have additional reasons for their conclusions, reasons with an independent basis. To take an exclusivist view of the independent-basis position is not only to read it as implying more than it does. It is also unfair to those who want to base their politics on their religious views and so seek a "religiously integrated existence."[36] In laying out Rawls's view earlier, I argued that it is not as exclusivist as it is sometimes taken to be. Rawls does endorse the independent-basis position, but he thinks this generates only a weak requirement. Citizens taking a position on the constitutional essentials for religious reasons must also have and be ready to offer reasons for drawn from the public political conception of justice. Citizens who want a religiously integrated existence can and should try to work out the relationship between religious and public reasons.

One of Wolterstorff's objections anticipates this reply. In a democracy citizens typically offer one another reasons and arguments on an ad hoc basis, and then vote without attempting to satisfy even the weak requirement Rawls endorses. In doing this, they cannot be violating the requirements of freedom, equality, and civility as those ideals are found in the consensus populi of liberal democracies since citizens behave this way in all the liberal democracies there are. So Rawls can get even the weak requirement only by using ideas of freedom and equality not found in the consensus populi. He can therefore derive even the weak requirement only by abandoning the strategy he purports to employ. One reply to this objection is that it ignores the extent to which Rawlsian constructivism is revisionary. It ignores the possibility that when the values of the consensus populi are interpreted, connected, and brought into

---

36   For further discussion of a "religiously integrated existence" and its bearing on Rawls's views, see Paul J. Weithman "Taking Rites Seriously," *Pacific Philosophical Quarterly* 75 (1994): 288–92.

reflective equilibrium, we will find that the political practices of contemporary liberal democracies depart significantly from moral ideals or requirements.[37] I will not pursue this reply here because, while important, it misses Wolterstorff's real point. His real point is that even the weak requirement is misconceived. Even the weak requirement seems plausible only if Rawls assumes the desirability and possibility of a society in which citizens cooperate on the basis of their common reasonability. But it is just these assumptions that Wolterstorff, like Quinn, calls into question.

A society in which citizens cooperate on the basis of their common reasonability is not desirable, Wolterstorff argues, because it asks too much of those who want a "religiously integrated existence."[38] These are citizens who want to be able to see all their actions and relationships as based on their religious commitments rather than on what they have in common with those who do not share their commitments. These citizens do not necessarily want to live in a Christian America. They do think that how they treat those who disagree with them should be based on their own religion rather than on their shared reasonability. This is, Wolterstorff thinks, a reasonable desire; asking these citizens to cooperate on the basis of their reason is to make an unfairly demanding request. In questioning the desirability of the well-ordered society implicit in the liberalism of reasoned respect, Wolterstorff raised a question that became, as we shall see, one of the most important objections of the conference.

The vision of citizens cooperating on the basis of their shared reasonability appeals to so many American political philosophers because so much of American politics is uncivil. This might be thought the result of the chronically undisciplined appeal to religion in American political argument. Incivility can be alleviated and reasoned respect promoted, it might be thought, only if religious citizens exercise some self-restraint. Wolterstorff argues that this misdiagnoses the problem and so prescribes the wrong cure. The incivility of American politics is a reaction, fueled by the resentment of religious citizens who rightly think they have been ignored.[39] Trying to remedy incivility,

---

37   See the articles of Sunstein cited at note 13, as well as the accompanying text.

38   It may also ask too much of those who want a tight integration of their political views with their secular comprehensive doctrines. I am grateful to Phil Quinn for this point.

39   Wolterstorff compares the religious violence of the seventeenth century with the nationalist violence of the twentieth to make the point that human beings do not necessarily fight about religion. They fight, he says, about what they care about. In light of his claim that religious conservatism and fundamentalism are reactions to politics which ignore religion, it might be equally illuminating to compare the nationalist politics of this century with the religious politics of this century. For an argument that outbreaks of nationalisms in the twentieth century are reactions to the politics of the nineteenth, see Isaiah Berlin, *The Crooked Timber*

alleviate resentment, and build mutual respect by constraining religious political argument will only exacerbate the problems those constraints are supposed to ameliorate. The antidote to incivility, Wolterstorff argues, is to allow religion to be heard. Audi argued that politics is an unwarranted distraction to churches and clergy. Wolterstorff, on the other hand, thinks religious citizens and organizations should devote sustained attention to working out the implications of their religion for political questions. This allows those who want religiously integrated lives to make thoughtful contributions to public debate.

A society in which citizens cooperate on the basis of their common reasonability is not possible, Wolterstorff thinks, as a matter of sociological fact. He argues that religious citizens and groups should develop the political implications of their views and should advocate them in public. The alternative, he conjectures, is not the liberalism of reasoned respect but a public life in which citizens appeal only to "their pocketbooks, their privacy, and their nation." A public forum from which sophisticated religious argument is absent, he predicts, will soon be "debase[d]" by "private and group egoism."

Adherents of the liberalism of reasoned respect might reply that they have no objection to citizens and churches working out the political implications of their religious views, Audi's cautions about undue distraction notwithstanding. Citizens can and should discuss politics, form their political opinions and reconcile them with their theological commitments. Churches can reason about the political implications of theological doctrines. Indeed, they might say, this active and widespread interest in politics is necessary for the maintenance of a healthy democratic culture. Where proponents of the liberalism of reasoned respect would say they differ from Wolterstorff is on the relationship between this activity and political argument in the public forum. Thus Rawls seems to agree with Wolterstorff that churches and universities should work out the implications of comprehensive moral view for politics, but he thinks this should take place in what he calls "the background culture". When citizens enter the public forum to debate the constitutional essentials, the constraints on public reason apply. It is in the public forum that the goods of civility and reasoned respect are to be realized. Rawls writes

> th[e] background culture contains comprehensive doctrines of all kinds: these are taught, explained, debated against one another, and argued about, indefinitely without end, as long as society has vitality and spirit. It is the culture of the social, not of the publicly political. It is the culture of daily life, with its many associations: its universities and churches, learned and scientific societies; and endless political discussions of ideas and doctrines are commonplace everywhere.[40]

of Humanity (New York: Knopf, 1991), 243–61.

40   John Rawls, "Reply to Habermas," *The Journal of Philosophy* 92 (1995): 140.

Wolterstorff would argue that if religious political argument is confined to the background culture it is sure to wither. The norms governing debate in the public forum tend, as a matter of sociological fact, to become normative for reasoning in the institutions which bear the background culture. Thus, Wolterstorff argues, the secularization of public political argument has led to the secularization of argument in the academy. So if there are to be distinctive values and ways of reasoning in the background culture, they must be represented in public political argument. A necessary condition of sophisticated religious political argument in the background culture is therefore the presence of religious argument in the public forum. Rawls suggests that the "vitality and spirit" of society and democratic culture depend upon the vitality and sophistication of argument, including religious argument, in the background culture. Wolterstorff would conclude that the maintenance of democratic culture depends upon the presence of religious political argument in the public forum as well.

Wolterstorff's reply to Rawls is reminiscent of some of Quinn's arguments, and makes explicit another of the conference's most important questions: Does the liberalism of reasoned respect undermine the cultural and social conditions necessary for realizing its own deepest aims? Proponents of the liberalism of reasoned respect think liberal societies should be ones in which citizens cooperate with one another on the basis of their common reason. When citizens cooperate on this basis, they argue, liberal democracies build mutual and reasoned respect and accumulate the social capital necessary to sustain pursuit of justice in the long run. Wolterstorff, on the other hand, argues that liberal democracies are faced with only two real options: a politics dominated by self-interest and factionalism, or one which encourages the religious to engage in serious political reflection and to present their religious arguments in public. Proponents of the liberalism of reasoned respect defend constraints on religious political activity and argument that, if followed, would effectively preclude the latter. Therefore, Wolterstorff would conclude, "their exclusions of the religious" undermine the only live alternative to the pluralistic conception of democracy they profess to oppose.

V.

The papers by Timothy Jackson and Jorge Garcia exemplify the religiously based political thinking Wolterstorff recommends. Jackson's "The Return of the Prodigal? Liberal Theory and Religious Pluralism" echoes and amplifies many of the themes sounded in Wolterstorff's paper. Jackson, like Wolterstorff, argues that the liberalism of reasoned respect is unfair to religious believers. He, like Wolterstorff, suggests that evacuating political discourse of religious arguments will open a vacuum that will likely be filled by selfishness. And he, like Wolterstorff, worries that the liberalism of reasoned respect may not have the resources to generate its own support in the long run. This form of liberalism presupposes that citizens must develop the capacities of autonomous agency and must learn to respect the rights of others. Citizens will develop these capacities and virtues, however, only if those responsible for educating them in childhood act from motives of self-sacrifice and benevolence. Self-sacrificial care of this kind is exercised in special relationships and communities. Jackson claims that Rortean and Rawlsian liberalism are unable to account for the value of these motives and of special relationships because it privileges impersonal justice.

The charge that Kantian moral thought cannot accommodate benevolence, self-sacrifice, and special relationships is one that is commonly made. Some have argued that the charge depends upon a misinterpretation of Kant's texts.[41] Rawls has long argued that his Kantianism is strictly political. The primacy he accords justice applies to the domain of the political and not to the whole of life; in other areas of life, values other than justice may have primacy. Jackson replies that the political and the non-political cannot be separated in the way that Rawls suggests. Rather than pursue this question, I turn to Jackson's sketch of a religious liberalism that can, he thinks, accommodate the motives of benevolence and self-sacrifice. He calls this the "l-a-m-p" version of liberalism, for "liberalism *as* *morally* *perfectionist*".

Like the liberalism of reasoned respect, the l-a-m-p version of liberalism accords the civic virtues an important place. According to Jackson's liberalism, these virtues "pivot around" a "robust fellow-feeling" rather than impersonal justice. He says that the pivot of the l-a-m-p version of liberalism is a family of dispositions associated with "personal care" for others. A liberalism according to which citizens should act from these dispositions is not one in which they cooperate in the pursuit of justice exclusively on the basis of their common human reason. They should attend first to one another's unique capacities and condition and should be ready to perform acts of self-sacrifice for them that are usually deemed supererogatory. A liberalism which demands what is usually taken to be supererogatory is one that aims at the perfection of citizens; only a liberalism which is morally perfectionistic in this way, Jackson thinks, can sustain "a stable society of decent citizens." Jackson recognizes that perfectionistic liberalism can take secular forms, but he himself defends a religious version. According to Jackson's liberalism, one motive for developing and exercising the virtues of self-sacrifice, personal care, and fellow-feeling is "gratitude for the redemption extended to humanity" in the self-sacrifice of Jesus. Jesus Christ was, he remarks, "a perfect liberal who refused to hide his lamp under a bushel."[42]

---

41   Barbara Herman, *The Practice of Moral Judgment* (Cambridge, Mass.: Harvard University Press, 1993), 184–207, esp. 190 ff.

42   Referring to Matthew 5:15.

Jackson does not argue that Christian theism is necessary for maintaining a liberal society. He does argue for the more modest thesis that liberalism can be a religious commitment implied by the commitment to follow Christ's example and to love one's neighbor. The conjunction of Christianity and liberalism is not, as popular accounts would have it, the shotgun wedding of religion with a moral view historically opposed to it. Rather, Jackson thinks, religion and liberalism have been in the same family all along. Liberalism inherited some of its central ideas from Christian accounts of equality. Contemporary liberal democracies survive because their citizens, knowingly or unknowingly, abide by the remnants of Judaeo-Christian morality. The liberalism Jackson defends in "The Return of the Prodigal?" is therefore not a forced marriage, but the reconciliation of a parent with an estranged child who has almost dissipated his inheritance.[43]

Jorge Garcia's "Liberal Theory, Human Freedom and the Politics of Sexual Morality" follows Jackson's paper. Garcia too begins by criticizing a version of secular liberalism for its inadequate treatment of the virtues. Unlike Jackson, Garcia does not argue that nonperfectionist liberalism assumes that citizens must act from virtues of which it cannot give an adequate account. He argues, rather, that liberal accounts of rights presuppose an account of the value of the liberties those rights protect. An account of the value of liberty, in turn, requires an account of what it is to exercise liberty well by choosing well. An account of choosing well requires an account of the virtues that liberals fail to provide. Garcia uses Thomas Nagel's recent argument for the right to engage in certain sexual behaviors as an example.[44] The argument suffers, Garcia thinks, from neglecting the virtues associated with responsible sexual behavior, virtues necessary for the good exercise of the rights Nagel is concerned to defend. If those rights are exercised badly, Garcia argues, the sexual liberties they protect cannot have the value Nagel thinks they do.

Garcia explores an alternative liberalism suggested by the writings of Pope John Paul II. According to this view "freedom is ill-used unless it operates to select in accord with what we really are and need. That is, genuinely free choice is realistic, facing up to our status as creatures and our need for God" and for "God's truth." What we really are and need dictates the liberties, and the scope of liberties, to which citizens are entitled and which governments are bound to recognize. It implies a right to freedom of conscience but not the rights to sexual behavior Nagel defends. Garcia considers the problems of putting liberal theory and human freedom on a theistic basis under conditions of religious pluralism. He thinks that in the United States "the great majority of people hold religious beliefs within the Jewish and Christian traditions." It

---

43   Referring to Luke 15:11–32.

44   Thomas Nagel, "Personal Rights and Public Space," *Philosophy and Public Affairs* 24 (1995): 83–107.

should therefore be possible to "achieve a broad and lasting base of support for a widely shared conception of justice based on human dignity that is rooted in our status as image of God." Proponents of the liberalism of reasoned respect would object that a society governed by such a conception of justice would not be one in which citizens cooperate on terms acceptable to their common reason. It is unlikely to be one of civility and reasoned respect, as they understand them. Garcia's concluding remarks suggest that he, like Wolterstorff, does not think civility as understood by proponents of the liberalism of reasoned respect is as valuable as they take it to be.

Jean Bethke Elshtain shares Wolterstorff and Jackson's worry that liberal theory, when embodied in practice, undermines the conditions necessary to sustain liberal democracy. Unlike them, she is skeptical that religious communities can do much to remedy the problem because she thinks liberalism has already done much to undermine religion. Elshtain, drawing on Hannah Arendt, argues first that citizens can sustain allegiance to political authority only if they regard authorities as augmenting the efforts of those who founded the political institutions under which they live. Liberal philosophy, especially the contractualist version so prominently associated with the liberalism of reasoned respect, encourages citizens to regard themselves as co-founders of those institutions. Once they regard themselves as co-founders, citizens think themselves unbound by the past, unbound by received interpretations of history and free to start anew rather than carry on the work of their predecessors. Since the Reformation, citizens' tendency to question the authority of the past has influenced the way they regard traditional religious authority, including the traditionally authoritative interpretations of religious texts. When embodied in practice, liberalism encourages, and the liberalism of reasoned respect would encourage, an attitude toward political authority that ultimately undermines other forms of authority as well. This, in turn, weakens the secondary associations, including religious associations, that might have helped strengthen the authority of democratic institutions and that de Tocqueville thought necessary for their survival.

VI.

As we have seen, proponents of the liberalism of reasoned respect attempt to specify the requirements of civic virtue. This Audi understands as the virtue or virtues necessary for "responsible participation" in democratic politics. Audi's guiding assumption, no doubt based on his observation of contemporary American politics, is that participation by religious persons and groups is a fact of political life in the United States. He takes his task as a philosopher to be the normative one of specifying how that participation should be constrained so that it is morally responsible. In doing so he relies on what Quinn described as "the strategy of exclusions tempered by exceptions." Observing the constraints is supposed to foster civility and reasoned respect, and to help accumulate what Rawls called the "political capital" needed to establish and maintain just institutions.

The last two papers in this volume, by John Coleman and David Hollenbach, could also be said to focus on civic virtue and its role in the accumulation of political capital, but the emphasis of these papers is importantly different. Coleman and Hollenbach would argue that the skills and the willingness to participate in politics are, like responsibility, important components of civic virtue. Widespread willingness to participate and widespread possession of the skills necessary to do so are, like an atmosphere of civility and reasoned respect, important among the resources liberal democracies need to sustain themselves. Coleman and Hollenbach would argue that philosophers should not assume that citizens will participate in politics; instead, they should begin by asking what makes them do so. Thus where proponents of the liberalism of reasoned respect try to defend the conditions of *responsible* participation, Coleman and Hollenbach try to discover the social preconditions of responsible *participation*.

Implicit in the papers of Coleman and Hollenbach is a view which might be called "civic democracy." This view has roots in the Catholic tradition; it finds expression in some of the writings of de Tocqueville and there are hints of it in the work of John Courtney Murray.[45] It represents a genuine alternative to the forms of liberalism that dominate contemporary political philosophy.

To see this, recall how proponents of the liberalism of reasoned respect conceive of citizens: as free coholders of political power equally possessed of certain rational interests and capacities. The centerpiece of this view is an ideal of political society in which citizens realize civility and reasoned respect by cooperating on terms acceptable to their common reason. Proponents of civic democracy do not reject liberalism's commitment to individual rights,[46] nor do they reject the economic egalitarianism of the liberalism of reasoned respect.[47] They do not reject the idea that society should be characterized by mutual respect among reasonable citizens. Instead some proponents of civic democracy, like Murray, suggest different conceptions of reasonability and civility;[48] others, like Coleman, suggest a different conception of citizenship. Coleman and Hollenbach's version of civic democracy has its centerpiece a

---

45 See John Courtney Murray, s.j., "The Church and Totalitarian Democracy," *Theological Studies* 13 (1952): 525–63.

46 See David Hollenbach, *Claims in Conflict: Retrieving and Renewing the Catholic Human Rights Tradition* (Mahway, N.J.: Paulist Press, 1979).

47 David Hollenbach, "Liberalism, Communitarianism and the Bishops' Pastoral Letter on the Economy," *Annual of the Society of Christian Ethics* (1987): 35. For the variety and underlying unity of views stressing civil society, see Jean L. Cohen and Andrew Arato, *Civil Society and Political Theory* (Cambridge, Mass.: MIT Press, 1994), 69–82; for the roots of these views in de Tocqueville, see 116.

48 See Murray, s.j., *We Hold These Truths*, 295–336.

conception of society, just as does the liberalism of reasoned respect. It is not a conception of *political* society, but of *civil* society.

Civil society is comprised, Hollenbach says, of "the many forms of community and association that are not political in form: families, neighborhoods, voluntary associations of innumerable kinds, labor unions, small businesses, giant corporations, and religious communities."[49] No social or moral theory could be complete without some discussion of civil society. Some of these associations, like churches, enable citizens to gather with others to pursue their deepest aims. The associations which comprise civil society are therefore important to social and moral life. Civic democrats insist that political theory should also pay a great deal of attention to civil society. They do so because they think that the vitality of secondary associations is essential to the health of liberal democracies. Any theory, like the liberalism of reasoned respect, which purports to analyze how societies should amass the capital they need to flourish in the long run must attend to the social role civil society plays in capital accumulation. Those theories must specify the central concepts of political philosophy accordingly. Thus Coleman thinks that citizenship is primarily exercised in civil society. Voting and deliberating with others about how political power is to be exercised are, he intimates, but parts of citizenship; to take this part for the whole, particularly when citizens vote self-interestedly, is to conceive of citizens as clients competing for the largesse of the bureaucratic state.[50] Tenable ideals of citizenship and civility, Coleman and Hollenbach might conclude, must therefore refer to the rational interests and capacities developed through participation in civil society.

Whether such a conception can be laid out and defended is a question that goes far beyond the scope of an introduction. Focusing on two of the distinctive components of civic democracy will bring out the implications of Coleman's and Hollenbach's work for the central issues of this volume.

The "Seedbeds of Virtue" Thesis. Civic democrats insist that the associations of civil society are important as places where citizens develop and exercise the civic virtues. In this, they differ from theorists who ignore the civic virtues. They also differ from those who think that the civic virtues should primarily be developed and exercised in "governmental processes."[51]

Coleman and Hollenbach insist that what holds of important secondary

---

49   Hollenbach, "Liberalism, Communitarianism and the Bishop's Pastoral," 30.

50   See pp. 296–97 of Michael Walzer, "The Ideal of Civil Society," *Dissent* 38 (1991): 293–304, an essay on which Coleman draws; for Walzer's distinctive conception of civility, see pp. 303–4.

51   For a clear expression of this view, see Sunstein, "Beyond the Republican Revival," 1541–42, where the phrase "governmental processes" is used; see also the passing discussions of civic virtue at 1547 and 1556. Sunstein's remarks at 1573 ff. instructively canvass his reservations about the view I call "civic democracy."

associations generally holds of religious associations as well. Both draw on recent empirical work by political scientist Robert Putnam, who argues that declining participation in civic life is correlated with declining political engagement.[52] David Hollenbach's "Politically Active Churches: Some Empirical Prolegomena to a Normative Approach" juxtaposes Putnam's work with a recent study by Sidney Verba, Kay Scholzman, and Henry Brady. That study showed that a particular sort of participation in civic life—church membership—is highly correlated with the possession of the skills needed for political participation. It also suggested that "churches play an especially key role in the political empowerment of those with lower social-economic status." John Coleman's "Deprivatizing Faith and Revitalizing Citizenship" conjoins Putnam's results with the conclusions of his own long-term study of paradenominational organizations. He notes that the decline in civic participation that has accompanied the privatization of religion is accompanied by a decline in interpersonal trust, one of the elements of social capital that Audi intimates will be built up when citizens observe his constraints.[53] He argues on the basis of his study that active engagement in these organizations can play an important role in revitalizing citizenship and in reversing the trends that Putnam discerns. Thus both Coleman and Hollenbach argue that churches and paradenominational organizations play important roles in accumulating the "social capital that is requisite for effective democracy." And both Coleman and Hollenbach would conclude that the conditions which foster citizen participation, hence the conditions of civic virtue, require far more active churches and religious organizations and far more public religious argument than some versions of the liberalism of reasoned respect would allow.

The Transformation-of-Politics Thesis. As we saw earlier, the pluralistic theory of democracy holds political processes to be processes through which citizens attempt to satisfy preferences that are fixed prior to their participation in politics. Some thinkers opposed to pluralistic democracy argue that political participation should be a transformative experience. Citizens should be ready to alter their preferences and change their minds, as they reason with one another about how to attain a common good.[54] One of the ways political participation fosters civic virtue is by encouraging this readiness and discouraging intransigence. Civic democrats agree with these opponents of pluralism in thinking that political participation can transform citizens' preferences and

52   Robert Putnam, *Making Democracy Work: Civic Traditions in Modern Italy* (Princeton, N.J.: Princeton University Press, 1993). On the importance of Putnam's work, see David D. Laitin, "The Civic Culture at 30," *American Political Science Review* 89 (1995): 168–73.

53   See note 31 above, and accompanying text.

54   See Joshua Cohen's seminal paper on the theory of deliberative democracy, "Deliberation and Democratic Legitimacy," *The Good Polity* (Cambridge, Mass.: Blackwell, 1991) ed. Hamlin and Pettit, 24.

thereby encourage civic virtue. But civic democracy, in Coleman's and Hollen-bach's version, parts company with these critics at a crucial point. Civic democrats deny that ideas about public affairs and the public good which citizens form in secondary associations are self-interested and exogenous preferences to be transformed by political participation. Rather the political views citizens develop in civil society are in dialogue with the public culture. They would argue that formation of these views draws on, interprets, and assimilates political values in the public culture. And they endorse *The Trans-formation-of-Politics Thesis*, according to which citizens can and sometimes should try to transform politics by drawing on the full range of views thus developed in civil society.

Coleman and Hollenbach would argue that citizens can and should try to transform politics by drawing on the moral resources of religious communities and other secondary associations. They point to episodes in recent political history in which religious institutions and other associations in civil society transformed the politics Eastern Europe and hastened the democratization of the Philippines and parts of Latin America. The abolitionist movement, they would continue, shows how religion can correct dominant and exclusivist understandings of democracy to bring the promise of American democracy within reach of a previously excluded group.[55] The civil rights movement illustrates the same point. In the 1980s, the Catholic bishops of the United States drew conceptions of human dignity and the common good from their own religious tradition in a sustained attempt to deepen the American under-standing of what sort of economy liberal democracy requires.[56] These episodes of political transformation or attempted political transformation were possible because members and official spokespersons of various religious communities did what Wolterstorff argued they should and Audi says they should not. They encouraged their members to think deeply about politics in religious terms and they presented their religious arguments in public.

Advocates of the liberalism of reasoned respect envision a society in which citizens relate to one another as such. This implies that the effort to establish just institutions is one in which citizens cooperate with one another on the basis of their reason. It also implies that when they engage in this cooperative effort, they should offer or be prepared to offer one another reasons of a special sort: the sort of reasons that legitimate the exercise of their common political power. Wolterstorff questioned whether the society envisioned by advocates of the liberalism of reasoned respect is either possible or desirable. Proponents

---

55   David A. J. Richards, "Public Reason and Abolitionist Dissent," *Chicago-Kent Law Review* 69 (1994): 787–842.

56   See *Economic Justice for All* (United States Catholic Conference, 1988). See also David Hollenbach, "Religion, Morality and Politics," *Theological Studies* 49 (1988): 68–89.

of civic democracy like Coleman and Hollenbach would join Wolterstorff in pressing these two questions against the version of that liberalism that Audi defends.

Consider first the question of whether Audi's version of the liberalism of reasoned respect could sustain itself in practice. According to Audi's *principle of ecclesiastical political neutrality,* churches are under a prima facie obligation not advocate policies which would restrict human conduct. They are obligated to obey this principle in order to preserve the integrity of churches, promote mutual respect, civility, civic virtue and, ultimately, the health of liberal democracy. The sociological data adduced by Coleman and Hollenbach suggest that there is a deep tension in so strong a version of the liberalism of reasoned respect. Those data support a version of the *"Seedbeds-of-Virtue" Thesis,* according to which churches and religious organizations are among the places where citizens acquire the skills necessary to participate in politics. Some of the skills they acquire are transferred: They are developed in situations in which citizens who develop them are not engaged with public affairs. Some of this development, however, occurs when churches mobilize their members on behalf of political causes. Furthermore, their data suggest that churches and religious organizations foster an interest in public affairs. They do so, not by exhorting their members to participate[57] but by engaging them with particular political issues. So if churches abided by Audi's principle they would not engage in many of the activities which foster political skills and interests in their members and so would not engage in many of the activities that foster important elements of civic virtue. Audi does not discuss which secondary associations might serve as the seedbeds of virtue if churches did not. It therefore seems that if churches behaved as Audi's institutional principle entails they should, the result would not be that religious citizens' vigorous engagement in politics would become responsible by Audi's lights. The result would be less engagement.

The *"Seedbeds of Virtue" Thesis,* supported by Coleman's and Hollenbach's data, also suggests problems with Audi's *principle of secular motivation.* This principle requires citizens to refrain from advocating laws which restrict human conduct unless they are motivated by adequate secular reason. Their data suggest that a significant number of Americans develop and sustain an interest in public affairs because of their religion. It may be that as a result of that interest, they immerse themselves in politics to such a degree that they acquire sufficient secular reasons for supporting the positions they do. Yet many may not. Even those who do will sometimes do so only as a result of engagement in politics that violates Audi principle. So the result of the *principle*

---

57   Audi permits exhortations of this sort; see "Separation of Church and State," 274–75. He also permits preaching against various forms of immorality; he thinks, however, that this must stop short of the advocacy of political positions.

of secular motivation, like the result of the *ecclesiastical principle of political neutrality*, would not be more responsible participation in politics. It would be less participation. The requirements of civic virtue would, if generally followed greatly reduce the opportunities for their own exercise. On the assumption that citizens' active interest in politics is necessary to maintaining the health of liberal democratic societies, it seems that Audi's principles would, if generally observed, sap the strength of liberal democracies. They would, if generally observed, lead to the dissipation rather than the accumulation of important elements of social capital. They would thereby undermine the conditions they are supposed to promote.

Audi's *principle of secular rationale* requires citizens to offer one another secular reasons in support of laws restricting human conduct. The *"Transformation-of-Politics" Thesis* implies that citizens should sometimes violate this requirement. The data which support it suggest that at certain crucial points in its history, religious groups had to offer explicitly religious understandings of liberal democracy if the promise of democracy was to be realized. On the uncontroversial assumption that American democracy benefited from the abolitionist and the civil rights movements, it seems that democracy in the United States would have been worse off had the principle of secular rationale been followed. This principle, like those of ecclesiastical political neutrality and secular motivation, would if followed have frustrated the ends Audi intends it to advance.

Coleman, like Wolterstorff and Jackson, argues that the society envisioned by those who defend the liberalism of reasoned respect is undesirable because it is unfair to religious believers. It might seem desirable when compared with the current incivility of American politics. But Hollenbach, like Wolterstorff, suggests that the incivility of some American religious conservatives is a reaction to their perception that they have been silenced. Like Wolterstorff, Hollenbach disagrees with Audi, thinking that the solution lies in more and better religious participation in politics rather than less.

The implications of Coleman's and Hollenbach's sociological arguments for the liberalism of reasoned respect are considerable. Those arguments suggest that Audi's version of it is undesirable because unfair to religious believers, and unable to sustain itself in practice. What Quinn referred to as Audi's "exclusions of the religious" withhold from liberal democracies some of the intellectual resources they need to survive and flourish. Coleman and Hollenbach therefore drive home Quinn's question about whether liberals ought to attack philosophical problems about religion and politics with "the strategy of exclusions tempered by exceptions."

Coleman's and Hollenbach's arguments might seem to have somewhat less damaging implications for Rawls's version of the liberalism of reasoned respect. Rawls, it might seem, can accommodate the two theses of civic democracy. As we saw in the discussion of Wolterstorff, Rawls distinguishes the public from the background culture, and associates secondary associations with the latter. With this distinction in hand, Rawls could grant that the associations of civil society, including religious associations, foster important elements of civic virtue and that they must be vital if liberal democracy is to flourish. He could grant that their vitality demands their sustained reflection on political issues and includes vigorous, religiously based political argument. He could grant that this argument can and sometimes should have a profound impact on citizens' reasoning about public affairs. Rawls would insist that his "exclusions of the religious" apply only to *public* reasoning about public affairs. They apply only to reasoning and argument that take place in public rather than in the background culture.

But to suppose that Rawls's version of the liberalism of reasoned respect can escape so easily is to miss the real point of Coleman's and Hollenbach's arguments. Their point is not that their findings are inconsistent with the liberalism of reasoned respect. Coleman and Hollenbach would concede that Rawls's distinction between the public and background cultures can be employed to show that they are not. They would also concede that some versions of that liberalism have the philosophical resources to accommodate, in one way or another, the insights of civic democracy. Their real point is that the insights of civic democracy should lead proponents of that liberalism to recognize the importance of questions they have not previously asked, and to rethink the importance of some they have asked. As Hollenbach says

> Given the correlation between religious and political participation . . . does it not make more sense to direct our discussions to the *kind* of political engagement we wish to see churches encouraging rather than to whether churches should be encouraging such involvement at all? . . . The center of the discussion ought to be how to achieve wise forms of political engagement by religious communities and their members (emphasis original).

In the last section, I indicate what proponents of the liberalism of reasoned respect would have to do to meet some of the challenges posed by Coleman, Hollenbach, and the other contributors to this volume.

VII.

First, the liberalism of reasoned respect is addressed to advanced democracies under conditions of religious and moral pluralism, with traditions of religious toleration and of democratic thought and practice. Its proponents do not defend constraints on religious political advocacy and activity primarily because they fear civil strife. Rather, they think that observing these constraints is an important part of civic virtue. When citizens honor the requirements of virtue, they cooperate with one another on the basis of their common reason. This helps to establish a climate of civility, mutual trust and civic friendship in which citizens regard one another as reasonable. It helps societies accumulate the political capital they need to establish just institutions. Contributors to this volume who criticize the liberalism of reasoned respect have not mistaken it for a view obsessed with stability or with avoiding religious warfare. They have read proponents of this form of liberalism as aiming at distinctive forms of civility and reasoned respect. Among the most important questions of the volume is whether those forms of civility and reasoned respect are as desirable as proponents of the liberalism of reasoned respect suppose. The use of civility and reasoned respect to justify constraints on religious political argument suggest that these goods play an important role in the liberalism of reasoned respect. Quinn, Wolterstorff, Jackson, Garcia, and Coleman all endorsed a conception of a well-ordered society that makes do with less civility and civic friendship, but which they think is fairer to religious believers. They thereby asked, in effect, why a society characterized by civic friendship, civility and mutual respect as Rawls and Audi conceive them are worth having. They asked, in effect, whether these forms of civility and respect are valuable enough to play the role they are assigned.

The liberalism of reasoned respect is sometimes represented as a moral theory which relies entirely on deontic concepts and which has no theory of the good. Whatever the reasons for this misinterpretation, it is one that proponents of this form of liberalism have moved steadily to correct. In recent years there has been a good deal more attention, by critics and proponents, to ideas of the good associated with liberalism generally, and with the liberalism of reasoned respect in particular.[58] To meet the challenge posed by Quinn, Wolterstorff, and the others, proponents of the liberalism of reasoned respect will have to elaborate and defend their conceptions of the good even further. They will have to be a good deal more forthcoming than they have been about why civility and reasoned respect as they understand them are to be valued so highly.

Proponents of the liberalism of reasoned respect can respond to this first challenge only by replying to two others. To see this, it is helpful to distinguish two senses of "civility." The first sense of "civility" is associated with politeness and opposed to hostility and rudeness. The requirements of civility in this sense can be specified largely by generalizing about courteous behavior. "Civility" in its second sense denotes the proper relationship among citizens. The requirements of civility in this sense must be specified in tandem with a properly defended conception of citizenship. Those who defend the liberalism of reasoned respect sometimes rest their arguments on the value of the first

---

58   See Henry S. Richardson, "The Problem of Liberalism and the Good," *Liberalism and the Good* (New York: Routledge, 1990), ed. Douglass, Mara, and Richardson, 1–28; also Richardson's "Beyond Good and Right: Toward a Constructive Ethical Pragmatism," *Philosophy and Public Affairs* 24 (1995): 108–41. See also William Galston, *Liberal Purposes* (New York: Cambridge University Press, 1991).

sort of civility. Sometimes they appeal to the value of the second. Contributors to this conference challenge the importance they attach to both.

Proponents of the liberalism of reasoned respect sometimes elaborate constraints on religious political argument because of their concern to promote civility in the first sense. The soundness of their defense depends upon the soundness of two political judgments: that the rudeness and hostility of so much contemporary politics results, in part, from undisciplined appeals to religion, and that constraining or silencing those appeals in the public forum will ameliorate the hostility that now prevails there. There is nothing exceptionable about relying on political judgments to discern what philosophical questions are most pressing and what problems political philosophy should address. But as we have seen, some contributors to this volume have challenged the soundness of the political judgments which motivate the constraints associated with the liberalism of reasoned respect, and have countered with political judgments of their own. Wolterstorff and Hollenbach suggest that religious incivility is a reaction to the privatization of religion and that civility in the first sense would be better promoted by more, and more thoughtful, religious participation in politics. To answer this challenge, those who defend the liberalism of reasoned respect need to defend the political judgments that motivate their "exclusions of the religious," giving a better analysis of incivility than they have so far.

Rawls and other proponents of the liberalism of reasoned respect derive the duties of civility from a normative conception of citizenship. Citizens, in this view, are conceived of in the first instance as free and equal holders of political power. That power, it is said, can be justified or legitimated only by reasons of a certain sort, reasons associated with a public conception of justice or, as in Audi's case, by secular reasons. Citizens who advocate the use of coercive power over one another must, on Audi's view, be moved by reasons of that sort. On Rawls's view, those who want to exercise it when constitutional essentials are at stake must be prepared to offer one another reasons of that sort in due course. The requirement that citizens be moved by or be prepared to offer one another reasons of the specified sort, when generally honored, insures that citizens cooperate with one another as coholders of political power concerned with its legitimate use. It insures that they relate to one another as citizens, and hence promotes civility in the second sense. Many of the contributors to this volume have questioned the value or feasibility of civility in this sense. As we saw, John Coleman goes a step further by challenging the conception of citizenship on which the liberalism of reasoned respect is based. To answer this challenge, proponents of this form of liberalism will have to say a good deal more than they have about why civility in this sense is so important.

Coleman's and Hollenbach's arguments pose the last of the volume's major challenges to the liberalism of reasoned respect. Proponents of this form of liberalism might argue that relations of civility in both senses are an important part of society's political capital. A store of this capital is needed if citizens are to cooperate in establishing just institutions and maintaining them in the long run. Coleman and Hollenbach argue that capital accumulation depends upon the vitality of secondary associations and not, or not only, upon the proper relations among citizens as they are conceived by the liberalism of reasoned respect. Those who defend this form of liberalism need not deny what Coleman and Hollenbach assert. In the last section I suggested how Rawls might try to accommodate the insights of their civic democracy. He would distinguish the public culture and public political argument from the associations of civil society, and from the reasoning and discourse that take place within and between them. He attends to the former, leaving the latter in the background. In this he is not atypical. Proponents of the liberalism of reasoned respect do not deny the importance of civil society, but neither do they devote much attention to it. The sociological findings on which Coleman and Hollenbach draw imply that the vitality of civil society and the orientation of its constituent institutions are matters about which liberals should be deeply concerned. The problem is that the liberalism of reasoned respect, in its current state of development, may not have the conceptual resources it needs to articulate and address these concerns.

Hollenbach argues, for example, that liberal democracies depend upon the political engagement of "churches and religious communities that have fully internalized th[e] synthesis of religion and the values of liberty." Advocates of the liberalism of reasoned respect may be reluctant to encourage such engagement because of liberal reluctance to foster religion of any sort. If they overcome this reluctance, they will have to spell out some criteria by which to distinguish churches and religious communities that have internalized this synthesis from those that have not. That criterion would have to be developed, stated, defended, and applied. A great deal of philosophical work would have to be done before proponents of the liberalism of reasoned respect could act on Hollenbach's suggestion. Yet it is not clear where in the liberalism of reasoned respect its proponents could look for the concepts they need to develop these criteria.

A more serious problem is that the liberalism of reasoned respect has little to say about how the proper ends of secondary associations might be ascertained, about what values are realized when they attain those ends, about the proper relationships between those values and democratic values, and about the conditions under which the state may exercise political power to influence secondary associations. It therefore has little to say about how the religious organizations might be encouraged to engage in the wise political participation Hollenbach and Coleman recommend. It therefore remains unclear how its proponents could elaborate their theory of value to show how or why the state can encourage the vitality of those secondary associations liberals have traditionally ignored.[59] This is not in itself to say that liberalism is inadequate to the task.[60] It is merely to point out another reason why proponents of the liberalism of reasoned respect need to elaborate their theory of value. It therefore points to another area of philosophical inquiry that they need to explore if they are adequately to address the problems religion poses for the most prominent form of contemporary philosophical liberalism.[61]

---

59   But see John Rawls, "The Idea of Public Reason Revisited," *University of Chicago Law Review* (forthcoming), n. 46. I am grateful to Dr. Rawls for making a pre-publication copy of this essay available to me.

60   Joshua Cohen and Joel Rogers, "Secondary Associations and Democratic Governance," *Politics and Society* 20 (1992): 393–472, is very instructive, though Cohen and Rogers do not discuss religious organizations.

61   I am grateful to Alasdair MacIntyre, Mark Murphy, John Rawls, David Solomon, Rebecca Konyndyk DeYoung, and the contributors to this volume for reading and commenting on earlier drafts of this essay.

The State, the Church, and the Citizen

Robert Audi
University of Nebraska, Lincoln

A liberal democracy, conceived as a free and democratic society, must protect religious liberty and should not establish or promote any particular religion.[1] These two points are widely considered to be among those that justify some kind of separation of church and state. But what kind, and how much? And if there should be a measure of separation between religious institutions and the state, should there be, in our conduct as citizens, a related separation between religious and secular considerations? The question is not whether religion and politics can be mixed; they *are* mixed and will continue to be mixed. But there is much to be said about what constitutes a good mixture and about how to achieve a democratic harmony in producing it.

There are broadly moral arguments that support liberal democracy—a liberal democratic state—as a form of government. A liberal state might be held to be the only kind that preserves freedom and provides adequate scope for individual autonomy. It may also be thought to be the only kind that can sustain legitimate government, which may be construed as the sort of government that rational citizens are willing to consent to. It may be held to contribute best—or to be essential—to human flourishing. And there are other rationales for preferring liberal democracy over alternative forms of government. I assume here that some such rationale will succeed. But it also seems to me that religious institutions—churches, for short—might, for internal reasons, want to subsist in a liberal state. They might, for one thing, religiously endorse a moral case for a liberal state. But they might also see such a state as best for their own flourishing, especially in a world of inescapable religious pluralism.

Individual citizens, religious and non-religious alike, often have a similar considered desire to live in a free and democratic society in which religious liberty is assiduously preserved. My task here is to explore some appropriate liberal democratic principles in all three areas of conduct: that of the state, that of religious institutions, and that of individual citizens.

I. Institutional Separation as Addressed to the State

If we think of the theory of separation of church and state as applied to governmental institutions in relation to religious ones, we find at least three

---

1   This is worded to leave open whether a liberal state might permissibly promote religion as such, a question treated below.

basic principles in any full-blooded liberal version of the separation view.[2] These are bound together by the ideal of religious liberty as a central element in a free society; but other ideals, such as those of equality of persons regardless of their religious affiliation, of unfettered democratic participation, of social pluralism, and, more generally, of human flourishing, can also unify and support the various elements in the institutional theory of separation of church and state.

The first principle—which I shall call *the libertarian principle*—says that the state must permit the practice of any religion, though within certain limits.[3] The second principle—*the equalitarian principle*—says that the state may not give preference to one religion over another. This principle not only rules out an established church—whose existence might be plausibly argued to be consistent with the libertarian principle—but also precludes such things as legally requiring a certain religious affiliation as a condition for public office. The third principle—*the neutrality principle*—is less commonly affirmed, but also belongs to any full-blooded liberal account of separation of church and state. It says that the state should neither favor nor disfavor religion (or the religious) *as such*, that is, give positive or negative preference to institutions or persons simply because they are religious. Why should a free and democratic society endorse these principles? This is a large question, and I shall cite only the most general supporting grounds. I take the principles in turn.

It seems beyond dispute that from the moral point of view a society without religious liberty is simply not adequately free. Moreover, freedom is required for democracy, at least in any sense of 'democracy' relevant here. Thus, if one's ideal is a free and democratic society, one wants a social (presumably consti-tutional) framework to guarantee at least this: (1) freedom of religious belief, understood to prohibit the state or anyone else from forcibly inculcating religious beliefs in the general population;[4] (2) freedom of worship, involving,

---

2   In describing and supporting these three principles I draw on—and greatly abbreviate—a section of my "The Separation of Church and State and the Obligations of Citizens," *Philosophy & Public Affairs* 18 (1989).

3   A liberal democracy need not protect, in the name of religious freedom, practices that violate basic human rights, as where people are burned to death in sacrifice. But there is no easy way to determine the range of these rights nor the appropri-ate sanctions for the state to impose should they be violated. The principles defended below are intended to constitute part of a framework of decision, but they are not by themselves sufficient for the task.

4   This restriction does not rule out teaching children moral principles that are commonly part of one or more religious traditions—a point that is not always appreciated, sometimes with the unfortunate effect that school teachers are reluctant to teach moral principles. I cannot here try to define 'religious', but it must for our purposes be taken sufficiently narrowly to permit a distinction between the moral and the religious, and the cases that most concern us are those presupposing that a religion is theistic. Non-theistic religions pose—other things

minimally, a right of peaceable religious assembly, as well as a right to offer prayers by oneself; and (3) freedom to engage in (and to teach one's children if one has any) the rites and rituals of one's religion, provided these practices do not violate certain basic moral rights. Clearly, then, a free and democratic society should adopt the libertarian principle. A society without the freedom it guarantees would offer inadequate protection against governmental coercion.

The case for the equalitarian principle is more complicated. The (or a) central premise is that if the state prefers one or more religions, its people might well find it hard to practice another, or would at least feel pressure to adopt or give preferential treatment to the (or a) religion favored by the state. The degree of pressure would tend to be proportional to the strength of governmental preference. That preference might be as great as requiring a certain religious affiliation for holding a government job, or as minor as inviting clergy from just one religion to officiate at small, local ceremonies. Any governmental religious preference, however, creates some tendency for greater power to accrue to the preferred religion, particularly if it is that of the majority. Even if the existence of certain disproportionate powers does not necessarily (or at least does not directly) restrict anyone's liberty, concentration of power in a religious group as such easily impairs democracy, in which citizens should have equal opportunities to exercise political power on a fair basis, and it may impair religious freedom in particular. Moreover, where a state establishes or prefers a given religion, we may expect (though it is perhaps not inevitable) that certain laws will significantly reflect the worldview associated with that religion. These are among the reasons why a free and democratic society should adopt the equalitarian principle. Even where the libertarian principle is respected, the equalitarian principle is needed for protection against governmental discrimination.

As to the rationale for the neutrality principle, recall that religious liberty, broadly conceived, includes the freedom to reject religious views. If the state shows preference for religious institutions as such (or for the practice of religion in general), there may well be pressure to adopt a religion, and quite possibly discrimination against those who do not. To be sure, some kinds of state preference for religious people or institutions as such are consistent with religious liberty; hence, the neutrality principle cannot be simply derived from the libertarian principle. There are many domains of state preference for the religious as such. Mandatory prayer sessions in public schools, religious exemptions from combat duty, and religious eligibility requirements for adopting children are examples.[5] Preferences of this sort may tend toward

---

equal—far less serious church-state problems.

5   Conscientious-objector status is debatable: Is allowing it only for religious reasons inadmissible preferential treatment, or is it required in recognition of

political domination by the religious, even if in principle they could be prevented from causing it. Thus, even if there is protection both from religious tyranny and from discriminatory exclusions of some disfavored groups on religious grounds, governmental preference of the religious as such is likely to give them advantages that threaten a proper democratic distribution of political power. It can also reduce the level of free *exercise* of liberty, as opposed to its mere legal *scope*.

There are, however, further reasons for a liberal democracy to adopt the neutrality principle even if such a society did not have to be committed to protecting the freedom not to be religious. (These reasons may of course also provide support for the equalitarian principle.) Once the state favors the religious over the non-religious, at least three problems arise. (i) Where there is a majority affiliation, the views and even the interests of this group are likely to dominate legislation and policy affecting religion, sometimes to the detriment of religious minorities, for instance in the treatment of religious schools and the celebration of major events, such as inaugurations and holidays. (ii) Religious disagreements are likely to polarize government, especially regarding law and policy concerning religion, say requirements for conscientious-objector status or, at the institutional level, for tax exemption. (iii) If a government prefers the religious over the non-religious, it will tend, through the pronouncements and social policies that express that preference, to influence churches, and, in deciding what to promote in the religious sphere, to begin to set criteria for what counts as being religious in the sense that qualifies institutions for preference. Once there are benefits to be had, there will be stretching to meet the criteria for getting them. This is a likely way to much "entanglement" of the government in religious affairs.[6]

It might be argued that the only reason to avoid reducing the exercise, as opposed to the scope, of freedom is a commitment to fostering pluralism. But the distinction is not sharp: apart from a courageous few, making the exercise of a freedom costly shades into narrowing its scope. Moreover, quite independently of a commitment to fostering pluralism, a liberal democracy should

---

religious freedom? Even if the latter holds, it is arguable that freedom of religion is being unwarrantedly preferred over freedom of secular conscience.

6   The language of this sentence will remind some readers of the much-discussed "Lemon test" for the propriety of legislation: "First, the statute must have a secular legislative purpose; second, its principal or primary effect must be one that neither advances nor inhibits religion; finally, the statute must not foster 'an excessive entanglement with religion.'" See *Lemon v. Kurtzmann* 403 U.S. 602 (1971). Apart from the point that it is obvious that "excessive" entanglement should be avoided, the first two clauses are deservedly controversial. This paper addresses some of the relevant issues, such as a possible voucher system for public education, in less vague terms (though some degree of vagueness is inevitable on such matters).

avoid reducing the exercise of freedom, if only because that tends to lessen creativity both in the lives of individuals and in the solution of social problems.

A further ground for the neutrality principle is the ideal of equal treatment not just among the religious but among citizens in general, an ideal that, like liberty, is an important element in a free and democratic society. Governmental preference for the religious as such is intrinsically unequal treatment of the religious and non-religious, however minor the resulting material differences. On balance, then, the neutrality principle seems required to guarantee protection from governmental favoritism, in the sense of preferential treatment of the religious over the non-religious. Even if this treatment does not involve discrimination in favor of one religious group, non-religious citizens will tend to *feel* it as discrimination and not as a legitimate expression of the will of a democratic majority. Freedom and democracy are best served by principles that keep the state from restricting *or* influencing religious institutions any more than is required for enacting laws and policies that are justified on non-religious grounds.

II. Religious Obligation

As individuals living in a liberal democracy, we are less constrained than governments and institutions by principles that restrict sociopolitical conduct. It is indeed arguable that a citizen in such a society may properly vote or engage in other political conduct on any conscientiously chosen basis. But some of the same grounds—including protection of religious liberty—that underlie separation of church and state at the institutional level may, at the individual level, warrant a measure of separation of religious and secular considerations. I want to explore the extent to which this is so. Despite the connections between these two levels and the bearing of liberal democratic theory on both, I think it is instructive to begin not (as is common) with the implications of some liberal theory of the state for the conduct of citizens but instead with the point of view of a morally upright religious citizen who wants to live in a free and democratic society.

Suppose that I am devoutly religious and that my religion implies much about how a good life is to be lived. I might subscribe to the Ten Commandments and to Jesus's injunction to love our neighbors as ourselves. I thus have far-reaching, religiously grounded prima facie obligations relevant to my conduct as a citizen, and I might try to lead my day-to-day life with such religious standards in mind.[7] May I, as a conscientious citizen, pursue these

---

7   Calling the kinds of obligations in question *religious* is not meant to presuppose the truth of theism. If it is objected that apart from God's existence there are no such obligations (at least for those who take them to be ordained by God), we could simply speak of *presumptively religious* obligations, referring to the kind reasonably taken to be incumbent on votaries of a particular religion as such,

obligations as vigorously as possible within the limits of the law? This is a plausible view; but let us go beyond the law, since the law may be either unjustifiably restrictive or unwarrantedly permissive. May I, as a conscientious citizen, pursue my religious obligations so far as possible within the limits of my moral rights? An affirmative answer to the second question also seems plausible, at least if the issue is *moral* propriety; for if I were violating anyone else's moral rights, I would presumably be going beyond mine. I will contend, however, that there are ideals of moral virtue which require of us more than simply acting within our moral rights. In particular, there are *ideals of civic virtue*, which arguably derive from moral ideals (though I cannot try to do a derivation here) and demand of us more than simply staying within our rights.

In setting out and defending the perspective just suggested, I shall first briefly consider the nature and dimensions of religious obligation. I shall then sketch a partial conception of civic virtue, with liberal democracy in mind as the context of its exercise. And against that background I shall suggest how civic virtue and religious obligation can be reasonably integrated.

Religious obligation has at least five kinds of evidential grounds. In describing these, and indeed in discussing religious obligation in relation to civic virtue, I shall be thinking above all of what might be called the Hebraic-Christian tradition; but the points that emerge will apply, to varying degrees, to other traditions, including, to some extent, certain non-theistic religious traditions. The five sources I have in mind are (1) scripture; (2) non-scriptural religious authority, especially that of the clergy, but including the authority of the relevant theological community; (3) tradition, which often implies presumptions regarding one's religious obligations and may in some cases be quite authoritative; (4) religious experience; and (5) natural theology. Divine command is of course distinct from any of these, but I am supposing for the sake of argument that evidences of it in human life will come from one of these sources. Several further comments are called for.

First, a source of religious obligation may require a kind of conduct directly—as by commanding it in the way God is Biblically described as having commanded the actions that Moses cited in the Ten Commandments—or indirectly, as where Jesus exemplifies a kind of conduct and the text presents it as incumbent on us. Second, there are both direct and indirect obligations that go with commitment to a religion; these include both *religious obligations* in the narrow sense, for example to engage in certain rituals, and *obligations of a religion* (some of which are non-religious in content), such as Christians' obligations to contribute to charity. Third, there are special obligations, such as those arising from what is revealed in a religious experience, which may

and proceed. The kinds of church-state issues under discussion would be largely unaffected.

fall not only on the person in question, chiefly the one having the experience, but perhaps also on those addressed in it. My whole family might, for example, be singled out in a religious experience of mine and might acquire a religious or other obligation through what I credibly report as revealed to me. Fourth, there are what might be called *supererogations*—types of conduct that are desirable (and so are often presented in a favorable light), but not obligatory.[8] All four cases concern me, but it will not in general be necessary to address them separately.

It is also important, in discussing religious obligation, to distinguish its grounds from its content. An obligation can have religious grounds without having religious content, such as theological or liturgical content. This is illustrated by the non-theological commandments of the Decalogue, for instance the prohibition of bearing false witness. Here a principle with secular content is presented as based on religious grounds. If, however, we take this distinction to imply that we should not call the obligations imposed by those commandments religious, we lose contact with an important constraint. An obligation whose non-fulfillment is religiously criticizable is to that extent a religious obligation. It is an obligation *of* a religion, even if not an obligation having religious content.

We should also distinguish those religious obligations that are *aligned* with non-religious ones, such as the obligation not to murder, from those that are religious in content (and from those that are neither), and I will generally use the term 'religious obligation' to refer to obligations clearly grounded wholly or primarily in a religious source.[9] I leave open whether these must be objective obligations, as opposed to being, say, reasonably *believed*, from the point of view of a person's religious commitments and relevant non-religious beliefs,

---

8   Perhaps those with resources giving everything they have to the poor is an example pertinent in this context, though the force of Jesus's directive is open to more than one interpretation.

9   This formulation applies both to *types* of conduct (the more problematic case) and their *tokenings*, the specific instances of those types by an agent at a time. A particular person's obligation to A—say to give money to a particular church-supported cause—could, at a specific moment, be grounded in secular considerations, such as the effectiveness of its famine relief work, even if the primary grounds of *the* obligation to A (for virtually all who have it) are religious. Then, the specific act token—donating a sum in writing a particular check—might be at least in part secularly grounded even though the same person might have written a similar check a week earlier entirely for a religious reason. Deeds of the same action type, such as donations to a church or synagogue, may be tokened at different times for different reasons, or different combinations of reasons, among the reasons there are for deeds of that type. When agent, time, and circumstance are fixed, there may, for a token of a religiously obligatory deed, be only a secular reason or only a religious reason or a happy marriage of the two.

to be objective obligations. This leaves open the possibility that there can be religious obligations even if the associated religious presuppositions (such as theism itself) should be mistaken, but it does not force us to attribute to a people just any religious obligation they believe they have, nor to adopt any specific account of the nature and force of any subjective religious obligations there may be. There are, for at least the religious traditions most important to this paper, internal standards for responsibly determining when one has a religious obligation.

It seems clear that the five sources of religious obligation I have listed are, though historically interdependent, logically independent, in the sense that "endorsement," by any one of them, of a proposition favoring some conduct does not entail its endorsement by any other source among the five.[10] Their close historical association may tend to hide their logical independence, but the latter is of great importance. It suggests the possibility both of conflicts between the sources and of mutual support among them. The support that a source gives to an action may be merely partial. One or more sources may provide some degree of support for a kind of conduct, yet not imply that it is obligatory; or two or more may be jointly but not individually sufficient; or we may have *obligational overdetermination*. Two or more sources may each be sufficient. It should not be surprising, then, if some religious obligations are stronger than others, whether because two or more sources coincide in requiring the act in question as against one prohibiting it, or because one is clearer or more weighty than some other single source. This differential strength of religious obligations is indeed reflected in the way they are sometimes presented in scriptures.[11]

Suppose, then, that multiple religious sources can converge on the same obligatory behavior, such as giving to the poor. Suppose further that a religious obligation can be aligned with a secular one—one that is secularly grounded (which in principle could also have religious content, since one might, for example, promise to pray with someone). We should now expect that there is sometimes not only a *plurality of obligational grounds* for a kind of conduct, but also religiously and secularly *mixed obligational overdetermination*, the kind that occurs when there are both sufficient religious reasons *and* sufficient secular

---

10   Such an entailment may hold for some propositions but apparently not for *every* proposition supported by a source. This is by no means beyond controversy; certainly scripture, religious authority, and tradition tend to overlap in regard to the obligations they imply are incumbent on believers. But my purposes here do not require that there be no exceptions to the independence claim.

11   Jesus says, e.g., that the greatest commandments are to love one's God with all one's heart and to love one's neighbor as oneself; and given the way in which the Ten Commandments are ordered and expressed by Moses, together with their role in the Hebrew Bible in general, there is some reason to think the order of their presentation may indicate a kind of relative importance.

reasons for a kind of conduct, for instance being honest. Logically, neither kind of ground is necessarily stronger, either evidentially or motivationally. Genetically, neither kind need be prior.

If we think of the Hebraic-Christian tradition, it is clear that there is much overlap between religiously and secularly grounded obligations. Nor is this tradition opposed to taking secular grounds seriously, or even to looking to them for purposes of, say, better understanding the conduct required by both sets of grounds, or of enhancing one's motivation to produce that conduct. Granting that a person's faith can and should inform aspects of secular life, including especially the treatment of other people, reflective secular living can also lead to enhanced understanding of one's faith. Taken together with the multiplicity and independence of religious grounds, their internal diversity, and the unclarity (in some cases) of their bearing on conduct, this complicated, mutually enriching relation between religious and secular grounds has important implications. Two implications in particular concern me: one regarding religious individuals themselves, the other concerning their relations to their non-religious fellow citizens.

Consider rational individuals aware of the independence of religious sources, of the overlap between religious and secular obligations, and of the extent of religious diversity within and, especially, among traditions, both religious and non-religious. Should we not expect such individuals to seek confirmation of, or at least mutual support among, some of these justificatory sources, as they bear on judgments of far-reaching obligation? Some of those judgments, after all, are controversial or unclear or difficult to live up to; hence, mutual support of a judgment by sources to which one is committed is normally felt to be at once confirmatory, clarifying, and motivating. Furthermore, if the support includes secular considerations, there is the special satisfaction of being able to maintain that one's religious perspective leads to a truth that can be appreciated independently of it—and that can perhaps be a route by which others may join one, from outside one's tradition, in some project this truth supports.

My suggestion, then, is that mature, rational religious people living in circumstances like those of a contemporary liberal democracy will seek at least a measure of reflective equilibrium among their beliefs and attitudes grounded in religious sources of obligation and, in some cases, among those *and* beliefs and attitudes which they hold or find plausible, that they take to be grounded in secular sources. Roughly, this effort is a search for a cognitive balance in which the elements in question—chiefly one's beliefs, attitudes, and desires—are mutually consistent and, so far as possible, mutually supportive. The more rational we are, and the more complicated the moral issues we face, the wider is likely to be the equilibrium we seek. It may, though it need not, extend to theology, ethical theory, and even scientific considerations.

In the social arena, a mature, rational religious person is likely to be sensitive not only to overlapping moral views, but to moral and other disagreements that have at least potential religious significance. It is likely to seem quite appropriate in such cases to seek common ground with fellow citizens with whom one disagrees in major moral or sociopolitical matters. Perhaps one's view is supported by secular grounds that people of any religious persuasion can accept, even if appealing to those grounds means revising some aspect of one's own outlook. Indeed, I may find that I should revise something in my religious view. After all, once I take seriously the possibility of my religious sources yielding mutually conflicting results, I will be a fallibilist about my views of what constitute my religious obligations. I may, to be sure, feel very confident of some particular obligation, such as the obligation to try to love others and to spread the word of God among those who have not received it; and the sense of fallibility need not reduce my confidence. But it may still moderate—and it certainly bears on—what I should be willing to *do* on the basis of that confidence.

Fallibilism about one's conception of one's religious obligations is particularly significant, I think, where two conditions hold: first, the issue is what we are morally permitted or obligated to do in *non*-religious matters, and second, one can find no good secular ground for one's religiously based view. For although no secular reason need be expected for engaging in the special rites and rituals appropriate within a religious community, there is something of a presumption that, for our *general* moral obligations, including obligations to prevent or promote certain kinds of social conduct, such reasons may be found. I shall return to this issue.[12] For now, it is enough to have argued that both an effort to achieve reflective equilibrium and an attitude of fallibilism are appropriate to mature, rational practitioners of a religion for which, as is typical, there are multiple, independent, and sometimes unclear or ambiguous sources of authority regarding human conduct.[13]

---

12 It is useful to compare John Rawls's notion of public reason in this context. The notion seems narrower than that of a secular reason, but usable for some of the same purposes. See his *Political Liberalism* (New York: Columbia University Press, 1993). Some of my case for constraints on the use of religious reasons applies also to certain secular reasons, especially those that cannot play a proper role in public policy debate in a liberal democracy. Some of the latter, e.g. certain esoteric reasons, would be construed as inappropriate for that role by my requirement of (justificatory) adequacy; but I cannot go into this matter here.

13 The notion of fallibilism here may raise the question of the appropriate attitude for those who believe in papal infallibility. It should be noted that this doctrine is restricted both as to content, covering above all moral matters, and as to manner of expression. It applies only to pronouncements *ex cathedra*. Since there might be some vagueness on both counts, a measure of fallibilism may be appropriate concerning any *interpretation* of what is regarded as infallible in content. My concern here is also quite specific sociopolitical matters; and on these even people who give authority an enormous role in their lives may wish to be fallibilistic regarding their own judgments of what they do should do as citizens.

III. Civic Virtue

The partial picture I have painted of a mature, rational religious person surely indicates some of the makings of civic virtue. But before pursuing the question of how religious and civic ideals are connected, let us ask what sort of thing constitutes civic virtue in a liberal democracy (which I shall assume is embedded in a just state). Is it enough for a person simply to obey the laws, or perhaps the just laws? I think not. One would not thereby do any charitable deeds and could be well-nigh hermetical. Virtuous citizens—certainly those in the Hebraic-Christian tradition—try to contribute in some way to the welfare of others, including others beyond their immediate community. In a society that is complex, pluralistic, and so, inevitably, somewhat divided, civic virtue implies trying to take reasonable positions on important issues, voting, discussing problems with others, and more. Civic virtue in a liberal democracy implies a degree of responsible political participation.

A liberal democracy by its very nature resists using coercion, and prefers persuasion, as a means to achieve cooperation. What we are persuaded to do, by being offered reasons for doing it, we tend to do autonomously and to identify with; what we are compelled to do we tend to resent. Thus, when there must be coercion, liberal democracies try to justify it in terms of considerations—such as public safety—that any rational adult citizen will find persuasive and can identify with.[14] This is one reason why religious grounds alone are not properly considered a sufficient basis of coercion even if they happen to be shared by virtually all citizens.

As an advocate for laws and public policies, then, and especially for those that are coercive, virtuous citizens will seek grounds of a kind that any rational adult citizen can endorse as sufficient for the purpose; and they tend to be motivated in this direction in proportion to the burdensomeness of the coercion, for instance more concerned regarding the rationale for military conscription than for requiring drivers to be licensed. This adequacy condition for justifying coercion implies intelligibility of a certain kind (allowances being made for technical considerations in some cases); more to the point here, it implies secularity. I hasten to add that if civic virtue does imply such a search, that is not in the least to suggest any attempt to abandon religious grounds or even to abstract from them as potential evidence or motivation. This brings us to the question of how civic virtue is related to religious commitment.

I have already suggested that there is in fact a great deal of overlap between the content of certain religiously based obligations and that of widely recognized secularly based moral obligations, and I think there is substantial

---

14   A weaker condition would require only the capacity to understand the grounds, but I doubt that this condition would be sufficiently strong. Actual identification, however, is not required; since we are not talking about ideally rational citizens, such things as confusion or prejudice can interfere.

overlap with respect to major moral principles, such as those prohibiting murder, assault, injustice (including political oppression), theft, and dishonesty, and those requiring some degree of beneficence toward other people, as where one can help others with no significant sacrifice to oneself. I now want to go further, starting with a conception of God that seems at least implicit in what we might loosely call standard Western theism: I have in mind chiefly Christianity, Judaism, and Islam, the Abrahamic religions, as they are sometimes called; and I am speaking from the point of view of natural theology, not the theology of any particular religion.[15] If we assume a broadly Western theism, we can take God to be omniscient, omnipotent, and omnibenevolent. Might we not, then, expect God to structure us and the world so that there is a (humanly accessible) secular path to the discovery of moral truths, at least to those far-reaching ones needed for civilized life? Let me try to develop this idea.

Granted, if God has created an ambiguous world in which evil looms so large that even many theists are tempted to conclude that this sorry world could not have been created by *God*, it would seem possible that there is no secular path to moral truths. But it is one thing for God to test us and provide conditions for our freely choosing to become children of God; it is quite another thing to make it virtually impossible for those who do not so choose, even to be moral in non-theological matters.[16] Why would God compound the incalculable loss suffered by rejecting one's Creator with the impossibility of even discovering how one should behave in the absence of such a supreme authority? If the freedom preserved by the religious ambiguity of the world is so valuable, should we not expect God to provide for access to rational standards, discoverable by secular inquiry, for the proper exercise of that freedom? If God cares enough about us not to compel us toward theism but instead to allow our free choice or rejection of it, would it not seem that we would be equipped with standards for use of our freedom in the ways appropriate to God's creatures?

Moreover, if one thinks, as a great many theists do, that natural theology yields a rational, non-religious route to religious truths, it is reasonable to expect that there might be a counterpart secular route to at least some basic moral truths.[17] It seems altogether appropriate that, in ethics as in religion, God

---

15 I use 'standard Western theism' with some hesitation. The idea may be in part a philosophers' construction, but there is a recognizable set of assumptions here. What follows will clarify the idea, which was introduced in my "The Place of Religious Argument in a Free and Democratic Society," *San Diego Law Review* 30, no. 4 (1993).

16 It would not be unqualifiedly impossible, since one might be moral from good fortune as opposed to being so as a realization of moral knowledge. I assume, what all but a few radical theists grant, that even if rejection of God can be a moral wrong it is not the only kind, nor does it make all the others insignificant.

should provide more than one path to truths essential for living a good life. Furthermore, if there is already plurality of grounds for some major theological propositions and, in a different way, for some important theoretical conclusions in science, and if plurality in those domains is suggestive of God's provision for our discovering, in our individual ways, genuine religious and scientific truths, why should there not also be plurality with respect to grounds for major ethical truths?

Even if one does not agree that given standard Western theism, we should expect there to be accessible, adequate secular reasons for major moral principles, one may well grant (on other grounds) that there are such reasons. I believe that there are. I cannot show this here, but there is one general consideration that is highly suggestive. Suppose, as is widely held, that moral properties supervene on natural ones, roughly in the sense that (a) the moral properties of a person or act are determined by its natural ones, in a way implying that two people or acts alike in all their natural properties cannot differ in their moral ones, and (b) moral properties are possessed in virtue of natural ones. A person is honest, say, in virtue of a tendency to tell the truth (for an appropriate range of motivating reasons), and an act is obligatory, for instance, in virtue of being an avoidance of running over a child.[18] Now, if there

---

17   It should be granted that a non-religious route to religious truths could lead, through them, e.g. through divine commands, to moral truths; but this pathway to moral truths, however impeccable logically, still runs through religious territory, and some rational citizens in a liberal democracy might be permissibly unwilling to follow it. For some, it might be religiously inappropriate to be so led by someone else; for others it might be objectionable to be led through religious premises at all.

18   If natural properties include theological ones, e.g. being commanded by God, then the case for the existence of secular grounds for moral truths becomes more problematic. But the relevant properties of God (as opposed to, say, power) are not usually considered natural. Moreover, if they are natural, it may be that moral properties could supervene on them *by virtue of* supervening more basically on other, "earthly" natural ones: God might, e.g., command honesty because of what it is to be honest as opposed to deceitful, i.e., because of the (ontically) constitutive natural properties of honesty. Thus the obligatoriness of honesty would supervene directly on its divine requiredness, which would in turn supervene on its appropriateness to relations among persons. Call this the *embeddedness* of natural base properties in theological properties (it can take various forms, which I cannot distinguish here). Alternatively, one might say simply that God commands honesty because it is necessarily right (or good or both). On this view, God infallibly sees the rightness of honesty through comprehending its natural basis, as opposed to determining that basis by sheer will, in a sense implying that, e.g., lying and murder could have been right. This line of thought may be the more plausible conception of divine moral commands and would be consistent with honesty's supervening on natural properties apart from embeddedness.

are natural properties determining moral properties, it is reasonable to think that in principle we can discover the presence of moral properties through discovering the presence of natural properties on which they depend. Natural properties are (as normally—and non-skeptically—conceived) accessible to secular reason.

Granted, it could be that we are sometimes unable to tell *what* moral properties a person or act has even when we know the person or deed has natural properties that underlie the former. A psychological basis of deceitfulness, for instance, need not wear its moral significance on its sleeve. We could, then, lack an appropriate principle for connecting the former with the latter. But this does not in general happen. If you have a thorough knowledge of my personality, views, and motives conceived non-morally, you are in an excellent position to discern my moral character; and we also have a good sense of what *sorts* of natural properties are relevant to moral decisions, for instance properties affecting pleasure and pain, freedom of movement, and the human capacities of those affected by those decisions.[19]

On the assumption that for major moral principles, there are secular reasons sufficient to warrant accepting them—a possibility that, incidentally, does not depend on the supervenience just hypothesized as supporting it—we can appreciate a further connection between the conception of God as omniscient and omnibenevolent and the possibility of a rational secular path to moral truths—*any* cogent argument, including an utterly non-religious one, for a moral principle *is* in effect a good argument for (1) God's knowing that conclusion—since God knows all truths—and hence, presumably, for (2) God's wishing or requiring conformity to it. How could God, conceived as omniscient and omnibenevolent, not require, or at least wish, our conformity to a true moral principle?[20] It may turn out that the theological significance of

---

19   What does commonly happen is that we cannot be sure what our obligations *on balance* are even when we know, from natural facts, what our prima facie obligations are. The secularly based moral map is thus limited—a point crucial for Kent Greenawalt, who argues that (as I would put it) where there is an appropriate kind of secular indeterminacy on certain moral issues individuals may properly rely, even in the political domain, on religions considerations to decide their conduct, including voting. See *Religious Convictions and Political Choice* (Oxford and New York: Oxford University Press, 1988). I would stress that there may be similar problems in the religious domain, e.g. where two prima facie commandments in the Decalogue conflict.

20   This is cautiously worded in part because it cannot be assumed without argument that religious (or moral) obligations outweigh all others, hence cannot simply be assumed that God must wish us, on balance, to prefer realizing a religious obligation over a moral one where the two conflict. The case of Abraham and Isaac of course comes to mind. Note, however, that even if we knew that God placed (one or more) religious obligations over moral ones, we could still have better reason for believing that God commands, say, protection

some moral arguments may be at least as great as the moral significance of some theological arguments.

I should think, moreover, that in some cases, good secular arguments for moral principles may be *better* reasons to believe those principles to be divinely enjoined than theological arguments for the principles, based on scripture or tradition. For the latter arguments seem (even) more subject than the former to cultural influences that may distort scripture or tradition or both, more vulnerable to misinterpretation of religious texts or to their sheer corruption across time and translation; and more liable to bias stemming from political or other non-religious aims. Granting, then, that theology and religious inspiration can be sources of ethical insight, we can also reverse this traditional idea. One may sometimes be better off trying to understand God through ethics than ethics through theology.[21]

If these considerations from philosophical theology and ethical theory are sound, then civic virtue on the part of the religious should embody a commitment to *theo-ethical equilibrium*—a rational integration between religious deliverances and insights and, on the other hand, secular ethical considerations. Thus, a seemingly sound moral conclusion that goes against one's scriptures or one's well-established religious tradition should be scrutinized for error; a religious demand that appears to abridge moral rights should be studied for such mistakes as misinterpretation of what it requires, errors in a translation of some supporting text, and distortion of a religious experience apparently revealing the demand; a major moral principle derived from only one of the five sources of religious obligation should, in many cases, be tested against one or more of the other four and perhaps also against some secular source. Given the conception of God as omniscient, omnipotent, and omnibenevolent, the possibility of theo-ethical equilibrium is to be expected, and a mature,

---

of one's children than to believe that God commands any particular action inconsistent with this. Should Abraham, however, *insofar as he (reasonably?) believed it was God requiring the sacrifice*, have believed sacrificing his son was inconsistent with protecting him? That is not clear: God's ways of protecting us are infinite. It might also be noted how the story ends. The morally forbidden action is not required after all, perhaps suggesting that despite appearances, there cannot be an inconsistency between religious and moral obligation. This, however, would be false comfort for Kantians and certain other moral theorists: Abraham has already done the immoral deed at the level of willing—and "in his own heart."

21   Cf. Lenn Goodman's view that "for monotheism goodness is constitutive in the idea of God" and that "Ethics is constitutive in framing our idea of God but does not exhaust its content, and theism is a source of moral resolve and sublimity of principle but far from being the sole source at which such values can be tapped. All human beings know a good deal about their obligations without turning to God." See *God of Abraham* (Oxford and New York: Oxford University Press. 1996), pp. 81 and 83.

conscientious theist who cannot reach it should be reluctant or unwilling to support coercive laws or public policies on a basis that cannot be placed in that equilibrium.[22]

If we take a commitment to theo-ethical equilibrium to be (or at least to merit being) a major element in the civic virtue of the religious, are we deifying reason? I think not. Notice that although secular reason can lead to modifying one's religious views, religious considerations can also lead to revision of one's secular moral views. This applies especially to moral theories, but it extends even to "intuitive" moral judgments. Moreover, a commitment to seeking theo-ethical equilibrium leaves open whether one gives either kind of reason evidential priority or any other kind of precedence. The precedence of either one, however, is not license to ignore the other. A conscientious religious person aware of the relationships outlined here should not in general approve of any deed that is either morally or theologically impermissible.

A commitment to seeking theo-ethical equilibrium may be thought to split the self into religious and secular personae,[23] but it need not, and it can have the opposite effect. That there are separate grounds of action does not require for their intelligibility different agents or subagents to grasp them; it does not even imply different obligations to act on them, as opposed to a single obligation with a plurality of supporting reasons. An action's being supported by two different kinds of grounds can indeed be a good occasion to connect them as allied considerations. Disparate grounds may even be merged into a unified point of view, especially when theo-ethical equilibrium is achieved or, where it is not, when the grounds support the same or complementary actions. Moreover, each of several disparate grounds may be embraced from the standpoint of the others, as where secular benevolence is a fulfillment both of divine command and of a secular ethical commitment.

It should also be stressed that reason can be considered a gift from God and thus divinely sanctioned for our use. Furthermore, even divine commands about its use—such as to love God with all one's mind—must be carried out using the very faculty they are to regulate. A certain autonomy of reason in governing human life is presupposed in any religious perspective. Extending

---

22 Depending on one's theology, this might apply to a secular ground having no religious counterpart that supports the same conclusion. On common theistic assumptions, however, if there is a cogent truth-entailing secular reason for a normative conclusion, then God believes that conclusion (like any other truth), and the absence of any specifically theological ground should not prevent one's acting on the conclusion.

23 Stephen L. Carter criticizes Kent Greenawalt, Bruce Ackerman, John Rawls, and me on this score, suggesting that "religious citizens are forced to split off vital components of their personalities." See *The Culture of Disbelief* (New York: Basic Books, 1994), 230. Here I reply from my point of view, but some of what I say might apply to the other positions, especially Greenawalt's.

a good measure of that autonomy to the ethical and religious domains seems consonant with piety.

The very notion of civic virtue, as contrasted with religious virtue, suggests that secular reason will play a major role in the former. One reaction would be to say that, if so, then the deeply religious are within their rights in rejecting civic virtue as understood here. My response to this is that they *may* be within at least their religious rights; but that depends on the very issue we are discussing. On what implications their overall religious view has for the treatment of other people, especially those outside their religious community. Thomas Aquinas's emphasis on natural law, and indeed Jesus's emphasis on loving one's neighbors, on nonviolence, and on forgiveness, would suggest that civic virtue, especially when taken as embodying a commitment to theo-ethical equilibrium, should not (from within at least the major Christian traditions) be rejected. If, on the other hand, the question is whether we are within our moral rights in rejecting the proposed ideal of civic virtue so conceived, I would say that the answer is not clear. A major second-order moral obligation that we all seem to have is to take (first-order) moral obligations and principles seriously and to seek accommodation with those with whom we are obligated to live in peace despite our disagreements, whether they are outside our own religious tradition or within it.

Supposing, however, that we would be within both our moral and our religious rights in rejecting this ideal of civic virtue, is doing so morally desirable, and would it be morally virtuous? My answer to both questions is negative. Whether, from a religious point of view, this answer is reasonable depends on the conditions for achieving theo-ethical equilibrium within that point of view and on what sorts of principles support giving such equilibrium a serious place in one's sociopolitical conduct. I have already suggested that given omniscience, omnipotence, and omnibenevolence as elements in the conceptions of God prevalent in standard Western theism, a major factor in the equilibrium should be good secular arguments for moral principles. To connect samples of these with any specific religion is too large a task to undertake here. But the next section will suggest some principles of conscience that commend themselves both as elements in civic virtue and as prima facie guides to achieving theo-ethical equilibrium.

IV. Some Principles and Practices of Civic Virtue

It may seem odd to speak of *principles* of virtue. But first, I am not here endorsing virtue ethics overall; and second, principles may have a major role even in a virtue ethics. Even if traits are morally fundamental, we can formulate principles on the basis of observing the conduct of virtuous agents in sufficiently diverse circumstances; and a habitually virtuous agent will often act on principles so derived.[24]

The first principle I want to discuss—which, in earlier work, I have called the *principle of secular rationale*—says that one has a prima facie obligation not to advocate or support any law or public policy that restricts human conduct, unless one has, and is willing to offer, adequate secular reason for this advocacy or support (say for one's vote). Five points of clarification are in order immediately. First, most laws and public policies do restrict human conduct to some extent, and the more restrictive the laws or policies in question, the stronger the relevant obligation. Second, my main concern is what I propose to call *positive restrictions*—roughly, coercion or restriction of the conduct of ordinary citizens—as opposed to *negative restrictions*, which are roughly the coercion or restriction of the enforcement of positive restrictions, chiefly by governmental or institutional officials. Negative restrictions are second order, being restrictions of restrictions, and amount to liberalizations. Third, the secular rationale principle seems to have some force even widened to apply to non-restrictive laws and public policies (those that, like laws enabling a certain kind of agreement to be a legal contract, impose no significant positive restrictions); but these less troublesome cases do not concern me here. Fourth, I am taking a secular reason as roughly one whose normative force, i.e., its status as a prima facie justificatory element, does not evidentially depend on the existence of God (or on denying it) or on theological considerations, or on the pronouncements of a person or institution *qua* religious authority.[25] And fifth, among the overriders of the obligation are special circumstances in which

---

24 In "Acting from Virtue," *Mind* 104 (1995), I discuss how virtues and principles interact in a virtuous agent and what it is to act from virtue. So far as principles in relation to virtue ethics are concerned, it is noteworthy that Aristotle himself says that there are some actions, such as murder, adultery, and theft, that do not admit of a mean, with the clear implication that they are "as a rule" wrong. See *Nicomachean Ethics* 1107a10 ff.

25 See "The Separation of Church and State and the Obligations of Citizenship," cited above. The principle applies with different degrees of force in different contexts. Moreover, the adequacy requirement rules out some *non*-religious reasons, e.g. those that are ill-grounded; but my concern here is with the specifically religious in relation to the political. I might add that the principle is not meant to require that an adequate reason be objectively correct in a sense implying that it is equivalent to a true proposition. A false proposition that is sufficiently well justified can count as an adequate reason. My paper just cited spoke of an adequate reason for something as one "whose truth is sufficient to justify" that, and at least one careful commentator on the paper has read this conjunctively rather than conditionally, i.e., as implying both truth and justificatory sufficiency, rather than (as intended) on the model of, e.g., 'You need a witness whose testimony for your side is sufficient to sway those in doubt', which does not imply that either the witness or the testimony is actual. An alternative wording is 'a reason which, if it should be true, justifies . . . '. See Philip L. Quinn, "Political Liberalisms and Their Exclusions of the Religious," *Proceedings and Addresses of the American Philosophical Association* 69 (1995), esp. pp. 38–39.

secrecy is necessary, as where one would be in serious danger if certain people knew what legislation or candidate one was supporting.

If, given God's omniscience, omnipotence, and omnibenevolence, there is as much reason to expect alignment between religiously well-grounded, and secularly well-grounded, moral standards as I have suggested, then following the principle of secular rationale may be reasonably expected not to put a religious person (at least in the tradition of standard Western theism) into disequilibrium except where there is an error, for instance where at least one of the two sets of grounds is erroneous (say, embodying a false premise or invalid inference). If, for example, a standard of punishment is irresolubly inconsistent with divinely required mercifulness, then perhaps revenge has been confused with retribution.

The principle of secular rationale is intended to benefit people *within* a religious tradition, for instance in different denominations and possibly even in the same denomination, as well as to facilitate good relations *between* different religious traditions, and between religious and non-religious people. Intramural strife can be deadly. It seems less likely to occur where this principle is adopted.

The second principle I suggest—which in earlier work I have called the *principle of secular motivation*—adds to the rationale principle that one also has a (prima facie) obligation to abstain from advocacy or support of a law or public policy that restricts human conduct, unless one is sufficiently *motivated* by some (normatively) adequate secular reason, where sufficiency of motivation here implies that some secular reason is motivationally sufficient, roughly in the sense that (a) this reason explains one's action and (b) one would act on it even if, other things remaining equal, one's other reasons were eliminated.[26] Notice that since an argument can be tacitly religious without being religious in content, one might fail to adhere to at least the second of these principles even in offering arguments that on their face are neither religious nor fail to provide an adequate secular reason for their conclusion. It might be argued, for example, that some people, in presenting a genetic argument for the personhood of the zygote, are not sufficiently motivated by the secular considerations cited in their argument, and (quite apart from whether it is objectively sound) would not find the argument convincing apart from their underlying religious beliefs.[27] The same might hold for a scientific argument

---

26   "The Separation of Church and State," esp. 284–86.

27   It has been claimed otherwise, e.g., by Vern Sima, in a letter to the *Lincoln Journal-Star* (October 23, 1993): "I belong to a church that teaches abortion is murder. I am open-minded enough to accept the church's unbounded wisdom. But what ultimately convinced me was scientific evidence and observation. What we have here is science confirming religious truths, not religious truths standing alone, even though that would be enough." This claim is not plausible to me because, for one thing, I cannot see why one would need to be open-minded to

aimed at preventing creationism from being discussed in a public school science course. The secular considerations it cites might not be motivating, and if it is proposed from anti-religious motivation, then even if it accords with the rationale principle, offering it does not accord with the motivation principle.

Consider, by contrast, arguing for a voucher system on the ground that parents, and especially religious ones, should be free to educate their children in academically adequate schools of their choice, including those that teach a particular religious point of view, and so should receive a voucher for each child, which can be used toward the costs of their children's attending any accredited school.[28] Here the *content* of the proposed legislation, unlike that of proposed restriction on abortion, includes a concern with religion and even envisages some likelihood of promoting its practice; but the *ground* given for the legislation is not intrinsically religious. One could support a voucher system on this ground without specially favoring the religious over, say, non-religious people who are simply dissatisfied with the general quality of public education.[29] If, however, pressing for a voucher system is to exhibit civic virtue as understood (in part) in terms of the principle of secular motivation, then some such secular consideration should be both (normatively) adequate and sufficiently motivating. If one's *only* reason for supporting vouchers is to promote the religious devotion of one's children (or other children), then even if one is expressing a kind of religious virtue, one is not exhibiting civic virtue.

Granted, if there *is* an adequate secular reason for a policy, no overall harm need be expected from the policy, and one might offer the reason as justifying one's conduct even if it does not motivate one. But let us apply the do-unto-others rule to that case. One would not like having a different religious group, with which one deeply disagrees, press for its religiously preferred policies

---

accept what one conceives as "unbounded wisdom" or why, if one thinks of the church's view as manifesting it, one would not be convinced *before* discovering the scientific evidence. The question is especially urgent given that the writer says the religious truth "would be enough," apparently meaning that the church's view would not *need* scientific confirmation to be acceptable. Detailed treatment of what constitutes religious argumentation is provided in my "The Place of Religious Argument in a Free and Democratic Society," cited above.

28 The accrediting may take account of certain factors that are not purely academic. It is one thing to give vouchers to support free parental choice, including religious choice; it is another to allow them where racial discrimination is practiced. It is a delicate and difficult question when criteria of admission are objectionable in a way that warrants differential governmental treatment.

29 It is noteworthy that in The Netherlands the government funds both public and sectarian schools, compensating, in part, for the differences this allows among publicly funded schools by requiring national examinations keyed to a core curriculum constituting 80 percent of what students study in the secondary school years. For a brief description see the article by Laurel Shaper Walters in the *Christian Science Monitor* for December 12, 1992.

solely for religious reasons of its own, even if a good secular reason could be offered. One's attitude may be modified only slightly where, although the secular reason motivates to some degree, it is inessential to determining support for the policies, which would have been promoted in its absence. One is especially likely to disapprove of the dominance of religious motivation if the policy or law in question is backed by severe punishments. As elsewhere in ethical matters, there can be a wrong way to do the right thing. The right way in cases of coercion must incorporate appropriate motivation.

The stress on secular reasons as evidential and motivational elements in civic virtue must not be taken to imply that such virtue requires no other constraints on appropriate reasons, such as prohibitions of racist grounds for public policy. This is not the place for an account of what makes certain reasons appropriate. Religious reasons, conceived (for instance) as reasons for human conduct that are ultimately grounded in God's nature or commands (or, at least from the point of view of religious persons, are rationally believed to be so grounded), are a major subject in their own right. There are some respects in which they are special in relation to liberal democracy even by contrast with other reasons—such as certain intuitive deliverances about other people—that are not accessible to any normal adult.[30] Here are some salient points.

First, the kinds of religious reasons of greatest concern in this paper are directly or indirectly taken to represent an infallible authority, in a sense implying that the propositions expressing them *must* be true.[31] Second, very commonly those who identify with what they regard as the ultimate divine source of religious reasons believe that anyone who does not is forsaken, damned, or in some other way fundamentally deficient. Third, religious reasons often dictate practices that are distinctively religious in content (such as prayer) or intent (such as preserving a fetus on the ground that it is a gift from God), and therefore are plausibly seen in some cases as forcing others to observe a religious standard. Fourth, for at least many religions, rational, relevantly informed outsiders are unable to discern effective checks on certain

---

30   Accessibility in the relevant sense is no simple matter. Ordinary sensory data of the kind needed to use a ruler and read a gauge are clearly accessible, and a clairvoyant sense about the future is clearly not. But it might be argued that anyone who is open-minded, considers natural theology, and attends certain religious services in a good faith effort to find God thereby has access to good theistic reasons for a certain view of the world. Many people who reluctantly or ambivalently leave their faith would claim to be counterexamples to this; but even if that judgment is accepted, the notion of accessibility is not precise and will remain controversial.

31   This does not imply that these propositions are necessarily true simpliciter but that it is impossible that they be *both* endorsed or accepted by God and false. Thus, one may presumably be as certain of their truth as one is that they are divinely endorsed or accepted.

possible tendencies for clergy (or, in some cases, votaries) to project, whether consciously or otherwise, their own views or preferences into their interpretations of one or another authoritative religious source, including even God[32]; and in this case there is, in addition to the possibility of some people's cloaking their prejudices with absolute authority, the possibility that the views and motives of those who follow them lack the minimal autonomy that citizens in a liberal democracy may hope for in one another. Fifth, owing to some of these points (among others), religious people often tend to be, in a way that is rare in secular matters, highly and stubbornly passionate about the importance of everyone's acting in accordance with religious reasons, and non-religious people often tend to be highly and stubbornly passionate about not being coerced to do so. Sixth, partly because religious liberty is a constitutive foundation (or at least a cogent rationale) for liberal democracy, citizens in such a state are naturally and permissibly resentful about coercion by religious factors (which may lead to restrictions of their specifically religious behavior), in a way they are not permissibly resentful concerning coercion by, for instance, considerations of public health. There may be other kinds of reasons to which each of these six points (or close counterparts) applies individually; but if there are any to which all of them apply, it is in a different way and is in any event a good prima facie reason to impose similar restrictions on the use of those reasons.[33]

It might still seem that motivation should not matter if the quality of one's reasons is good enough. This is a very difficult issue to settle, if it can be settled. But I would stress that insofar as we are thinking of the advocacy or other public behavior as supposed to be action *from virtue* we should look not just at what kind of act it is and what can be said for it abstractly, but also at how it is grounded in the agent's *character*.[34] As Kant distinguished acting merely

---

32 Stephen Carter puts a related point vividly when he says, "I have always been deeply offended by politicians, whether on the left or on the right, who are ready to seize on the language and symbols of religion in order to grub for votes" (*The Culture of Disbelief*, p. 47).

33 It is worth noting two points here. (1) Nothing I have said about religious reasons entails that religion is necessarily either "esoteric" or in any way irrational, or even that there cannot be cogent arguments for God's existence from non-religious premises. (2) To Unitarianism—particularly the more common non-theistic forms—these points apply far less than to many other religions. There may indeed be forms of Unitarianism and other broadly religious outlooks that are not plausibly considered a religion—though they would be *religious*, in the sense John Dewey noted, in which appropriate attitudes, e.g. of reverence, can mark a perspective as religious even if it is not part of *a religion*. Dewey's distinction among the notions of religion, the religious, and *a* religion is a major topic of definition I cannot address directly in this paper.

34 In "Acting from Virtue," cited above, I provide an account of such action which supports the conception of it employed here.

in conformity with duty and acting *from* duty, and Aristotle distinguished—as any virtue theorist should—actions that *express* virtue from those not virtuously performed but merely "in the right state," i.e., of the right type, we should distinguish actions from civic virtue and actions merely in conformity with it. There is no question that morally one may, within one's rights, advocate a coercive course of action without being motivated by an adequate secular reason; my contention is that to do so is not always consonant with civic virtue.

The point here may be more readily seen by reflecting on the difference between what we *say* to others and what we *communicate* to them. This difference is particularly relevant to public debate on major human issues. We speak with different voices on different occasions and for different purposes. Even when they say the same thing, human voices can differ as radically as the timbres and resonances of different musical instruments sounding the same note; and, as it is the causal basis of those notes, and not their pitch, that produces the quality of the instruments sounding them, with human speech it is the causal basis of what we say, including our motivation, and not the content of what we say, that yields our voice.

Our voice is determined more by why and how we say what we do than by what we say.[35] And we tend to listen for voicing as well as content. We try to hear more than just *what* people say, and quite commonly we accept—or reject—what others say because of how they voice it as well as because of what it is. Just criticism, delivered in a patronizing voice, is sometimes resisted precisely because of that voicing; a rejection of what we say, expressed impersonally and respectfully, may evoke fruitful revision of our view. Quite often, a disparity between content and voice, as where a scientific argument concerning abortion is religiously motivated and presented in a religious voice, can, though the proponent is entirely sincere, produce suspicion or resentment.

Part of civic virtue consists in having an appropriate *civic voice*; part of civic harmony in a framework of pluralism and disagreement consists in using that voice as the primary mode of communication in debating fundamental issues of citizenship. It need not be any citizen's only voice, not even for public argumentation, and certainly not for self-expression. But it is achievable by

---

35   Our voice is, however, likely to be also determined *in part* by what we say, and other things being equal a civic voice is not fully achieved if one is proposing religious reasons as grounds for public policy decisions. It may be possible, however, to present such reasons in a context that preserves a certain balance, e.g. by noting that, in addition to sufficient secular reasons for a piece of legislation such as permitting state aid handicapped children in religious schools, many religious citizens will feel better able to provide for their children services they believe God requires. Thus, the emphasis on achieving a proper civic voice as part of civic virtue leads to no simple rule about the admissible content of advocacy of laws or public policies.

any rational citizen committed to liberal democracy; and if I am right about the prospects for achieving theo-ethical equilibrium, then a civic voice is available, in part through adherence to the principle of secular motivation, to most rational religious people without compromise of their basic religious commitments.[36]

Is the mixed voice produced by combined religious and secular motivation consonant with civic virtue? It certainly may be. Overdetermination need not produce discord; it can yield harmony. The cooperation of different elements can, moreover, produce a more powerful and, especially in a democracy, a more authoritative voice—a point worth noting both by those who would restrict political argument to publicly accessible considerations and by those who think secular reasons are not needed.[37]

There are saintly people whose actions may make it seem odd to take civic virtue to imply secular motivation and a mistake to conceive acting from civic virtue as grounded—at least in part—therein. Consider Mother Teresa. Doesn't her loving treatment of the sick manifest civic virtue? It certainly may. But to answer adequately we must distinguish civic virtue proper, as a *civically grounded* state of character, from civic virtue in a looser, behavioral sense: a *civically directed* disposition to do things having civic value. Similarly, we must distinguish action performed from civic virtue, and civically directed action. Virtues are best classified by their grounds, roughly the crucial elements of motivation and cognition that explain what the agent is doing in manifesting those elements of character, and why. Virtues are not best classified in terms of a person's typical external conduct—good though that is in indicating the presence of a virtue.

---

36   One has a voice as a writer and can have a civic voice as such. In some ways the voice of a writer is less easily, in some more easily, discerned; but the same general points seem to hold.

37   I have in mind, e.g., the emphasis in Rawls, *Political Liberalism*, on restricting the reliance on "comprehensive views." My position is, on this count, less restrictive than his; mine allows that they may figure crucially both evidentially and motivationally, and both in general public discussion and in advocacy and support of laws and public policies, provided (evidentially) adequate secular reasons play a sufficiently important role. For a detailed discussion of Rawls's restrictions, particularly as they bear on whether he is in the end an "Enlightenment liberal," see Jean Hampton, "The Common Faith of Liberalism," *Pacific Philosophical Quarterly* 75, nos. 3–4 (1994): 186–216. Other recent critical discussions of value are Jürgen Habermas, "Reconciliation through the Public Use of Reason: Remarks on John Rawls's *Political Liberalism*," *Journal of Philosophy* 92, no. 3 (1995): 109–31 (replied to by Rawls in the same issue, 132–80); and Joshua Cohen, "A More Democratic Liberalism," *Michigan Law Review* 92 (1994): 1503–46. For criticism of both Rawls's and my views on the constraints appropriate to public political behavior, see Michael J. Perry, *Religion in Politics: Constitutional and Moral Perspectives* (New York: Oxford University Press, 1996).

To see why virtues are best classified by reference to their grounds, recall that action conforming with virtue may stem from other sources, from prudence to treachery to dissembling to self-deception. Mother Teresa could be expected to have *both* religious reasons and secular motivation, such as simple human compassion, even if the virtue she acts from in most of her daily conduct is religiously grounded devotion to others. On my view, however, she has little if any moral *need* to exercise civic virtue in her charitable work. She is not promoting restrictive laws or policies; her work restores and liberates people, rather than restricting them.

Nor do I claim that civic virtue is intrinsically better than religious virtue; they are good in different ways. Mother Teresa's charitable work is, however, perfectly compatible with her having civic virtue; and one can act from two virtues, just as one can act from two motives.[38] Civic virtue is needed above all where one is advocating or otherwise supporting laws or public policies that would restrict human freedom. Much of human life does not involve such conduct; much that does can be guided by cooperating religious and secular motives.

Given the importance of such cooperating religious and secular motives, it is appropriate to formulate a second-order principle that facilitates the application of, and adherence to, the principles of secular rationale and motivation. This higher-order principle is based on the idea that there is much to be gained, intellectually and motivationally, from seeking theo-ethical equilibrium in deciding a wide range of important questions. For those who are religious, then (and possibly even as a heuristic principle for some who, though not religious, can think sympathetically and fruitfully in religious terms), I propose a *principle of theo-ethical equilibrium*: where religious considerations appropriately bear on matters of public morality or of political choice, religious persons have a prima facie obligation—at least insofar as they have civic virtue—to seek an equilibrium between those considerations and relevant secular standards of ethics and political responsibility. I take this obligation to seek equilibrium to be strongest where support of a law or public policy that would restrict human conduct is in question, but I believe that some obligation may remain even apart from such cases.

Much is still left unspecified here. How readily should the bearing of religious considerations on the matter at hand be discernible? How much effort should one expend in connection with decisions regarding law or public policy to discern whether this is any such bearing? And what ethical and political standards must one consider? A great deal could be said, but I leave the issue for another occasion. I certainly would add, however, that one may seek a still wider equilibrium, for instance where the application of a moral

---

38   This and other claims about virtue in this paper are defended, at least implicitly, in my "Acting from Virtue," cited above.

standard to a concrete case requires a knowledge of many facts. It should be no surprise that a principle of virtue is not quantifiable and requires finding an Aristotelian mean between excess and deficiency.

V. Separation of Church and State as Addressed to the Church

My concern so far has been with governmental activities as they affect religion and, even more, with standards of sociopolitical conduct appropriate to conscientious citizens in a free and democratic society. But a full-blooded liberal theory of institutional separation has another component, also based on ideals underlying liberal democracy. For many of the same reasons why the state should not interfere in religion, churches should not interfere in government. The point is not legal or even constitutional. I am not suggesting, for example, that church donations to political candidates must be illegal in a liberal democracy—though presumably they should be *if* churches have tax-exempt status. My point is that protection of religious liberty, and certainly of governmental neutrality toward religious institutions, is better served if, normally, churches as such abstain from political action.

This political-neutrality proposal goes somewhat beyond what one would expect in the institutional counterparts of the principles of secular rationale and secular motivation. For a church might often both have and be sufficiently motivated by a moral consideration bearing on a political issue. This ecclesiastical moral engagement is surely desirable in a liberal democracy, and it is quite likely to occur if, in moral matters, churches abide by an *institutional principle of theo-ethical equilibrium*, which says that religious institutions, at least insofar as they are committed to citizenship in a free and democratic society, have a prima facie obligation to seek such equilibrium in deciding to advocate or support laws or public policies that restrict human conduct. This equilibrium principle is a plausible candidate for a principle of institutional civic virtue and is quite far-reaching. (Indeed, a counterpart principle has some application to secular private institutions for which it is appropriate to bring religious considerations into the relevant range of public policy decisions.) Why should we go beyond the principle to the suggested neutrality proposal, which calls not for theo-ethical equilibrium as a constraint on political conduct, but for political neutrality on the part of churches?

One ground for the neutrality proposal is that in their official institutional actions churches are commonly understood to be acting *as* religious institutions whose major concerns and bases of action are always religious. That common understanding, however, does not always apply, and even when it does it has limited force. It is simply not true that religious institutions can properly have or be motivated only by religious reasons. For at least a great many churches, it can be quite proper both to take a moral position as such and to consider a moral conclusion as such to be sufficient for a political position. I think it turns out, then, that we need a more fine-grained understanding of the proper role of churches in a free and democratic society than we can achieve simply by extending the rationale, motivation, and equilibrium principles to institutions.

Let me tentatively suggest, then, a *principle of ecclesiastical political neutrality*: in a free and democratic society, churches committed to being institutional citizens in such a society have a prima facie obligation to abstain from supporting candidates for public office or pressing for laws or public policies that restrict human conduct.[39] This principle applies not just to institutions as social entities but (if this is different) to their official representatives acting as such.[40] Even for churches not committed to citizenship in a liberal democracy, a case can be made that it would be good for them to recognize such an obligation of neutrality, but here I restrict attention to the former case. A number of other comments (far more than I have space to make) are also required.

First, I do not take the neutrality obligation to be likely to prevail under just any social conditions. Under conditions of tyranny, freedom and democracy might be restorable only if churches *do* support candidates for (public) office. A clear threat of such tyranny, as in pre-Nazi Germany, may also warrant such support. Nor do I take the obligation in question to be specifically religious or theological, since it need not be grounded in religious or theological elements and indeed not every religious tradition need contain elements that would sustain it. Whether the obligation has a sufficient moral basis depends in part on whether there are (as I think there may very well be) sufficient moral grounds for liberal democracy as the best form of government.[41] But even apart

39   The notion of institutional citizenship needs explication, but I think it is significantly analogous to individual citizenship, though unlike an individual citizen a church has its own citizens—indeed, citizens forming a *community* rather than merely a group. There is a serious challenge here which the notion of institutional citizenship can meet only in part: according to Gerald Frug, as interpreted by Jean Bethke Elshtain, "American liberal thought and practice have no robust way to thematize entities intermediate between the state and the individual." See her "Catholic Social Thought, the City, and Liberal America," in Kenneth L. Grasso, Gerard V. Bradley, and Robert P. Hunt, eds., *Catholicism, Liberalism, and Communitarianism* (Lanham, Md.: Rowman and Littlefield, 1995), 109 and, for an indication of her own perspective, 111–12. A number of the essays in this volume also bear on the problem. Christopher Wolfe's "Subsidiarity: The 'Other' Ground of Limited Government" and Michelle Watkin's and Ralph McInerny's "Jacques Maritain and the Rapprochement of Liberalism and Communitarianism" may be especially pertinent to the problem and to this paper in general.

40   Nothing less than the holism-individualism issue lurks here; for our purposes an individualistic reading of the principle is best, but the normative issues could be similarly treated if one plausibly formulated the principle as applying directly to institutions as such.

41   If the obligation is moral, it is presumably not contingent on churches' being committed to good institutional citizenship. That commitment itself would

from how this question is resolved, there are considerations of good institutional citizenship and of prudence that support the principle of ecclesiastical political neutrality for churches living under conditions of freedom and democracy.

This neutrality principle will be too strong if we construe 'political' in the broad sense of 'contested in the arena of politics'; it must be taken rather narrowly, so that moral issues are not included, even if they enter into distinctly political debates, but not so narrowly that pressing for restrictive laws or public policies—e.g. policies requiring periods of prayer or meditation in public schools—does not count as political. The difference between the political and the moral can be masked by the application of a single term, such as 'the abortion issue', to both moral questions of ethical permissibility and political questions of legal protection. Paradigms of political questions are what specific persons or particular party will hold governmental power, what specific structure should be enacted for taxation, welfare, criminal justice, health care, and military systems, and what policies should govern relations, including immigration, with other countries. But there are many other political questions, and some of these have major moral dimensions.

The separation of church and state does not require, nor do any sound principles demand, that churches should not publicly take moral positions, even if there is political controversy about them. Publicly taking moral positions is indeed a positive religious obligation in many religions. There are, to be sure, different ways of supporting moral positions; and some are closer than others to political statements, as where government officials of only one party are cited as immoral despite the prominence of comparable offenders who are officials in another party. These matters call for discretion and do not admit of codification.

In applying the ecclesiastical neutrality principle it is important to distinguish—as with other politically significant institutions, such as universities—between *internal* and *external* political activities and, in both cases, between *official* and *unofficial* political statements and positions. The former activities are directed toward members, the latter toward an external group, such as society as a whole (these are the pure cases; there are myriad mixtures raising special problems I cannot take up here). The principle of ecclesiastical political neutrality applies differently to the latter than to the former activities. A church's publicly promoting political candidates is, prima facie, poor institutional citizenship; its doing so internally need not be, though it may tend to

presumably be an institutional prima facie moral obligation. Moreover, at least if the obligation is moral I would take its prima facie character to imply not just that there is a reason for the conduct in question but that when that reason is overridden there should be an appropriate explanation, say in terms of one relevant value's outweighing another in the context, as illustrated by the case in which resisting tyranny justifies direct political action by a church.

corrupt its spiritual mission or may put undue pressure on its members or both.[42] It also matters considerably whether the political activity is official or unofficial, say carried on in private conversation as opposed to a letter to parishioners. Here again the internal-external distinction is relevant; public support by clergy of a candidate for office may, especially when official, exert pressure on church members, on ordinary citizens, on candidates for public office (who may, e.g., curry favor or solicit opposing clerical statements), or on government officials (who may, for instance, think they are hearing, in the voice of one or more clergy, the wishes or views of the members of the relevant religious group).

The principle of ecclesiastical-political neutrality would not prevent churches' encouraging their members' *participation* in politics; and it does not unduly restrict political participation by religious citizens, or imply that they should not consider such participation an aspect of their religious commitments. A minister or rabbi could, under this principle, both publicly oppose nuclear dumping in the oceans and, during religious services, preach against political apathy. Civic indolence may be criticized both as a failing in a religious obligation to improve the world and as a moral vice in citizens. It is only taking political positions from the pulpit (and in other institutional ways) that the principle implies would be (prima facie) objectionable. Thus, a church-sponsored group, such as one opposing an unjust war, or a service committee that, in its humane activities, defies government policy, is not necessarily an official representative of the church's position. Even then, the group may distinguish its moral from its political aims, and prudence often dictates doing so.

To be sure, there are moral statements which, combined with certain obvious facts about politicians, government officials, or foreign powers, imply condemnation or approval of them. But there is a crucial difference between affirming moral truths which, *with* certain facts, imply political judgments, and, on the other hand, making political judgments themselves. Matters of fact may be controversial; and in any case, when the suggested distinction between the moral and the political is observed, the political bearing of factual issues is left to the individual judgment of those in the congregation or audience. That

---

42   Again, Stephen Carter nicely expresses part of my point: of a young minister he once heard who preached in detail about El Salvador, he says, "For her, politics should lead faith, rather than the other way around—a proposition that is by no means the special reserve of the left. Her sermon, like many that were preached in support of Ronald Reagan's presidential candidacy, exemplified the problem of the political tail wagging the scriptural dog" (*The Culture of Disbelief*, 69). I differ with Carter, however, on how religious motivation should enter politics. The religious dog should be joined by a secular one, sufficient for the task even if less important to one and less vociferous than its religious companion. Given theo-ethical equilibrium, they will pull together.

judgment constitutes an important filter between clerical deliverances and political action. Even people who accept the moral judgments in question, find it obvious what the relevance of the facts is, and draw an obviously implied political conclusion will have traversed a certain inferential distance. Doing so is an exercise of autonomy.[43]

I do *not* believe that the principle of ecclesiastical political neutrality should be written into law; but if it is not conscientiously observed, then candidates for public office may be unduly influenced to serve the special, even the distinctively religious, interests of certain churches, particularly if there is a majority church. Furthermore, the polarities afflicting relations between certain religious groups are more likely to surface in government decision making, where the public interest should be the overriding concern.

Admittedly, some polarization may arise from *any* public political disagreement, particularly when institutions themselves square off. But whereas, in a free and democratic society, political controversy is inevitable, religious polarization is not. Moreover, some clergy represent themselves as having, or in any case are generally taken to have, special insight into matters of human conduct; this (among other factors) increases the chance of sociopolitical polarization if religious institutions as such enter into politics and (certain kinds of) public policy debate, even if they do it only or chiefly within their own congregations.

Granted, however hard we try to avoid basing political positions on religious considerations, there is no sharp distinction between moral and political issues, and certainly an admirable moral sermon on, for example, the duties of charity, could have obvious implications for legislative decisions on welfare policy. But if, in borderline cases, the moral and political intermingle, there is still a generally plain difference between, say, giving a moral sermon about the quality of contemporary movies and endorsing candidates, political parties, or politically contested public policy positions.

---

43   For valuable discussion of the general problem here see David Hollenbach, S.J., "The Political Role of Religion: Civil Society and Culture," *San Diego Law Review* 30, no. 4 (1993). At one point he says, "[S]ome fundamentalist Christians draw policy conclusions about the rights of homosexuals or about prayer in the public schools directly from the *Bible*. . . . Some more conservative Catholics regard the legal banning of abortion as similarly entailed by the moral teachings of the pope and the Catholic bishops. From what has been said above about the need for believers to enter into dialogue with others in society as they develop their vision of the larger meaning of the social good and its consequences for policy, it is evident that I do not accept this understanding of the relation between religious belief and policy conclusions as immediate and direct. Roman Catholic thought, like much Protestant thought as well, maintains that religious belief must be complemented by the careful use of human reasoning, both philosophical and social-scientific, in the effort to reach decisions about policy that are both religiously and humanly adequate" (p. 898).

One might object to the ecclesiastical neutrality principle that the clergy are obligated to help bring into being a morally acceptable democracy and thus to promote, for example, economic justice, which might in turn require criticizing the government's policy on federal minimum wages.[44] Two distinctions are essential here. The first is between their obligations as citizens and their distinctively clerical obligations; the second is between the obligation to promote these ideals *in general*, especially as broadly moral, and the obligation to promote them *politically*, through specific parties or policies. I heartily acknowledge obligations of citizenship—and freedom of action—on the part of clergy. But I take it that argument is needed to show that the clergy *as such* are obligated to promote democracy, particularly if the promotion is to be political; and I have argued that they are prima facie obligated not to promote candidates for office or specific laws or public policies that restrict human conduct. I agree that they should oppose, for instance, economic injustice; but proposing a specific wage structure or a detailed strategy of disarmament is quite another matter. Similarly, powerful opposition to racial injustice is to be expected of, for example, clergy in the Hebraic-Christian tradition, and it may be quite specific in terms of, say, real or imaginary examples of wrongdoing held up as abominable. But support of one political party's particular way of dealing with the problem, as opposed to a competing strategy proposed by another party, is quite different; that is (typically) one kind of thing the ecclesiastical neutrality principle is intended to restrict.

I believe it is—or should be—the moral and spiritual power of churches by which they improve society rather than their direct exercises of political power; and I fear that churches' regularly exercising political power might produce religious fractures and quite possibly religious domination. Such domination, particularly in certain domains of life, would wrongly limit the freedom of the religious and the non-religious alike. If there is a Protestant or Catholic or Jewish or Moslem position on a political issue, candidates may not only bend over backwards to win church endorsement on that issue, but also covet it in other areas. To some extent, this already occurs in the U.S.; and if there is, for instance, little enough disagreement, or ingenious enough compromise, or a wise enough clergy, or a sufficiently educated citizenry, democracy may still thrive. But it is more likely to thrive if the clergy judiciously abide by a reasonable standard of political neutrality.

The ecclesiastical principle of political neutrality must not be thought to be supported only by considerations of religious liberty and democratic ideals. It may also protect the integrity of religious institutions themselves. Politics

---

44   Essentially this objection has been posed by Paul Weithman, and in responding to it I draw on my "Religious Commitment and Secular Reason: A Reply to Professor Weithman," *Philosophy & Public Affairs* 20 (1991). For a more detailed statement of his view see his "Taking Rites Seriously," *Pacific Philosophical Quarterly* 73, nos. 3–4 (1994): 272–94.

and public policy are a complex and absorbing business, and to acquire the knowledge of them requisite to speak with the authority properly befitting a corporate church voice (or even an influential clerical voice) can easily reduce the time and commitment needed for spiritual and moral matters. It is one thing to criticize economic injustice in a general way; it is quite another to make a responsible judgment that the minimum wage should be raised or, say, increased to $5.55. The neutrality principle can thus help to prevent dilution of the clergy's religious function. As Moses gave the commandments of the Lord, the first is "You shall have no other Gods before me" (Exodus 20:3 and Deuteronomy 5:7); and Jesus taught that one cannot serve God and mammon (Matthew 7:24). Politics should be a worthier pursuit than money and other false gods, but we must still ask how well one can serve God and the state.

At this point I would reiterate that the ecclesiastical neutrality principle is institutional; it does not imply that clergy should not take personal and even public positions on topics connected with politics or public policy, or even concerning personalities in government. Granted, in some churches what the clergy say even privately might be taken for church doctrine; but there is still a great difference between what is so interpreted and what is publicly announced as church doctrine or policy, or paid out from church coffers. Even in making avowedly personal statements or in giving private counsel, however, clergy who believe in freedom and democracy should follow an individual *principle of clerical political neutrality* to the effect that clergy (as individuals) have a prima facie obligation to (i) observe a distinction between their personal political views and those of their office, especially in making public statements; (ii) prevent any political aims they may have from dominating their professional conduct as clergy; and (iii) abstain from officially (as religious leaders) supporting candidates for public office or pressing for laws or policies that would restrict human conduct. Domination by political aims is possible even where (e.g. in a sermon) one specifies that one is not speaking for one's church institutionally; but disclaimers of that kind can help in keeping official statements distinct from personal conviction.

This principle is quite consistent both with the point that applying religious principles and insights to issues of law and public policy can be highly beneficial and with the clergy as individuals following the rationale and motivation principles—with all the freedom to use religious reasons that implies. The judicious application of religious principles and insights may have heuristic value in leading to discovery of new points; it may serve as a moral corrective, for instance in bringing out injustices; it may strengthen moral motivation; it may reduce strife and recrimination among disparate social groups, as where tolerance and forgiveness are stressed as part of a religious commitment; it may enhance the aesthetic and cultural aspects of civic life; and it may encourage a vivid and salutary modeling of the forms of life people cherish as part of their religious faith. Nonetheless, it is appropriate that clergy exercise restraint—*clerical virtue*, we might say—in touching on political issues, even in unofficial conduct and particularly in public. If they do not, they invite peers who disagree to use religious leverage for opposite ends; and the public, quite possibly including their own congregations, may suffer. There is certainly a risk of inducing political discord in congregations that might otherwise enjoy a deeper unity.

Departures from the clerical principle of political neutrality also raise, in addition to the danger of dilution of function, the risk of influencing one's congregation toward placing political aims over spiritual and non-political moral ones, such as those concerning relations with family and friends. It easily seems more important to put others' houses in order than one's own; and even to the righteous the latter task, typically involving so many more people, can seem much more important.

VI. Some Problems of Application

Application of the principles of secular rationale, secular motivation, theo-ethical equilibrium, and ecclesiastical and clerical neutrality can be complicated because there may be considerable difficulty in determining whether a reason one has for doing or believing something is secular, or constitutes an evidentially adequate ground, as well as in deciding whether it is fact motivating. These difficulties merit extensive study. Here I simply offer three suggestions. First, we should be guided by paradigms of both kinds of reason. There is much to be learned from asking, of what seem our most cogent reasons, why they justify, and, of our most moving reasons, why they influence us. Second, wherever the two kinds of reason diverge on a major issue, we should inquire why. Third, in borderline cases where the secular status of a reason is in question we should consider whether it would be taken to be secular by a reflective person who sincerely and comprehendingly claims to be non-religious and considers it carefully.[45]

The difficulty of determining whether a reason one has is motivating is especially likely to occur before the relevant action or long afterwards. But what the motivation principle (beyond the rationale principle) requires of conscientious citizens contemplating support of restrictive laws or policies is at most this: first, trying to formulate all the significant reasons they have for each major option—itself often a very useful exercise; second, where one or more reasons is religious, considering the motivational weight of each reason taken by itself as well as in the context of the others (if none is religious, the principle does not imply any need to go any further into motivation, though

---

45   The determination of evidential adequacy is also a difficult matter, but is not peculiar to my position on religious and politics. Any plausible political philosophy must employ some such notion. It is perhaps some help to say that standard deductive and inductive logic are highly relevant, as is whatever logic of moral discourse there may be that goes beyond them.

some other principle may); and third, attempting to ascertain, by considering hypothetical situations and felt motivational or cognitive impulses or tendencies, whether each reason is motivationally sufficient. We should ask ourselves, for example, what really impresses us as supporting the proposition; what occurs to us first (or most spontaneously) on the matter; whether we would believe something if we did not accept a certain premise for it; and whether a given reason taken by itself seems persuasive to us, in the sense of providing a sense of surety. We should also listen carefully to our own voice. If we are adhering to the principle of secular motivation, and if we would speak with a truly civic voice, at least one secular reason should emerge as suitably motivating us.

In short, my two main first-order principles of civic virtue imply that one should ask of one's reasons certain evidential, historical, and hypothetical questions. Applying the (second-order) principle of theo-ethical equilibrium can often help in this task, as well as in applying the principles of ecclesiastical and clerical neutrality. One must, with all three of these principles, use practical wisdom in deciding how much effort to expend in a given case of contemplated action.

Practical wisdom is also crucial in determining how much of one's public discourse should be couched in religious terms; for even if one is scrupulously abiding by the secular motivation principle, one may still have and present religious reasons for one's sociopolitical views. The principles of secular rationale and secular motivation concern advocacy and support of a certain range of laws and public policies; they do not restrict freedom of speech or preclude the use of religious reasons in many other ways, including support of a purely moral conclusion, as where abortion is said to be immoral because it destroys a gift of God. Neither the crucial premise for this moral conclusion nor the conclusion itself entails that abortion should be illegal in a free and democratic society, and stating it, even publicly, does not automatically count toward supporting a coercive law or public policy. There are, moreover, ways to offer the argument even in public policy contexts (e.g., by taking care to bring these limitations out) that do not imply supporting restrictive laws or public policies.[46]

One may, however, easily be wrong in thinking that bringing religious reasons to bear on a public policy issue will make one more convincing; one may instead polarize the discussion. It can well turn out that advancing religious reasons for a controversial social policy leads the opposition to advance conflicting religious reasons. This, in turn, can lead to suspicions about the motivation or the cogency of even the secular reasons on each side; and while people who seek theo-ethical equilibrium may often be prepared to

---

46 Here one can be conscientiously mistaken: one can falsely but excusably believe a reason to be secular.

revise their secular as well as their religious views, this disposition is not always present, and deadlock may occur where compromise would have been possible.

Fortunately, if the motivation principle is widely accepted by the parties to a dispute—indeed, perhaps even if it is not—and if one is in good communication with people who disagree on the issue at hand, one will likely get substantial help from them. Whenever religious reasons seem motivationally too strong, people who disagree should be expected to help one probe one's grounds. Others hear our voice better than we do. They may also think of revealing questions about us that we ourselves overlook, or observe words or deeds that teach us something we did not realize about our own thinking or motivation.[47]

It could be that most people are not usually good at forming reasonable judgments regarding even what reasons they have, much less which of these reasons, if any, are motivating.[48] If this is so, the effort to find out may be all the more needed. If, through self-examination, I can't tell what my reasons for a belief or desire of mine are, I should probably wonder whether I have any normatively adequate reasons; and I am likely to make better decisions if I try to find some good reasons for the relevant beliefs or desires. If I can't tell pretty accurately which reasons motivate me and about how much they do so at least relative to other reasons, I cannot adequately understand myself or reasonably predict my own behavior.

This is a good place to emphasize three points about the rationale and motivation principles. First, they are each independent of the principle of theo-ethical equilibrium. They do not entail it, and although the principle of theo-ethical equilibrium is helpful in applying them, neither principle is presupposed by the view that civic virtue requires (for religious people) seeking theo-ethical equilibrium; I simply present them as good candidates for a role in realizing that virtue. Second, the principle of secular motivation

---

47   Paul J. Weithman, in "The Separation of Church and State: Some Questions for Professor Audi," *Philosophy & Public Affairs* 20 (1991), and others have questioned how feasible it is to try to follow the principle of secular rationale. See also Lawrence B. Solum, "Faith and Justice," *DePaul Law Review* 39, no. 4 (1990): esp. pp. 1089–92. Also relevant is Weithman's "Liberalism and the Privitization of Religion: Three Theological Objections Considered," *Journal of Religious Ethics* 22 (1994). The above is only the beginning of a reply to such worries. For another pertinent discussion see Jonathan Jacobs, "Theism and Moral Objectivity," *American Catholic Philosophical Quarterly* 66, no. 4 (1992).

48   One might think that a person must have *some* motivating reason for a belief or action. But this is not so, if we distinguish reasons from causes or, more subtly, reasons *for which* one believes or acts from mere (explanatory) *reasons why* one does. Wishful thinking is a non-rational source of beliefs, and actions not performed intentionally need not be done for a reason, as where one quite unwittingly offends someone.

allows that one may *also* have religious reasons and be motivated by them. The ideal for religious citizens is indeed a cooperation between the religious and the secular, not the domination of the former by the latter. Third, my use of such separationist principles by no means presupposes that religious reasons cannot be evidentially adequate. My principles also allow that religious reasons may be motivationally *sufficient* for a political stance (though not motivationally necessary, since secular reasons could not then be motivationally sufficient—they would be unable to produce belief or action without the cooperation of religious elements).

The rationale and motivation principles even allow the person's judging the religious reasons in question to be more important than the secular ones, or being more *strongly* motivated by them, or both; this is perfectly consistent with being sufficiently motivated by an adequate secular reason. Holding such judgments is also compatible with adhering to the clerical principle of political neutrality. The principles simply aim at preventing a certain kind of domination by religious reasons in contexts in which they should be constrained; and adhering to the principles makes it much easier to speak with an appropriate civic voice. To be sure, in public advocacy of laws and policies that restrict human conduct it seems *generally* best to conduct discussion in secular terms; but there may be special contexts in which candor or other considerations require laying out all of one's main reasons.[49] If one does articulate religious reasons in a public debate, it should help to be able to express both commitment to the principle of secular rationale and reasons that accord with it. This would show a respect for a religiously neutral point of view that is sharable with any rational citizen.[50]

While the rationale and motivation principles (and indeed everything I have contended here) are entirely consistent with religious reasons' being evidentially adequate, the evidential adequacy of those reasons is not a presupposition of liberal democracy—nor, of course, is their evidential inadequacy.[51] Indeed, it may be that the absence of both presuppositions is a

49   There are many issues here. Some are addressed in "The Separation of Church and State and the Obligations of Citizenship" and "The Place of Religious Argument in a Free and Democratic Society," cited above. Kent Greenawalt discusses the issues in *Religious Convictions and Political Choice* (Oxford and New York: Oxford University Press, 1988) and *Private Consciences and Public Reasons* (New York: Oxford University Press, 1995).

50   The notion of neutrality is also informatively discussed by Rawls, *Political Liberalism*, and Carter, *The Culture of Disbelief*; see also Robert van Wyk, "Liberalism, Religion, and Politics," *Public Affairs Quarterly* 1 (1987), and "Liberalism, Religion, and Politics Again: A Reply to Gordon Graham," *Journal of Social Philosophy* 25 (1994). (Some of van Wyk's criticism of my view is at least implicitly answered in this paper.)

51   The Declaration of Independence is one famous document supporting liberal democracy that seems to imply otherwise; but I am not certain that it must be so

negative commitment of liberal democracy, a special kind of neutrality regarding religious matters. It would be inappropriate for a liberal theory to contain either epistemological claim, just as it would violate the neutrality of a liberal state toward religion to support anti-religious practices or institutions, as such.[52] This epistemological neutrality need not be a positive plank in even a fully articulated democratic constitution, but it is an important strand in much liberal democratic theory.

Religious commitment is not, in its mature embodiments, a monolithic position of blind obedience, but a complex, multi-layered fidelity to a multifarious array of texts, traditions, authoritative directives, religious experiences, and people in and outside one's own religious community. A mature religious commitment may require sensitivity, reflection, self-renewal, and, often, the practical wisdom to reconcile conflicting elements. Any educated religious person, however, who comes to the obligations of citizenship in a liberal democracy is already aware of plural bases, both religious and secular, of moral and sociopolitical obligation and of the fallibility of even one's careful interpretations of those sources and obligations. The cultivation of civic virtue should reflect this sense of multiplicity and tension. That same sense helps in seeing the need for institutional separation of church and state, with each keeping an appropriate distance from the other and concentrating on its proper function.

Neither the institutional separation of church and state I have defended nor any reasonable separation of the religious and the political in the conduct of individuals need retard the forces of progress, whether they are inspired religiously or morally or in both ways. Injustice in all its forms may be fought. Corruption and dishonesty may be rooted out. The ignorant may be taught. The practice of the arts and humanities, and of religion and the sciences, may be promoted among all peoples. The sick may be given comfort, the poor relief, the lonely fellowship.

In religious traditions that recognize God as omniscient, omnipotent, and omnibenevolent, there is good reason to expect that one can, by and large, achieve an equilibrium between religious and secular considerations in relation to major moral and sociopolitical principles crucial for guiding civic life in a free society. Seeking that equilibrium is in any case a worthy goal. That quest can contribute both to understanding each set of sources of obligation and to one's justification for affirming the obligations in question. Far from reducing one's inclination to be a politically active citizen, it can add to one's

---

read, nor do I take it to be as authoritative on this matter as the work of, say, John Stuart Mill.

52   This point (among many others relevant to this paper) is brought out by Kent Greenawalt in *Private Consciences and Public Reasons*, cited above.

motivation to fulfill one's civic obligations. It can add to one's motivation to also enhance communication with others in different traditions. Both in achieving such equilibrium and in our efforts to exhibit civic virtue the principles of secular rationale and secular motivation, and the related ecclesiastical and clerical neutrality principles, are among the reasonable guides we may follow. They can also help in cultivating and in using an appropriate civic voice. To achieve such equilibrium, and to realize civic virtue, is to contribute to the liberty, mutual respect, and cooperative exchange of ideas that best nourishes both religious practice and moral conduct. Perhaps it is also part of the civic realization of the injunction of beneficence: the injunction to love one's neighbor as oneself.[53]

53   This paper has benefited from discussions at the University of Notre Dame Conference on Liberalism and Religion, from audience discussions at the Center for Ethics at Emory University, the University of Memphis, and Vanderbilt University, and from comments by Lenn Goodman, Kent Greenawalt, James Gustafson, Hugh McCann, Michael Perry, Philip Quinn, Timothy Jackson, Mark van Roojen, and Paul Weithman. It draws significantly on my contribution to *Religion in the Public Square*, jointly authored with Nicholas Wolterstorff (Lanham, Md.: Rowman and Littlefield, 1996), and I gratefully acknowledge permission to reprint parts of that work.

Abstinence and Exclusion: What Does Liberalism Demand of the Religiously Oriented (Would Be) Judge?

Sanford Levinson

I.

Few subjects interest me more than the relationship between religion and liberalism. I confess, though, that almost none seems to be more difficult in terms of figuring out acceptable solutions. It is not simply the case that there is quite obviously no scholarly consensus as to what is the proper relationship. Rather, I discover that even when examining my own views, I am scarcely satisfied with my conclusions. Indeed, one reason I eagerly accepted the invitation to participate in the conference out of which this volume developed was precisely the opportunity it presented to see where I now stand regarding the intersection of religion and liberalism. During the New York newspaper strike in 1966, James Reston was quoted as asking, "How do I know what I think until I read what I write?" It is easy to identify with Reston's plaintive question. One writes not only to spell out arguments but also, and perhaps ultimately more importantly, to try to figure out what arguments one really is comfortable making and, of course, whether one is still comfortable with arguments presented in the past.

I thus begin by referring to a prior essay of mine that examined "religious language and the public square."[1] In this essay, a review of Michael J. Perry's book *Love and Power: The Role of Religion and Morality in American Life*, I noted that a prominent strain of liberal thought (about which I shall have a bit more to say presently) had developed the argument that entry into the public square should in effect be conditioned on a willingness to speak only in the language of an areligious secularity. Among other things, this means that cosmopolitan academics, who probably oppose the "English-only" movement in the United States as insufficiently respectful of the multicultural nature of our society, often have little hesitation in endorsing a "secular-only" version of public discourse that, from the perspective of those who speak other languages, seems at least as dismissive of those from different cultures as is the view that English is the only acceptable mode of discourse within American life. One

---

1   See Sanford Levinson, "Religious Language and the Public Square," *Harvard Law Review* 105 (1992): 2061 (review of Michael J. Perry, *Love and Power: The Role of Religion and Morality in American Politics* (New York: Oxford University Press, 1991).

question is whether this is a genuine paradox that self-styled cosmopolitans ought to address.

In any event, I suggested in my review that liberal democracy, at least in its American version, should be interpreted as "giv[ing] everyone an equal right, without engaging in any version of epistemic abstinence, to make his or her arguments, subject . . . to the prerogative of listeners to reject the arguments should they be unpersuasive." From the perspective of those who, like myself, define themselves as secular, "[i]t seems enough. . . to disagree vigorously with persons presenting theologically-oriented views of politics. To suggest as well that they are estopped even from presenting such arguments seems gratuitously censorial."[2] The elegant phrase "epistemic abstinence" is not my own; I borrowed it from an important article by Joseph Raz[3] that was itself a critique of an earlier argument by Thomas Nagel that the effective functioning of a liberal society, defined in part as a society including a variety of (conflicting) fundamental perspectives or, in Rawls's language, "comprehensive views," "requires that a limit somehow be drawn to appeals *to the truth* in political argument."[4]

As I understand the argument, it is as follows: Even if a reasonable person might believe that some argument is true, resting, presumably, on ontological and epistemological predicates that might well establish satisfactory truth conditions, that person should, nonetheless, refrain from offering it (or, under some formulations, even privately being motivated by it) if the argument is religious rather than secular, precisely because many of one's fellow citizens do not share the assumptions necessary to establish the truth conditions of a religion-based argument. (I am assuming, for purposes of argument, that one finds notions like "truth conditions" meaningful, as Nagel appears to do; other problems are presented if one follows, say, Richard Rorty instead of Nagel and adopts one or another version of "post-modernist anti-foundationalism" that tries to dispense with such language.)

One cannot, I think, overemphasize the importance of the point that arguments such as Nagel's are, in form at least, totally different from what might be termed classic anti-religious arguments. Those arguments were based on a basically high-Enlightenment dismissal of religious notions as either superstitious poppycock, ontologically, or, slightly more moderately, as resting on insupportable epistemological assumptions about the ability to know God's will. In any case, anti-religionists in the past were prone to assert that religion-based argument—especially the kind found in Protestant America, which is

---

2   Ibid., 2077.

3   Joseph Raz, "Facing Diversity: The Case of Epistemic Abstinence," *Philosophy & Public Affairs* 19 (1990): 3.

4   Thomas Nagel, "Moral Conflict and Political Legitimacy," *Philosophy & Public Affairs* 16 (1987): 218 (emphasis in original).

often based more on some notion of revealed truth rather than, say, on the working out of natural law premises as in Roman Catholicism—could not possibly serve as a predicate for offering truthful sentences about how we should live our lives. This was true even though, on occasion, there was an overlap between the conclusion of a religion-based argument and the findings of more authoritative secular systems of argument; any such overlap, however, was completely contingent, a happy accident rather than anything that might count as verification of religious premises. To oppose religious language in the public square, from this perspective, is exactly like rejecting, say, astrological argument or other "irrational" views.

However, the most interesting contemporary arguments, at least within the academy, are less overtly dismissive of religion. Indeed, relatively few are heard today who forthrightly adhere to classical anti-religionism. It may be that the willingness of many leftish academics to defend, in the name of "multiculturalism," a variety of less than wholly plausible views of reality when articulated by some suitably sympathetic group, such as Native Americans, has in effect disabled them from engaging in classic religion-bashing. There are, to be sure, writers like the literary theorist Jonathan Culler[5] or University of Minnesota law professor Suzanna Sherry,[6] who are willing to assert unabashedly anti-religious positions, but I believe that they are relative outliers in contemporary American culture. Even Stephen Carter, in his denunciation of what he termed "the culture of disbelief,"[7] took care to subtitle his book *How American Law and Politics Trivialize Religious Devotion*. "Trivialization" may be objectionable, but it is far different from an out-and-out attack on such devotion as, say, representing submission to delusional fantasy.

More typical of the contemporary debate, I think, is the comment of New York University law professor David A. J. Richards, who writes that "religiously based values . . . may be valid and true,"[8] but, nonetheless, goes on to argue that a precondition of a liberal political order is that religious believers

---

5   See Jonathan Culler, *Framing the Sign: Criticism and Its Institutions*, chapter 4: "Political Criticism: Confronting Religion," 69–82 (Norman: University of Oklahoma Press, 1988).

6   See Suzanna Sherry, "Outlaw Blues," *Michigan Law Review* 87 (1989): 1418, 1427 (describing "such things as divine revelation and biblical literalism [as] irrational superstitious nonsense"). One doubts that my friend Professor Sherry is significantly more admiring of non-literal biblicism.

7   Stephen L. Carter, *The Culture of Disbelief: How American Law and Politics Trivialize Religious Devotion* (New York: Basic Books, 1993), reviewed in Sanford Levinson, "The Multicultures of Belief and Disbelief," *Michigan Law Review* 92 (1994): 1873.

8   David A. J. Richards, "Book Review," *Georgia Law Review* 25: 1189, 1197 (reviewing Kent Greenawalt, *Conflicts of Law and Morality* [New York: Oxford University Press, 1987] and *Religious Convictions and Political Choice* [New York: Oxford University Press, 1988]).

voluntarily refrain from offering religious arguments in recognition of the fact that many of their co-citizens do not share their perspectives and, therefore, do not recognize religious materials as an authoritative source of true arguments. This "abstinence" obviously does not mean that the abstainer disbelieves the arguments that he or she is agreeing to suppress. Rather, these "true" arguments (from the perspective of the religious believer and "possibly true" even from the perspective of the now-generous religious skeptic) are in effect sacrificed by the believer as the price for maintaining the liberal (and pluralistic) political order.

As Michael Perry pointed out, there is an important asymmetry in regard to the "terms of trade" that secularists and religionists must offer one another in order to participate in a liberal polity. Secularists are in effect free to make whatever truthful arguments they believe to be relevant to any important issue of the day; this freedom holds even if, as a matter of fact, almost no one within the polity is educated enough to be able to follow the arguments, as in the case, say, of arguments that rest on the resolution of complex scientific controversies. But what of those who view their "basic moral/religious convictions [as] (partly) self-constitutive" and, therefore, "a principal ground . . . of political deliberation and choice"? According to Perry, to ask those who view the world through the prism of religious convictions to "'bracket' such convictions" as the price of engagement in liberal politics is to ask them "to bracket—to annihilate—essential aspects of one's very self."[9] Perry regards this demand as intolerable. And, as already suggested, the theme of my review-essay on Perry, although critical about certain aspects of his argument, nonetheless agreed with him on this basic point. But, to put it mildly, many questions remain, and I turn now to consideration of some of those questions.

II.

I cannot help but notice the obvious fact that I am the only lawyer who is part of this enterprise. Even if I were inclined to ignore the presumed desire of its organizers that I draw on some aspect of my legal training, sheer prudence would dictate that I not try to compete with the truly distinguished philosophers and political theorists who can be found elsewhere in this volume. If I have a comparative advantage, it is surely not my ability to explicate Rawls, Nagel, or Raz or to offer any new philosophical insights to the genuinely knotty problems that confront anyone trying to figure out the relationship between religion and liberalism. One comparative advantage that I do have, though, is almost certainly having read more legal cases than most of the other authors.

One temptation is to do what lawyers are presumably skilled at, which is

---

9   Michael Perry, *Morality, Politics and Law: A Bicentennial Essay* (New York: Oxford University Press, 1988), 181–82.

to try to explicate the current doctrines of the United States Supreme Court in regard to religiously motivated legislation or other governmental decisions. For better or worse, though, I will not succumb to any such temptation, not least because these doctrines are, by common consensus, hopelessly confused. If truth be known, I detest reading most of the relevant Supreme Court cases, which tend to be a series of 5-4 decisions in which highly idiosyncratic views of one or another justice lead to results in a given instance that seem either patently inconsistent or simply absurd, when one decision is placed next to another.

But there is another advantage to reading cases beyond becoming aware of the doctrines that courts purport to be applying. That advantage is simply the confrontation with fascinating facts that supply a concreteness sometimes lacking in the writings of philosophers. It is, I think, through responding to concrete examples that one's intuitions are best examined. I thus invite you to look with me at some very specific examples of the use of religious language in the public square and to put them within the context of a particular question: To what extent, if at all, do the rules of what might termed the "liberal-polity game" require the exclusion of certain kinds of religion-based arguments, even from the perspective of one like myself who would profess to be maximally inclusive (or, more precisely, as inclusive as is reasonably possible)?

I draw my primary example from Professor Kent Greenawalt's most recent book, *Private Consciences and Public Reasons*.[10] Greenawalt is surely among the most distinguished contributors, as both philosopher and lawyer, to the general debate about liberalism and religion and, more specifically, about the extent to which membership in a liberal polity presupposes the exclusion of certain kinds of arguments from the public realm. One of the things that makes his writings especially interesting is that he speaks as a professed religious believer. Although Greenawalt is willing to tolerate a wide range of arguments from ordinary citizens and the use of religious perspectives in deciding, for example, how to vote in elections, he goes on to argue that many public officials operate under different, and more constrained, standards. Thus, to take what for him is the easiest example, judges ought to suppress any explicit reference to their own personal religious perspectives—and, concomitantly, avoid using them as purported *justifications* for a particular outcomes—even if their religious views in fact constitute part of the *explanation* for the judge's reaching a particular decision.[11] He would, I believe, substantially agree with

---

10   New York: Oxford University Press, 1995.

11   See Greenawalt, *Private Consciences and Public Reasons*, chapter 13, "Judicial Decisions and Opinions." Probably the best known critic of positions like Greenawalt's is Stephen L. Carter. See "The Religiously Devout Judge," *Notre Dame Law Review* 64 (1989): 932. The most extensive scholarly article in the law review literature is Scott C. Idleman, "The Role of Religious Values in Judicial Decision Making," *Indiana Law Review* 27 (1993): 433.

the statement of a Wisconsin judge that, "[w]hile the law may have had part of its origin in the same customs and necessities as did traditional religion, it is a distinct entity from religion, functioning in a different manner and *being guided by different principles.*"[12]

As a presumed negative example, Greenawalt cites a case from the South Dakota Supreme Court involving a bitter dispute between former spouses over visitation rights regarding their two children.[13] In particular, the conflict concerned the non-custodial mother's lesbianism, and the custodial father's objection to an order by the court below that allowed the mother to have unsupervised overnight visitations with her daughter. The Supreme Court reversed the court, demanding that the court below engage in a "home study, to be assured that the children are not placed in an unsafe or unstable environment."[14] What is of central interest to me, given the central topic of this essay, is a concurring opinion filed by Justice Henderson. The crux of that opinion is the following sentence: "Until such time that she can establish, after years of therapy and demonstrated conduct, that she is no longer a lesbian living a life of abomination (*see* Leviticus 18:22), she should be totally estopped from contaminating these children."[15]

Such language is relatively rare in our judicial reports, but, as Scott Idleman well shows, Judge Henderson is certainly not unique.[16] And, of course, as with white ravens and black swans, all we really need is one actual occurrence of such language to raise the question whether it violates what might be termed the "essence" of the adjudicatory role within a liberal society. Or, on the contrary, is simply a legitimate, albeit statistically unusual, variation of that role?

Needless to say, I am not interested in exploring whether or not what Justice Henderson says is true, though I suspect that no reader will be surprised at learning that I do not agree with him and find his homophobia appalling. But for our purposes that is beside the point, for one must assume that he believes his statements to be true, in precisely the same way that, say, Vice President

---

12   *City of Milwaukee v. Wilson,* No. 77-670 (Wis. Ct. App. Jan. 19, 1979) (LEXIS, States library, Wisc. file), aff'd, 291 N.W.2d 452 (Wis. 1980), quoted in Idleman, "The Role of Religious Values in Judicial Decision Making," 433 n. 2 (1993).

13   *Chicoine v. Chicoine,* 479 N.W.2d 891 (S.D. 1992).

14   Ibid., 894.

15   Ibid., 896.

16   See Idleman, "The Role of Religious Values in Judicial Decision Making," n. 11, 476–77, nn. 147–56. One of Idleman's examples is another opinion of Henderson's, this time in dissent: "[C]hildren are entrusted to parents as part of God's great plan," and "the Law should be ever so cautious in interfering with that edict," citing, according to Idleman, "numerous passages from the Old and New Testaments." Id. at n. 155, quoting from *In re* S.L. and L.L., 419 N.W.2d 689, 697–98 (1988).

Al Gore believes himself to be stating other than nonsense when he writes of the "moral principles defining our relationship to both God and God's creation"[17] and goes on to suggest that his own particular environmental views are importantly linked to a religious "faith [that] is rooted in the unshakeable belief in God as creator and sustainer, a deeply personal interpretation of and relationship with Christ."[18] The question is whether Judge Henderson (or the Vice President) should feel under a duty to maintain a public silence about the religious roots of their views or whether we should properly censure them for not excluding·them from the public square. (And, of course, public silence · might not be enough; as Robert Audi argues, we might also want to require them to be genuinely motivated by secular concerns and not merely to suppress the "real" grounds for their political or judicial positions.)

Let us look more closely at Justice Henderson's harsh, Leviticus-based, attack on Ms. Chicoine's lesbianism. Child custody and visitation decisions are based, at least in theory, on the "best interests of the child." Application of this standard presumably requires the conscientious judge to believe that there are, in fact, such interests that are cognizable though testimony by child psychologists, moral philosophers, or whomever. Indeed, one important question almost inevitably raised in child-custody disputes is precisely who counts as an "expert" on the child's best interest, and one need not be overly postmodernist to recognize in the question an echo of Foucault's emphasis on the endless battle over discourse legitimacy. This is, of course, just another way of restating the central question that runs through this entire volume.

Can, for example, a minister testify as an "expert" on what constitutes a child's best interest? Is one such interest living a maximally sin-free life and thus escaping, among other things, the risk of eternal damnation?[19] Surely, if one accepts the ontological reality of eternal damnation, then it would seem to follow that it would be in one's best interest to avoid it, assuming that there is anything that might count as reliable knowledge about methods of damnation avoidance. And what if one simply accepts the possibility that there *might* be such a possibility or that there *might* be such knowledge? Should society make a Pascalian wager on its actuality? Or are such considerations necessarily inadmissible in an American court of law?

One strongly suspects that Judge Henderson is neither an ontological nor an epistemological skeptic about damnation. He obviously believes that it

17   Al Gore, *Earth in the Balance: Ecology and the Human Spirit* (Boston: Houghton Mifflin, 1992), 256.

18   Ibid., 368.

19   On the role of religion in child custody disputes, see Donald L. Beschle, "God Bless the Child?: The Use of Religion as a Factor in Child Custody and Adoption Proceedings," *Fordham Law Review* 58 (1989): 383; Note, "The Establishment Clause and Religion in Child Custody Disputes Factoring Religion into the Best Interests Equation," 82 *Michigan Law Review* 82 (1984): 1701.

violates the best-interest standard to place a child in a context suggesting, in any way, that non-heterosexuality is a morally available option in living one's life, rather than an "abomination." Whether one agrees with them or not, millions of Americans not only endorse his substantive view, but also the propriety of looking to the Bible for guidance in the resolution of such questions. Is this relevant? Or should a condition of his being a judge be a duty to ignore—to exclude—what he regards as the best evidence of moral truth or falsity, including valuable guidance as to how children should be raised, if that evidence is religion-based rather than secular? That is, is his opinion *worse*, because it evokes Leviticus, than would be an opinion that offered only secular reasons for the adoption of similarly homophobic views? Concomitantly, would Gore's environmentally protective views be even more attractive, to those of us who indeed find them so, if he refrained from justifying them by reference to his religious beliefs?

Indeed, let me ask perhaps the question in the strongest possible way: Would Henderson (or Gore, were he a federal judge offering such comments as I have quoted in the course of an opinion explaining his perhaps tortuous construction of a statute in the most environmentally protective manner) merit impeachment if he refused to cease from looking to, and then publicly articulating, the religious bases of his decisions? Would such refusals constitute the deviation from "good behavior" that properly merits exclusion from public office? Only slightly less strong is the question whether Judge Henderson's citation of Leviticus would be sufficient to justify a senator's voting against his confirmation to the federal judiciary after being nominated by a president who, obviously, did not find the language disqualifying. One suspects, for example, that Henderson might be extremely attractive to a president supported by the so-called Christian Coalition, but then, so was Gore's open religiosity presumably attractive to President Clinton.

In spite of my inclusiveness, which would allow citizens Henderson and Gore to write religion-saturated letters to the editor and perhaps even candidate Gore to make similar speeches to the public while seeking their votes, I am certainly inclined to agree with Professor Greenawalt that "[o]f all officials, judges are the most carefully disciplined in restraining their frames of reference. Asking them to try to decide exclusively, or nearly exclusively, on the basis of authoritative materials and publicly accessible [i.e., non-religious] reasons is not too great an imposition."[20] But how, precisely, does one enforce such an "imposition," especially if it is the case that Greenawalt's view is itself controversial rather than a truly accepted convention that, by being accepted, is made uncontroversial?

Consider, for example, the following statement: "Sometimes I think the environment in which we operate is entirely too secular. . . . [T]hose of us who

---

20   Greenawalt, *Private Consciences and Public Reasons*, 149.

have faith should frankly admit that we are animated by that faith, that we try to live by it—and that it does affect what we feel, what we think, and what we do."[21] This was said by President Clinton, who has also ostentatiously endorsed Professor Carter's book and *its* call for greater respect of those who are serious rather than "trivial" in integrating their religious perspectives into the performance of their public duties. Carter in turn has noted his respect for those who engage in "prayerful consideration" aimed toward "discerning and then enacting the will of God."[22] So let us assume that we are indeed presented with a judge who refuses to cordon off his or her religious beliefs. What ought to be our response, especially if we share Professor Greenawalt's view that this refusal indeed is problematic? Can we do anything beyond writing critical, albeit almost certainly ineffective, criticisms?

As already suggested, one way to enforce such an *cordon sanitaire* is impeachment; as a practical matter, though, that is a spectacularly inefficacious procedure within American government. One might also hesitate to pay the costs of the full scale *kulturkampf* that would undoubtedly attend an impeachment effort based on a judge's religiosity. A far better solution, practically speaking, is to prevent the appointment in the first place by denying Senate confirmation to a presidential appointee (assuming, of course, we are talking about federal level of the polity). As demonstrated by the nomination of Clarence Thomas, this is no easy process either. Still, the example of Robert Bork stands as evidence that "difficult" does not mean "impossible." Thus one can well imagine vigorous senatorial interrogation of Henderson and other nominees before voting on their confirmations.[23] The question, obviously, is whether we are pleased or dismayed by the prospect that senators would believe that they could legitimately inquire into a nominee's religious views and then take the answers to these inquiries into account when deciding whether or not to confirm the nomination.

There is, to be sure, precedent for such inquiries, though many would scarcely place them among the happier aspects of the American past. Thus William J. Brennan, in his own confirmation hearings in 1957, was asked, by Wyoming's Senator Joseph O'Mahoney (who was himself Catholic), whether Brennan "would . . . be able to follow the requirements of your oath [to enforce the Constitution] or would you be bound by your religious obligations?"[24] O'Mahoney asked his question at the behest of the National Liberal League,

21   Remarks by President Clinton in a Photo Opportunity during White House Interfaith Breakfast, U.S. Newswire, Aug. 30, 1993, quoted by Fred Barnes in "Rev. Bill," *New Republic* (January 3, 1994): 11.

22   Carter, *The Culture of Disbelief*, 77.

23   What follows is drawn, in part, from Sanford Levinson, "The Confrontation of Religious Faith and Civil Religion: Catholics Becoming Justices," 39 *DePaul Law Review* 1047 (1990).

24   Nomination of William Joseph Brennan: Hearings Before the Committee on the

though the "liberalism" of the league is open to at least some doubt insofar as its opposition to Brennan was based less on its commitment to separation between religion and state than to the purported unseemliness of the United States's, "a predominantly Protestant country," having to suffer the presence of a Catholic on its Supreme Court. Brennan knew his role in this subtle degradation ceremony. Expressing no objection to the question per se, he told the Senate first that he did not recognize within Catholicism any obligations "superior" to his constitutional oath and, secondly, that "what shall control me is the oath that I took to support the Constitution and laws of the United States."[25] This may simply reflect his belief that *all* laws passing muster under the Constitution were also sufficiently moral to pass muster under Catholic doctrine. To put it mildly, that itself is a highly controversial—many would say wildly implausible— doctrine of constitutional interpretation.

In any event, with Justice Brennan providing our precedent, we might ask Judge Henderson and other nominees if they would ever allow their religious views to "interfere" with their task of judgment. Stephen Carter offers his own version of what he calls *"the separation question"*: "If we confirm you and you become a judge, will you be able to separate your religious beliefs from the task of judging?"[26] Would, for example, they promise to refrain from seeking guidance as to legal meaning in Biblical materials or other obviously religious sources? Perhaps they would promise to avoid seeking even "prayerful guidance" as to God's will before deciding a controversy brought before them for authoritative legal adjudication. Indeed, as with Brennan's public testimony that the judicial oath dominated over any potentially conflicting loyalties, we might seek acknowledgment from any nominee that "epistemic abstinence" is a requirement of conscientious judging at least within our society and properly refuse to confirm any nominee who felt unwilling to pledge such abstinence.

The immediate question before us is whether it is *permissible* to reject a nominee solely because of an unwillingness to promise "abstinence." I find it hard to see how one can offer a strongly negative answer to this question, at least if one accepts Greenawalt's premises. To reject the notion that it is even *permissible* would be, I think, to accept Stephen Carter's position that "reliance by judges on their personal religious convictions is as proper as reliance on their personal moral convictions of any other kind."[27] So perhaps the question is whether judges should be asked to pledge abstinence from *any* materials believed to be true if they do not fit within some quite narrow version of acceptable sources of positive law.

Judiciary, United States Senate, 85th Cong., 1st. Sess. 32.

25   Ibid., 34.

26   Carter, "The Religiously Devout Judge," 932 (italics in original).

27   Carter, "The Religiously Devout Judge," 933.

This question itself raises profound jurisprudential questions that are well beyond the scope of this particular essay. Very briefly, though, one might note the differences among quite different arguments. First, one could assert that a judge ought have recourse to *nothing* beyond a limited set of strictly denominated legal materials, which entails, among other things, that the judge *qua* judge must always distinguish, in John Marshall's words, between the tasks of "the jurist" and "the moralist."[28] This position requires formal indifference to the possibility that the "best" meaning of a given law, based on these limited materials, is immoral. A competing position says that a judge *can* properly look to the guidance of secular morality at least in all cases when there is some genuine dispute about the meaning of a patch of legal text. The decision rule might be, "always construe disputed passages in such a way as to achieve the most attractive moral result"—but that the judge can *never* look to sectarian sources for guidance as to what counts as "the most attractive moral result." One could, of course, accept the decision rule set out under "b," but go on to argue, as Stephen Carter seems to, that the judge ought to feel free to consult *any* sources she deems personally deems authoritative as to the meaning of morality, including, of course, religious ones. A final position, of course, is the classic "just law" argument that nothing violating the substantive dictates of justice can count as law, whatever the formal provenance (as, for example, in majority will, presidential command, or whatever). Once again, one could distinguish between secular and religious sources of insight as to the meaning of justice.

Assume that adopts some version of the second principal, such as that of Greenawalt's as described above. That is, even what Carter calls "the religiously devout judge" ought to operate under a self-denying ordinance in all but the most exceptional of circumstances. We must then confront an even stronger question, going well beyond the *permission* that Greenawalt presumably gives one to vote against a nominee who gave the wrong answer to the "separationist question." Should a "Greenawaltian" be *required* to vote against the nominee? After all, isn't this the way that operative conventions are in fact preserved, by sanctioning those who would deviate from them? Assume that the Senate is willing to confirm a nominee who forthrightly indicated that "prayerful guidance," mixed with study of Scripture, would constitute one standard source for the decisions that she would render, and opinions that she would write, as a judge. Would that confirmation not serve as powerful evidence for the proposition that, contrary to Greenawalt, we as a society now

---

28   The Antelope, 23 U.S. (10 Wheat.) 66, 121 (1825). Not at all coincidentally, the case involved slavery. In an opinion upholding the rights of slaveholders, Marshall insisted that "this court must not yield to feelings which might seduce it from the path of duty, and must obey the mandate of the law." (Ibid., 114.)

believe that it *is* "too great an imposition" on judges to require that they exercise restraint in "their frame of reference"?

Interestingly enough, Greenawalt offers several caveats to his own argument: Thus it might be acceptable for a judge to rely on his or her religious views if otherwise authoritative materials generated a perfect equilibrium or were otherwise radically indeterminate; reliance might also be acceptable in the presumably extraordinary situation where "the judge finds 'the law' to be so abominable she feels a duty to subvert it in some way . . ."[29] Otherwise, though, Greenawalt appears to accept the desirability of restraint, which would seemingly entail the possibility that a senator would indeed be under a duty to reject an otherwise attractive nominee who failed to agree to abstain in all but the most extreme situations.

It should be obvious that the suggestion of such a duty (which I emphasize is my own rather than Greenawalt's) could be read by those who disagree as indicative of liberals' own participation in the *kulturkampf*. I take it that most of us would be outraged if a senator were to inquire into the possibly atheistic beliefs of a nominee and to announce that such atheism would itself serve as a basis for rejection. Perhaps the senator would revive eighteenth-century arguments as to the potential untrustworthiness of those who did not fear divine punishment for misbehavior. But would any argument justify rejecting a "secular humanist" simply on the grounds of lack of sufficient religious commitment? I take it that the question is truly "rhetorical," admitting of only one answer.

There is, of course, one way to avoid the comparison between our Gospel-oriented, prayerful nominee, on the one hand, and the secular humanist nominee, on the other, and that is to evoke the Establishment Clause of the First Amendment. Would it not be precisely an illegitimate "establishment" if religious belief were made a prerequisite for public office? Indeed, one scarcely needs the Establishment Clause to make this argument. After all, Article VI of the original unamended Constitution explicitly stated that "no religious Test shall ever be required as a Qualification to any Office or public Trust under the United States."[30] This seems clearly to rule out requiring any belief in God and, perhaps, even asking any questions about whether one believes in God. But is the Test Oath Clause symmetrical in preventing any inquiry about religious belief even of someone who has indicated, whether in speeches and books like those of Presidents Clinton and Gore or published judicial opinions like those of Judge Henderson, that religious views (and sources) will indeed be viewed as relevant to one's behavior in office? I can see no good reason for

---

29   Greenawalt, *Private Consciences and Public Reasons*, 149.

30   See Gerard Bradley, "No Religious Test Clause and the Constitution of Religious Liberty: A Machine That Would Go of Itself," *Case Western Reserve Law Review* 37 (1987): 674.

avoiding inquiry into any aspect of a nominee's life that he or she has publicly indicated might be relevant to later conduct while in office.

Perhaps the more fundamental question, though, is if such a "symmetrical" Test Oath Clause, read to preclude any taking account of a person's religious views into a determination of fitness to serve in public office, is normatively attractive. After all, even if one agrees that that is what the Oath Clause means, one might still go on to bewail its presence in the Constitution and advocate its repeal by amendment. I confess myself troubled by a reading of the Clause that would render legally impossible the interrogation of Judge Henderson as to the linkage between either the book of Leviticus and the United States Constitution or the book of Leviticus and the determination of what counts as the best interest of a child. And I confess as well that I would hold Judge Henderson's use of Leviticus against him. If the Test Oath Clause prohibits this, then, I suggest, so much the worse for the Clause.

One must ask, of course, whether one would be so opposed to Judge Henderson if one were attracted by his substantive values. So what ought the response to a "Judge Gore" be? It seems like a patent double standard to hold Henderson's citation of Leviticus against him if one is not also perturbed by the hypothetical Judge Gore's reference to his reading of Biblical passages (and values) as the source for his environmentally protective views. To be sure, it is easy for most of us to offer religion-independent defenses of environmentalism, whereas almost all anti-homosexual arguments seem, at bottom, to rest on religious grounds. But should the availability of non-religious arguments for a given position make irrelevant the offering by a particular judge of religious ones? It is hard for me to see why the answer should be yes. Presumably the point is whether a given judge will honor the duty to confine his or her attention only to what is stipulated to be a properly confined range of materials. On the other hand, if one is resistant to disqualifying the putative "Judge Gore" from a position on the federal judiciary, then perhaps one should reconsider the basis of opposition to Judge Henderson. Perhaps one should simply say that one is appalled by his substantive views, whatever their derivation. If he held an acceptable set of views, again regardless of their derivation, then one would vote for him. But this does not seem a satisfactory resolution, either. It is almost impossible to escape the belief that law and what Ronald Dworkin has famously called "legal integrity" rest at least in part—and what the percentage that part constitutes is perhaps the most pervasive debate in jurisprudence—on the process by which a judge decides independently of the result achieved. So we necessarily return to the place within legal process of recourse to explicitly religious norms.

What makes Justice Henderson's opinion so interesting is its unabashed tone of religion-based moralism. Indeed, in another part of his opinion, dealing with the lower court's division of the marital property, Justice Henderson denounces the award to the former wife of some $42,000 in cash. "This compounded and perpetuated an existing wrong," thundered Henderson, "for it rewards a rejection of the good things in the sacrament of marriage. I would pray that God help the decent hard working young farmers and ranchers of this state."[31] One rarely reads language like this in the opinions of more "sophisticated" judges.

Consider, though, another example of religious reference in a judicial opinion, this one drawn from an opinion written by one of the most sophisticated judges in American history, Justice William O. Douglas. The case involved the criminal prosecution, under the Mann Act prohibiting so-called "white slavery," of a Mormon "fundamentalist" who had refused to accept his church's 1890 repudiation of polygamy—itself the result of the most systematic religious persecution in American history—and, therefore, continued to adhere to Brigham Young's teachings about the necessity of plural marriage.[32] Justice Douglas, writing for the majority of the Court, had shockingly little trouble upholding the conviction of Harlan Cleveland for transporting one of his wives across a state line "for immoral purposes." (He had, presumably, traveled from Southern Utah to Northern Arizona, which continue to this day to be havens for groups of old-line Mormons.) Douglas, who would later face censure for his own marital circumstances, quoted language from earlier decisions that denounced polygamy as, among other things, "contrary to the spirit of Christianity and of the civilization which Christianity has produced in the western world."[33] (One might compare this to Chief Justice Burger's evocation forty years later of "Judaeo-Christian moral and ethical standards" to justify Georgia's criminalization of what he termed "homosexual sodomy.")[34] To be sure, Douglas also goes on to state, in his own language, that "[t]he establishment or maintenance of polygamous households is a notorious example of promiscuity,"[35] and the moral revulsion presumably felt by most right-minded Americans amply justified, as a constitutional matter, Congress's using its power to regulate interstate commerce to punish the hapless Mormons. An eloquent (and lonely) dissent was written by Frank Murphy, the one Catholic member of the Court during that era. Although he carefully noted that it is "not my purpose to defend the practice of polygamy or to claim that it is morally the equivalent of monogamy,"[36] he went on to describe it as "one of the basic forms of marriage," offering as evidence for this proposition "the writers of the Old Testament" and its perpetuation even in the twentieth century "among certain pagan and non-Christian peoples of the world."[37]

---

31 479 N.W.2d 898.

32 *Cleveland v. United States,* 329 U.S. 14 (1946).

33 Ibid., 19, quoting *The Late Corporation of the Church of Jesus Christ of Latter-day Saints v. United States,* 136 U.S. 1, 49 (1890).

34 See *Bowers v. Hardwick,* 478 U.S. 118, 196, 197 (1986).

35 329 U.S. 19.

36 Ibid., 25.

Douglas's language is far more ambiguous than is Henderson's. There is not a scintilla of doubt that Henderson is writing in his own voice. It would be an extraordinary law clerk indeed who would dare write the language that appears in the *Chicoine* opinion. Douglas, on the other hand, is writing in more indirect discourse. That an earlier Court had denounced polygamy as un-Christian is not necessarily evidence for the proposition that Douglas believes its violation of Christian doctrine is a good reason for him to suppress it. One might think that *his* reason had to do with the "promiscuity" purportedly linked with polygamy. As I have discovered in many conversations about *Reynolds v. United States*,[38] the (in)famous case in which the Supreme Court upheld the prosecution of a Mormon bigamist against claims that this violated his free exercise of religion protected by the First Amendment, there are many academics today who readily denounce bigamy on secular grounds, such as its purported entrenchment of patriarchy. They therefore need make no reference to any religious norms against the practice.

Still, one can ask whether Justice Douglas should have quoted the language cited. And even if one gives him the benefit of a "that's the way they talked in the unenlightened old days" defense, should any person who finds unproblematic the presence in 1966 of such language in judicial opinions be readily confirmed for the bench? Things can become even more complicated, though. Consider, for example, a nominee who (sincerely) says that she herself has no religious commitments but that she views the judicial role as enforcing our "fundamental social norms"? And, the nominee goes on, given the particular history of the United States, identification of such "fundamental norms" requires that due attention be paid to the religious roots of basic American values and practices. From this perspective, an essential role of the judge is that of the cultural anthropologist. It is truly difficult to understand most societies, and impossible to understand the United States, without paying due heed to the role of religion. If one treats Christianity (or that peculiarly American amalgam "Judeo-Christianity") simply as a culture, it is hard to see why its norms should be ignored by any anthropologically sensitive judge in favor of some other set of cultural norms, unless, of course, one were willing to make the argument that non-religious cultures necessarily offer greater access to certain important social and moral "truths" than is the case with religiously based cultures. Perhaps there is good reason to believe that. Is it relevant, though, that the public articulation of any such view would surely be enough to doom one's career in public life, including, one strongly suspects, prospects for Senate confirmation to the judiciary?

I offer one final example of the kinds of issues that both interest and perplex me. Armstrong Williams, in an interview with Clarence Thomas, asked him

37   Ibid., 26.

38   98 U.S. 145 (1878).

whether he thought he should use his position on the Court to advance the interests of the black community.[39] Thomas answered as follows:

> You cannot embrace racism to deal with racism. It's not Christian. [Thomas went on to compare using the law to favor blacks as similar to the hypocrisy of] "the self-righteous religious leaders who wanted to stone the prostitute" [in the Bible]. Jesus said go and sin no more. That is what I have to do.
>
> At stake is the principle of equality, including equality before law that is, or ought be, the domain of the Supreme Court. Behind that precept is a high moral imperative: to do unto others as you would have them do unto you. I cannot do to white people what an elite group of whites did to black people, because if I do, I am just as bad as they are . . . I can't break from God's law just because they did. . . .
>
> From the minute they put the first slave on the first ship, they violated God's law. From the first drop of the venom of racism to the slave codes to the Jim Crow law, they broke God's law. If I type one word at my word processor in one opinion against them, I break God's law. . . . If I write racism into law, then I am in God's eye no better than they are.

Whatever one's position on the merits of affirmative action (or on the merits of his appointment), I think it is difficult indeed not to be moved by the intensity of Justice Thomas's comments and his commitment to maintain fidelity to his highest loyalties. That being said, is one *only* moved, or is there also a proper element of disquiet, at the extent to which Thomas either believes that he knows what "God's law" in fact is, or interweaves into his role as a judge the apparent duty of fidelity to it? Forget Anita Hill. Should these comments alone, had they been made to the Senate, have disqualified Thomas? Is it possible, on the contrary, that they would actually count as a reason for supporting his nomination?

My general posture in considering issues is ambivalence, and I scarcely feel, at the conclusion of this essay, genuinely closer to a resolution than I was at the outset. Yet part of my contract with those who invited me to participate in this collective discussion—and with the reader who has stuck with me this far—is presumably to offer conclusions, however tentative. If forced, then, I am willing to defend the following three propositions:

(1) Greenawalt is right in suggesting that judges must be especially resistant of the temptation to treat religious sources as containing any privileged statements of moral truth; and

---

39   The quotations below come from a version of the article published in the *Charlestown Post and Courier*, August 17, 1995, that is available on LEXIS. It was sent to me by Professor Richard Duncan, a fellow participant in a marvelous e-mail discussion group on law and religion that features a remarkable (and courteously expressed) range of opinions.

(2) this justifies, first interrogation, and then a negative vote in regard to any nominee whose statements lead one to doubt whether this temptation will in fact be resisted. However,

(3) it is tolerable to treat religious cultures as providing insight into what might be described as the positive morality of our social order, so long as one recognizes that religious cultures are indeed only a part of the American mosaic, and that non-religious cultures must be given "equal concern and respect."

Hanging over this entire discussion, of course, is whether any public officials other than judges have a duty to make the pledge of abstinence when performing their public roles. I confess that I find it harder than do some to draw bright lines between judges and legislators or executive officers. My skepticism comes in part from the basic perspective of legal realism, which I share, that one cannot necessarily distinguish between "law" and "politics" and, therefore, that the judicial function often in fact overlaps with the legislative insofar as both judge and legislator "make policy" even if the method by which this is done is quite dramatically different. This being said, I am, like Greenawalt, unwilling to be censorious of ordinary citizens or even political candidates who present religious sources as the basis, at least in part, for their advocacy of certain political positions. But, again like Greenawalt, I am truly uncertain as to what successful candidates, who now inhabit public office, should be allowed, within the limits of an adequate liberal theory, to articulate as the basis for using the coercive power of the state to require or prohibit certain activity. Fortunately, my contract did not require that I answer *all* of the issues raised by our subject, and, like a restrained judge, I reserve fuller discussion for another occasion.

Religion and Women's Human Rights

Martha C. Nussbaum

The *mullahs* say: "When they will die we shall not bury them." Villagers say, "Wherever they want, they go. They do not cover their heads. They talk with men. They will be sinners." I said: "If Allah does not see us when we stay hungry then Allah has sinned." —*A Bangladeshi wife, participant in a literacy and skills program sponsored by the Bangladesh Rural Advancement Committee*[1]

I. The Liberal Dilemma

Political liberals characteristically defend two theses, which appear to be closely related. First, liberals hold that religious liberty, or more generally the liberty of conscience, is among the most important of the human freedoms and must be given a very strong degree of priority in the basic structure of a political regime. This is frequently understood to entail that the freedom of religious exercise can permissibly be infringed only when there is an imminent threat to public order.[2] Second, liberals hold that human beings have various other rights, including rights to freedom of movement, freedom of assembly, freedom of speech, the right to equal political participation, the right to be treated as equals under the law, both civil and criminal, and, finally, various rights to the integrity and inviolability of the person.

In a sense, there would seem to be a strong complementarity between the first thesis and the second. For we know well that the rights on the list given in the second thesis have all too often been denied to individuals on grounds of religious membership; one clear sign of a regime's failure to honor the first thesis will be its discriminatory behavior toward religious groups with respect to a wider spectrum of human rights. Thus the German Nazi regime, unlike that of medieval Spain, was not preoccupied with the specific task of impeding the Jews' freedom to worship. They pursued their campaign through the denial of other human rights, such as the equal right to contract a marriage, the right to mobility, assembly, and choice of occupation, and, of course, ultimately, the right to life. It would be correct to hold that true religious liberty

---

1   Cited in Martha A. Chen, *A Quiet Revolution: Women in Transition in Rural Bangladesh* (Cambridge, Mass.: Schenkman, 1983).

2   See John Rawls, *A Theory of Justice* (Cambridge, Mass.: Harvard University Press, 1971), 205–21; on 213, Rawls holds that restrictions of religious liberty can be justified only when the consequences for the security of public order are "reasonably certain or imminent."

required that these other basic freedoms not be impaired on a discriminatory basis.

On the other hand, the two theses can also generate a tension, which poses difficult questions for contemporary law and political thought. For the world's major religions, in their actual human form, have not always been outstanding respectors of basic human rights or of the equal dignity and inviolability of persons. Some, indeed, have gone so far as to create systems of law that deny the equal rights of persons and justify violations of their dignity and their person. Apart from law, influential religious discourse in many parts of the world threatens the bodily integrity and equal dignity of persons—and some-times, even, their equal liberty of worship. Consider the following seven examples:

1. In a village in rural Bangladesh in the early 1980s, low-income women leave their homes to meet in a group organized by the Bangladesh Rural Advance-ment Committee. They are learning to read, to keep accounts, and to pursue various forms of work outside the home—all important ingredients in improv-ing nutrition and health for themselves and their children. The local *mullahs* (Islamic religious leaders) make speeches saying that women who work outside the house and talk with men other than their husbands are whores. They threaten them with religious and communal ostracism (refusal to offici-ate at any of the woman's social or religious functions), and even with physical violence. ("If you go into the field, your legs will be broken.")[3] Although most of the women continue with the literacy project, they fear for their status in the community, their well-being (which, so far, is entirely dependent on their relation to men), and their physical safety.[4]

2. In Pakistan, again in the early 1980s, a young blind girl named Safia Bibi complained of rape. Since she was a minor, her father filed a complaint. Under the recently promulgated Hudood Ordinance, rape convictions require four male witnesses; and complainants who fail to produce the necessary testimony may then be prosecuted for fornication (*zina*). The Sessions Court found Safia in violation of the Zina Ordinance, sentencing her to three years hard labor in prison, despite her blindness. After a storm of national and international protest, the Federal Shariat Court set the case aside on technical grounds, but refused to prosecute the accused rapist.[5]

---

3   See Chen, *A Quiet Revolution*, 174.

4   In this case, the fact that the women were soon understood to be augmenting the family income won the day for them; husbands and in-laws soon ceased resis-tance, and the authority of the *mullahs* declined in importance. One woman concludes, "We do not listen to the *mullahs* any more. They . . . did not give us even a quarter kilo of rice. Now we get ten maunds of rice [i.e. through their new employment]. Now, people help us" (Ibid., 176).

3. In China in 1995, government spokesmen promote a new policy to deal with the fluctuations in the labor market during this time of economic growth. It is, that women should be the first to be fired in any case where an employer has to downsize. The so-called "women go home" policy is defended by ample reference to the Confucian religious tradition,[6] since Confucius held that women's nature fits them only for domestic duties.[7]

4. In Madhya Pradesh, India in 1978, a Muslim woman named Shah Bano was thrown out of her home by her husband after forty-four years of marriage. As required by Islamic personal law, he returned Rs. 3000 (about $300), which had been her marriage settlement from her family. Rather than accept this settlement, she sued for maintenance under Section 125 of the Criminal Procedure Code, which requires a person of adequate means to protect relations from destitution and vagrancy.[8] As a result, she was awarded Rs. 180 ($18) per month, hardly a princely sum, but an improvement. Her husband, however, appealed this judgment to the Supreme Court of India, holding that as a Muslim he was bound only by Islamic law. In 1985, the Supreme Court held that the provisions of the Criminal Procedure Code regarding maintenance of destitute relations were applicable to members of all religions, and that a person should not lose simply by being a Muslim. In his opinion Chief Justice Chandrachud alluded to a provision of the Constitution that had instructed the state to "endeavour to secure" a uniform civil code; he deplored its failure to have done so.[9] The Muslim Personal Law Board and other religious leaders vehemently criticized the ruling, using public rhetoric to persuade followers that their religion was in grave danger, unless the government should decide

5   See the account of the case in Radhika Coomaraswamy, "Women, Ethnicity, and the Discourse of Rights," in *Human Rights of Women: National and International Perspectives* (hereafter HRW), ed. Rebecca J. Cook (Philadelphia: University of Pennsylvania Press, 1994), 50–51.

6   Some people do not think of Confucianism as a religion, presumably because metaphysical belief plays no role in it. It is, however, an organized system of ritual practice, not simply a set of attitudes to life; in its approach to ethics, it is distinct from philosophical ethical systems, and closely related to religions such as Judaism, in the center role given to ritual.

7   Oral communication, at conference on Chinese Women and Feminism, Beijing, June 1995, sponsored by the Ford Foundation.

8   Relations enumerated are spouse, minor children, adult handicapped children, and aged parents.

9   India has a uniform criminal code, but not a uniform civil code, many civil matters being handled by individual religious systems of law; the confusion in this case arises from the fact that the Muslim woman who could not find redress in Muslim civil courts was able to appeal to a provision of the national criminal procedure code; see further on this situation below.

to exempt Muslim women from the provisions of Section 125.[10] Responding to this campaign, the government of Rajiv Gandhi passed the Muslim Women's Act of 1986, depriving divorced Muslim women of their right of maintenance under the criminal code[11]—while at the same time recommending that by the year 2000 the nation adopt a uniform civil code.[12] Hindu political activist subsequently complained that the new law discriminated against Hindus by giving Muslims "special privileges."[13]

10   On the controversy, see Kavita R. Khory, "The Shah Bano Case: Some Political Implications," in Robert Baird, ed., *Religion and Law in Independent India* (Delhi: Manohar, 1993), 121–37, pointing out that in reality the Islamic community was highly divided about the judgment. See also Sen, "Secularism and Its Discontents," in *Unravelling the Nation*, ed. Kaushik Basu and Sanjay Subrahmanyam, 1995; and Sen, *On Interpreting India's Past* (Calcutta: the Asiatic Society, 1996), 22–23; Kirti Singh, "Obstacles to Women's Rights in India," in HRW, 384–85; relevant documents are collected in Asghar Ali Engineer, ed., *The Shah Bano Controversy* (Delphi: Ajanta Publishers, 1987). See also Veena Das, *Critical Events* (Delhi: Oxford University Press, 1992), chapter 4. On general issues about the Indian legal system and its history, see John H. Mansfield, "The Personal Laws or a Uniform Civil Code?" in Baird, ed., *Religion and Law*; Tahir Mahmood, *Muslim Personal Law, Role of the State in the Indian Subcontinent* 2d ed. (Nagpur, 1983).

11   The Act, however, contains an option: At the time of marriage, a couple may elect to submit themselves to the maintenance provisions of the Criminal Procedure Code instead of the Islamic law; previously, Islamic law was enforced on all Muslims, regardless of their choice, and that is still the case, in effect, for most matters. Such options have been a matter of great dispute. Under the Shariat Act, individuals will be governed by the Shariat only if they make an election in its favor, but that choice will be binding on their descendants, who have no choice in the matter. See Mansfield, "The Personal Laws," 169.

12   On the pros and cons of a uniform code, see Sen, "Secularism," 22 ff., citing constitutional debates; Mahmood, *Muslim Personal Law*, 115–30 on Muslim opinion. Although Dr. Ambedkar, the leader of the team of constitutional framers, expressed a preference for "uniformity of fundamental laws, civil and criminal," this uniformity was not incorporated in the constitution, and his preference was included only as an unenforceable "Directive Principle of State Policy," stating that "the State shall endeavour to secure for the citizens a uniform civil code throughout the territory of India." It was stated that this principle was "fundamental in the governance of the country " and that "it shall be the duty of the State to apply" it, but that it "shall not be enforceable by any court." (*Constitution of India*, Article 44.) At the same time, however, Article 13 (1) provides that all "laws in force" shall be void insofar as they are in conflict with the constitutionally enumerated Fundamental Rights; among which (Articles 14 and 15) are the right of all persons to the equal protection of the laws and a guarantee of non-discrimination on the basis of "religion, race, caste, sex, place of birth or any of them." It is thus possible to hold that the personal laws were already rendered void by article 13 (1): see discussion below.

13   Cited in Sen, "Secularism," 22, who observes: "This line of reasoning has many

5. In 1955, the Indian Parliament passed the Hindu Marriage Act, which for the first time gave women the right to divorce and remarriage, which men had long enjoyed. (Indeed, men could previously marry an unlimited number of times without getting divorced, although the reforms of 1955 and 1956 ruled out polygamy for Hindu men.) Conservative Hindu members of Parliament claimed that the bill had been passed to "wound the religious feeling of the Hindus" and was "against the fundamental principles of Hinduism."[14]

6. In contemporary Iran, the penalty for women who do not adhere to the dress code is between 34 and 74 lashes with a whip. The actual penalties are more varied. Some women get off with a cash fine. "But, just as commonly, women who do not adhere to the dress code are punished with acts of extreme cruelty: their feet may be put in a gunny sack full of mice and cockroaches, their faces splashed with acid or cut with razor blades."[15] So terrifying are the penalties that in 1991 a thirteen-year-old girl who had been found in violation committed suicide by throwing herself out of a fifth-floor window. On August 15, 1991, the Prosecutor-General, Abolfazl Musavi-Tabrizi, addressing the controversy occasioned by this death, declared that "anyone who rejects the principle of the *Hijab* [dress code] is an apostate and the punishment for apostasy under Islamic Law is death."[16]

7. In 1993, two groups of women attempted to hold prayer services at the Western Wall ("Wailing Wall") in Jerusalem. Although they did not challenge the traditional separation of male and female prayer spaces—and thus were not in violation of any explicit provision of religious law—they did wear prayer shawls and read from the Torah scroll, which is not conventionally appropriate within Orthodox Judaism. The official in charge, representing the Ministry of Religious Affairs, forbade them to continue, holding that it would undermine custom and violate the religious feelings of orthodox worshippers. They were even labeled "provocateurs" for their organized singing. The Supreme Court of Israel dismissed the women's petition for freedom of religious exercise, recommending that the government establish a commission to look into the issue.[17]

problems. . . . Any unfairness that is there is surely one against *Muslim women*, rather than against *Hindu men*."

14   Singh, "Obstacles," 380, quoting from *Lok Sabha Debates* Part II Vol. IV (1955): 6889.

15   Akram Mirhosseini, "After the Revolution: Violations of Women's Human Rights in Iran," in *Women's Rights, Human Rights* (hereafter WRHR), ed. Julie Peters and Andrea Wolper (New York: Routledge, 1995), 75.

16   Ibid., citing Rinaldo Galindo Pohl, Special Representative of the United Nations Commission on Human Rights in the Islamic Republic of Iran, report on January 2, 1992.

In all these cases we see an apparent dilemma for the modern liberal regime. For if the people who claim to speak for the religious traditions in these examples are to be accepted as their representatives and their claims as legitimate claims of religious liberty (and we shall see that this is not an uncomplicated matter), then there really is a tension between respect for religious liberty and respect for the basic human rights of many citizens. This tension finds its sharpest form wherever the religious traditions have arrogated to themselves, and have been permitted, the right to make law; but it arises, as well, in more informal ways, when the highly influential discourse of religious leaders poses problems for the equal worth of basic liberties—usually already guaranteed in the constitutions (or the legal traditions) of the nations in question, as well as in their commitment to the Universal Declaration of Human Rights and, in most cases, the Convention on the Elimination of All Forms of Discrimination Against Women, a multilateral treaty ratified by 131 countries.[18] If the government defers to the wishes of the religious group, a vulnerable group of individuals will lose basic rights; if the government commits itself to respecting equal human rights of all individuals, it will stand accused of indifference to the liberty of conscience. Often government actors, for example Rajiv Gandhi and the Israeli Supreme Court, make a mere pretense of serious engagement with the problem—satisfying the religious group, since it is far more politically powerful than women, but saying, at the same time, that something must surely be done about this by someone in the future.

Nor is this dilemma troubling only for the liberal state: It vexes the religions themselves as well. An especially poignant statement of its force can be found in the Pope's recent address to the United Nations. On the one hand, this address contained a very strong injunction to respect the world's major religions and a ringing defense of "the fundamental right to freedom of religion and freedom of conscience, as the cornerstones of the structure of human rights and the foundation of every truly free society."[19] These sentiments are exactly those of John Rawls, who writes that "the question of equal

---

17   HC 257/89, 2410/90, *Hoffman et al. v. Officer of the Western Wall*, judgment delivered January 26, 1994, reported in Carmel Shalev, "Women in Israel: Fighting Tradition," in WRHR 94–95.

18   Data as of January 1994, cited in HRW, 254. See also UN *Human Development Report 1995* (New York: UN Development Program, 1995), 43. Among the countries that will be discussed below, Iran, Pakistan, Saudi Arabia, and the Sudan have not ratified the Convention; some of the others, including India, China, and Bangladesh, of the others (and many European nations as well) have ratified it only with some "reservation"; the United States has signed it but has not ratified it.

19   Pope John Paul II, Address to the United Nations General Assembly, October 5, 1995.

liberty of conscience is settled. It is one of the fixed points of our considered judgments of justice."[20] At the same time, however, the Pope vigorously endorsed the U.N.'s Universal Declaration of Human Rights as "one of the highest expressions of the human conscience of our time" and spoke of a worldwide movement toward universal respect for the dignity and inviolability of the human person. His more recent "Letter to Women," issued just before the Beijing Women's Conference, makes it clear that he considers many of the rights at issue in my examples to be central human rights: he mentions freedom from sexual violence (including marital rape), equality in family rights, equality in political duties and responsibilities, equality under the law, and equality in the workplace.[21] Although his list does not contain all the rights that all advocates of women's rights have sought, it includes enough of them to generate the dilemma, simply by its juxtaposition with the urgent claim to respect the answers given by each religious tradition.

The other papers in this volume focus on domestic American issues of religious discourse and liberal politics. The dilemma I propose to study does arise in the U.S. as well; as I pursue the international issues I shall orient myself toward the other papers by sketching my own view of those debates. But, given that the United States has a Bill of Rights that is effective, not merely aspirational (as are relevant constitutional provisions in many other nations)[22], and given that by now the major religions in the U.S. have long accepted some fundamental shared ideas about the equal dignity and liberty of persons, such a focus cannot address the most problematic aspects of the relationship between political liberalism and religion. We simply do not hear any influential religious voice in the United States proposing, at this time, that women's legal testimony be judged unequal to that of men, that women be severely

---

20   Rawls, *Theory*, 206.

21   Pope John Paul II, "Letter to Women," dated June 29, 1995, released July 10, p. 2: "As far as personal rights are concerned, there is an urgent need to achieve real equality in every area: equal pay for equal work, protection for working mothers, fairness in career advancements, equality of spouses with regard to family rights and the recognition of everything that is part of the rights and duties of citizens in a democratic state. . . . The time has come to condemn vigorously the types of sexual violence which frequently have women for their object and to pass laws which effectively defend them from such violence." Elsewhere, the Pope has spoken explicitly about marital rape, making it clear that he believes it to fall among the violent acts that should be legally prohibited.

22   Other constitutional guarantees of rights may be merely aspirational for two distinct reasons: because they include a long list of rights, including many economic and social rights, that are extremely difficult to enforce; or because they do not attempt to enforce the very same rights that are enforced in the United States. I am speaking here of the second contrast: guarantees of equal protection, mobility and assembly rights, speech rights, rights of religious exercise, and others are merely aspirational for many citizens in many nations.

punished for dressing this way or that, that their legs be broken for walking outside the house, that they be denied a right to divorce equal to that granted a man. None of these cases is totally discontinuous with our own past and even present; the practical difficulty of complaining of rape, for example, and the punishment meted out to women who do so complain, are real and recent, in some cases current. Further back in our history all the mentioned inequalities in family law could be attested, often buttressed by appeals to religion.[23] Certainly Christianity and Judaism are far from blameless in the global history of women's unequal treatment, as my Israeli case attests; they have merely been on a rather short leash recently in Europe and America. My international examples manifest, I believe, what parts of most religious traditions (as well as many non-religious traditions) will try to do when they are not on such a short leash. I believe, therefore, that a focus on current international issues is valuable in order to give us a vivid sense of the reality of our topic. Without this focus, we might fail to acknowledge that religions (like many non-religious political actors) can propose and seriously defend gross atrocities; we might therefore fail to ask what liberals who care about religion should say when they do.

Such atrocities frequently involve women, but they are obviously not limited to them; a similar paper could be written about the religions' treatment of other religions, or about issues of caste and hierarchy within the religions. But the example of women will give us a very useful focus for debate.

It is useful to focus on this topic for another reason as well: because these atrocities do not always receive the intense public concern and condemnation that other systematic atrocities against groups often receive, and there is reason to think that liberal respect for religious difference is involved in this neglect.[24] The worldwide mobilization against South African Apartheid has not been accompanied by any similar mobilization to divest stock holdings in nations that treat women as unequal under the law. Indeed, these inequalities are often cheerfully put up with, as part of legitimate difference—as when our troops were asked to fall in with Saudi customs regarding women's dress while serving in the Gulf. During a debate on South African divestiture at Harvard University in 1983, a prominent liberal political thinker argued that the case of apartheid was unique in today's world because a group of persons was not merely being discriminated against but was being treated as systematically unequal under the law. Unique in the world? That was false in 1983 and is even more false today. One reason for the reluctance of Western liberals to face this

23   See Mary E. Becker, "The Politics of Women's Wrongs and the Bill of 'Rights': A Bicentennial Perspective," *University of Chicago Law Review* 59 (1992): 453–517; reprinted in *The Bill of Rights*, ed. G. Stone, et al.

24   An honorable exception to the neglect is certainly Rawls, who in "The Law of Peoples" argued that women's equality was one area in which it was legitimate to interfere with the religious or traditional practices of a nation.

fact and to take appropriate political action is surely the political hopelessness of it all—for how could we hope to convince our nation to take economic action against so many oil-rich nations? There may be several other reasons. Among them however, is surely the role of religion in the debate: Liberals who do not hesitate to criticize a secular government that perpetrates atrocity are anxious and reticent when it comes to vindicating claims of justice against major religious leaders and groups. They are hesitant, I suggest, because they hold that the liberty of conscience is among the fixed points in our considered judgments of justice, and are at a loss to see how they could in good conscience ask religious people to acquiesce in a judgment about sex equality that is foreign to that religious tradition. This suggests that a sorting out of the liberal dilemma may contribute to greater political clarity in an area where we urgently need clarity.

I shall be focusing on cases in which religions threaten basic human rights. This is because it is these cases that generate the dilemma with which I am concerned, not because I believe that this is the primary relation religions have had to human rights. It is obvious that religious discourse has been among the major sources of support for human rights around the world, and I have focused on the Pope's statement partly in order to keep this fact before our minds. The dual role of the religions in these areas will concern me when I turn to the philosophical unraveling of the dilemma; for the time being, however, I shall continue to focus on cases where human rights are at risk.

In what follows, I do not ignore, though I shall not directly address, the difficulties involved in defining the notion of a "human right" or specifying the conditions under which a person can be said to have a right to a certain type of treatment. Obviously enough, since I shall be urging legal change in order to do justice to women's human rights, I do not accept a positivist analysis, according to which a person has a right if and only if the law in her country has recognized such a right. I understand a human right to be a claim of an especially urgent and powerful sort, one that can be justified by an ethical argument that can command a broad cross-cultural consensus, and one that does not cease to be morally salient when circumstances render its recognition inefficient. A human right, unlike many other rights people may have, derives not from a person's particular situation of privilege or power or skill, but, instead, just from the fact of being human. In my understanding, there is a very close relationship between a list of basic human rights and the Rawlsian list of "primary goods," that is, things that all persons may be presumed to need in order to carry out their plans of life, whatever the plan is. Human rights are, in effect, justified claims to such basic goods. Other much-discussed questions, concerning the precise relationship between rights and interests, rights and theories of the good, rights and duties, do not affect the analysis to be presented here and can therefore be deferred.[25] If this way of proceeding leaves the philosopher open to accusations of woolly abstractness, she may justly reply that economists standardly use notions (such as *preference* and *develop-*

ment) that are similarly in need of further clarification, and that have, unlike these much-analyzed philosophical notions, received, in the literature of the profession, relatively little of the clarification they need.

II. Women's Human Rights: The Problem Areas

The Women's Convention defines "discrimination against women" as:

> any distinction, exclusion or restriction made on the basis of sex which has the effect or purpose of impairing or nullifying the recognition, enjoyment or exercise by women, irrespective of their marital status, on a basis of equality of men and women, of human rights and fundamental freedoms in the political, economic, social, cultural, civil or any other field.

By ratifying the Convention—as most of the nations under discussion have—states pledge (a) to embody "the principle of the equality of men and women" in their national Constitutions or other appropriate legislation; (b) to legislate against discrimination against women, providing appropriate sanctions; (c) to "establish legal protection of the rights of women on an equal basis with men" and to ensure this protection through "competent national tribunals and other public institutions"; (d) to ensure that public authorities do not discriminate against women; (e) to take "all appropriate measures" to eliminate existing discrimination "by any person, organization or enterprise"; (f) to change or abolish any existing discriminatory "laws, regulations, customs and practices"; (g) to repeal all provisions of the penal law that are discriminatory.[26] Article 5 of the Convention elaborates these duties by explaining that state parties agree to confront and modify "customary and all other practices" that are based on the idea of the inferiority or superiority of one sex to the other, or on ideas of stereotyped roles for men and women. Let us keep these norms in mind, as we briefly survey eleven problem areas for women's human rights in which religious discourse, and often action, have been major influences. In the United States, and in most of the papers in this volume, the focus of debate has been on the role of religious *discourse*, since the scope of the religions for direct political action is relatively circumscribed and its limits are well understood. As we turn to the international realm, we must focus on practices as

25   For a sense of my own relation to them, see my "Human Capabilities, Female Human Beings," in *Women, Culture, and Development: A Study of Human Capabilities*, ed. M. Nussbaum and J. Glover (Oxford: Clarendon Press, 1993) (hereafter WCD); and "The Good as Discipline, the Good as Freedom," forthcoming in *The Ethics of Consumption and Stewardship*, ed. D. Crocker, discussing the very close relationship between my list of the basic human capabilities and Rawls's list of primary goods.

26   Women's Convention, Article 2, quoted in full in R. J. Cook, "State Accountability Under the Women's Convention," in HRW, 230.

well as discourse, assessing discourse both as a political force in its own right and as a part of programs of political action.

Cultures are complex. It is generally very difficult to determine to what extent the religions in a nation reflect influences from other aspects of the culture and to what extent they influence the culture. In nations such as Iran, we can contrast the situation prior to the control of religious fundamentalists with the current situation; usually such assessments are more elusive, and we must exercise caution in drawing conclusions. The problem is compounded, in a nation such as India, by sharp regional variations that reflect many different cultural and political factors; differences across religions are less sharp than such regional differences, though religion appears to have some independent explanatory weight.[27]

Our assessments are made more complex by the fact that when religions act politically their religious discourse is often powerfully colored by issues of political power. Thus, the Hinduism represented today in India by the BJP (Bharatiya Janata Party, the leading Hindu nationalist party) is not very much like the inclusive, loosely defined, polytheistic Hinduism of earlier tradition; political and cultural forces are likely to have shaped the BJP's selection of religious principles and emphases.[28] Very different political aims shaped Mahatma Gandhi's characterization of the essence of Hinduism, when he said, "If I were asked to define the Hindu creed, I should simply say: Search after truth through non-violent means."[29] Where women are concerned, the same has been true over the years. The Hindu tradition offers many different and contradictory pictures of women's agency, from Draupadi's strength and sexual initiative in the *Mahabharata* (including a choice to marry five husbands simultaneously!) to the enlightened sensualism of the *Kama Sutra*,[30] in which women of good social situation enjoy considerable sexual freedom (a freedom freely depicted in many works of Hindu visual art), to the misogyny of the *Laws of Manu*, in which women are depicted as both whorish and childish, totally unfit for independent choice.[31] An investigation of cultural context

27   See J. Drèze and A. Sen, *India: Economic Development and Social Opportunity* (Oxford: Clarendon Press, 1995.

28   See Amartya Sen, "Secularism."

29   Cited by Jawaharlal Nehru in *The Discovery of India* (Calcutta: Signet Press, 1956 centenary edition; Oxford: Clarendon Press, 1989), 75; see discussion in Sen, *Interpreting*, 13–14.

30   This work, which Westerners often encounter as a pornographic curiosity, is, of course, a central text of the religious tradition, of deeply serious pedagogical intent.

31   For an account of the misogynist texts, see Roop Rekha Verma, "Femininity, Equality, and Personhood," in WCD, 433–43. The reader of these texts will quickly discover that the tendency of some Hindu feminists to blame all repressive tendencies in Hinduism on the Islamic cultural influence is in error.

would be likely, here too, to reveal political influences at work shaping and reshaping the religious tradition; more important for our purposes, the contemporary choice to stress one aspect of the tradition rather than another itself often betrays political aims.[32]

Similarly, the Islamic fundamentalism characteristic of the Iranian regime has little in common with the tolerant and pluralistic form of Islam espoused by Iranian writer Alberuni, who traveled to India in the eleventh century, or with that implemented politically by the tolerant Moghul emperor Akbar in the sixteenth century.[33] Islam contains fundamentalists who are intolerant of other religions, but it also contains some of the earliest expressions of toleration and the transcendence of sectarian boundaries—in, for example, the great medieval religious poet Kabir, who wrote, "Kabir is the child of Allah and of Ram: He is my Guru, he is my Pir."[34] In India today, Muslims include liberals and conservatives, feminists and traditionalists. Similarly the contemporary Iranian regime interprets Islam in ways that do not reflect the entirety of that tradition, ways that may not be unconnected with its political goals. Many devout Muslims today support more liberal views and policies. Judaism and Christianity contain similar complexities, as is well known.

Thus the criticisms we may make of "religious practices" and "religious discourse" will be criticisms of human beings, often vying for political power; they do not presuppose that any of these religions has an unchanging and unchangeable core of misogyny, or even that the misogynistic elements are religiously central rather than political in origin. Nonetheless, since we are interested in the rights of individuals, we must approach the religions where they, or their representatives, threaten these rights.

1. Life and Health

Women's lives are unequally at risk in many parts of today's world. Statistics continue to show that women suffer unequally from hunger and malnutrition and from unequal access to basic health care. It has been estimated that tens of millions, and perhaps hundreds of millions, of women are not alive today who would be alive had they received nutrition and health care equal to that given men. (Some of these numbers may be attributed to infanticide, but far more are attributable to neglect and malnutrition.)

India, Pakistan, China, and Bangladesh have especially large numbers of

---

32   For one clear example of this, see Khory's study of reactions to the Shah Bano case, "The Shah Bano Case." She summarizes: "the Shah Bano case is representative of the way in which group divisions within Indian society are increasingly manipulated for political reasons."

33   See Sen, "Secularism," 32–39.

34   See Ibid., 41, citing the translation by Rabindranath Tagore in *One Hundred Poems of Kabir* (London: Macmillan, 1915), Verse LXIX; see also Kshiti Mohan Sen, *Hinduism*, chapters 18 and 19 (Harmondsworth: Penguin Books, 1960).

such "missing women."[35] Although it is difficult to pin down the origins of practices of unequal feeding and care, cultural systems that portray female life as unequal in worth to male life must bear some of the responsibility for this egregious situation. Religious discourse has played a substantial role here. Although it is difficult to distinguish between a religion and the cultural traditions that surround it, the Hindu, Islamic, and Confucian traditions have all with some plausibility been accused of denigrating the value of female life in ways that have undermined women's claim to basic goods of subsistence.[36]

Of equal or greater importance, religious discourse has played a major and undisguised role in confining women to the home in many parts of the world, and in denying them opportunities to earn wages outside. Islamic ideas of women's proper role returned thousands of women to the home in Iran; they keep women in the home in Bangladesh, India, and many other nations. Hindu caste traditions, similarly, are often invoked to resist a woman's attempt to seek outside employment. It is especially common that middle-rank "upwardly mobile" caste families will invoke norms of the Brahmin ideal of woman in order to forbid their women employment, thus defining the family as "Brahminizing."[37] Confucian values, as we have seen, are also publicly invoked to return women to the home from the public sector. But the fact is that wage labor outside the home is highly correlated with a woman's ability to command food and other goods within it. Sometimes the connection is direct: in Rajasthan Metha Bai, a young widow, was starving because her Brahminizing in-laws refused to let her earn money to feed herself and her children, threatening to beat her if she went out.[38] Sometimes it is more indirect, through a perception of a woman's importance to the future of the family. Because housework is usually not perceived as making a great contribution to the family's well-being, whereas cash wages are, women who work

35 See J. Drèze and A. Sen, *Hunger and Public Action* (Oxford: Clarendon Press, 1989); A. Sen, "Women's Survival as a Development Problem," *Bulletin of the American Academy of Arts and Sciences* 43 (1989), shortened version in *New York Review of Books*, Christmas issue 1990; for a focus on India and more recent comparative data, see Drèze and Sen, *India*. Drèze and Sen establish that there is no evidence that the female disadvantage is greater among Muslims than among Hindus. For a summary, see Nussbaum, "Introduction" in WCD.

36 On Islam, see Chen, *A Quiet Revolution*; Valentine Moghadam, *Gender, Development, and Policy: Toward Equity and Empowerment*, UNU/WIDER Research for Action series, November 1990; on the Confucian tradition, see Xiarong Li, "Gender Inequality in China," in WCD 407–25; on Hindu traditions, see Roop Rekha Verma, "Femininity, Equality, and Personhood," in WCD, 433–43, with ample references to traditional texts.

37 See Martha Chen, "A Matter of Survival: Women's Right to Employment in India and Bangladesh," in WCD, 37–57.

38 See Chen, "A Matter of Survival," 37; for some progress in Metha Bai's situation, see "Introduction," 14.

outside do better at commanding food in times of shortage, and the general perception of a daughter's worth is similarly affected by her future employment opportunities.[39] The number of "missing women"[40] in Pakistan is 5.2 million (12.9 percent of the number of actual women), in India 36.7 million, in Bangladesh 3.7 million, in China 44 million, in North Africa 2.4 million, in Iran 1.4 million. Religious discourse is implicated in these deaths.

At times, religion directly urges female death. The Indian practice of *sati*, or the immolation of a widow following her husband's death, is certainly religious in origin. The practice has dwindled but has not disappeared completely. On September 4, 1987, in Deorala, Rajasthan, an eighteen-year-old university student named Roop Kanwar was burned alive on her husband's funeral pyre.[41] (Her husband, when he died, was an unemployed university undergraduate.) Some say that she died willingly, others that she was coerced by family pressure.[42] Pilgrims flocked to Deorala, revering Roop as a goddess and believing that offerings at her shrine would cure cancer. A huge public controversy erupted. Three months later the Indian Parliament passed a tough new law extending the domain of criminal culpability with respect to *sati*, even though an old law already made the practice illegal; Rajiv Gandhi, decisive in this case, pronounced the practice "utterly reprehensible and barbaric." Traditionalist Hindus attacked the government. "A leading Hindi journal pointed an accusing finger at secular, western-educated intellectuals, arguing that only godless people who did not believe in reincarnation would denigrate Roop's brave act."[43]

It is an understatement to say that most Indian widows do not commit *sati*. Even the much publicized "dowry deaths" are few, and largely middle-class. Rare dramatic cases involving upper-class or middle-class women tend to attract more press coverage and more public protest than the "endemic but quiet deprivations"[44] that are the lot of a large proportion of widows, especially

---

39   See A. Sen, "Gender and Cooperative Conflicts," in I. Tinker, ed., *Persistent Inequalities: Women and World Development* (New York: Oxford University Press, 1990).

40   The number is arrived at by taking as the "base line" the sex ratio in Sub-Saharan Africa, where there is great misery, but (given that women are major agricultural producers) little evidence of discrimination at the level of basic nutrition, and then asking, "How many more women than are now in Country C would be there if it had the same sex ratio as Sub-Saharan Africa?"

41   For an account of the case, see Coomaraswamy, "Women, Ethnicity, and the Discourse of Rights," in HRW, 48–50.

42   Pressure can be either spiritual or financial; in the past many such cases clearly involved financial motives by family members eager to avoid dowry payment and also by in-laws eager to avoid having another mouth to feed.

43   Coomaraswamy, "Women, Ethnicity, and the Discourse of Rights," 49.

44   Drèze and Sen, *India*, 173.

in rural areas. A large majority have very insecure and limited property rights; because they remain in their husband's place of residence, they can expect little care or support either from their birth family or from their in-laws, who frequently mistreat them; they may have no freedom to work, even if this causes malnutrition or even starvation.[45] As Metha Bai said to Martha Chen, "I may die, but still I cannot go out. If there is something in the house we eat; otherwise we go to sleep."[46] Many factors are implicated in this situation, including a traditional gendered division of labor and customs of patrilocal residence and patrilineal inheritance. Religious discourse about widowhood (according to which the widow is virtually dead at the husband's death) is, then, not the only cause of these ills; it is, however, among the causes.

2. The Right to Bodily Integrity

Women suffer many abuses that violate their bodily integrity. These include domestic violence, rape, marital rape, sexual abuse, and genital mutilation. While religious discourse does not frequently call directly for violence against a disobedient spouse, it can frequently promulgate norms of male authority— and also pictures of female wantonness and childishness—that give support to these practices. (This is as true of Western as of non-Western religions.) Nations that allow the religions to take charge of family law often move very slowly to counter this problem. In India women have long sought a civil law against domestic violence; a major obstacle to this is the fact that, in the absence of a uniform civil code, such laws would have to be separately made for Hindus, Muslims, and Parsis.[47] Stranger-rape is, again, usually not directly urged by religious authorities; and yet norms of female purity and submissiveness are frequently used to justify the rape of women who defy such conventions. The Iranian Prosecutor-General believes that any woman who violates the dress code deserves death; he is not likely, then, to deter the common practice of police rape of women under detention for such violations. More generally, the requirements on rape evidence under Islamic laws that prevail in many nations (four male witnesses) make an accusation a virtual impossibility; in Pakistan, with its Catch-22 according to which an unsuccessful accusation of rape constitutes a confession to fornication, very few women will complain of rape, and few men will be deterred from raping.

The very concept of marital rape is foreign to many religious traditions, which give a husband limitless sexual access to the wife. The concept of marital rape is a very recent one in European and North American culture and religion

---

45 See Drèze and Sen, *India*, 172–75; Chen, *The Lives of Widows in Rural India*, forthcoming.

46 See Chen, "A Matter of Survival," 37.

47 See Indira Jaising, "Violence against Women: The Indian Perspective," in WRHR, 51–56.

as well, a fact on which we should not pride ourselves. Indeed, the notion of "restoration of conjugal rights" that is frequently invoked in Indian family courts is of British origin and was retained in the Hindu Marriage Act and the Special Marriage Act of 1954. Nonetheless, at this point, religious law and discourse, including the Hindu and Islamic, are heavily implicated in maintaining marital rape as an option for men.

There has been opposition. In *T. Sareetha v. T. Venkata Subhaiah* (1983),[48] a judge of the Andhra Pradesh High Court, in an especially eloquent opinion, held that the remedy of "restitution of conjugal rights" "violates the right to privacy and human dignity guaranteed by and contained in Article 21 of our Constitution." The measure, he continued, "deprives a woman of control over her choice as to when and by whom the various parts of her body should be allowed to be sensed" and "when and how her body is to become the vehicle for the procreation of another human being."[49] The Supreme Court reversed, however, holding that the Hindu Marriage Act contained sufficient safeguards to prevent such abuses, since a woman who had left her marital home would not be forcibly returned if she could pay a fine. The decree of restoration was even praised as one that "serves a social purpose as an aid to the prevention of break-up of marriage."[50] The Court did not take cognizance of the likely financial position of such women, many of whom would be forced to return to marriages from which they had fled, or effectively respond to the constitutional questions raised by the lower court judge. In other related decisions, the Court opined that a Hindu woman's duty is to live with her husband in the matrimonial home.

Similar cases can be found on the Islamic side. In Bangladesh, a woman who had suffered from domestic violence left the conjugal home and filed for divorce; her husband brought suit for "restoration of conjugal rights."[51] A lower court held that the woman had "no right to divorce at her own sweet will and without any reasonable excuse." In this case, however, the High Court vindicated her rights, commenting on the inconsistency between the "restoration" remedy and the equality provisions in Bangladesh's constitution:

> The very concept of the husband's unilateral plea for forcible restitution of conjugal rights had become outmoded and . . . does not fit with the State and Public Principle and Policy of equality of all men and women being citizens equal before the law and entitled to be treated only in accordance with the law as guaranteed in Articles 27 and 31 of the Constitution. . . . A reference to Article 28(2) of the Constitution of Bangladesh guaranteeing

48   A.I.R. (1983) A. P. 356.

49   Citations from Singh in HRW, 387–88.

50   A.I.R. (1984) S. C. 152; see Singh, "Obstacles," 388.

51   *Nelly Zaman v. Ghiyasuddin*, 34 D.L.R. 221 (1982), discussed in Sara Hossain, "Women's Rights and Personal Laws in South Asia," in HRW, 465–94, at 478–79.

equal rights of women and men in all spheres of the State and public life would clearly indicate that any unilateral plea of the husband for forcible restitution of conjugal rights as against a wife unwilling to live with her husband is violative of the accepted State and Public Principle and Policy.

In these two contested cases we see our liberal dilemma. Both India and Bangladesh have sought to combine a secular liberal constitution, including guarantees of sex equality, with religious courts of family law. In both cases it remains ambiguous to what extent the equality provisions of the constitution apply to the protected family sphere. In such a situation, women's constitutional rights are bound to be fragile and contestable; sometimes things will work out one way, sometimes the other.

Female genital mutilation is frequently defended with discourse that appeals to its basis in Islam. It would appear that these appeals are at the very least tendentious: The practice long preexisted the arrival of Islam in Africa, and the one textual reference to the practice in the *hadith* classifies it as a *makrama* or nonessential practice. Even here, the attitude expressed by Mohammed is ambiguous and dissuasive of any extensive mutilation.[52] Nonetheless, the discourse is religious, and it is powerful in defending the practice and branding the attack on it as Westernizing. FGM is usually performed on young girls, often as young as five or six years old, without their consent even were consent at that age a meaningful notion. FGM, both in the form of clitoridectomy and in the form of infibulation,[53] involves, as commonly practiced, the permanent loss of capacity for orgasm, and is strongly linked with many other health problems: infection from the unsanitary conditions in which it is performed; hemorrhage and abscess; later difficulties in urination and menstruation; stones in the urethra and bladder due to repeated infections; exces-

---

52 See Nahid Toubia, "Female Genital Mutilation," in WRHR: 236. Mohammed told his listeners to "circumcise" but not to "mutilate," for not destroying the clitoris would be better for the man and would make the woman's face glow—a directive that many interpret as calling for "a male-type circumcision where the prepuce is removed, making the clitoris even more sensitive to touch" (236).

53 In clitoridectomy, part or all of the clitoris is removed and, frequently, part or all of the labia minora; in infibulation, the clitoris is removed, the labia minora are cut off, and incisions in the labia majora create raw surfaces which are then stitched together to heal as a hood of skin which covers the urethra and most of the vagina. In general, 85 percent of the women who undergo FGM have clitoridectomies, 15 percent infibulations. In countries such as the Sudan, Somalia, and Djibouti, 80 to 90 percent of FGM procedures are infibulation, and infibulation is also common in Egypt, Mali, Eritrea, Gambia, and Ethiopia. When I speak of FGM I am not including merely symbolic operations in which capacity for sexual functioning is not impaired. Worldwide, approximately 2 million girls per year suffer FGM—around 6,000 per day (see Toubia, "Female Genital Mutilation").

sive growth of scar tissue at the site, which may become disfiguring; pain during intercourse; infertility (with its devastating consequences for a woman's other life-chances); obstructed labor.[54] It is not surprising that FGM is illegal in most of the nations in which it is practiced or that international human rights activists should view it as a major violation of human rights.

3. The Right to Employment

Women should have the right to seek employment outside the home without intimidation or discrimination. Religious discourse, as I have already indicated, is prominently used in opposition to women's efforts to seek and retain employment outside the home. In the Rajasthan inhabited by Metha Bai, in the Bangladeshi village described by Martha Chen, in Islamic Iran, in the contemporary Chinese workplace—in all of these places religious norms about women's proper place are working to deny women equality and in many cases totally to deny them access to employment. At the time of Iran's Islamic revolution, the regime fired more than 40,000 women working as elementary and high-school teachers, as well as many others; women's employment fell in five years by 50 percent and reached a low point of 6.2 percent.[55] The 1995 UN *Human Development Report* gives 19 percent as the figure for women's economic activity, but this figure includes unpaid agricultural labor and is therefore difficult to compare with the earlier figures. The Ayatollah Mutahari, one of the architects of Islamist policy, wrote that:

> The specific task of women in this society is to marry and bear children. They will be discouraged from entering legislative, judicial, or whatever careers may require decision making, as women lack the intellectual ability and discerning judgement required for these careers.[56]

These views of women are just the ones that were defended by appeal to Christian norms in earlier American cases—for example, the famous *Bradwell* case in 1873 in which a woman was denied the right to practice law, in an opinion that mentioned "the divine ordinance" as a source for the view that women were naturally unsuited for the professions.[57] Employment rights are

---

54   See Toubia, "Female Genital Mutilation," 227–29. Toubia was the first female surgeon in the Sudan, is an advisor to the World Health Organization, vice-chair of the Women's Rights Project of Human Rights Watch, and the director of the Global Action against FGM Project at the Columbia University School of Public Health.

55   Mirhosseini, "After the Revolution," 73.

56   Ayatollah Mutahari, *The Question of the Veil*, quoted in Mirhosseini, "After the Revolution," 73.

57   *Bradwell v. Illinois*, 83 U.S. (16 Wallace) 130 ff. (1873).

a central source of genuine equality for women in a modern liberal regime. They are also, frequently, essential for well-being and often for survival.

4. Mobility and Assembly Rights

It is obvious that women who are confined to the home and threatened with harm or opprobrium by religious leaders should they walk outside are being deprived of an essential right. It is difficult to conceive of the meaning and extent of this deprivation. Cornelia Sorabji, the first woman to take a degree in law at Oxford and the first woman admitted to the bar in India, dedicated her career to representing women who were not permitted to see a man other than their husband. (As a Parsi, Sorabji was in an unusually advantaged position, since Parsi women at that time were considerably less restricted than Hindu and Muslim women.) She reports that when she brought a rose to one young wife, and mentioned having plucked it from a bush outside, the wife reacted with puzzlement. Having been married as a small child, she had never been in contact with growing things of any kind; she believed that roses lie on the ground and are picked up like stones.[58] The Bangladeshi women described by Martha Chen are not exactly in that position—for one thing because they are too poor not to have to go outside for some purposes. But their lives were utterly circumscribed by religious threats of ostracism and physical violence if they walked around in the streets and talked to males. The Iranian dress code, again, is a great restriction on women's full mobility, as are other provisions of the regime, such as the requirement that women sit in the back of the bus.

In all countries governed in whole or part by Islamic law, women are under some form of male guardianship, and this, again, imposes various limits on mobility. To take many trips, especially trips abroad, women must secure written permission from a male. In Saudi Arabia, for example, women may not leave the country without permission of a father or husband—and female visitors are not allowed in unless accompanied by a male family member.[59] In 1990, the Saudi government justified a ban against women driving as flowing from Islamic morality and principles.[60] In the Sudan, the Personal Law for Muslims Act directs the husband to grant permission "within reason" for a woman to visit parents and relatives for short periods; but she may never travel on her own. If she is under 50, she must be accompanied by a male

---

58 Cornelia Sorabji, *India Calling* (London: Nisbet and Co., 1934), 68. Though rich and pampered, this woman (one of three or four wives of the local Thakur), was also illiterate, "the theory being that if women learnt to write they would get themselves into trouble" (67).

59 Marsha A. Freeman, "The Human Rights of Women in the Family," in WRHR 149–64.

60 Ann Elizabeth Mayer, "Cultural Particularism as a Bar to Women's Rights," WRHR 176–88.

relative to whom she could not legally be married; if she is over 50, another sort of "trustworthy companion" may, with the guardian's permission, be selected. Exit visas require written permission of the guardian.[61]

As to assembly rights, it is of course true that in regimes that are not liberal and democratic nobody has very secure freedom of assembly, especially when political protest is involved; but assembly rights are also denied to women, further, on a discriminatory basis. When Saudi women demonstrated against the ban on driving, the government responded by prohibiting all future demonstrations by women.[62] In Egypt, the prominent Arab Women's Solidarity Association was suppressed in 1992, with reference to religious norms: The organization had "threatened the peace and political and social order of the state by spreading ideas and beliefs offensive to the rule of Islamic *shari'a* and the religion of Islam."[63] Particular reference was made to the group's criticisms of established laws regulating marriage and divorce. In China it is similarly impossible for any independent women's organization to exist, but it is unclear to me whether religious discourse has been used to justify the repression.

Even in the constitutional democratic regimes, such discrimination in assembly rights is well known. The women described by Chen drew the opposition of the *mullahs* primarily on the ground that they were going to meet in an organized group to mobilize for common action. Even had the women complained of a constitutional violation, it is unlikely that this complaint would have been effectual, given the way religious power dominates the local scene.

5. Rights of Political Participation and Speech
Again, these rights are severely curtailed for all citizens in many of the nations under discussion. Are they unusually curtailed for women, in ways that show the influence of religious norms? The Egyptian case involves suppression of speech as well as assembly. All countries that impede women from going outside the home create barriers to political speech and participation, as do those that create barriers to women's literacy. Nations that effectively enforce constitutional guarantees of free press and free political speech, for example, India, do not often suppress women's speech or speech about women's issues in a discriminatory way. On the other hand, the fear of offending religious authorities does at times pose acute threats to speech—consider various democratic governments' willingness to ban *The Satanic Verses*, and the relative absence of official protest against the *fatwahs* directed against authors Salman Rushdie and Taslima Nasrin, both critics of Islamic traditions regarding

---

61   See Asma Mohamed Abdel Halim, "Challenges to Women's International Human Rights in the Sudan," in HRW, 397–421.

62   See Mayer, "Cultural Particularism," 180, with documentation.

63   Mayer, "Cultural Particularism," 180–81.

women. The most pervasive impediments to women's speech in the democratic nations are, however, the indirect and unseen obstacles imposed by poverty, malnutrition, impediments to mobility outside the home, illiteracy, and an exhausting round of duties. In the nondemocratic nations, speech is not free for anyone, but it is especially unfree for women who might be inclined to criticize the prevailing view of women's role—recall the Saudi ban on demonstrations by women.

As to political participation: in Iran, women were for a time banned totally from employment in government, and are heavily discouraged from entering politics. Only 3 percent of parliamentary seats are held by women (as contrasted with 12 percent in Jamaica, 16 percent in Nicaragua, 18 percent in Trinidad and Tobago, 24 percent in South Africa, 20 percent in Guyana, 33 percent in Denmark, 39 percent in Finland and Norway, 34 percent in Sweden, 29 percent in the Netherlands, 20 percent in Germany),[64] and there are no female ministers. Although it is well known that women play leading roles in government in India, Pakistan, and Bangladesh, their situation is far from representative of the average women in their nations: in Pakistan 2 percent of parliamentary seats are held by women, in India 7 percent, in Bangladesh 10 percent. It is very difficult to gauge actual participation in elections, but we can infer that poverty, illiteracy, and lack of mobility are grave impediments to women's equal participation. Religious doctrines to the effect that women are unsuited for political functions are invoked in many nations and play at least some part in bringing about this situation.

6. The Right of Free Religious Exercise

Once again, there is no recognition of such a right in many of the nations under discussion, a fortiori none for women. But my Israeli case shows the liberal dilemma arising in a very sharp form in a parliamentary democracy that faces strong pressures from orthodox religious groups. The women's free exercise of a right to worship was indeed infringed, with appeal to majority religious norms; it seems very likely that the behavior of the guard would have been declared unconstitutional under U.S. law. The fact that Israel currently has no written constitution (a fact explained in large part by the difficulty of knowing how to speak about religion in one) creates a permanent unclarity about basic rights, including religious rights. The case indicates that, whatever the tensions and confusions between the claims of free exercise and the claims of nonestablishment in our own jurisprudence, we have chosen a wise course in giving both of these values strong protection, since they support one another. It is very difficult to maintain free exercise for minorities when one has

---

64   Note that the U.S., at 10 percent, lies closer to Iran than to many of the European nations. France, at 6 percent, Great Britain at 7 percent, and Japan at 8 percent are even lower, and (South) Korea is as low as any democratic nation, at 1 percent.

established a single religion and given it considerable political and legal power.

7. Rights of Property and Civil Capacity

Article 15 of the Women's Convention insists on women's equality with men before the law, on their full legal capacity and on their equal opportunities to exercise that capacity. Women are to have equal rights to make contracts, equal treatment before courts and tribunals, equal property rights and rights to administer property. This is simply not the case for very many of the world's women, frequently on account of religious discourse and religious law. Under traditional Islamic law, women are expressly and explicitly unequal. A woman must have a male guardian to perform many contracts, including a marriage contract for herself. A woman's testimony in court is regarded as half as weighty as the testimony of a man; in the case of rape and adultery, women are forbidden to give evidence. Witnesses to contracts and other documents may be either two men or one man and two women. States vary in the degree to which this religious discourse and the laws based upon it have full effect: Some, like Iran, Pakistan, and the Sudan, are quite thoroughly Islamicized— though even among these there are differences of degree; in others, such as Egypt, there is an unpredictable mixture of elements; in India and Bangladesh, there is a putative distinction between private law, which is governed by religious norms, and other affairs, which are in the charge of the secular state. In none are women's human rights to legal equality fully respected.

Once again, the Indian situation provides instructive examples of the conflict between constitutional guarantees of sex equality and religious legal systems. Since we have focused until now on Hindu and Muslim law, let us turn, for a change, to the situation of India's Christian women. Christians in India are governed by a bewildering variety of distinct regional codes. Catholic Christians in Goa, for example, are still governed by the Portuguese Civil Code. Until recently, Christians from Kerala were governed by the Cochin Christian Succession Act of 1921 and the Travancore Christian Act of 1916. In 1983, a Syrian Christian woman named Mary Roy challenged the Travancore Act in the Supreme Court, on the grounds that it violated the sex equality guarantee by denying equal inheritance rights to daughters and sons. The Supreme Court agreed that the act was unconstitutional and ruled that Christians in Kerala should henceforth be governed by the Indian Succession Act of 1925, which grants daughters and sons equal rights. The Christian community in Kerala has continued to protest this judgment as an inappropriate interference with their religious prerogatives.[65] Such clashes between consti-

---

65   See Bina Agarwal, *A Field of One's Own: Gender and Land Rights in South Asia* (Cambridge: Cambridge University Press, 1994), 223–25; see also M. Chen, *Windows*, chapter 9.

tutional rights and religious law are common throughout the Indian legal system.

8. Nationality

The Women's Convention insists (in Article 9) that women and men be fully equal in matters of their own and their children's nationality. All nations that, relying on Islamic law, require a woman to obtain a guardian's permission before moving abroad are in violation of this fundamental right. In addition, quite a few nations have laws forbidding women from passing their own nationality on to her children. Although a landmark case testing such a law derives from Botswana and involves no religious element,[66] religious discourse is heavily implicated, elsewhere, in the maintenance of this form of discrimination against women.

9. Marriage Rights

This is an especially large and complex area of women's inequality; religious norms and laws play a direct role in it. Religious systems of family law, Islamic, Hindu, Jewish, and other, may severely limit women's degree of choice in and consent to marriage, their rights to control the lives of their children during a marriage and to child custody if the marriage ends, their access to divorce and the type of evidence required to get a divorce, their right of maintenance after a divorce. Polygamy, insofar as it continues to exist, is a structurally unequal practice: Plural marriages are unavailable to women.[67]

A few examples of these practices must suffice to indicate the whole. In the Sudan (whose Personal Law for Muslims Act is closely based on the *shari'a*) a woman's guardian had absolute authority to decide on a marital partner—until a rash of suicides by young girls forced a change. Now the woman's consent is required. In the Sudan again, a man may divorce a wife simply by saying, "You are divorced." A woman must go to court and establish a basis, such as impotence, cruelty, or inability to provide. Most religiously grounded systems of personal law are asymmetric in a similar way. In most systems of Islamic

---

66   *Attorney General v. Unity Dow,* Court of Appeal Civil Appeal No. 4/91 (1992): Unity Dow challenged the Botswana nationality law, under which by marrying an American she lost her ability to transfer Botswana nationality to the children of the marriage, and thereby the free university education to which the children would otherwise be entitled. Justice Agudah, deciding in Dow's favor, cited the Women's Convention as binding, saying that it "has created an international regime" that must be considered in considering whether national laws were constitutional. See Freeman, "The Human Rights of Women," 163.

67   And also, in India today, to non-Muslim men—a fact that has given rise to some interesting free exercise jurisprudence in Indian courts. Polygamy is of course not required in Islam, but criticisms of the practice are met with intense opposition.

law, a woman is guardian of a male child only until he is seven years old—although in a recent Bangladeshi case the judge ruled that a mother might retain custody of her eight-year-old son, who was afflicted with a rare disease. (The mother, a doctor, was able to give him expert care, and she had also financed his medical treatment.) The judge remarked, "The principle of Islamic law has to be regarded, but deviation therefrom would seem permissible as the paramount consideration should be the child's welfare."[68] Under India's Hindu law, the father is regarded as the natural guardian of the child, except for children under the age of five, or when the father is away. Only an illegitimate child can remain in its mother's custody.[69] As to the important issue of maintenance, so dramatically exposed in the Shah Bano case, the uniform civil code in India that might adjust the plight of such women is very far in the distance, even as the year 2000 rapidly approaches.

The right to adopt a child, a right important to many women, is another matter that is decisively affected by the domination of religion in codes of personal law. The Hindu Adoptions and Maintenance Act, passed in 1956, was for many years the only statutory law of adoptions in India. This law applies only to Hindus. Thus for many years only Hindus could adopt a child, and only a Hindu child could be adopted. Attempts in both 1972 and 1980 to enact a uniform adoption act met with determined resistance from Muslim leaders, who hold adoption to be forbidden by the Koran. (This is not a universal opinion: Tunisia in 1958 enacted a law of adoption whose provisions were very similar to the 1972 Indian Adoption Bill.) The 1980 bill was passed—thus granting Jews, Christians, Parsis, and others adoption rights—but only after Muslims were explicitly exempted.[70] Tariq Mahmood, of the Faculty of Law at the University of Delhi, summarized the matter well in a public letter to the Indian Council for Child Welfare:

> Even if it is accepted that Islamic law prohibits adoption, how can the Muslims prevent enactment of a secular law of adoption which will be applicable only to those who wish to adopt a child? If Islamic law does not permit adoption, the Muslims need not make use of the Indian adoption law. That law will certainly not impose on any person a duty to adopt. . . .
> If Islam does not recognize a social or economic concept, the state cannot compel every Muslim to keep away from it. If that were possible, our banking laws should not be available to any Muslim, since Islam does prohibit interest on money. . . . The demand that a special saving clause exempting the entire Muslim community from its application be inserted in the Bill cannot be accepted. There are some Muslims who do not share

---

68   *Abu Bakar Siddiq v. A. B. Siddiq*, 38 D.L.R. (AD) (1986), discussed in Hossain, "Women's Rights," 479.

69   Hindu Guardianship and Minority Act, reported in Singh, "Obstacles," 382.

70   See Mahmood, *Muslim Personal Law*, 110–14.

the belief that their personal law prohibits adoption; and there are many who do not consider personal law as a part of their religion at all. To them the benefit of the adoption law cannot be denied.[71]

This sensible conclusion seems right for the whole area of family law: Loyal members of a religious group should remain at liberty to follow its teachings in such matters, but this does not justify imposing such teachings on people who do not so choose, especially where imposition is unequal and where it violates a fundamental right of choice.

10. Education Rights

Nothing is more important to women's life chances than education. With literacy, a woman may consider her options and to some extent shape her future. She may question tradition and discover how women in other parts of the world are managing to live. She may discover that women are actually able to achieve well in many of life's functions; that the female body is not as weak as has sometimes been said. With literacy, she may do her own accounts, read a bill, read an important notice that comes to her in the mail,[72] enter trades that require literacy.

Women's educational opportunities and achievements are dramatically limited in many nations in the world. Adult female literacy rates, in the developing countries, range from 96.7 percent (Guyana) and 94.2 percent (Cuba) all the way down to 5.8 percent (Niger) and 8.0 percent (Burkina Faso). Among the nations under discussion here, we find Pakistan at 22.3 percent, India at 35.2 percent, Bangladesh at 24.4 percent, Afghanistan at 12 percent, the Sudan at 30 percent; China does considerably better, at 69 percent;[73] Saudi Arabia, at 40 percent, is extremely low among the countries sharing its general level of economic development, as is Iran at 55 percent. [74] In all these cases, women are doing considerably worse than men. In Pakistan, the female literacy rate is 56 percent that of males, in India 55 percent, in Bangladesh 51 percent, Afghanistan 29 percent, the Sudan 56 percent, China 79 percent, Saudi Arabia 66 percent, Iran 74 percent.[75]

---

71 Mahmood, *Muslim Personal Law,* 113, citing his letter of 15 September 1974, addressed to Mrs. Tara Ali Beg, President, Indian Council for Child Welfare.

72 Metha Bai almost lost her small farm because a mortgage notice arrived, and she put it aside, knowing that since she was unable to read it. Fortunately, after attending the Widow's Conference organized in Bangalore by Martha Chen, and with the help of Seva Mandir, a local N.G.O., she learned how to consult the local women's bank for assistance, and her late payment did not cause her to forfeit the land.

73 See Drèze and Sen, *India,* on this contrast and its importance for overall welfare.

74 Data from *Human Development Report 1995,* UNDP; the data are from 1992.

75 Drèze and Sen, *India,* emphasize that the Chinese achievement has its basis in

The reason for disproportionately low female attainments are not always religious, but in many cases one can see clearly that religious discourse has played a major part. The *mullahs* in the village described by Chen set out to oppose women's literacy—by insults to the women's moral character and, if necessary, by threats to their physical safety. As Cornelia Sorabji's memoir attests, denial of literacy has strong conventional links to *purdah* and to general notions of women's purity that are at least in part religious. In Afghanistan, Islamic fundamentalists insist as a matter of policy that women should attain no more than a first-grade education.[76] In India, women's education is opposed or neglected for all sorts of reasons, some economic, some customary; but the major religions certainly play their role in creating an image of a woman's role. Although regional differences in policy and culture are important in explaining these differences, religion also seems to play at least some independent causal role.[77] In Iran, related ideas of women's proper role have led to severely curtailed educational opportunities at the level of higher education. Women are excluded from 79 of 157 courses of study in the university, including 55 of 84 courses in math and technology; they are forbidden to study, among other things, archaeology, cinematography, and graphic design.[78]

And one must ask, as well, what is being taught when girls are taught. In the ultraorthodox communities of Jerusalem, all children, attending state-supported schools, are permitted to follow a curriculum that contains absolutely no information about world history or about the life of the world outside (just as at home TV and radio are entirely forbidden). They do learn modern math and science, but women are carefully shielded from any image of a woman's role that is not within the domain of what the ultraorthodox community considers proper. They will not be in a position to choose their own way of life as the result of their very own reflection.

11. Reproductive Rights

This is such a familiar contested area that it seems unnecessary to discuss it at length. International human rights activists concur, with few exceptions, that women's access to contraception is an extremely important ingredient of their own well-being, both because of reproductive control and because of AIDS. They agree, further, that promoting women's control of their own reproduc-

---

the policies of the older regime, highly egalitarian toward women, and long preexist the current era of market expansionism; in Iran, the discrepancy between female and male education becomes much sharper as we move higher up: Iranian women have only 47 percent the tertiary education (i.e., college) of males.

76   See Moghadam, *Gender, Development, and Policy.*

77   See Drèze and Sen, *India.*

78   Mirhosseini, "After the Revolution," 74.

tion (along with women's education more generally) is the most effective way to control world population without unacceptable infringements of liberty.[79]

Both Islamic and Roman Catholic discourse has been involved in opposition to such policies, as the Cairo conference made clear, although the primary emphasis of the Catholic position was access to abortion. I know of no corresponding discourse from the Jewish or Hindu traditions, though obviously the ultraorthodox Jewish community, in Israel and to some extent elsewhere, does have a strong pronatalist bias and for its own members opposes contraception. It seems plausible that unimpeded access to contraception is a basic human right of women. It is especially urgent to protect this right for women who have no economic or social alternative to marriage, and no recourse against enforced intercourse within it.

As for abortion, the issue cuts both ways where women's human rights are concerned. On the one hand, many defenders of such rights do hold that abortion rights, at least in the first trimester, are basic to women's equality; I myself would defend such a right for the U.S. on such grounds.[80] On the other hand, abortion has very often been used sex-selectively, to destroy female fetuses; in that sense it can also be a dangerous instrument of women's inequality. Right now it is possible to prevent the abuse without restricting abortion rights, by forbidding access to amniocyntesis and by forbidding late abortions, as some governments have done; but this balancing act will not endure long into the future, as information becomes more readily available and at an earlier date. Some Indian feminists therefore favor removing the abortion right—indeed, some would like to jail women who seek abortions.[81] The issues are so difficult and have generated such intense, subtle, and lengthy debate that it would be foolish of me to attempt, here, to pronounce as to what an advocate of women's human rights should say.

III. Addressing the Dilemma

The other papers have focused on the question, "What forms of religious discourse shall we promote or encourage in a liberal society as morally acceptable and appropriate?" Insofar as they are responding to John Rawls's formulation of the issue they focus not on the use of religious discourse in electoral politics but on its use in debate about constitutional fundamentals, for example by judges deciding constitutional cases. Nowhere is the issue

---

79   See Sen, "Population: Delusion and Reality," *New York Review of Books* (September 22, 1994), a document that was highly influential in the wording of documents prepared by the Cairo Population conference.

80   For the equality-based defense of abortion rights, see Cass R. Sunstein, *The Partial Constitution* (Cambridge, Mass.: Harvard University Press, 1993).

81   See Vina Mazumdar's contribution to J. Glover and M. Nussbaum, eds., *Reproductive Technology and Women's Equality*, forthcoming.

raised of actually suppressing religious speech or making it illegal. I must now, however, broaden the focus of debate, addressing practices as well as speech and issues of illegality as well as issues of moral acceptability: for my examples make clear, I think, that there are some forms of religious discourse and practice that should be utterly unacceptable as constitutive structural elements within a society; others that should be criminalized within a society; and, finally, others that we should simply deem immoral and inappropriate.

My starting point is a simple one: It is that human beings should not be violated and that the protection of the basic human rights should have a very strong degree of priority, even when this interferes with traditional religious discourse and practice. To those who object that violating others is part of the free exercise of their religion, we should reply as we do when a murderer claims that God told him to do it (and he may sincerely believe this to be true): Never mind, we say, there are some things we do not allow people to do to other people. Or, as the Bangladeshi wife said in my epigraph, if Allah really said that (as may be doubted) then he is dead wrong.[82]

Beyond this, we can say more about the list of basic rights that has just been enumerated. These rights, like (and closely related to) John Rawls's list of primary goods, would appear to be necessary for all people if they are to carry out their plans of life, whatever they are. They therefore have a strong claim to be recognized politically as basic in a pluralistic society, whatever the commitments of its constitutive religious groups. Because of their fundamental role, a liberal society should commit itself to protecting these rights for all individuals, regardless of whether it contains groups that don't like individuals (their own members, or members of other groups) to have these rights. The list is somewhat more extensive than Rawls's list, and closely related to the list of basic human capabilities that I have defended elsewhere.[83]

In the view I shall develop, the fundamental bearer of rights is the individual human being. This seems right, since a violation of a person is no better when it comes from some group to which the person belongs than when it comes from the state. The hunger of A made not less but more morally offensive when we learn that A is a loving girl child in a family in which there is, overall, enough food to go around. The rape of B is made not less and quite likely more offensive when we discover that the rapist is B's husband and therefore a member of an allegedly altruistic organic unit together with B. Nor is the bodily integrity of B a merged part of a larger whole; B's body is B's body, the only one she will ever have. Women have very often been violated by

---

82   Compare a moment in Lincoln's Second Inaugural, where, commenting on the use of religious discourse by southern slaveholders, he observes that it "may seem strange that any men should dare to ask a just God's assistance in wringing their bread from the sweat of other men's faces."

83   See "Human Capabilities" and "The Good as Discipline" for the most recent versions.

groups to which they have belonged, such as the family, the religious body, the community. It is all the more important for them, then, to insist that each and every human is a worthy object of moral concern.[84]

The rights, furthermore, should not be regarded as isolated atoms, which can be given or withheld independently of one another. Since they interact and support one another in so many ways, we should think in terms of a total system of liberties and opportunities, and refuse to compromise on any one item not only because of its intrinsic worth but also because of the way it affects the other items on the list. Education is closely correlated with meaningful opportunities for employment, and both of these with nutrition and health. The right to protect one's bodily integrity is closely connected to, and derives support from, equality in family law and rights to mobility and assembly. The right to contraception is closely associated with increased abilities to pursue education and employment, with political participation and with health. And so forth. We want, then, to secure to individuals not only one or two liberties, but a total system of liberties; and not merely the liberties in name only (as some words in a constitution) but their fully equal worth, meaning the capability to avail oneself of them.

In this section I shall present a view (no more than a sketch) of what should be the case; much of this will seem like pie in the sky. In a concluding section I shall ask what practical action is available.

1. What roles for religion should be off-limits as elements of the constitutional and legal structure?

Most basically, no systems of religious law should be permitted as elements in a constitutional order (or, where there is no written constitution, a democratic legal system). It is especially obvious that a thoroughly sectarian regime, such as those of Iran, the Sudan, and Pakistan, is unacceptable and by itself violates the liberty of conscience. Such systems hardly even raise our liberal dilemma, since their violations of other human rights are accompanied by equally serious violations of the liberty of conscience—for members of minority religions above all (witness, as one egregious conscience example, the Iranian persecution of the Bahá'í), but also for non-orthodox members of the dominant religion. Such regimes are by definition a human-rights abuse and should be the targets of protest the world over.

What should we say about a tolerant liberal regime with an established church that carefully protects the rights and liberties of all citizens—as is the case, in general, in today's Britain and Scandinavia? Such arrangements, I would argue, are always morally problematic: In the British case, the unsavory

---

84   See my "The Feminist Critique of Liberalism," forthcoming in *Women's Voices, Women's Lives: The Amnesty Lectures 1996*, ed. M. Forey and J. Gardner (New York: HarperCollins).

history of discrimination against dissenters and Roman Catholics colors the social meaning of the innocuous and bland pronouncements of the Anglican Church; its established status, even if it does nothing wrong, may still be expected to affect the self-respect of members of these minorities despite liberal policies. This suggests that establishment by itself raises problems for a liberal political understanding.[85] On the other hand, the problems are certainly different in kind from those that obtain where recognition of equal protection of the law for all citizens is not a fundamental political commitment.

Particularly interesting and complex, in terms of our questions about women, is the situation in countries such as Bangladesh and India, where a basically liberal constitutional order has allowed the religions to take charge of part of the legal system, creating systems of religious law; or Israel, where the same thing has happened in a parliamentary democracy without a written constitution. These regimes are problematic in a number of ways. First, they may still violate the free-exercise side of our dilemma, as in Israel's refusal to permit non-religious marriage and in its attitude toward non-orthodox Jewish worship, as described in my example. (I don't even mention the inequality in life chances between Jew and non-Jew.) Second, they treat citizens unequally on the basis of the chance of their birth into a given religious community. Shah Bano did worse because she was a Muslim than had she been a Hindu. Third, they encourage the maintenance of practices that are in direct violation of equality provisions recognized in many constitutions, and implicit in the legal system of some nations that lack a written constitution. It is quite absurd for India to guarantee women all sorts of rights in a constitution, and then turn the all-important sphere of family law over to codes that explicitly deny women the equal protection of the laws. All such courts should be abolished, as in violation of basic rights and liberties of citizens. Finally, as we can see, such systems are highly divisive and politically unworkable; the endless negotiations in which the Indian government has engaged could have been avoided, as they were for the criminal law, if India had had a single civil code from the start.

Indeed, the Indian case is especially interesting for the way in which constitutional guarantees point in diametrically opposed directions on the issue of separate religious codes of personal law. On the one hand, by placing the directive that the state shall "endeavour to secure" a uniform civil code in Article 44 of the Constitution, among the unenforceable Directives of State Policy, the framers expressed the judgment that it would be unwise to move too hastily against existing personal laws. In the constitutional debates, Muslim leaders had repeatedly held that retention of the personal laws is "a part

---

85   Nor is the British legal system fully symmetrical: Blasphemy laws protect Christianity and no other religion, just as in Pakistan blasphemy laws protect only Islam.

of the fundamental right to religious freedom."[86] The words "endeavour to secure" were chosen deliberately, so as to contrast with the words "shall enact," and essentially the idea of Article 44 was that the state should gradually prepare the population to accept a uniform code at some future date. On the other hand, it is perfectly plain that the enumerated Fundamental Rights include a right for all persons to the equal protection of the laws and also a right to non-discrimination on the grounds of religion, caste, sex, or place of birth; and Article 13 (1) rendered void all "laws in force" that were inconsistent with the enumerated Fundamental Rights, while Article 13 (2) forbade the state to introduce any new law abridging a Fundamental Right. Thus a contradiction was created, since the existing (and also the subsequently introduced, i.e., reformed) personal laws of both Hindus and Muslims do violate the constitutional guarantee of sex equality and, in some respects, the guarantee of religious equality as well. It would thus appear that the framers deliberately left in place a route whereby such personal laws could be deemed unconstitutional—although in a 1952 decision in *State of Bomba v. Narasu Appa Mali*, two especially eminent judges held that the term *"laws in force* did not include the personal laws, which they held to be distinct from other "laws in force" in that they are not just the result of legislative enactments but are grounded in religious texts. This seems perfectly beside the point. What I would argue, in effect, is that nations should all follow the course suggested by Articles 13 (1) and 13 (2) in combination with the list of Fundamental Rights, and that the personal laws be treated no differently from any other law.

Does this nullify the whole project of having distinct systems of personal law? Modern defenders of secularism insist that the ideal of secularism requires only symmetrical treatment of the religions and that this can in principle be fulfilled in quite a few different ways.[87] We must remember, however, that the fundamental bearer of rights is the individual citizen, and that any system of personal law that groups individuals in accordance with their religious origins runs a great risk of disadvantaging those individuals who do not particularly rejoice in that classification, whether because they are non-religious or because they do not agree with the dominant group in their own religion. (In India, religious classifications do not require any statement of membership, belief, or enthusiasm: one is classified by origin, and everyone is put into one box or another.) In principle, a guarantee of non-discrimination on religious grounds, such as the one already present in India's constitution,

---

86 See Mahmood, *Muslim Personal Law*, 80 ff., citing Mohammad Ismail. Some Muslim leaders took the rather different position that the uniform code was a good thing but "in advance of its time." Ironically, some speakers invoked the Raj, holding that one of the "secrets of success" of the British rulers was their willingness to retain the personal laws (Pocker Saheb, cited in Mahmood, *Muslim Personal Law*, 82).

87 See Sen, "Secularism."

would nullify only those portions of the separate religious codes that treat citizens unequally on grounds of their religious background and membership. Given the ubiquity of such differences, however, the guarantee of non-discrimination cuts deeply into the very idea of separate codes, since if they treat people the same in important matters there seems little point in maintaining them.

More important for our purposes, a guarantee of non-discrimination on the basis of sex, such as the one enacted in the list of Fundamental Rights in India's constitution renders unconstitutional many of the main provisions of most of the separate codes, as regards marriage, divorce, and maintenance. In all the heated debate about Indian laws of marriage and divorce, the fundamental interest of women in equality before the law was rather neglected—Muslims claiming violation of religious freedom if they were held to the uniform provisions of maintenance under the criminal code, Hindus claiming that the exemption of Muslims from these provisions violated their equality rights as Hindus. In effect, they were haggling over how not to be required to pay a destitute woman $18 per month. The woman's fundamental rights under the constitution were not taken to represent fundamental interests of either religious group. But such debates can and should be cut short by pointing to the fundamental role of the constitutional guarantee of sex equality. Let that first be upheld, and then we will see in what the demands of the religions differ. If the codes were really held to the full equality of citizens' rights, in short, a good deal of the point of their existence (at least as represented by their most zealous defenders) would rapidly disappear.

Such uniformity, as the Indian Constitutional debates showed, cannot be implemented overnight in nations that contain groups with traditional hostilities. On the other hand we should also remember that all these groups are internally diverse, and the representative voice is not always the one that cries loudest. Once again, the Indian situation is revealing. At every step in the unfolding debate about personal law, opposition to a uniform civil code was vigorous from some quarters of both Muslim and Hindu communities. On the other hand, at every stage also, defenders of constitutional uniformity included prominent members of these religious traditions. Muslim lawyer Chowdhry Hyder Hussain strongly defended a uniform civil code already in 1949, arguing that separate codes were a vestige of British rule and "wholly a medieval idea [that] has no place in the modern world."[88] Twenty years later another distinguished Muslim jurist, M. C. Chagla, held that an acceptable legal system was one that "applies to every individual whatever his religion or his community. . . . The Constitution was enacted for the whole country, it is binding on the whole country, and every section and community must

---

88   Chowdry Hyder Hussain, "A Unified Code for India," A.I.R. (j) 68, (1949): 71–72, cited in Mahmood, *Muslim Personal Law*, 115.

accept its provisions and its directives."[89] Such influential voices, which have been heard continuously throughout the post-Independence period, show that strong rights-oriented constitutionalism is not generally opposed by Muslims, any more than it is by Hindus.

The claim that the uniform protection of the rights of individuals infringes legitimate prerogatives of free religious exercise is itself a contentious and highly political claim, which should not be accepted in the first instance. Religious liberty is a right of individuals, like other rights; how can the religious liberty of an individual possibly be infringed by the determination to protect all individual rights of the religion's members on an equal basis? The liberty to treat your co-religionists unequally is simply not a legitimate prerogative of religious freedom. The fact that prominent spokesmen for the major religions agree with this liberal principle should be insisted on, as one makes this argument. The liberal should emphasize this individualistic concept of basic rights and religious liberty, insisting on uniform codes of law that give individuals broad latitude to choose forms of life in accordance with the dictates of their religion. (The right to divorce does not force anyone to get divorced; the right to contraception does not force contraceptive use; the right to adopt, as Muslim jurist Mahmood eloquently insists, does not force anyone to adopt a child against his or her religious principles.) We should not accept the idea that denying any fundamental right of any individual is a legitimate prerogative of a religious group. As liberal Muslim Zoya Hasan commented on the Shah Bano case, "It is not [a] question of the personal law of the community, but that of the abandoned getting social justice."[90]

In general, then, when any democratic government or government actor takes an action or makes a law that violates the equal rights of its citizens in response to pressure from a religious party or group, this action should be deemed unconstitutional or (where there is no written constitution) incompatible with the basic rights of citizens in a liberal democratic regime. This is what should have happened with the action of the Israeli guard at the Western Wall; it is what should have happened, and did, in the case of Shah Bano—before Rajiv Gandhi's helpful intervention. It is what happened in the court in Andhra Pradesh in the case of "restoration of conjugal rights"—until the Supreme Court intervened, defending women's inequality. It is what happened in the High Court in Bangladesh, in a similar case. It is what happened in Bangladesh, again, in the child custody case, in which the judged dared to opine that deviation from Islamic law "would seem permissible" for the sake of a child's welfare."[91] It is what happened in India's Supreme Court in the

89   M. C. Chagla, *Proceedings of the 26th Congress of Orientals* (1964): 79–80, and "Plea for a Uniform Civil Code," *Weekly Round Table* 25 March 1969: 7, both cited in Mahmood, *Muslim Personal Law*, 116.

90   Engineer, *Shah Bano*, 158.

case of Mary Roy, when the unequal inheritance rights mandated by the Travancore Christian Act were declared unconstitutional. It is what happened in the nationality case in Botswana, not religious but a precedent for many cases involving religion, because the Women's Convention was interpreted as binding on state actors. (I shall shortly comment on exemptions that may possibly be granted to religious organizations in their internal operations, arguing that these are not necessarily unconstitutional but should face something like our "strict scrutiny.")

In a related way, the Israeli public school set-up should be held unlawful, and presumably would be unconstitutional if Israel had a constitution enumerating basic rights in keeping with the Women's Convention. There are many issues here, including the egregious separate and unequal treatment of Arab children. But let me focus for now on the case of Jerusalem's ultraorthodox community, permitted to receive state funding for schools that produce gross ignorance of the modern world. This is inappropriate for all sorts of reasons, but in keeping with my theme let me simply focus on the fact that such systems prevent women from having access to information about their role in the world and norms of sex equality in modern democratic constitutions. They are thus a kind of *purdah*, and this ought to be deemed a violation of education rights. Were a religious school to operate in this manner in the U.S., it probably would not win accreditation by any regional or local agency, much less receive public funding.

Special issues arise when a nation-state contains within its borders a distinct national minority that has in effect been conquered and subdued and now claims the right to a separate legal system. Will Kymlicka has given an extensive analysis of the situation of tribal populations in Canada, urging that in such cases broader latitude be granted to such groups to form distinct political communities. If such groups rule illiberally, violating individual rights, he holds that it is legitimate for constitutional arrangements to immunize them from judicial review at the federal level. Liberals should hold that such a minority acts unjustly, should speak out against such injustices, and should promote the development of international human rights policies that would ultimately give international courts the power to handle complaints of rights violations from such communities. But intervention from the federal level in the internal affairs of a minority would be justified, he argues, only in cases of "gross and systematic violation of human rights, such as slavery or genocide or mass torture and expulsions, just as these are grounds for intervening in foreign countries."[92] Remarks elsewhere in the chapter indicate that

---

91   Notice, however, that the opinion did not address the fundamental issue of sex inequality; the judge rested the argument on the highly unusual circumstances.

92   Will Kymlicka, *Multicultural Citizenship: A Liberal Theory of Minority Rights* (Oxford: Clarendon Press, 1995).

Kymlicka does not regard the denial of legal and political rights to women as the type of "gross and systematic" violation that would justify intervention.[93]

This position seems to me totally inadequate. It is of course desirable that ultimately international courts should become strong defenders of individual rights. But what is to happen in the meantime with women who are not only suffering what ought to be called gross and systematic rights violations but, precisely on account of those deprivations (of political voice, mobility, assembly, education, often equal nutrition and health care), are unable to move their own community in the direction of change? Should this subgroup within the nation even be thought of as "their" community, just because they are in it and unable to leave? We think that the family is a type of community. Nonetheless, if a husband beats a wife or tries to prevent her from voting or going out of the house, we do not hesitate to intervene—or if we do hesitate, we shouldn't. I see no reason why a tribal or religious group should have any more latitude than a family should in abridging the fundamental rights of adult citizens.

It is of course another matter to decide how to implement that judgment politically. Kymlicka seems right that such cases are less tractable than the Indian case, where the two largest religious groups have been intertwined for years and each has considerable political power at the federal level. In India, it seems just right for defenders of a unified civil code to say, with Muslim jurist M. C. Chagla, that Muslims who wish to influence the law are already empowered to do so: "After all fifty million Muslims[94] have a voice in the election of that Parliament through adult suffrage."[95] The election of 1996 showed the world exactly how decisive that power can be: Muslim parties form a major part of the coalition that eventually managed to form a government, after the BJP was unable to do so. In Kymlicka's case, by contrast, the tribal peoples are few, uninfluential, and bitterly opposed to cooperation with the former oppressor. But I fail to understand how the sad history of a group can provide a philosophical justification for the gross denial of individual rights and liberties to members of the group. What is a "group" anyway? As Joyce's Leopold Bloom said of that equally overrated concept "nation," it is neither more nor less than "the same people living in the same place"[96] (or, as the case may be, not in the same place). A "group" is, then, not a fused organism, but a plurality of individuals, held together in some ways but usually differing in many others. The voices that are heard when "the group" speaks are not magically the voice of a fused organic entity, they are the voices

---

93   See p. 165, arguing that intervention with the policies of Saudi Arabia denying political rights to women and non-Muslims would be unjustified.

94   Today, 110 million.

95   Chagla, "Plea for a Uniform Civil Code," in Mahmood, *Muslim Personal Law*, 116.

96   Joyce, *Ulysses*, in the "Cyclops" episode in which Bloom confronts an anti-Semitic Irish nationalist in Barney Kiernan's bar.

of the most powerful individuals; these are especially likely not to be women. So why should we give a particular group of men license to put women down, just because they have managed to rise to power in some group that would like to put women down, if we have concluded that women should have guarantees of equal protection in our nation generally?[97] To do so is condescending to that group—we don't hold them up to the same moral standard to which we hold ourselves—and it is grossly unfair to the women, who are simply being told that because they are tribal women, or whatever, they don't enjoy the same guarantees of liberty that other women do. (And what of the "group" of women? Are they not as much a group as the tribe? And do they not have their own sad tale to tell?)

No religious group, then, may maintain a separate system of law that either violates the basic rights of any citizen, as specified above, or involves the religions in asymmetry vis-à-vis one another. If all this is firmly guaranteed, then the case for permitting religions some latitude in areas such as marriage and divorce contract may at least be argued. For example, it ought to be possible, as it is virtually everywhere, to enter into a religious marriage contract—provided that the state guarantees equality of treatment to all citizens regardless of religion in areas such as consent, divorce, and maintenance, provided that secular marriage also exists (as is not the case in Israel), and is regulated in an even-handed way by the state, and provided that individuals of religious origin may choose whether or not to avail themselves of religious marriages when they marry. In such cases, the devotional and spiritual meaning of religious marriage and divorce may still be great; what is important is that these rules do not impose an obligation on citizens in violation of their equal rights and liberties. (Thus a religious Roman Catholic may decide to regard the availability of secular divorce as spiritually unimportant and may focus on annulment as the only way in which a marriage may be validly terminated; what is important is that the state does not impose these Roman Catholic views on all people of Catholic origin—as is presently the case in similar situations in India—but maintains a uniform secular system of divorce for all citizens.)

One more aspect of this issue must now be mentioned. It is, that religious leaders should be held equal to everyone else under the law. This is not always the case. In Thailand, Buddhist monks can be tried only by courts composed of themselves; they may not be indicted by the general legal system. They tend, however, to hang together. In a recent case, a monk charged with sexual harassment and refusing to support an illegitimate child (he had allegedly told various women that their spiritual status was in grave jeopardy if they did not sleep with him) could not be publicly prosecuted, and the other monks refused

---

97   Kymlicka's principle suggests that the United States should permit segregated schools in the South because of the sad history of quasi-national division.

to prosecute him. Only after a prolonged scandal did the Ministry of Education order the monk to take a DNA paternity test[98] or risk being defrocked, and even then its authority to do anything is in doubt.[99] Needless to say, this should not be permitted to happen.

Should religious organizations and their members be treated as unequal under the law for certain purposes? United States constitutional law has standardly granted special latitude to religion, by contrast with other forms of commitment and affiliation. Religious reasons for military service,[100] or for refusing to work on a particular day,[101] are granted a latitude that is not granted to other forms of conscientious commitment, such as the familial or the artistic or even the ethical. This remains controversial for the way it appears to privilege religion over non-religion and thus, it might seem, to violate the Establishment Clause. The future of this issue remains uncertain, and this is not the place to make a normative argument on such a complex and vexed matter. Suffice it to say that such privileges given to religion, though highly contestable, can be strongly supported by pointing to the special importance of the liberty of conscience as a fundamental right, and the consequent need to give religious freedom special protection from the incursions that, throughout history, have threatened it.

Religious bodies have also claimed exemption from certain laws of general

---

98   Only one woman dared to come forward to claim that Yantra had fathered her child, but many had complained of sexual harassment.

99   "Yantra may be drummed out of monkhood," *The Bangkok Post*, February 4, 1995; "Phra Yantra's back to the wall," *The Bangkok Post*, February 5, 1995. The later article summarizes: "The nagging Yantra fiasco has in fact shown that there is no official agency with real authority and willingness to deal decisively and rightly with such a high-profile scandal. . . . The buck has been passed to and from with no one fully *authorised* or equipped to deal with the case." For these articles, and discussion of the case, I am grateful to Suwanna Satha-Anand, Philosophy Department, Chulalongkorn University.

100   See *United States v. Seeger*, 380 U.S. 163 (1965): The intent of the law is understood to be "to embrace all religions and to exclude essentially political, sociological, or philosophical views." The Court held that where a set of beliefs "occupies a place in the life of its possessor parallel to that filled by the orthodox belief in God" the person may be considered for the exemption.

101   A classic case is *Sherbert v. Verner*, 374 U.S. 398 (1963), in which it was held that a state's refusal to grant unemployment benefits to a woman who had been dismissed because she refused, for religious reasons, to work on Saturday violated the Free Exercise Clause. As Justice Stewart pointed out in his concurring opinion, the state would be within its rights to refuse unemployment benefits to a woman whose dismissal from employment resulted from inability to find a Saturday baby sitter: "[T]he Court . . . holds that the State must prefer a religious over a secular ground for being unavailable for work." Stewart argues that this creates grave difficulties for the Establishment Clause.

applicability, including non-discrimination laws. A Catholic Church may refuse to accept a Jew as a member just because she is a Jew; such action, usually
unconstitutional, seems perfectly legitimate here. More contentious is the
demand of religious groups to be exempted from the reach of other non-discrimination statutes—for example, those dealing with gender and sexual
orientation. The state does not require the Roman Catholic Church to admit
women to the priesthood on equal terms, although in almost all other occupa-
tions a denial on the basis of sex would be illegal. Some local non-discrimination laws on sexual orientation, for example that of the city of Denver, have
exempted religious institutions. These are borderline cases, difficult to distinguish from those of private clubs and educational institutions, whose liberty
to discriminate on grounds of religion and gender has steadily eroded. Again,
the legal questions are complex; we can only gesture in the direction of a
recommendation. But a promising approach would be to insist that any form
of discrimination on the basis of gender, race, or sexual orientation should face
heightened scrutiny under the Equal Protection Clause—or the analogue of
this in the legal system in question: Only a compelling state interest can justify
such restrictions. On the other hand, it should be possible to hold in some cases
that the protection of religious liberty may supply such a compelling interest,
so long as the law in question is narrowly tailored to protect that particular
interest.[102]

A further area of controversy is the role of state benefits and subsidies:
Should the state be permitted to grant tax-exempt status to an institution that
does engage in discriminatory activity? In *Norwood v. Harrison*, 413 U.S. 455
(1973), the Court held that a state-supported textbook program was unconstitutional as applied to schools with racially discriminatory policies. In *Bob Jones
University v. United States*, 461 U.S. 574 (1983), the Court upheld the Internal
Revenue Service's denial of tax-exempt status to that racially discriminatory
and religiously grounded institution. A religious institution that refused to
admit women might possibly receive similar treatment, and state subsidies to
such institutions might be struck down, although this is unclear. The question
is, however, what other practices of religious institutions qualify as discriminatory for these purposes? Hardly any religion fails to allow women in as
members; the question is, how does it treat them when they are there? Should

---

102   In *Evans v. Romer*, the case dealing with the constitutionality of Colorado's
Amendment 2, which denied local communities and state agencies the right to
pass non-discrimination laws for sexual orientation, Judge Bayless, ruling that
the law did not survive strict scrutiny, recognized the interest in religious liberty
as a compelling interest but pointed out that the way to protect that interest in a
"narrowly tailored" way was to do as Denver had done and exempt religious
organizations from the law. (These issues were not addressed in the Supreme
Court's discussion of the case in *Evans v. Romer*, since strict scrutiny was not at
issue and the entire mode of argumentation was different.)

the Roman Catholic Church lose its tax-exempt status because women are not admitted to the priesthood? Should the University of Notre Dame lose federal funds because only a male can serve as its President? Such questions may well be answered in favor of broad latitude for the religious group, but they must be honestly confronted and debated. If we take them off the table we suggest that such forms of discrimination, unlike racial discrimination or religious discrimination, are permissible and innocuous expressions of cultural variety—and that, I think, is an assumption from which women have suffered far too long. If we debate these questions openly, we will come to a better shared understanding of the limits of religious liberty even in voluntary organizations, within a liberal regime committed to the protection of fundamental rights.

2. What types of religious discourse and practice should be legally prohibited?

In general, putting to one side the small class of exemptions discussed above concerning non-discrimination in employment and membership, religious organizations and actors should be held to the same standards as everyone else. This means that any form of religious discourse that constitutes a threat of violence against an individual or group should be, and probably already is, illegal under the state's system of criminal law. It is obvious that proposing a *fatwah* is an illegal act and that all who had a part in it are international criminals and villains; but since they are also the makers of the code of criminal law in their country, we can't use their case to speak about how a constitutional democracy should operate its legal system.[103]

Let us therefore turn to less high-profile cases. The *mullahs* who threatened to break women's legs should have been arrested. The fact that they are *mullahs* should give them no special rights; insofar as they are advocating leg-breaking, they are no different from Mafia crime bosses making similar threats. What is their crime? Presumably assault: Take, for example, the Model Penal

---

103 There is an interesting question, however, whether the *fatwah* would not be protected under the current U.S. law of free speech. In *Brandenburg v. Ohio*, 395 U.S. 444 (1969), the Court required three things in order for speech to forfeit protection: (1) express advocacy of law violation, (2) the advocacy must call for *immediate* law violation, and (3) the immediate law violation must be likely to occur. The *fatwah* may not satisfy (2); and yet a number of individuals connected with the publication and translation of Rushdie's book have, over the years, been murdered. See the discussion in G. R. Stone, L. M. Seidman, C. R. Sunstein, and M. V. Tushnet, *Constitutional Law*, 3d ed. (Boston: Little, Brown, 1996), 1127, citing Schwartz, "Holmes versus Hand: Clear and Present Danger or Advocacy of Unlawful Action?" *Supreme Court Review* 1994: 209, 240–41, who argues that the *Brandenburg* test would protect the Ayatollah's speech. If one holds, as I do, that the Ayatollah's speech should be punishable, one may feel that the *Brandenburg* test is too protective.

Code's definition, according to which one sufficient condition for assault is that the person "attempts by physical menace to put another in fear of imminent serious bodily injury." (211.1.c) Given that the actions of the *mullahs* restrained women from going outside to seek education, we might also focus on the crime of "felonious restraint," which occurs if a person "(a) restrains another unlawfully in circumstances exposing him to risk of serious bodily injury or (b) holds another in a condition of involuntary servitude." (212.2); and "false imprisonment," defined as a misdemeanor committed by a person who "knowingly restrains another unlawfully so as to interfere substantially with his liberty." Other statutory solutions could involve notions of stalking, harassment, and so forth that have more recently been developed. Probably their threat of social ostracism should receive similar treatment, since in the situation it was like a death threat.

In a grey area is discourse that incites other people to commit violent acts against women. This is a large and heterogeneous class, including direct instruction to commit *sati* (which has recently been rendered criminal under the new post-Roop Kanwar law); speeches saying that women who do thus and so (say, dress in a certain way or talk immodestly) deserve to die; speeches saying that such women are whores and fair game for rape; speeches simply saying that such women are whores; speeches saying that widows are virtually dead and their wishes do not count; speeches saying that women are childlike and immoral and in need of stern home discipline; and a host of others. Such incitements are a major cause of battery, rape, and even death of women: At what point should the religious speaker be held to have committed a criminal offense? It seems obvious that the strongest case for criminality exists when the incitement is directly targeted at a particular individual and is an incitement to immediate action—say, a woman is told that it is right for her to commit *sati* now; or a brother whose sister has gone off to work in the big city and comes home in short skirts is told that a woman like her deserves to die without further ado;[104] or a man is told by a religious leader that he should assert his domestic authority more, and a little thrashing when he gets home today won't hurt; or village men are urged by *mullahs* to feel free to beat up these particular women as they go to school. Even where no threat is involved, expressions of hate targeted narrowly against a particular individual may legitimately be criminalized.[105]

---

104   There was a recent case of this type in an Arab family in Northern Israel, in which a woman who came home to visit her family was murdered for allegedly bringing shame on the family by her short skirts, etc.

105   See C. Sunstein, *Democracy and the Problem of Free Speech* (New York: The Free Press, 1993), 202–4, arguing that the Stanford speech code would be constitutional even in a public university. Under the Stanford code, speech qualifies as regulable "harassment" if it "(1) is intended to insult or stigmatize an individual or a small number of individuals on the basis of their sex, race, color, handicap,

Where threatening speech or hate speech is more general, we should be cautious. Much speech against women's equality is political speech, and general expressions of a political sentiment, however, odious, should receive a very high degree of protection. And yet, a country may legitimately, in keeping with its particular history, judge that some forms of speech expressing hatred and stirring up hostility are too dangerous not to be made illegal. Most European nations, including Britain with its Race Relations Act, set narrower limits to hate speech than does the United States. In Germany, anti-Semitic speech is illegal, even if it is clearly political or religious speech and would obviously, as such, be protected under the U.S. constitution. Such a course seems right, given Germany's particular history. A nation in which millions of women are "missing" might legitimately judge that some forms of speech denigrating the value of female life are to be forbidden, even if the speech is religious and, indeed, the expression of a deeply rooted religious tradition. In practical terms, such laws are likely to cause more problems than they solve— for the religious groups in question, unlike the Nazis, are not defeated and mostly dead, and therefore will make no end of trouble, with clever use of ideas of free speech. Nonetheless, it seems important to point out that there is a moral case to be made for such laws. This is obviously a large and immensely controversial topic, which deserves separate treatment.

3. What types of religious discourse should be deemed immoral and criticized as inappropriate in the public sphere?

Here, finally, we approach the topic of most of the U.S.-focused papers. In a constitutional or otherwise democratic regime that has adopted a guarantee of sex equality or ratified the Women's Convention, it should be straightforwardly immoral and inappropriate to speak in ways that contradict or undermine these fundamental rights. Thus, any discourse that denies women's equal humanity (or, indeed, the equal humanity of all citizens); any discourse that portrays women as by nature whorish or childish or unfitted for citizenship; any defense of practices that violate women's human rights as guaranteed in the constitution, such as marital rape or female genital mutilation, all

religion, sexual orientation, or national and ethnic origin, (2) is addressed directly to the individual or individuals whom it insults or stigmatizes, and (3) makes use of insulting or 'fighting' words or nonverbal symbols." To qualify under (3), the speech must by its "very utterance inflict injury or tend to incite to an immediate breach of the peace," and must be "commonly understood to convey direct and visceral hatred and contempt for human beings on the basis of" one of the grounds enumerated in (2). I cannot comment extensively on the complexities involved in applying this useful paradigm to the cases I have been talking about; but one surely is the contestability of "hatred and contempt": For speech that might legitimately be seen by women as expressing hatred and contempt of them may be seen by the speaker as expressing a protective kind of love, the kind of love one has for a child who is prone to error.

this should be deemed highly inappropriate. (And I do mean to include here any religious speech attacking contraception in international fora, since, as I have said, I take contraception to be a basic human right of women.) We could legitimately view a history of such speech as a reason against confirming a judge for office; a religious leader who uses such speech in the public realm should be strongly criticized as a subverter of the constitution.

As for other forms of religious discourse, my view is essentially that of John Courtney Murray (and close to the view defended in the new paper edition of Rawls's *Political Liberalism*):[106] that such discourse is appropriate, provided that it can be made publicly assessable and intelligible to citizens who do not share the speaker's religious starting point, and provided that it takes care to indicate its harmony with the fundamental principles of the constitution (or the principles implicit in the democratic political culture, if there is no written constitution). Thus, the Pope's address to the United Nations seems to me fully appropriate, since he is always at pains to make his moral argument available to others who may come to the issue from a different metaphysical starting point and since he is careful to show its consistency with fundamental principles of, in this case, international law and morality.

Special care should be taken, however, to avoid offense to minorities: thus a judge in India who cites the *Ramayana*, however compatibly with the principles set forth above, may send a political signal that many will construe, in the present climate of opinion, as denigrating Muslims and expressing the sentiment that India is basically a Hindu society;[107] a judge who cites the *Laws of Manu*, even as a storehouse of wisdom of the ages, could be suspected by some feminists of holding its views regarding women, even if the portion he has cited has nothing to do with women's issues. In India, it is probably wiser to cite Shakespeare.

Are these acceptable constraints? Certainly they will not be acceptable to many participants in many religions, since they involve the curtailment of traditional prerogatives. We should insist, however, that there is a basic core of international morality that constrains all religious actors in the public realm, that to be held to this morality in the ways I have described is no more violative of religious free exercise than is the requirement to obey the criminal law.

When charges of "Westernizing" and "colonializing" (even, at times, "Christianizing")[108] burst in upon us, we liberals should insist, once again, that

106   New York: Columbia University Press, 1996, l–lii.

107   Sen, "Secularism," notes, however, that the attitude to Rama taken in Hindu activist politics (that he is the central god of the tradition) is far from universal: in Bengal Rama is traditionally thought of as simply a good king, not divinity incarnate. (Thus, even the idea that the *Ramayana* is in any sense a religious text is contestable.) Furthermore, in the classic Bengali dramatic poetry of Madhusudhan Dutt, Rama's adversary Meghad is the hero, while Rama and his brothers are not even especially admirable.

the loudest voices in a religious tradition do not define the totality of its possibilities; that political actors use religious appeals as a vehicle for their own power, not always as legitimate attempts to capture the essence of the tradition in question; that all religions are plural and contain argument and dissent; finally, that all religions contain the voices of women, which have not always been heard in the statements that are usually taken to define what the religion is and requires. Attention to women's perspectives is surely a highly important part of pluralistic religious discourse. All this may at least ease the burden of guilt liberals will surely feel for having taken so definite a stand on the liberal dilemma.

IV. What Can Be Done

I said that some of my recommendations sound like pie in the sky; so they do. And yet, this does not mean that there is no scope for action aimed at making these constraints real.

One form of action in which liberals concerned with religion can very definitely engage is the encouraging of pluralistic and comparative religious discourse on these topics, discourse that brings to light and publicizes the plurality of views on all these matters within the religious traditions, and also brings members of the different traditions together for consultation and comparative discussion.[109] In the process, many appeals to religion that do violate women's rights will be exposed as at the least narrow and partial accounts of a tradition, and often as simple misrepresentations—as has been happening with the relation of Islam to female genital mutilation. This is one area where the old adage that it is best to drive out bad speech with more speech seems to be just right. And this is why the general issue raised by our volume seems so urgent for the future of the world's women: For religious discourse, if a villain in many of my examples, is also, in multiple and powerful ways, a major source of hope for women's future. We should therefore not accept any solution to the liberal dilemma that unduly marginalizes religious speech, or asks people to cut themselves off from humanitarian motivations that may motivate them in a specifically religious form. I believe that my own proposal does not do this.

It is, moreover, a legitimate function of a liberal state to encourage the liberal

---

108   Chen reports that one of the forms of abuse used by the *mullahs* against the reading women was the charge of being Christian. To which one woman replied, "If we can get food, we will become Christian." (p. 176) Note, however, that in India Christian women, insofar as they have historically separate legal codes, do relatively badly in some important matters.

109   For one good recent example, see the volume *Religion and Human Rights*, ed. John Kelsay and Sumner B. Twiss (New York: The Project on Religion and Human Rights, 1994).

elements in the religious traditions. Here I agree with John Courtney Murray and with Rawls: By giving prominence to the type of religious speech that accords with constitutional fundamentals and to its speakers, a state legitimately strengthens the political consensus around these fundamentals and dramatizes to citizens the fact that religious argument in the major traditions can support them. Thus in India, it would be highly advisable for major state actors to spend time insisting (as intellectuals such as Tariq Mahmood and Amartya Sen have long insisted) that both Islamic and Hindu traditions are diverse and plural and contain prominent liberal elements. Such public emphasis weakens the claim of anti-liberal parties and individuals to speak for the entirety of a religious tradition.

Beyond this, it seems crucial for all who are concerned with these facts to promote and support local forms of group action that are the most promising avenues of change. This means supporting NGO's like the Bangladesh Rural Advancement Committee (organizer of the literacy project), which are free from government pressure and able to pursue a highly effective grass roots agenda,[110] At the same time, we should also try to bring pressure to bear on our governments and on multinational corporations to alter this situation, as was done so successfully in the case of South Africa. Women who are fighting these injustices on the spot need such external reinforcement. Frequently, too, the fact that an international body or a foreign government has made compliance with certain human rights practices a condition of some form of economic or diplomatic cooperation gives women a way to support such changes without fear. Blaming change on the Americans is a convenient way out for people who are not in a position to risk personal defiance; we should create many such opportunities.

Meanwhile, in acute cases, individuals who suffer human-rights violations on account of being female should be granted political asylum. This happened for the first time in the U.S. in June 1996, when a woman from Togo, about to be forced to undergo genital mutilation, was admitted by the INS, in a ruling that stated "that women have little legal recourse and may face threats to their freedom, threats or acts of physical violence, or social ostracization for refusing to undergo this harmful traditional practice, or attempting to protect their female children."[111] Obviously, however, we should not rely on this remedy, which is arbitrary in its benefits (it helps only those people who can get on a

---

110   It is for this reason that NGO's were regarded with much more alarm than governments by the powers that be in Beijing.

111   "U.S. Gives Asylum to Woman Who Fled Genital Mutilation," Celia W. Dugger, *The New York Times*, June 2, 1996. The case was unusual for two reasons: the woman was nineteen, old enough to take action for herself, rather than age five or six, the usual time for the operation—because her wealthy progressive father had forbidden the procedure during his lifetime; and, second, because she could get hold of enough money to purchase a plane ticket to the U.S.

plane and go somewhere), and which can hardly address problems that affect millions of people.

The best way to promote the role for religious discourse defended in this paper is to produce active, unintimidated, educated democratic citizens. Such citizens will demand that religious discourse play a role compatible with constitutional guarantees of human equality. And this means that their role toward their own religious tradition will also be active and reflective, not merely submissive to the powerful interpreters of the moment. In many parts of the world, women have not been encouraged to become such citizens. But this situation is changing. At the conclusion of the literacy project, same women said that they no longer took advice from the local religious leaders. One woman said that she still went to get advice. Asked whether she found the advice helpful, she replied:

> I will think myself whether he gives me good suggestions or bad ones. If he gives me a good suggestion, I will try to understand how far it is good for me. Or whether it is a bad suggestion.

This is exactly the response that a society truly committed to a religious liberty should encourage.[112]

---

112   For comments that have helped me in rewriting this paper, I am grateful to Martha Chen, Richard Posner, Mark Ramseyer, Amartya Sen, David Strauss, Cass Sunstein, and Paul Weithman.

Political Liberalisms and Their Exclusions of the Religious[1]

Philip L. Quinn

Writing a Presidential Address provides a fine opportunity to set aside for a while the small puzzles that tend to preoccupy us in our increasingly specialized discipline and to spend time on larger issues of general interest. I have taken full advantage of my opportunity. I shall be speaking about the role of religion in the politics of a pluralistic democracy. A growing literature in political philosophy addresses this issue, but it is also much discussed in other academic disciplines, particularly law, political science, religious studies, and theology. And, of course, educated citizens of a pluralistic democracy such as ours have a stake in and should, though they often do not, take an interest in the course of academic discussions of this issue. So I do not worry about there being considerable interest in my topic, both within and beyond philosophy.

I do however worry about the prospects for making a contribution that has any real chance of advancing the discussion. Politics and religion are a dangerous mixture; combining them, even in academic discussion, risks generating more heat than light. Any substantive view on the proper role of religion in democratic politics will, in present circumstances, be highly controversial. My position will, I am sure, be no exception to this general rule. I shall be dissenting from the views of a great many philosophers, including those of three past divisional presidents of this association. I cannot hope to advance the discussion if doing so requires coming up with arguments that are apt to produce consensus on my views. But perhaps discussion of controversial issues can be advanced without producing much progress toward agreement. Hence maybe I can hope to advance the discussion if no more is required of me than to enrich a lively conversation by adding a distinctive and reasonable voice to it. What I aim to accomplish is at least to satisfy this modest requirement.

Several prominent philosophers who support one version of political liberalism or another have recently proposed excluding religion from our political life in various ways. Richard Rorty is an example. In a recent discussion of Stephen Carter's book, *The Culture of Disbelief*, Rorty advocates what he describes as the happy, Jeffersonian compromise that the Enlightenment reached with the religious, which "consists in privatizing religion—keeping it

1   Editor's note: Philip Quinn's paper was his Presidential Address to the American Philosophical Association's Central Division, delivered April 28, 1995. It originally appeared in *Proceedings and Addresses of the APA* 69 (1995): 35–56, and is reprinted here by permission of the editor of the *Proceedings*.

out of what Carter calls 'the public square,' making it seem bad taste to bring religion into discussions of public policy."[2] And he attributes to contemporary liberal philosophers the view that "we shall not be able to keep a democratic political community going unless the religious believers remain willing to trade privatization for a guarantee of religious liberty."[3] But of course many religious believers do not regard the proposed exclusion of religion from the public square as an acceptable compromise or a source of happiness. It strikes them as unreasonable and unfair. Thus a question political liberals need to answer is this: Can any exclusion of religion from the public square be defended by showing that it is neither unreasonable nor unfair? I am going to take a few steps toward an answer to this general question by examining critically three fairly specific proposals by contemporary liberals for excluding religion from politics.

In order to provide a unifying thread to my discussion, I shall focus on proposals involving claims that there are moral duties to refrain from appealing to religious reasons in certain political contexts. I shall concentrate on the question of whether ordinary citizens of pluralistic democracies have such duties, leaving aside the question of whether public officials such as legislators or judges have role-specific, special duties of this sort and the question of whether ecclesiastical officials such as bishops have related special duties. I shall also restrict my attention to discussion of these topics by philosophers and legal theorists, passing over in silence a large and interesting literature in religious ethics and moral theology because of limitations of time and space.

The first proposal I wish to consider comes from Robert Audi. In recent publications, he has formulated and defended two principles of individual conduct that would, if scrupulously followed by all citizens of a democratic society, have the effect of excluding some religious believers from full participation in political debate and action on some important issues. In order to understand these principles, one needs first to grasp Audi's idea of what is involved in having an adequate secular reason to advocate or support a law or public policy. He tells us that "a secular reason is, roughly, one whose normative force, that is, its status as a prima facie justificatory element, does not (evidentially) depend on the existence of God (for example, through appeals to divine command) or on theological considerations (such as interpretations of a sacred text), or on the pronouncements of a person or institution qua religious authority."[4] I shall refer to reasons that are not secular in this sense as religious reasons. Audi goes on to say that "an adequate reason for a

---

2 Richard Rorty, "Religion as Conversation-Stopper," *Common Knowledge* 3, no. 1 (1994): 2.

3 Ibid., 3.

4 Robert Audi, "The Separation of Church and State and the Obligations of Citizenship," *Philosophy and Public Affairs* 18 (1989): 278.

law or policy is a proposition whose truth is sufficient to justify it."[5] Combining the notions of secularity and adequacy yields the result that an adequate secular reason to advocate or support a law or public policy is a proposition such that (i) it is evidentially independent of religious reasons and (ii) its truth confers justification on the law or public policy.

Audi employs the idea of adequate secular reason in formulating his two principles. The weaker is the principle of secular rationale. It says that "one should not advocate or support any law or public policy that restricts human conduct unless one has, and is willing to offer, adequate secular reason for this advocacy or support."[6] A slightly different formulation says that "one has a prima facie obligation not to advocate or support any law or public policy that restricts human conduct unless one has, and is willing to offer, adequate secular reason for this advocacy or support."[7] The stronger is the principle of secular motivation. It says that "one should not advocate or promote any legal or public policy restrictions on human conduct unless one not only has and is willing to offer, but is also *motivated by*, adequate secular reason, where this reason (or set of reasons) is motivationally sufficient for the conduct in question."[8] An alternative formulation says that "one also has a prima facie obligation to abstain from such advocacy or support unless one is sufficiently *motivated* by adequate secular reason."[9] According to Audi, these principles are not merely counsels of prudence; they are not merely specifications of what it would be best for religious believers to do if they hope to persuade or form alliances with their nonreligious fellow citizens. They are, he says, "principles of conscience,"[10] and are intended to express "constraints on conscience."[11] And he concludes that "a conscientious citizen strongly committed to preserving religious and other liberties should probably strive to follow the stronger principle, which requires that one do one's best to have sufficient secular motivation, particularly for actions in support of laws or policies that would restrict human conduct."[12] Of course many conscientious citizens devoted to preserving religious and other liberties would not always succeed in complying with Audi's stronger principle even if they always tried to follow it. Ordinary citizens cannot be expected to be perfect judges of the adequacy of

---

5   Ibid.

6   Ibid., 279.

7   Robert Audi, "The Place of Religious Argument in a Free and Democratic Society," *San Diego Law Review* 30 (1993): 691–92.

8   Audi, "Separation," 284.

9   Audi, "Place," 692.

10   Audi, "Separation," 278.

11   Audi, "Place," 691.

12   Audi, "Separation," 286.

secular reasons or flawless in understanding and managing their own motivations.

An interpretive issue must be resolved before Audi's principles can be evaluated. At one point he remarks that he has "not meant to suggest that, for example, there is no *right* to base one's vote on a religious ground. But surely we can do better than guide our civic conduct merely within the constraints imposed by our rights."[13] This remark suggests that the prima facie obligations specified by the two principles may never be actual obligations because they are always overridden by a right not to comply with the principles. Since Audi describes his views on individual conduct as laying out "what we ought to do in something like an ideal case,"[14] we might do well to understand his two principles not as principles of obligation but as principles fleshing out a supererogatory ideal of good citizenship. If they are construed as counsels of perfection, compliance with them would always be better than failure to comply but would never be obligatory. However, thus construed, they would lack constraining power. What is more, this interpretation does not fit well with other things Audi says. After all, he formulates the two principles as specifications of prima facie obligation and describes them as principles governing "duties as citizens."[15] And, in discussing the principle of secular motivation, he says that "I leave open whether, as I am inclined to grant, there is a moral *right* to act otherwise; but I assume that rights do not exhaust oughts—that there are things one ought not to do even if one has a right to do them."[16] It seems to me that Audi is best understood as claiming that the secular motivation principle is a principle of obligation specifying what one ought to do, all things considered, in at least some cases and hence determining one's actual obligations in those cases. In short, I think Audi intends his principles to have considerable constraining power—real teeth, so to speak—and I shall proceed on that assumption.

If Audi's intentions are understood in the way I have proposed, I do not find it plausible to suppose that every conscientious citizen strongly committed to preserving religious and other liberties should probably strive to follow the secular motivation principle in all cases. Reflection on an example will help to explain my view. Imagine a person sufficiently motivated to take part in peacefully advocating more restrictive abortion laws solely by the belief that God has made it known through the teaching authority of the Roman Catholic Church that almost all abortions are wrong. Because this person is not motivated by any secular reason, she is a fortiori not motivated by adequate secular reason, and so she violates the principle of secular motivation. But I think it a

---

13   Audi, "Place," 700.

14   Ibid.

15   Audi, "Separation," 278.

16   Ibid., 284.

mistake to suppose that she fails on this account to be a conscientious citizen, particularly if we further specify the case by adding that she firmly opposes illegal violence of the sort involved in bombing abortion clinics or killing physicians who perform abortions. Furthermore, if she is to come into compliance with this principle, she must either cease her advocacy or acquire a sufficient secular motivation for it. As Audi emphasizes, the intent of the principle "is to require that one either not perform the relevant acts or see to it that one's secular, for instance purely moral, motivation is strong enough so that (other things being equal) one would do the thing in question even if one had no further motive."[17] But our advocate of restrictive abortion laws might also believe that, apart from religious reasons, there simply are no true propositions that confer justification on more restrictive abortion laws or their advocacy and so consider it unconscientious to try to comply with the principle by acquiring secular motives, which by her lights either would fail to confer justification or would be false beliefs. She might therefore be able to comply with the principle in good conscience only by ceasing to engage in her advocacy of restrictive abortion laws, and I do not think it reasonable to suppose that she is under an obligation to refrain from advocacy in her circumstances. More generally, I doubt that good citizens must in all or even most cases abide by self-denying ordinances according to which being motivated by beliefs of certain sorts is a precondition of political speech in support of restrictive laws or policies.

There is, of course, room in Audi's position for him to agree with my view of this and similar cases. He could acknowledge that in such cases one ought, all things considered, to exercise one's moral right to act otherwise than as the principle of secular motivation directs. In other words, he could say that the principle specifies in such cases only a prima facie obligation but not one's actual obligation. So perhaps the principle of secular motivation will exclude fewer people from political participation than one might have initially supposed. However, if it is to have any teeth at all, it will have to exclude some people who are not sufficiently motivated by adequate secular reasons. I regard the principle as dubious for this reason alone.

Audi's weaker principle of secular rationale also appears to be problematic. One difficulty is technical. Consider two secular moralists who offer contrary nonreligious reasons in support of the policy on abortion enunciated in *Roe v. Wade*. One argues that, though it does not protect a woman's right to make early abortion decisions free from state interference, there being no such right, it does maximize utility. The other argues the opposite, contending that the policy does not maximize utility but does adequately protect the right in question. Since both these claims cannot be true, both cannot be adequate reasons if we follow Audi in holding that an adequate reason is a proposition

17   Ibid.

whose truth is sufficient to justify a law or policy. So at least one of our secular moralists must not have and be offering an adequate secular reason to support the policy being discussed. And because even this fairly liberal policy is restrictive in comparison to some alternatives, at least one of them must therefore be failing to comply with the principle of secular rationale. But it seems excessively harsh to suppose that either fails to comply with a principle of conscience binding on good citizens. After all, each may be perfectly reasonable, even if both cannot be correct, in accepting the propositions she offers in support of the policy under consideration. Such disagreement about reasons is commonplace in moral argument between reasonable people.

No doubt this technical problem in Audi's account can be solved. One might, for example, weaken his condition for adequacy by stipulating that reasons are adequate for purposes of advocacy or support of restrictive laws or policies if they are reasonably held and would justify the law or policy in question if they were true. But then we must ask why citizens who have religious but not secular reasons that satisfy a condition of this sort should ever consider themselves by conscience bound not to advocate or support laws or policies their reasonably held beliefs would, if true, serve to justify. Such self-denial on the part of religious believers would be an extraordinary thing to demand. What could justify such a demand for self-denial?

Some people fear that religious argument is apt to be dangerously divisive. This fear seems to be behind Audi's remark that "conflicting secular ideas, even when firmly held, can often be blended and harmonized in the crucible of free discussion: but a clash of gods is like a meeting of an irresistible force with an immovable object."[18] No doubt religious conflict has in the past been dangerous and continues to be so in some parts of the world. However it does not seem that religious disagreement in a democracy must be dangerous or that it is a danger in all democratic societies. Students in Holland told Kent Greenawalt in 1991 that "very few people took religion seriously any longer, that tolerance was high and religious tension was virtually nonexistent, that religious arguments for political positions would be wholly ineffective."[19] If these students are correct, there is no need in Holland at present for exclusionary principles of constraint of the sort proposed by Audi. And, following

---

18   Ibid., 296. It also seems to animate Jeffrey Stout's argument that we should probably not try to revive the theological presuppositions of the traditional moral conscience. Stout asserts that "the risks of reviving religious conflict like that of early modern Europe are too great," and supports his assertion by pointing to contemporary evidence "from Belfast to Beirut, from Teheran to Lynchburg, Virginia." See Jeffrey Stout, *Ethics after Babel: The Languages of Morals and Their Discontents* (Boston: Beacon Press, 1988), 223.

19   Kent Greenawalt, "Grounds for Political Judgment: The Status of Personal Experience and the Autonomy and Generality of Principles of Restraint," *San Diego Law Review* 30 (1993): 674.

Greenawalt, I think we should acknowledge that what principles of constraint on the use of religious reasons in political argument, if any, are needed to prevent dangerous conflict will "depend on time and place, on a sense of present realities within a society, its history and its likely evolution."[20] If that is the case, an argument that Audi's principles are needed for this purpose in the United States at the present time should rest on appeals to empirical realities and possibilities here and now instead of appealing to an abstract ideal of good citizenship and its duties. I doubt that a good argument in such empirical terms will be forthcoming because current political debate in the United States exhibits failure to comply with Audi's principles on a massive scale and yet shows no tendency to reignite the Wars of Religion of the early modern era. Of course, current political debate in the United States contains more verbal conflict than it would if Audi's principles were agreed to by all parties. But constrained verbal conflict is probably healthy in a deeply pluralistic democratic society provided it rarely spills over into violence and does not seriously threaten the stability of fundamental constitutional arrangements.

But perhaps the self-denial required of the religious by the principle of secular rationale could be argued for on the grounds that in a religiously pluralistic society religious reasons cannot justify laws or policies that restrict conduct in terms of considerations all citizens can share or cannot reasonably reject. Such an argument is suggested by Audi's remark that "adherence to the principle of secular rationale helps to ensure that, in determining the scope of freedom in a society, the decisive principles and considerations can be shared by people of differing religious views, or even no religious convictions at all."[21] However, if the fact that religious reasons cannot be shared by all in a religiously pluralistic society suffices to warrant any exclusion of religious reasons for advocating or supporting restrictive laws or policies, then much else ought in fairness also to be excluded on the same grounds. For example, justification of a restrictive law or policy by an appeal to its maximization of utility should be excluded because many citizens reasonably reject utilitarianism. Indeed, it would seem that the appeal to any comprehensive ethical theory, including all known secular ethical theories, should be disallowed on the grounds that every such theory can be reasonably rejected by some citizens of a pluralistic democracy. And if justification of restrictive laws or policies can be conducted only in terms of moral considerations no citizen of a pluralistic democracy can reasonably reject, then in a pluralistic democracy such as ours very few restrictive laws or policies can be morally justified, a conclusion that would, I suspect, be welcomed only by anarchists.

At one point Audi raises the possibility of going beyond the principle of

---

20   Ibid.

21   Audi, "Separation," 290.

secular rationale to something stronger. He says that "if there is secular reason which is esoteric in a sense implying that a normal rational person lacks access to it, then a stronger requirement is needed; one might thus speak of public reason, as Rawls and others do."[22] But he has made it clear that in saying this he "was taking account of the possibility that the secular may be esoteric, and not asserting that secular beliefs sometimes are."[23] He has not acknowledged that many secular beliefs are on a par with religious beliefs in not being shared by all citizens or in being reasonably rejected by some citizens. If such features of religious beliefs are grounds for demanding that citizens who have religious but not secular reasons for restrictive laws or policies refrain from advocating or supporting such laws or policies, they are equally grounds for demanding that citizens whose secular reasons for such laws or policies also possess these features refrain from advocating or supporting such laws or policies. In other words, religious believers will rightly regard Audi's principle of secular rationale as making an unfair demand on them unless it is coupled with corresponding principles that make similar demands on people whose secular reasons are no better off than their religious reasons in terms of being shared or not being reasonably rejected. If the exclusion of the religious in Audi's variety of liberalism is to be fair, it must be accompanied by other exclusions.

As Audi's allusion to him indicates, John Rawls stresses the distinction between public and nonpublic reasons, rather than the contrast between secular and religious reasons, in formulating his idea of public reason. An advantage of this way of proceeding is that it allows Rawls both to include religious beliefs within public reason in some circumstances and to exclude many secular beliefs from public reason. Thus, although public reason does impose limits on the kinds of considerations to which it is legitimate to appeal in certain political contexts, it need not be systematically unfair in its exclusion of the religious. Rawls aims at an account of public reason in which all reasonable comprehensive doctrines, whether they be religious or not, are treated in the same way.

For Rawls, public reason is connected with an ideal conception of citizenship for a constitutional democratic regime. As such, "it presents how things might be, taking people as a just and well-ordered society would encourage them to be."[24] Yet it is not an ideal for the whole of life of a democratic citizen; it is only meant to regulate a citizen's participation in political affairs. And

---

22   Audi, "Place," 690.

23   This remark, contained in a letter to Michael Perry, is quoted in Michael J. Perry, "Religious Morality and Political Choice: Further Thoughts—and Second Thoughts—on *Love and Power*," *San Diego Law Review* 30 (1993): 716.

24   John Rawls, *Political Liberalism* (New York: Columbia University Press, 1993), 213. Nonpublic reasons are said to "comprise the many reasons of civil society and belong to what I have called the 'background culture,' in contrast with the public political culture" (p. 220).

even within the political sphere "the limits imposed by public reason do not apply to all political questions but only to those involving what we may call 'constitutional essentials' and questions of basic justice."[25] Constitutional essentials consist of "fundamental principles that specify the general structure of government and the political process: the powers of the legislature, executive and the judiciary; the scope of majority rule; and equal basic rights and liberties of citizenship that legislative majorities are to respect: such as the right to vote and to participate in politics, liberty of conscience, freedom of thought and of association, as well as the protections of the rule of law."[26] When what is at stake in politics is these things or questions of basic justice, "the ideal of public reason does hold for citizens when they engage in political advocacy in the public forum, and thus for members of political parties and for candidates in their campaigns and for other groups who support them. It holds equally for how citizens are to vote in elections when constitutional essentials and matters of basic justice are at stake."[27] Yet it is not a supererogatory ideal, asking for conduct above and beyond the call of duty. The ideal of citizenship with which it is connected "imposes a moral, not a legal, duty—the duty of civility—to be able to explain to one another on those fundamental questions how the principles and policies they advocate and vote for can be supported by the political values of public reason."[28] And such explanations are to be given "in terms each could reasonably expect that others might endorse as consistent with their freedom and equality."[29] The content of public reason will therefore have to be restricted under conditions of pluralism if mutuality of endorsement is to be hoped for or achieved.

The restrictions Rawls proposes become clear when he specifies the content of public reason. It has three components, all of which are tied to distinctly liberal political conceptions of justice. A liberal conception of justice does three things: "first, it specifies certain basic rights, liberties, and opportunities (of the kind familiar from constitutional democratic regimes); second, it assigns a special priority to these rights, liberties, and opportunities, especially with respect to claims of the general good and of perfectionist values; and third, it affirms measures assuring all citizens adequate all-purpose means to make effective use of their basic liberties and opportunities."[30] To say that a conception of justice is political is to say three things: "that it is framed to apply solely to the basic structure of society, its main political, social and economic institutions as a unified scheme of social cooperation; that it is presented inde-

---

25   Ibid., 214.

26   Ibid., 227.

27   Ibid., 215.

28   Ibid., 217.

29   Ibid., 218.

30   Ibid., 223.

pendently of any wider comprehensive religious or philosophical doctrine; and that it is elaborated in terms of fundamental political ideas viewed as implicit in the public political culture of a democratic society."[31] The three components of public reason are the substantive principles of justice of a liberal political conception, the guidelines of inquiry of a liberal political conception, which specify "principles of reasoning and rules of evidence in the light of which citizens are to decide whether substantive principles properly apply and to identify laws and policies that best satisfy them,"[32] and rules determining the kinds of considerations to which it is legitimate to appeal in advocacy and voting on matters of constitutional essentials and basic justice. Since the purpose of public reason is to justify laws and policies regarding such matters to all citizens of a pluralistic democratic society, the rules will have to exclude considerations about which there is reasonable disagreement in such a society. As Rawls states them, "we are to appeal only to presently accepted general beliefs and forms of reasoning found in common sense, and the methods and conclusions of science when these are not controversial"[33] and "we are not to appeal to comprehensive religious and philosophical doctrines—to what we as individuals or members of associations see as the whole truth—nor to elaborate economic theories of general equilibrium, say, if these are in dispute."[34] Within the bounds of public reason, then, we may appeal to the substantive principles and guidelines of inquiry of a liberal political conception of justice, and to political values associated with it, as well as to shared common sense and undisputed science, but we may not appeal to comprehensive doctrines, religious or secular, or to disputed science. And the duty of civility requires us to stay within the bounds of public reason when we are trying to justify laws and policies bearing on constitutional essentials and questions of basic justice unless we are in special circumstances Rawls later discusses or others like them.

Rawls considers it desirable that the substantive principles and guidelines of inquiry of a liberal political conception of justice should be complete in the sense that its values, when suitably combined or balanced, will "alone give a reasonable public answer to all, or to nearly all, questions involving the constitutional essentials and basic questions of justice."[35] If this is to occur, the

---

31   Ibid.

32   Ibid., 224.

33   Ibid.

34   Ibid., 224–25. Because Rawls excludes secular comprehensive doctrines from public reason while Audi does not insist upon a parallel exclusion of secular reasons, there is one way in which Audi's view is more permissive than that of Rawls. But since they do not benefit from this permissiveness, religious believers are apt to see it as an instance of secularist bias.

35   Ibid., 225.

resources of public reason must be rich enough to justify answers to all, or nearly all, such questions. But since public reason denies itself the resources of all comprehensive doctrines, including comprehensive liberal doctrines, it is not obvious that it has enough content to yield such answers in almost all cases. It must be applied to hard cases to determine whether it yields reasonable public answers.

Rawlsian political liberalism thus excludes the religious by drawing the boundaries of public reason so that comprehensive religious doctrines fall outside them for the most part. But it also excludes comprehensive secular doctrines in the same way and so cannot be accused of unfairly privileging the secular over the religious. Instead it privileges liberal conceptions of justice over their rivals by including the substantive principles, guidelines of inquiry, and political values of a liberal conception of justice, or a family of such conceptions, but not those of competing, nonliberal conceptions, within the bounds of public reason. Those whose comprehensive doctrines endorse such nonliberal conceptions of justice can be expected to object that their views are being unfairly excluded from the domain of public reason. Of course, if there were an overlapping consensus of all the reasonable comprehensive doctrines present in a pluralistic and democratic society on a liberal conception of justice, or on a family of them, there would be no unfairness in such an exclusion. But even if one agrees with Rawls that the *hope* for such an overlapping consensus on a liberal conception is not utopian,[36] one should be willing to acknowledge that no such consensus exists in our society here and now. Hence those whose reasonable comprehensive doctrines do not at present support any liberal conception of justice will find it natural to object that they have no sufficient reason to honor the limits of public reason or to affirm the duty of civility, as these things are specified by Rawlsian political liberalism. Though I have considerable sympathy with this objection, I am not going to press it on this occasion. My interest is in political liberalism's exclusion of the religious and not in whether its other exclusions may be unfair.

I am, however, going to press an objection based on the way in which Rawls uses public reason to discuss a hard case. In a footnote that has already attracted some attention and is bound to attract more, Rawls considers the question of abortion. It is worth quoting at length:

---

36   Ibid., 158–68, presents a reply by Rawls to the objection that the hope for an overlapping consensus is utopian. His argument proceeds in two stages. The first shows how liberal arrangements that are merely an acceptable modus vivendi at first might come to enjoy the status of being the object of a constitutional consensus. The second shows how a constitutional consensus might evolve into an overlapping consensus. The argument, if successful, shows that evolution to an overlapping consensus on a liberal conception of justice, or a family of them, is, in some sense, possible. As far as I can tell, it does not show that evolution to an overlapping consensus is likely, will occur, or is inevitable.

Suppose first that the society in question is well-ordered and that we are dealing with the normal case of mature adult women. It is best to be clear about this idealized case first; for once we are clear about it, we have a guide that helps us to think about other cases, which force us to consider exceptional circumstances. Suppose further that we consider the question in terms of these three important political values: the due respect for human life, the ordered reproduction of political society over time, including the family in some form, and finally the equality of women as equal citizens. (There are, of course, other important political values besides these.) Now I believe any reasonable balance of these three values will give a woman a duly qualified right to decide whether or not to end her pregnancy during the first trimester. The reason for this is that at this early stage of pregnancy the political value of the equality of women is overriding, and this right is required to give it substance and force. Other political values, if tallied in, would not, I think, affect this conclusion. A reasonable balance may allow her such a right beyond this, at least in certain circumstances. However, I do not discuss the question in general here, as I simply want to illustrate the point of the text by saying that any comprehensive doctrine that leads to a balance of political values excluding that duly qualified right in the first trimester is to that extent unreasonable; and depending on details of its formulation, it may also be cruel and oppressive; for example, if it denied the right altogether except in the case of rape and incest. Thus, assuming that this question is either a constitutional essential or a matter of basic justice, we would go against the ideal of public reason if we voted from a comprehensive doctrine that denied this right. However, a comprehensive doctrine is not as such unreasonable because it leads to an unreasonable conclusion in one or even in several cases. It may still be reasonable most of the time.[37]

As it happens, I agree with the conclusion Rawls arrives at by means of this reasoning concerning the qualified right to decide whether or not to abort during the first trimester of pregnancy. But the question I want to ask is whether public reason alone dictates the conclusion he and I share. I do not think so.

Let us assume that the question of abortion is a matter of constitutional essentials or basic justice. On that assumption, the duty of civility requires us to respect the limits of public reason in answering it. The conception of justice that well-orders our society provides the political values we are to balance in coming to an answer. Let us further suppose, to simplify the discussion, that two of the values Rawls mentions, due respect for human life and equality of women as citizens, are so great that the balance between them is enough to determine our conclusion, leaving it unaffected when all other political values are taken into account. How are these two values to be balanced for the first trimester of pregnancy? Let us suppose that one of the two values is overriding

---

37   Ibid., 243–44.

and the other overridden: Either the value of equality of women is overriding and the value of respect for human life is overridden or vice versa. Rawls claims that the value of equality of women is overriding, arguing that the right to abortion is needed to give that value substance and force. Some who agree with Rawls about the values at stake will claim that the value of respect for human life is overriding and argue that a fetal right to life is required to give substance and force to that value. There is a conflict of intuitions about how two great values are to be balanced in a hard case. Does public reason have the resources to resolve it?

I think it does not. Comprehensive doctrines lie outside the limits of public reason. So those who oppose Rawls cannot appeal to comprehensive religious or metaphysical doctrines according to which the fetus is during early pregnancy a full-fledged person to support their intuition that the value of respect for human life is overriding. But, by the same token, those who side with Rawls cannot appeal to comprehensive doctrines according to which the early fetus is not a full-fledged person to support their intuition that the value of respect for human life is overridden. If they are to honor the limits of public reason, both sides must accept the discipline of restricting their appeals to generally accepted common sense beliefs and uncontroversial science. However, common sense is divided on or simply perplexed by the question of abortion and probably will remain so, and uncontroversial science is and is likely always to be silent on the question of whether the early fetus is a person and so should be protected by a strong right to life. Hence it seems that resources of public reason cannot get us beyond a standoff between the two sides in this debate, a standoff that is likely to persist.

If this is correct, there appear to be two ways of describing the situation. One could say that public reason in this case yields no reasonable balance of the values of respect for human life and equality of women because its resources are too weak to determine any reasonable balance. Or one could say that public reason permits two reasonable balances of those values because its resources are too weak to single out just one reasonable balance. In either case, public reason does not determine a unique reasonable balance of the values in question and so is incomplete to that extent. And that being the case, one may not infer, as Rawls does, that any comprehensive doctrine whose balance of those values excludes the duly qualified right to abortion in question is to that extent unreasonable. But neither may one infer that any comprehensive doctrine whose balance supports such a right is to that extent unreasonable. My suspicion is that public reason will fairly often fail to determine a balance of liberal political values that can be seen to be reasonable by all citizens of a democracy as deeply pluralistic as ours is. I have little confidence in its resolving power, its ability to provide "guidance where guidance is needed."[38]

---

38   John Rawls, *A Theory of Justice* (Cambridge, Mass.: Harvard University Press,

Of course Rawls uses the example in the footnote to illustrate how political values may be balanced within public reason, not as a full argument about abortion and certainly not as a decisive argument. Indeed, as he has subsequently made clear, such a balancing of values yields only a *pro tanto* political justification that "may be overridden by citizens' comprehensive doctrines once all values are tallied up."[39] This is because "it is left to each citizen, individually or in association with others, to say how the claims of political justice are to be ordered, or weighed, against nonpolitical values" and "the political conception gives no guidance in such questions, since it does not say how nonpolitical values are to be counted."[40] Thus Rawls acknowledges that public reason cannot determine, by itself, a unique reasonable balance of political and nonpolitical values. What is more, as I see it, it does not even in hard cases determine a unique reasonable balance of political values.

Rawls himself acknowledges that public reason may sometimes fall short of providing uniquely reasonable answers to troubled questions. The ideal asks us to try for a balance of values we think can be seen to be reasonable by fellow citizens.

> Or failing this, we think the balance can be seen as at least not unreasonable in this sense: that those who oppose it can nevertheless understand how reasonable persons can affirm it. This preserves the ties of civic friendship and is consistent with the duty of civility. On some questions this may be the best we can do.[41]

If we are to test the proposition that our opponents can understand how reasonable persons can affirm the balance we favor, however, we may have to introduce into the discussion enough of our comprehensive doctrine to enable them to see that the part of it on which we rely in arriving at the balance we favor is itself not unreasonable and does support that balance. Thus there are circumstances in which the appeal to comprehensive doctrines, including

1971), 20. Jean Hampton and Peter de Marneffe have recently arrived by independent arguments at similar critical conclusions about the way Rawls treats the abortion issue. According to Hampton, "the abortion issue would seem to be a paradigm case of an issue on which reasonable people can reach different conclusions, by virtue of the fact that they weight the relevant considerations differently" (Jean Hampton, "The Common Faith of Liberalism," *Pacific Philosophical Quarterly* 75 (1994): 209). And according to de Marneffe, "The issue of abortion suggests, then, that there are important liberal positions on the scope of basic liberty that cannot be adequately defended in terms of liberal political values alone" (Peter de Marneffe, "Rawl's Idea of Public Reason," *Pacific Philosophical Quarterly* 75 (1994): 235).

39   John Rawls, "Reply to Habermas," *Journal of Philosophy* 92 (1995): 143.

40   Ibid.

41   Rawls, *Liberalism*, 253. In a footnote, Rawls expresses indebtedness to Robert M. Adams for instructive discussion of this point.

religious doctrines, may be consistent with the duty of civility and the ideal of public reason and, what is more, may even serve to support the ideal.

Rawls agrees that there are such circumstances, which is why he endorses an inclusive view of the limits of public reason "allowing citizens, in certain situations, to present what they regard as the basis of political values rooted in their comprehensive doctrine, provided they do this in ways that strengthen the ideal of public reason itself."[42] He gives two examples. The first is a case of a serious dispute in a nearly well-ordered society. Suppose the dispute concerns the constitutionality of state aid to church schools. In the course of such a dispute, citizens on different sides of the issue might come to doubt the sincerity of one another's allegiance to fundamental political values, such as separation of church and state that order the society. According to Rawls, "one way this doubt might be put to rest is for leaders of the opposing groups to present in the public forum how their comprehensive doctrines do indeed affirm those values."[43] The second example is a case of a society that is not well ordered and in which there is profound disagreement about constitutional essentials. Rawls mentions in discussing this case the abolitionists of the nineteenth century and civil rights leaders, such as Martin Luther King, Jr., who appealed to comprehensive religious doctrines in the public forum. As Rawls sees it, "the abolitionists and leaders of the civil rights movement did not go against the ideal of public reason; or rather, they did not provided they thought, or on reflection would have thought (as they certainly could have thought), that the comprehensive reasons they appealed to were required to give sufficient strength to the political conception to be subsequently realized."[44] And once we have grasped the principle underlying these examples, we can construct others, even if they are only hypothetical, that satisfy the proviso that an appeal to comprehensive doctrine must strengthen, or least must not go against, the ideal of public reason. It would not be contrary to the spirit of the Rawlsian enterprise to be open to altering the proviso.

Indeed, Rawls has altered it in a forthcoming paper in which he moves from the inclusive view of public reason to what he calls "the wide view of public political discourse." Its principle is that "in public political discourse citizens (though not judges and other government officials) may freely introduce their reasonable comprehensive doctrines, with one crucial proviso: namely, that in due course they support the political measures they propose in terms of the principles and values of a public political conception of justice." The new proviso separates the wide view from what Rawls calls "the open view," according to which anything goes in public political discourse. He explicitly rejects the open view, saying that "political liberalism cannot, then, accept the

42   Ibid., 247.

43   Ibid., 249.

44   Ibid., 251.

open view, for this abandons the ideal of public reason: namely, that citizens in a democratic regime owe one another a public and mutually acceptable justification for their political actions on fundamental questions."[45] I suppose the new proviso is not vacuous because there are, for example, comprehensive religious doctrines whose adherents can support some political measures they propose only by appeal to principles or values, for instance, an interpretation of scriptural texts that is authoritative only for a particular religious denomination, that are not included within any public political conception of justice. Since adherents of such comprehensive doctrines cannot justify some of their political actions in terms acceptable to their fellow citizens who do not regard such scriptural texts, thus interpreted, as authoritative, the wide view precludes them from introducing their comprehensive doctrines into public political discourse about measures or actions of this sort. If this supposition is correct, then, even on the wide view, the ideal of public reason will rule out some appeals to comprehensive religious doctrines, and so Rawlsian liberalism will remain committed to excluding the religious from the public forum to some extent. Religious pacifists whose opposition to war is justified only by nonpublic reasons drawn from their comprehensive doctrines would seem to be precluded by the wide view's proviso from appealing to those reasons to support a constitutional amendment they might propose to prohibit the United States from waging any wars.

As I have tried to show, the political liberalisms of philosophers such as Audi and Rawls involve exclusions of the religious from political activity under certain conditions. For Audi, what is involved is exclusion from advocacy or support of restrictive laws or policies if one has only religious motives or reasons for such advocacy or support. For Rawls, what is involved is exclusion of religious comprehensive doctrines from the things to which it is legitimate to appeal in ultimately justifying answers to questions about constitutional essentials and matters of basic justice. To be sure, both philosophers soften the exclusions, so to speak, by allowing for or explicitly making exceptions. But one cannot help wondering whether the strategy of exclusions tempered by exceptions is one liberals must adopt or the best one for them to adopt. A growing literature suggests an alternative. Since much of it is in books by legal theorists or in law reviews, I expect that it will not be familiar to most philosophers. For this reason, I shall not try to present or discuss its details. I shall instead report briefly on the direction in which it seems to me moving—a direction I find attractive—with the hope that some of you will be drawn to look at it for yourselves.

---

45   John Rawls, "Public Reason Revisited," *University of Chicago Law Review* (forthcoming). My quotes are from pp. 12 and 16 of the copy of the manuscript in my possession. I am grateful to Rawls for permission to attribute the wide view to him in advance of the publication of this paper.

One important contribution to this literature is Kent Greenawalt's book, *Religious Convictions and Political Choice*. Greenawalt argues that "when people reasonably think that shared premises of justice and criteria for determining truth cannot resolve critical questions of fact, fundamental questions of value, or the weighing of competing benefits and harms, they do appropriately rely on religious convictions that help them answer these questions."[46] In a footnote, however, Rawls maintains that his ideal of public reason is consistent with Greenawalt's views, though Greenawalt thinks otherwise. Rawls may be right because, as he says, the requirements of public reason "are limited to our conduct in the public political forum and how we are to vote on constitutional essentials and questions of basic justice."[47] Some of Greenawalt's most convincing examples of cases in which reliance on religious convictions is appropriate do not concern constitutional essentials or matters of basic justice; these include issues concerning our treatment of nonhuman animals and problems in environmental ethics. To be sure, Greenawalt considers abortion to be a case in which reliance on religious convictions is appropriate, and Rawls is willing to assume that the question of abortion is either a constitutional essential or a matter of basic justice. But even if reliance on religious convictions is appropriate in answering for oneself the question of abortion, it does not follow immediately that reliance on such convictions is appropriate in determining one's conduct in the public political forum when the question of abortion is at issue or how one is to vote on that question. Besides, Greenawalt has recently told us that factors he discerns on the contemporary American religious and political scene "counsel some restraint about casting public political issues in terms of competing religious grounds."[48] Even if this is only a counsel of prudence and has nothing to do with moral duty or obligation, it leaves Greenawalt on the side of those who think it good that there should be some exclusion of the religious from our political life.

For my purposes, the most interesting contribution to this literature is the work of Michael J. Perry, and responses to it, starting with his book, *Love and Power*. In that book Perry proposed a model of ecumenical political dialogue that was meant to be inclusive of the religious. He describes it as "an ideal of religious (and nonreligious) participation in political dialogue—specifically, in the political dialogue of a religiously and morally pluralistic society."[49] Ecumenical political dialogue has existential prerequisites because, according to Perry, "a certain constellation of attitudes and virtues or habits of character

---

46   Kent Greenawalt, *Religious Convictions and Political Choice* (Oxford and New York: Oxford University Press, 1988), 12.

47   Rawls, *Liberalism*, 244.

48   Greenawalt, "Grounds," 675.

49   Michael J. Perry, *Love and Power: The Role of Religion and Morality in American Politics* (Oxford and New York: Oxford University Press, 1991), 141.

is prerequisite to fruitful participation in the practice of ecumenical political dialogue."[50] Two of them are fallibilism and pluralism. To be a fallibilist "is essentially to embrace the ideal of self-critical rationality."[51] In other words, fallibilists treat their own beliefs as questionable and revisable in the light of reason. To be a pluralist "is to understand that a morally pluralistic context, with its attendant variety of ways of life, can often be a more fertile source of deepening moral insight—in particular, a more fertile soil for dialogue leading to deepening moral insight—than can a monistic context."[52] In other words, pluralists attribute positive value to moral diversity because they consider it instructive. Many religious believers today are fallibilists and pluralists and so can participate fruitfully in ecumenical political dialogue.

But some religious believers even today regard fallibilism and pluralism as vices rather than virtues when they are extended to moral and religious matters. Even before Perry's book had been published, David M. Smolin, a law professor who identifies himself as an evangelical Christian, complained about the religious exclusiveness of the ideal of ecumenical political dialogue in correspondence with Perry. According to Smolin, Perry's prerequisites of fallibilism and pluralism have the effect of "excluding from dialogue a number of culturally significant religious communities in America, including various Christian groups (evangelicals, fundamentalists, pentecostals, traditionalist Roman Catholics) and theologically conservative representatives of other monotheist[ic] religions (Orthodox Jews, and certain Muslims)."[53] In the conclusion of the book, which contains a brief response to Smolin, Perry backed off a bit, suggesting that "perhaps fallibilism and pluralism are better understood, not as prerequisites *to* ecumenical political dialogue, but as attitudes or positions for which it is sometimes fitting to contend, depending on the particular question at issue, *in* ecumenical political dialogue."[54] This retreat indicates, I think, that Perry had grown uncomfortable with an ideal of the middle ground according to which some religious believers can participate happily in ecumenical political dialogue but others are or feel themselves to be excluded from participation.

There is, however, another chapter in the story of the development of Perry's views on this topic. Pressing his case in print, Smolin wrote that "Perry has used his own vision of good religion as the standard for admission to political and legal debate."[55] After expressing agreement with Smolin on

---

50 Ibid., 99.

51 Ibid., 100.

52 Ibid.

53 Ibid., 139, quoting a letter from David M. Smolin to Michael J. Perry.

54 Ibid., 140.

55 David M. Smolin, "Regulating Religious and Cultural Conflict in Postmodern America: A Response to Professor Perry," *Iowa Law Review* 76 (1992): 1076–77.

several points, Sanford Levinson, who is not an evangelical Christian, set forth his own criticism of the limited tolerance of Perry's ecumenical politics, arguing that "Perry seems to impose his own version of 'epistemic abstinence' on those religions that are less modernist (and politically liberal) than his own."[56] Levinson went on to ask whether the search for criteria that would exclude certain types of discourse from the public square is misguided. His question is this: "Why doesn't liberal democracy give everyone an equal right, without engaging in any version of epistemic abstinence, to make his or her arguments, subject, obviously, to the prerogative of listeners to reject the arguments should they be unpersuasive (which will be the case, almost by definition, with arguments that are not widely accessible or are otherwise marginal)?"[57] Second thoughts have prompted Perry to give an answer to this question that is worth quoting in detail:

> I now see that we Americans should not accept any exclusivist ideal, either of public political argument or of political choice—not even any "middle ground" ideal. Instead we should accept the inclusivist ideal, according to which neither any controversial moral belief nor supporting belief—including (and this is what I want to emphasize here) any support-ing religious belief—is excluded. This includes any supporting religious belief. There is no good reason to accept any middle ground exclusivist ideal. In particular, there is no good reason to exclude religious beliefs— religious beliefs that, in the view of those who embrace them, support controversial moral beliefs—as a basis for political choice *even when no other basis is available*.[58]

And, to lay my own cards on the table, I think Perry, who is a liberal Roman Catholic, has here come close to the position it would be best for all contem-porary American liberals to endorse.

Two sets of considerations make Perry's inclusivist ideal more attractive to me, all things considered, than the ideal of public reason proposed by Rawls or its close kin.[59] One I share with Robert M. Adams; the other I share with Jeremy Waldron. I shall sketch both briefly.

---

56   Sanford Levinson, "Religious Language and the Public Square," *Harvard Law Review* 105 (1992): 2075.

57   Ibid., 2077.

58   Perry, "Religious Morality," 713. The restriction to "we Americans" is important. There would clearly be at least prudential or strategic reasons for some exclu-sions if the introduction of religious beliefs into public political argument without limits were to produce or exacerbate destructive social conflict on a large scale. But I judge that such conflict is unlikely here and now.

59   For example, the one proposed in Lawrence B. Solum, "Constructing an Ideal of Public Reason," *San Diego Law Review* 30 (1993): 729–62. As I understand it, the ideal Solum endorses does not completely exclude nonpublic reasons. But it

Adams points out that "nothing in the history of modern secular ethical theory gives reason to expect that general agreement on a single comprehensive ethical theory will ever be achieved—or that, if achieved, it would long endure in a climate of free inquiry."[60] Though the substantive principles of justice of liberal political conceptions are not comprehensive, they are, when stated with precision, theoretical. For example, they go well beyond what might be regarded as the shared common sense of Americans to make distinctively liberal claims about justice that not all reasonable American citizens share or are likely to come to share. By parity of reasoning, then, nothing in the history of modern secular political theory should lead us to expect that an overlapping consensus on a single liberal political conception of justice, or a small family of such conceptions, will ever be achieved or would long endure in a pluralistic democracy if achieved. Because the chances of agreement in ethical theory are so slim, Adams concludes that "the development and advocacy of a religious ethical theory, therefore, does not destroy a realistic possibility of agreement that would otherwise exist."[61] Similarly, on my view, allowing nonpublic reasons, whether religious or secular, into political debate about restrictive laws or policies or about matters of constitutional essentials or basic justice is unlikely, here and now, to destroy a realistic possibility of agreement that would otherwise exist. So I am skeptical about there being any assured real (as opposed to merely possible) costs associated with being guided by Perry's inclusivist ideal rather than the Rawlsian ideal of public reason. And if there are none, the inclusivist ideal is more attractive than its rival because, being less restrictive, it allows all citizens to express themselves and their deepest values more fully in the political sphere and is apt to mitigate the problem of alienation from the political. Adams suggests that "Rawls underemphasizes the combative aspects of a democratic polity and tends to overestimate the level of theoretical agreement in political ethics needed for an attainably just society."[62] I concur. Of course we let ourselves in for some-

---

"implies that nonpublic reasons could only be given in two circumstances: (1) if the nonpublic reason were the foundation for a public reason, and (2) if the nonpublic reason were an additional sufficient justification for a policy that would be given an independent and sufficient justification by a public reason" (p. 748). These conditions restrict the use of religious reasons in much the same way that Audi's principle of secular rationale does, though they also restrict the use of nonpublic secular reasons in a way that Audi's principle does not. They also insure that Solum's ideal is less inclusive than Perry's ideal. Solum also argues for these restrictive conditions in "Inclusive Public Reason," *Pacific Philosophical Quarterly* 75 (1994): 217–31.

60   Robert M. Adams, "Religious Ethics in a Pluralistic Society," *Prospects for a Common Morality*, ed. Gene Outka and John P. Reeder, Jr. (Princeton, N.J.: Princeton University Press, 1993), 97.

61   Ibid., 91.

thing more like debate than like dialogue on many issues if we adopt the inclusivist ideal, but I consider that no bad thing when there is disagreement in a pluralistic democracy.

There are benefits to be gained from adopting an inclusivist ideal of public political discourse that permits more than argument from shared premises by shared modes of reasoning. For one thing, it is open to the possibility that agreement may emerge from political discourse that does not presuppose it. As Jeremy Waldron points out, "moves may be made in political argument that bear no relation to existing conventions or commonly held opinions, but which nevertheless gain a foothold as soon as they are considered and discussed by persons with open minds."[63] Even if this does not occur, there is the possibility that one's own view may be improved in its subtlety and depth by contact and confrontation with an alien religion or metaphysics that one is initially inclined to reject. In this connection, Waldron says:

> I mean to draw attention to an experience we all have had at one time or another, of having argued with someone whose world view was quite at odds with our own, and of having come away thinking, "I'm sure he's wrong, and I can't follow much of it, but, still, it makes you think. . ." The prospect of losing that sort of effect in public discourse is, frankly, frightening—terrifying, even, if we are to imagine it being replaced by a form of "deliberation" that, in the name of "fairness" or "reasonableness" (or worse still, "balance") consists of bland appeals to harmless nostrums that are accepted without question on all sides. That is to imagine open-ended public debate reduced to the formal trivia of American television networks.[64]

Even if one considers Waldron's portrait of the imagined replacement tinged with rhetorical excess or finds it merely depressing, rather than terrifying, one can appreciate the loss of value to which he is pointing.

Commitment to Perry's inclusivist ideal, as stated above, probably needs to be qualified in one way. Liberals typically subscribe to norms of respect for fellow citizens as free and equal persons. So a narrowly drawn moral but not legal restriction on contributions to public political discourse that express disrespect, such as certain forms of hate speech, or that assert or imply a lack of equality of groups of citizens, such as racist and anti-Semitic speech, is certainly in the spirit of liberalism and may be required to capture its limits of moral toleration.[65] History teaches that religion has not, to put it mildly, been

---

62   Ibid., 112.

63   Jeremy Waldron, "Religious Contributions in Public Deliberation," *San Diego Law Review* 30 (1993): 838.

64   Ibid., 842.

65   Perry, of course, knows that giving reasons of certain sorts is a failure to show

altogether free of lack of respect for others as free and equal persons.[66] So in the end liberalism will probably have to practice a minimal exclusion of the religious. If it does so, then in the interests of fairness the many secular doctrines that are committed to such lack of respect will also have to be excluded. Spelling out the details of such a restriction in such a way that it could survive testing against examples would, of course, be a large task. And the claim that the restriction should be moral but not legal would have to be defended against the arguments of those nonliberals who are prepared to support legal prohibitions of such forms of speech. I do not on this occasion have time or space even to begin these projects of explication and defense.

There are, then, political liberalisms that advocate extensive exclusions of the religious from the public forum, but there are also political liberalisms that put forward a more inclusive ideal. Being both a liberal and a religious believer myself, I naturally favor liberalisms of the latter sort. I think religious believers who are now American citizens should not acknowledge prima facie obligations to be sufficiently motivated by or even to have and be willing to offer adequate secular reasons for advocating or supporting restrictive laws or policies. Nor should they affirm a duty of civility according to which they may not appeal to their comprehensive religious doctrines to justify answers to questions about constitutional essentials or basic justice unless they satisfy some restrictive proviso. And they should not think that political liberalism is the exclusive possession of secular forces opposed to religion, even if they cannot help being aware that plenty of liberals are in fact hostile to religion.

As I see it, among religious people only liberals will even be tempted to acknowledge such obligations or to affirm such a duty of civility. Religious conservatives, particularly those who belong to the so-called Religious Right in the United States, will predictably decline to acknowledge or affirm such things. If religious liberals were to give in to the temptation, political debate in the public square in the United States would continue to be polarized between secular liberals and religious conservatives. Secular liberals would have an excuse for thinking in terms of the stereotype according to which all religious people are illiberal, and religious conservatives would have an excuse for thinking in terms of the stereotype according to which all liberals are secularists. But if religious liberals were to resist the temptation, they

---

equal respect. On p. 711 of "Religious Morality" he cites the example of a Nazi offering a Jew as a reason for acting as the Nazi does his sincere belief that the Jew has an inferior nature and credits Charles Larmore with having brought the point to his attention. But this knowledge did not prompt him to qualify the statement of the inclusivist ideal I have quoted.

66   Closest to home, in my own case, are the many shameful episodes in the history of Christianity in which Christians have failed to show respect, most notably to Jews. It is no consolation that secular ideologues such as the Nazis have done worse.

would have a way to challenge this polarization. They would be in a position to argue for liberal laws and policies from religious premises and thereby show secular liberals that some religious people are their allies, and they would also be in a position to dispute the political agenda of the Religious Right on religious grounds. I am convinced that such a challenge would be good for the health of the American body politic.

According to an attractive ideal of good citizenship, being a good citizen of a political community involves having some allegiance to the values that are most deeply embedded in it. I, for instance, think the Establishment Clause of the First Amendment to the Constitution of the United States expresses one of the deepest values of the political community to which we belong, and so I am prepared to acknowledge that peacefully advocating repeal of the Establishment Clause in order to clear the way for making Christianity the official religion of the United States would represent a failure to live up to that ideal. But I do not think American citizens have a prima facie moral obligation to refrain from peacefully advocating the repeal of the Establishment Clause. Hence I do not concede that American citizens have a prima facie moral duty to live up to the ideal in question. Though I endorse this ideal, I also believe that living up to it is supererogatory. The ideal imposes no moral requirements on American citizens, and one is not a bad citizen if one fails to live up to it. However one is a better citizen if one lives up to it than if one does not, and so I would want to encourage religious citizens to refrain from advocating repeal of the Establishment Clause or trying to make the United States into a "Christian nation," whatever that might mean. And I would make similar claims about other, less dramatic cases in which it is morally permissible but less than ideal for citizens to introduce their religious concerns into politics.

If we look away from the debates about liberal theory in the academy, we will notice that, in the rough and tumble of American politics, liberalism has recently suffered serious reverses. If they are to overcome these setbacks, liberals need new allies. They might find some in America's religious communities if their ideals were more inclusive. Thus it may be important for the future of American liberalism that something like the inclusivist ideal should prevail in the practice, even if it remains disputed in the theory, of liberalism for our time and place. I hope it will prevail.[67]

67   I owe thanks to many people for help at various stages in the preparation of this Address. For suggesting or giving to me things to read, I am grateful to Michael Byron, Thomas D'Andrea, Jean Hampton, Alasdair MacIntyre, Suzanne Marilley, Michael Perry, John Robinson, and Paul Weithman. For comments on a draft, I am indebted to Robert Audi, C. F. Delaney, Martin Golding, Jeff Jordan, J. B. Kennedy, Janet Kourany, Richard Kraut, Stephanie Lewis, Alasdair MacIntyre, Suzanne Marilley, Kevin Meeker, Mary Mothersill, Martha Nussbaum, David O'Connor, John Rawls, Hans Reinders, Robert Rodes, Jr., Richard Rorty, Nevan Sesardic, Eleonore Stump, Paul Weithman, and several members of an audience at Notre Dame. Responding adequately to all the points raised by the

people who gave me comments would involve expanding the address to such an extent that the Editor of the APA *Proceedings* might well balk at publishing it. So I have set aside for use on other occasions the comments that suggest, quite correctly, that much more needs to be said on certain topics I treat briefly in the Address.

Why We Should Reject What Liberalism Tells Us about Speaking and Acting in Public for Religious Reasons

Nicholas Wolterstorff

§1. Psalm 72 in the Hebrew Bible and the Christian Old Testament opens as follows:

> Give the king your justice, O God,
>   and your righteousness to a king's son.
> May he judge your people with righteousness,
>   and your poor with justice.
> May the mountains yield prosperity for the people,
>   and the hills, in righteousness.
> May he defend the cause of the poor of the people,
>   give deliverance to the needy,
>   and crush the oppressor.

My own reflections on the moral and political significance of poverty have been decisively shaped by this and similar passages in the psalms, the prophets, and the gospels—all of which I accept as canonical scripture. I interpret what I read in these passages, about justice to the widows, the orphans, the aliens, and the poor, as implying that involuntary avoidable poverty is a violation of *rights*. Not, as such, a failure of charity on the part of the well-to-do—though such failure may well be involved. A violation of the rights of the poor, *qua* poor. What comes through, to my interpreting ear, is that to be a human being is to bear the unconditional natural right to fair and non-degrading access to the means of livelihood.

So far forth, this says nothing about the state. So let me add that in our society I see no option but for the state to function as the last-resort guarantor of this right. In other times and places it was different: The king was the last-resort guarantor, or the bishop. Should the state in our society not function as the last-resort guarantor of fair and non-degrading access to the means of livelihood, it is failing in its duty to secure justice.

My question in this paper is how I ought to espouse this religiously based view in public, and how I ought to act on it in the political domain, when so many of my fellow citizens accept neither the Christian nor the Hebrew Bible as canonical, and when so many of those who do accept these writings as canonical regard it as quaint and dangerous on my part to treat what they say about the moral and political significance of poverty as relevant to contemporary politics. You will understand, of course, that I am taking this particular

162

case as an example of the general point: How should citizens espouse their religiously-based political views in the public space and act thereon?

The question arises for me because so many of my fellow citizens do not agree that the poor *qua* poor have rights. They believe that the poor *qua* poor are candidates for charity, not holders of rights. And they believe that the failure of the state to act as last-resort guarantor of fair and non-degrading access to the means of livelihood is not a failure on its part to secure justice, but a responsible refusal on its part to act as a charitable organization. If my views on these matters were universally shared by my fellow citizens, we would still have to discuss the difficult question of how best to secure the rights of the poor *qua* poor. But we wouldn't have to debate the moral and political significance of poverty. The only question in the region would be, how best to transmit our consensus to our children.

Of course, disagreement with my views on the moral and political signifi-cance of poverty is not only to be found among those of my fellow citizens who do not accept the Christian or Hebrew scriptures as canonical. It is also to be found among my fellow Christians. So there's work facing me on *two* fronts. Not only do I have to consider how to conduct my public, inter-com-munity, discourse, but also how to conduct my intra-community discourse.

Within my own community, I will talk about the status of scripture, and about principles of scriptural interpretation, and about the exegesis of specific passages. Then I will move on to the Christian tradition, where I will highlight a large number of ringing passages about the rights of the poor *qua* poor. I will observe that the tradition was still alive in John Locke—where I, at least, would have expected it to be dead. (See his *Second Treatise*, §135).[1] Along the way I will bring some live poor people into the room—so that their faces can be seen and their voices heard. Talk and argument about such matters, in the absence of faces and voices, is a frail reed. I'm sure I wouldn't succeed in persuading all of my fellow believers. But I think I would get some to come along—since many of them have formed their views in oblivion of scripture and tradition rather than on the basis thereof, while yet officially acknowledging their relevance.

§2. The most pervasive and influential answer to my question to be found on the American scene is that offered by political liberalism. I think that answer is mistaken. But given its popularity, it's with an analysis and appraisal of the liberal answer that we must begin.

Unfortunately, anyone who chooses to talk about liberalism faces the

---

1   I have done some of this intra-community argumentation in my essay, "Has the Cloak Become a Cage? Charity, Justice, and Economic Activity" in Robert Wuthnow, ed., *Rethinking Materialism: Perspectives on the Spiritual Dimension of Economic Behavior* (Grand Rapids, Mich.: Eerdmans Publishing Co., 1995), 145–68.

necessity of saying what is that about which he has chosen to talk. A shared understanding cannot be presupposed.

At the core of liberalism, as I shall be taking it, is a certain understanding of society and its members. The liberal regards the normal adult members of society as free and equal in the following way: *equally free* in that each has it in his or her power to act as moral agent; *equal* in that each has the inherent right, subject to appropriate qualifications, to pursue what he or she regards as good and obligatory; and *equal* also in that none bears a right by 'nature' which the others do not also bear.

With this understanding in hand, the liberal then focuses his attention on the political dimension of society. Here two strands of thought can be identified. In the first place, the liberal tries to formulate a general criterion of political justice for a society whose members understand themselves as thus free and equal—he tries to formulate, in Rawls' phrase, "a political conception of justice" for such a society. I speak, in this indefinite way, of the liberal as "trying to formulate a general criterion" for political justice, because, when it actually comes to the criterion offered, one finds considerable diversity among liberals. Classical liberals, such as John Locke, focused entirely on the rights of individuals in formulating their criterion of political justice. And as to the rights of individuals, they focused almost entirely on their *negative* rights— that is, on their right to freedom from interference in the pursuit of such goals, and the application of such principles, as they have chosen for themselves. But if we grant to John Rawls his wish to be regarded as a liberal, then we must regard classical liberalism as but one of many liberal options. For though Rawls also thinks entirely in terms of the rights of individuals, he most certainly does not hold that the formulation of a political conception of justice, for a society which regards its normal adult members as free and equal, can confine itself to the specification of negative rights. *Fairness* is what he regards as the appropriate principle.

I will be arguing that liberalism is unfair to at least certain kinds of religion. But before I get to that, let me put in a plea for fairness to liberalism. Many of the accusations which in recent years have been lobbed at liberalism are unfair. It is charged that liberalism denies the existence of moral agents other than individuals. That's unfair. Liberalism does not deny the existence of non-individual moral agents; it simply doesn't pay any attention to them in its theory. Ignoring is not denying. It is charged that liberalism denies that agents other than individuals have rights. That's also unfair. Liberalism does not deny the rights of entities other than human individuals; rather, in its theory it pays them no attention. It is charged that liberalism denies all but negative rights. That's unfair. It's true that in its formulation of a political conception of justice, classical liberalism makes reference to no other rights than these; but it doesn't deny that there are others. And even that is not true for liberalisms such as Rawls'. It is charged that liberalism denies the existence of responsibilities and regards morality as consisting entirely of rights. That too is unfair. It's true that liberalism formulates its political conception of justice entirely in terms of rights; but that's fully compatible with holding that the moral life as a whole incorporates responsibilities along with rights. Indeed, any position other than that would be incoherent. It is charged that liberalism is "based on an atomistic, abstract, and ultimately incoherent concept of the self as the subject of rights."[2] Again, unfair. Liberalism says that the normal adult members of society are free and equal; it's entirely consistent with that to be as social and concrete in one's understanding of the self as one wishes. I don't doubt that liberalism encourages a *mentality* against which several of the above charges stick. But that, then, is the thing to say; not that to be a liberal just is to hold all these nasty positions. Let's be fair to liberalism!

I mentioned that two strands of thought can be identified in what the liberal says about the political dimension of society. Having identified the first, let me now move on to the second. Liberalism was born in the situation of a single society containing a diversity of religions, and was motivated by the conviction that there had to be a new and better way of relating the political dimension of society to that diversity than was then extant. The policy which liberalism advocated is regularly described as political toleration, or political neutrality. That's not an incorrect description. But it's important, for my purposes, to be a good deal more precise than that. Let me distinguish two aspects of the toleration, or neutrality, that the liberal advocates.

In the first place, definitive of liberalism, as I shall be taking it, is a certain view as to how government and its agents ought to treat the various religions to be found in society—when that society regards its normal adult members as free and equal. Call it the *separation* view. It would be possible to hold that government and its agents ought to treat all religions *impartially*. But that's not the liberal position. The liberal position is rather that government is to do nothing to advance or hinder any religion. The difference between the two positions can most easily be seen by taking note of the difference in result on the issue of state aid to schools. The impartiality position says that if the state aids any school, it must aid all schools, and aid them all equitably—no matter what their religious orientation. The separation position says that the state is to aid no school whose orientation is religious. The First Amendment in the United States Bill of Rights specifies that the government shall neither establish any religion nor infringe on the free exercise of any. That formulation is ambiguous as between the impartiality and the separation positions. Nonetheless, the U.S. Supreme Court, in its decisions over the past fifty years, has consistently interpreted the amendment as an affirmation of the separation position. It has ruled as if Jefferson's *wall of separation* metaphor had been incorporated into the constitution.[3]

---

2   Jean Cohen and Andrew Arato, *Civil Society and Political Theory* (Cambridge, Mass.: MIT Press, 1992), 9.

It is also definitive of liberalism, as I shall be taking it, to embrace a certain view as to the proper basis of public political debate, and of political decision making, in a society which incorporates a diversity of religions—when that society regards its normal adult members as free and equal. The view is that those members are neither to base their political debate in the public space, nor their political decisions, on their own particular religious convictions, nor on such religious convictions as they might all share. When it comes to such activities, they are to allow their religious convictions to idle. They are to base their political debate in the public space, and their political decisions, on the principles yielded by some source *independent of* any and all of the religious perspectives to be found in the society. To this, the liberal adds one important addendum: The source must be such that it is *fair* to insist that everybody base his or her public political discourse, and political decisions, on the principles yielded by that source. This addendum eliminates what would otherwise be obvious candidates for the political basis. A good many of the nationalisms of the contemporary world are rich and thick enough to serve as the basis of the political debates and decisions of the members of a society; in addition, they are often relatively independent of the religions to be found in the society. But rarely if ever will it be fair to insist that the life of the polity be based on some nationalism; for it never happens anymore that all the citizens of a single polity belong to the same nation, the same 'people.'

In this paper I will have nothing further to say about liberalism's under-standing of the normal adult members of society as free and equal. Neither will I have anything further to say about the first of the two major strands which I identified within liberalism, namely, liberalism's attempt to formulate a criterion of political justice appropriate for a society which thus understands its normal adult members. I will focus entirely on the second strand. And of the two elements in that strand, liberalism's embrace of the *separation* position with respect to governmental action, and liberalism's embrace of the *independent-basis* position with respect to political debates and decisions, I will speak mostly about the second. For the sake of convenience, I shall call the second strand as a whole, with its two components, the *neutrality* postulate.

§3. Why does liberalism affirm the independent-basis position? That is, why does the liberal insist that, in a society which regards its normal adult members as free and equal, political debate in the public space be conducted on the basis of principles yielded by some source independent of all the religions in society, and why does he insist that political decisions be made on the basis of such independent principles?

An obvious question to ask at the outset is, what are we to understand as

---

3   An exception to this generalization is the recent *Virginia v. Rosenberger* decision. It remains to be seen whether this represents a change of direction.

the scope of "political"? It's open to the liberal to carve out, within the sphere of what is ordinarily and loosely called "political," a sphere of the *truly political*, or of the *politically fundamental*—call it what you will—and to specify that he means his thesis to apply only to that inner sphere. Rawls does that; citizens in public are to appeal to the independent basis when dealing with matters of constitutional essentials and basic justice. But nothing that I have to say will depend on reaching precision on this point. And in any case, the dynamics of liberalism lead to a very expansive view on the matter. Rawls' willingness to limit the scope of his normative thesis to matters of constitutional essentials and basic justice is grounded on his conviction that though in principle *all* political debates in the public space, and all political decisions, ought to be conducted in accord with the thesis, it's much less *important* that we do so when we move beyond constitutional essentials and matters of basic justice. (The difficult but unavoidable question of what constitutes *public* space is also one which I cannot treat on this occasion.)

My question, once again, is why the liberal embraces the independent-basis position. What are his reasons? One reason which liberals have offered ever since the emergence of liberalism in the seventeenth century is that it's just too dangerous to let religious people debate political issues outside their own confessional circles, and to act politically, on the basis of their religious views. The only way to forestall religious wars is to get people to stop invoking God and to stop invoking canonical scriptures when arguing and determining politics—unless perchance the independent basis should yield various propositions about God, and should yield the conclusion that some canonical scripture is reliable on certain matters.

I must confess my inability to see any cogency in this reasoning. I think that if I had been living in the seventeenth century, I would have found it cogent. But I live in the twentieth century. And so far as I can see, the slaughter, torture, and generalized brutality of our century has mainly been conducted in the name of one and another secularism: nationalisms of many sorts, communism, fascism, patriotisms of various sorts, economic hegemony. The common denominator is that human beings tend to kill and brutalize each other for what they care deeply about. In seventeenth-century Europe, human beings cared deeply about religion. In our century, most seem to have cared much more deeply about one and another secular cause. Liberalism's myopic preoccupation with religious wars is outdated.

The other side of the matter is also worth mentioning: Many of the movements in the modern world which have resulted in reforms and revolutions that the liberal admires have been deeply religious in their orientation: the abolitionist movement in nineteenth-century America, the civil rights movement in twentieth-century America, the resistance movements in fascist Germany, in communist Eastern Europe, and in apartheid South Africa. These movements are regularly analyzed by Western academics and intellectuals as if religion were nowhere in the picture.[4] The assumption, presumably, is that religion plays no explanatory role in human affairs; it's only an epipheno-menon. Thus does ideology shape scholarship! The truth is that even the *free and equal* doctrine, which lies at the very heart of liberalism, had religious roots—in Protestant dissent of the seventeenth century.[5]

However, thinkers in the liberal tradition have offered other and more substantial arguments for the independent-basis position than the argument that the offering of religious reasons in political debate is dangerous. Let me look briefly at Locke's main argument; and then, somewhat more expansively, at Rawls'.

§4. Locke's argumentation was epistemological—part and parcel of his general epistemology.[6] Though Locke had a good deal to say about awareness, or "perception," as he called it, this being what he identified as knowledge, the focus of his epistemology as a whole was on *belief*, and more specifically, on *entitlement* to believe. Doing what we ought to do, by way of the formation and maintenance of our beliefs, was what he mainly had his eye on. Belief is more important than knowledge, Locke says, because there's much more of it: Knowledge is short and scanty. And entitlement in beliefs is important because in many situations we are obligated to do better, by way of gaining true beliefs and eliminating false ones, than we would be doing if we just allowed beliefs to be formed in us haphazardly.

Accordingly, Locke set out to formulate a criterion for entitlement in beliefs. Not a *general* criterion for entitlement, however. Though much of Locke's rhetoric is universalistic, a number of passages, both in the *Essay concerning Human Understanding* and in the *Conduct of the Understanding*, make clear that Locke had no interest whatsoever in offering a criterion of entitlement appli-cable to all beliefs. He was concerned exclusively with situations of maximal concernment—"concernment" being his word. That is, he was concerned exclusively with situations in which one is obligated to do *the best* to find out the truth of the matter, and to believe in accord with the results of one's endeavor. His strategy was to articulate a practice of inquiry whose employ-ment constitutes, in his judgment, doing the best. It follows that, on matters of maximal concernment, one is entitled to one's belief (or non-belief) if and

---

4   See, for example, Chapter 1 of Cohen and Arato, *Civil Society and Political Theory*, which talks as if there were no churches in Eastern Europe at the time of the overthrow of communism!

5   A recent discussion of this point is David Richards, "Public Reason and Aboli-tionist Dissent," *Chicago-Kent Law Review* 69 (1994): 787–842. The irony, of course, is that a doctrine born out of religion should be turned by Rawls and cohorts against that which gave it birth!

6   The matters which follow are discussed much more amply in my recent *John Locke and the Ethics of Belief* (Cambridge: Cambridge University Press, 1996).

only if one has employed the optimal practice, and one believes or refrains from believing in a manner appropriate to the results of the employment.

Locke sometimes describes this supposedly optimal practice as "listening to the voice of Reason." At other times he describes it as "getting to the things themselves." The point of the latter formulation is that, by employing the practice, one gets to the things themselves *instead of resting content with what people tell one about the things.* One circumvents tradition.

The essential elements of the practice are easily described. We can think of it as having three stages. With some proposition in mind concerning the matter in question, one first collects evidence concerning the truth or falsehood of the proposition, this evidence to consist of a non-skewed and sufficiently ample set of beliefs which are certain for one because their propositional content corresponds directly to facts of which one is (or was) aware. Secondly, by the exercise of one's reason one determines the probability of the proposition on that evidence. And lastly, one adopts a level of confidence in the proposition corresponding to its probability on that evidence. To employ this practice, says Locke, is to do the best.

Whether or not a matter is of maximal concernment to a person is a function of the whole contour of that person's obligations—with the consequence that which matters are matters of maximal concernment varies from person to person. Locke insisted on an extremely important limitation on this principle of variation, however. Matters of religion and morality are of maximal concernment to everybody. Accordingly, everybody is under obligation to employ the optimal practice on such matters.

Locke himself believed that by employing the practice we could arrive at a substantial set of beliefs about God; he furthermore believed that by employing the practice we could establish the reliability of the New Testament. Thus Locke was definitely not a proponent of secularism. His thought, rather, was that when it comes to forming beliefs on matters of religion and morality, it is our obligation, instead of appealing to the moral and religious traditions into which we have been inducted, to appeal to the deliverances of our generic human nature—to the yield of our human "hard wiring."

It just follows that when debating political matters, we are not entitled to appeal to our own particular religious tradition. It would be wrong to do so. It would be wrong to do so whether or not the matter was political. That's not to say that everything we have come to believe, by virtue of being inducted into some religious and ethical tradition, is off-limits in political debate. If, by employing that generically human, optimal, practice, one succeeds in arriving at some of the content of one's tradition, then one is entitled to appeal to that content in one's political debates. But one is then entitled to do so only because it's part of the yield of that generically human practice. Though religion is not necessarily excluded from the debate, everything other than *rational* religion most definitely is.

This Lockean defense of the independent-basis principle of liberalism was enormously influential in the centuries between him and us. Today, however, almost nobody accepts it—at least, almost nobody in academia. The defense rests directly on the epistemology of classically modern foundationalism. "We hold these truths to be self-evident." Constitutional assemblies making epistemological pronouncements! The intertwinement of traditional liberalism with classical foundationalism is there for all to see. But almost everybody today rejects classically modern foundationalism. I do so as well. With that rejection, the traditional defense of the independent-basis principle is rendered null and void.

No point in beating the dead horse—not on this occasion, anyway. Let me rather close our discussion of Locke by remarking that as long as the Lockean practice was widely thought to yield a substantial rational religion, along with rational evidence for the reliability of the Christian scriptures, American religious leaders were relatively content with liberalism. That was the situation throughout the nineteenth century. It was when skepticism on those scores began to spread—impelled especially, in my judgment, by the emergence of Darwinian evolutionary theory and the rise of biblical criticism—that tensions began to mount between religion and political liberalism.

§5. In his recent book, *Political Liberalism*,[7] John Rawls tacitly concedes the untenability of Locke's way of defending the independent-basis principle of liberalism. For he concedes the existence in our society of a plurality of significantly different religions with adherents who are *entitled* to their adherence. The test of entitlement does not pick out one from the diversity; nor can it serve as guide for newly devising a "rational" religion, or some "rational" secular perspective, which will then be the sole entitled member of the mix. "The political culture of a democratic society," he says, "is always marked by a diversity of opposing and irreconcilable religious, philosophical, and moral doctrines. Some of these are perfectly reasonable, and this diversity among reasonable doctrines political liberalism sees as the inevitable long-run result of the powers of human reason at work within the background of enduring free institutions" (3–4). It must be conceded that Rawls' *reasonableness* is not identical with what I mean by "entitlement." But in the course of his discussion it becomes clear, so I judge, that if "reasonable" in the above passage is interpreted as *entitled*, Rawls would happily affirm what would then be said.

How, then, does Rawls defend the independent-basis principle of liberalism? Locke held it to be a truth of the matter about normal adult human beings that they are free and equal. Though I did not explicate this part of his thought in my discussion above, Locke offered arguments for this position. He thought that societies which did not regard their normal adult members thus were

---

7   New York: Columbia University Press, 1993.

mistaken—deeply mistaken. Rawls shies away from all such ontological claims. In their stead, he employs a *consensus populi* strategy.

In the contemporary world there are societies which regard their normal adult members as free and equal. Rawls thinks American society is such a society; he holds, so far as I can tell, that all constitutional democracies are such societies. So consider such societies. And attend then to the shared political culture of such societies; attend to the "political mind," as one might call it, of such societies. Identify the fundamental organizing ideas in those political minds. And then "elaborate" or "unfold" (27) those ideas into principles of justice capable of serving as the basis of deliberations and determinations concerning matters of constitutional essentials and basic justice. Of course the identification of those ideas, and the elaboration of those ideas into principles of justice, must not be whimsical or arbitrary. The principles one arrives at must be ones that one can reasonably expect all citizens of such societies to endorse *who use the light of our common human reason*. The principles must "win [their] support by addressing each citizen's reason" (143).

The principles of justice thus arrived at will be "freestanding" (10) with respect to all the comprehensive perspectives present in society. For they will not have been derived from any one of those perspectives, nor from any overlapping consensus among those perspectives. They will have been de-rived instead from the shared political culture of the society. However, if the society is to be at all stable and enduring, the comprehensive perspectives present within the society—or at least the reasonable ones among them—must each find the principles of justice acceptable from its own standpoint. Citizens must "within their comprehensive doctrines regard the political conception of justice as true, or as reasonable, whatever their view allows" (151). This is necessary if the society is to be stable and enduring and no one position is to enjoy a hegemony which stifles opposition by coercion or persuasion. But the source of the principles is to be independent of one and all comprehensive doctrines. The principles are to be *arrived at*—to repeat—by rational reflection on the political culture of constitutional democracies.

It is principles of justice thus arrived at that are to serve as the basis of political debate in the public space, and political decisions—at least on matters of constitutional essentials and basic justice. The "question the dominant tradition has tried to answer has no answer," says Rawls; "no comprehensive doctrine is appropriate as a political conception" (135). Not at least for demo-cratic societies with constitutional regimes. In such a society, no one of the reasonable comprehensive doctrines can "secure the basis of social unity, nor can it provide the content of public reason on fundamental political questions" (134). One of the great merits of Rawls' discussion is that, under "comprehen-sive doctrines," he includes not only religions but comprehensive philoso-phies. No comprehensive vision—be it religious or not, be it of God and the good, or only of the good—no comprehensive vision can properly serve as the basis of public reason on fundamental political questions.

Rawls acknowledges that liberalism may well seem paradoxical at this point. Speaking on behalf of the objector, he asks:

> why should citizens in discussing and voting on the most fundamental political questions honor the limits of public reason? How can it be either reasonable or rational, when basic matters are at stake, for citizens to appeal only to a public conception of justice and not to the whole truth as they see it? Surely, the most fundamental questions should be settled by appealing to the most important truths, yet these may far transcend public reason! (216)

His answer is that it would be inconsistent with the society's understanding of its adult members as free and equal for the members to conduct their fundamental political debates and make their fundamental political decisions on any basis other than that of the consensus populi. Democracy, he says,

> implies . . . an equal share in the coercive political power that citizens exercise over one another by voting and in other ways. As reasonable and rational, and knowing that they affirm a diversity of reasonable religious and philosophical doctrines, they should be ready to explain the basis of their actions to one another in terms each could reasonably expect that others might endorse as consistent with their freedom and equality. Trying to meet this condition is one of the tests that this ideal of democratic politics asks of us. Understanding how to conduct oneself as a democratic citizen includes understanding an ideal of public reason (217–18).[8]

§6. What Rawls tells me is that if I step outside my own religious community and enter the public debate about the treatment of the poor in our society, I must at no point appeal to my religious convictions. In my debates with others I must not cite them as reasons; in my political actions—in my voting, for example—I must not employ them as reasons. I must base my discourse and actions on the consensus populi—more precisely, on the results of analyzing the core ideas in the political consensus populi of constitutional democracies

---

8   Cf. Ibid., 217: "when may citizens by their vote properly exercise their coercive political power over one another when fundamental questions are at stake? Or in the light of what principles and ideals must we exercise that power if our doing so is to be justifiable to others as free and equal? To this question political liberalism replies: our exercise of political power is proper and hence justifiable only when it is exercised in accordance with a constitution the essentials of which all citizens may reasonably be expected to endorse in the light of principles and ideals acceptable to them as reasonable and rational. This is the liberal principle of legitimacy. And since the exercise of political power itself must be legitimate, the ideal of citizenship imposes a moral, not a legal, duty—the duty of civility— to be able to explain to one another on those fundamental questions how the principles and policies they advocate and vote for can be supported by the political values of public reason."

and elaborating those ideas into principles of justice—both the analysis and the elaboration having been conducted in such a way that one can reasonably expect all who use their common human reason to accept the principles of justice that emerge. When the coercive power of the state is involved, as ultimately it always is when political issues are under consideration, I would violate the equal freedom of my fellow citizens if I did not debate and act on the basis of reasons which I can reasonably expect at least the reasonable and rational among them to accept. And to fail to treat them as free and equal is out of accord with the consensus populi of the constitutional democracy of which I am a citizen.

May it be that I have interpreted Rawls more sternly than he intends? He does say, after all, that "the ideal of citizenship imposes a moral . . . duty . . . *to be able to explain* to one another on those fundamental political questions how the principles and policies they advocate and vote for can be supported by the political values of public reason" (219, my italics).[9] The ideal imposes a duty *to be able* to explain, not *to explain*. Possibly this is what Rawls has in mind. It's a position which has some plausibility with respect to one's own deliberations and decisions; it has none whatsoever, though, when it comes to the offering of reasons in public. Suppose that the reasons I offer in the public square for the policies I favor and the actions I take are ones that it would be unreasonable of me to expect all my reasonable fellow citizens to accept—parochial religious reasons. There are consensus populi reasons which I am *able to offer* to the same end—in some sense or other of "able to." But I don't in fact offer those reasons. Perhaps I'm not interested in offering them; perhaps I'm not aware that I could offer them. I offer what I acknowledge to be parochial religious reasons. If there's an issue here of the violation of the equal freedom of my fellow citizens, surely it's the reasons which I *actually offer* that is the relevant phenomenon, not the reasons I *could have* offered. Consider an analogy from epistemology. If I hold a belief on the basis of reasons, then it's the reasons *on the basis of which* I actually hold the belief that determine its entitlement, not my possession of reasons on the basis of which I *could have* held it.

Or perhaps what Rawls has in mind is not just that I *be able to* offer reasons that I can reasonably expect all my reasonable fellow citizens to accept, but that I be *ready and able* to offer such reasons. That is suggested by this passage: "As reasonable and rational, and knowing that they affirm a diversity of reasonable religious and philosophical doctrines, they *should be ready to explain* the basis of their actions to one another in terms each could reasonably expect that others might endorse as consistent with their freedom and equality" (218; my italics). If this is what Rawls has in mind, it would be appropriate to ask

---

9   *Cf.*,Ibid., "What public reason asks is that citizens *be able to explain* their vote to one another in terms of a reasonable balance of public political values" (243; italics added).

what constitutes *readiness*. I'm ready and able to offer such reasons, but I don't in fact do so.

Appropriate, but not especially relevant. The relevant response is that I, as one who holds the views indicated at the beginning of this paper, would find myself silenced were I to accept even this qualified stricture. As I have indicated, my own views on the rights of the poor have been formed by reflecting on the scriptures which I accept as canonical. I am now told that if I want to present and debate those views in the political arena, I must find an entirely different basis. I must base them on the consensus populi, rationally analyzed. Either that, or be ready and able to appeal to base them on that. I see no hope whatsoever of success in that project. A large proportion of my fellow citizens deny that the poor have any such rights as I believe they have. Should someone extract principles of justice from the consensus populi which entail that the poor do have such rights as I believe they have, I would, on the basis of that entailment, conclude that her analysis was a *mis*-analysis. I cannot *appeal* to the consensus populi; the challenge facing me is to try to *reform* it.

The fact that I would find myself silenced will not seem to most people a decisive objection to Rawls' strictures! So let me move on to highlight other difficulties. The strategy Rawls proposes for arriving at the consensus which is necessary if his stricture is to be met has no chance whatsoever of succeeding. The stricture is that, with respect to fundamental political issues, we are to debate in the public arena and to act (or to be ready and able to debate and act), on the basis of principles of justice that we can reasonably expect all those of our fellow citizens who are reasonable and rational to accept. The strategy for obtaining those principles of justice is the analysis/elaboration strategy. Suppose, then, that someone has followed that strategy; she has analyzed our political mentality into its constituent ideas and has elaborated those ideas into principles of justice. I submit that no matter what those resultant principles of justice may be, the reasonable thing for her to expect is *not* that all reasonable people who use their common human reason will agree with her results, but that *not all* reasonable people will agree. It would be utterly *unreasonable* for her to expect anything else than disagreement. The contested fate of Rawls' own principles of justice is an illustrative case in point. There's no more hope that all those among us who are reasonable and rational will arrive, in the way Rawls recommends, at consensus on principles of justice, than that we will all, in the foreseeable future, agree on some comprehensive philosophical or religious doctrine.

But what about the stricture itself, and Rawls' reason for it: Failure to satisfy the stricture represents failure to treat one's fellow citizens as free and equal? Well, in the first place, there's something very much like a fallacy of composition in Rawls' reasoning at this point. We must each stand ready to defend our political beliefs and actions, says Rawls, in terms that we can "reasonably expect that others might endorse as consistent with their freedom and equality" (218). So suppose it's true that, when conversing with Ryan, I must, to honor his freedom and equality, offer (or be ready to offer) reasons for my political beliefs and actions which I can reasonably expect him to endorse if he uses "our common human reason"; and suppose it's also true that, when conversing with Wendy, I must, to honor her freedom and equality, offer (or be ready to offer) reasons for my political beliefs and actions which I can reasonably expect her to endorse if she uses "our common human reason." It doesn't follow that the reasons I offer to Ryan must be the same as the reasons I offer to Wendy. To Ryan, I offer reasons that I hope he will find persuasive; to Wendy, I offer reasons that I hope she will find persuasive. They need not be the same reasons. They need not even be reasons that I myself accept! Ad hoc reasons would satisfy Rawls' stricture. Contrary to his assumption, the reasons don't have to be reasons for all comers.

But is it true—and this, finally, is the fundamental point—is it true that offering to Wendy reasons for my political views which I know or learn she doesn't accept, and which, accordingly, I cannot reasonably expect her to accept, is to violate her freedom and equality? And is it true that to vote, and otherwise act politically, on the basis of reasons which I do not expect all those affected to accept, is to violate their freedom and equality?

A distinction here is important. What's wrong with explaining to Wendy my religious reasons for thinking that involuntary avoidable impoverishment is a violation of rights, even though I don't expect her to accept those reasons? How does doing that violate her freedom and dignity? In no way whatsoever, so far as I can see. The 'silencing' component in Rawls' stricture—if that's the right interpretation—is just out of place. At most what he ought to say, as, so we have seen, perhaps he means to say, is that I should always have *additional* reasons available—reasons that I reasonably expect Wendy to accept.

But even this I fail to see. In our constitutional democracies we try to persuade each other on political issues, usually on an ad hoc basis: Offering to Republicans reasons that we think might appeal to them, if we can find such; offering to Democrats reasons that we think might appeal to them, if we can find such; offering to Christians reasons that we think might appeal to them, if we can find such; offering to America-firsters reasons that we think might appeal to them, if we can find such; and so forth. Rarely do we succeed in reaching consensus even among reasonable people of all these different stripes; but we try. Then, finally, we vote. Are we, in voting under these circumstances, all violating somebody's freedom and equality? On certain understandings of freedom and equality we probably are; "freedom" and "equality" are extraordinarily elastic terms. But it cannot be the case that we are violating those concepts of freedom and equality which are ingredients in the political culture of constitutional democracies, since it is characteristic of all constitutional democracies to take votes and act on the will of the majority.

A final point: In our society, the independent-basis principle of liberalism engenders a paradox. It's my own conviction that, when it comes to the political issue of poverty, I ought to act and vote on the basis of my religious convictions—that conviction being itself a religious conviction on my part. Should someone try to stop me from voting, and acting politically, on the basis of my religious convictions, that would violate the free exercise of my religion. Accordingly, if honoring the freedom and equality of citizens did require adherence to the independent-basis principle, then honoring the freedom and equality of citizens would also require non-adherence. Let it be added that I am not unique in my refusal on religious grounds to divide my life into secular and religious components.

In summary, the Rawlsian defense of the independent-basis principle of liberalism fares no better than the Lockean defense. Yet these, though not the only defenses of the principle, seem to me the best.

§7. It's worth briefly taking note of the fact that the other half of the neutrality postulate of liberalism, namely, the separation principle, also has consequences in our society which violate the freedom and equality of citizens. The state, in all contemporary constitutional democracies, funds a large part of the educational system. One can imagine a constitutional democracy in which that is not the case; in the contemporary world, however, it always is the case. The separation principle specifies, then, that such state-funding must not in any significant way aid any religion—nor any comprehensive non-religious perspective.

Now suppose there are parents present in society for whom it is a matter of religious conviction that their children receive a religiously integrated education. There are in fact such parents present in contemporary American society. Were the state to fund an educational program in accord with the religious convictions of those parents, it would, obviously, be aiding their religion, and thereby violating the separation principle. But if the state funds other schools but refuses to fund schools satisfactory to those parents, then those parents, in a perfectly obvious way, are discriminated against. If those parents are forbidden by law to establish schools which teach in accord with their convictions, then the discrimination is embodied in law. If they are not legally forbidden to establish such schools, then the discrimination is located in the economics of the matter. Were those parents to establish schools which teach in accord with their convictions, they would have to pay for those schools out of their own pockets while yet contributing to the general tax fund for schools. Obviously the free exercise of their religion is thereby infringed on—in a way in which that of others is not.

There's a common pattern to the liberal's impression that his independent-basis principle and his separation principle both deal fairly with religion—to his impression that the neutrality postulate honors the freedom and equality of the religious members of society as much as it does the non-religious members. That common pattern is this: The liberal assumes that requiring religious persons to debate and act politically for reasons other than religious reasons is not in violation of their *religious* convictions; likewise he assumes that an educational program which makes no reference to religion is not in violation of any parent's *religious* convictions. He assumes, in other words, that though religious people may not be in the *habit of* dividing their life into a religious component and a non-religious component, and though some might be *unhappy* doing so, nonetheless, their doing so would not be in violation of anybody's religion. But he's wrong about this. It's when we bring into the picture persons for whom it is a matter of religious conviction that they ought to strive for a religiously integrated existence—it's then, especially, though not only then, that the unfairness of liberalism to religion comes to light.

§8. My argument up to this point has been entirely at the level of ethical, political, and epistemological theory. Let me now be so bold as to engage in some social analysis. I understand Stephen Carter, in his recent book, *The Culture of Disbelief*,[10] to be pointing to a prominent feature of our actual civil and political society here in the United States. What he observes is that there is a strong impulse in very many Americans to disapprove of bringing religious conviction into discussions which take place in the public space—and it makes no difference whether those discussions be on political issues or others. "We are," says Carter, "one of the most religious nations on earth, in the sense that we have a deeply religious citizenry; but we are also perhaps the most zealous in guarding our public institutions against explicit religious influences. One result is that we often ask our citizens to split their public and private selves, telling them in effect that it is fine to be religious in private, but there is something askew when those private beliefs become the basis for public action" (8). This seems to me indubitably correct. There has been, in our country, a widespread embrace of the independent-basis thesis of liberalism—and more generally, of its neutrality postulate. There has been a silencing of religion in the public square.

What has rushed in to fill the void is not noble discussions about principles of justice which have been extracted in Rawlsian fashion from the consensus populi. For nobody *cares about* principles of justice thus obtained. What has rushed in to fill the void is mainly considerations of economic self-interest, of privatism, and of nationalism. These today dominate our discourse in the public square. For people do genuinely care about their own economic well-being, they do genuinely care about protecting their private lives, and many of them do genuinely care about their nation.

As a consequence, public discussion of political issues has been profoundly debased—assuming, as I do, that discussion of political issues purely in the flat secular terms of economic self-interest, of privatism, and of nationalism, is a debased discussion. Let alone not mentioning God, none of these even so much as alludes to anything at all transcendent. Indeed, of the three, only

---

10   New York: Basic Books, 1993.

nationalism even so much as extends beyond the self; and it extends beyond egocentric self-ism only by introducing group self-ism into the picture. I do not regard the embrace of the neutrality postulate as the only cause of the debasement of public dialogue. The spread of capitalism, intensively and extensively, also bears responsibility,[11] as do the contemporary media. But apart from religion, what people in contemporary society care most deeply about is their pocketbooks, their privacy, and their nation. If the reigning ethos says that it is wrong to introduce religion into the public space, then it is these other concerns that people will appeal to. What else? In all the great religions of the world there are strands of conviction which tell us that pocketbook, privacy, and nation are not of first importance. In all of them there are strands of conviction which tell that, in the name of God, we must honor the other— even when that other is not only other than ourselves but other than a member of our nation. Silence religion, and the debasement represented by private and group egoism will follow.

Adherence to the neutrality postulate has a debasing effect on religion as well. What we are witnessing today on the American scene, as the utterly natural and predictable response of religious people to the silencing of religion in the public space, is outbursts of resentment. We had better expect such outbursts to continue. Many religious people feel profoundly that their voice is not being heard—as of course it isn't. But an outburst of resentment is very different from a reasoned and civil discussion. Yet how are religious communities supposed to develop a reasoned voice on political matters when the neutrality postulate is in full sway? In their churches and synagogues and mosques? Does anybody seriously believe that churches, synagogues, and mosques can possibly engage in reflection of a depth which could compete with the sustained reflection that takes place in the public academies of the land? The only thing that can compete with the academy is the academy. But when it comes to the academy, we must note that though no one raises an eyebrow when those who are committed to comprehensive utilitarianism use the resources of the public academy to work out the political implications of their view, a similar use of the resources of the public academy by Christians, Jews, or Muslims would raise an uproar. This is the effect of the liberal silencing of religion in the public square, coupled with the tag-end of the Enlightenment view, that while religion is irrational, utilitarianism and such like, though they may be mistaken, are eminently rational, and thus appropriate for the public academy. I think we must expect, in a society committed to the neutrality postulate, that religious people, *qua* religious, will by and large either have little to say on matters of politics, or little to say beyond simplistic

---

11   See my argument in "The Schools We Deserve," in Stanley Hauerwas and John H. Westerhoff, eds., *Schooling Christians* (Grand Rapids, Mich.: Eerdmans Publishing Co., 1992), 3–28.

sentiments expressed in tones of resentment. The system disadvantages serious religious reflection on political issues.

I think there's reason to believe that the fate of liberalism itself is threatened in a society shaped by the neutrality postulate of liberalism. I suggested that at the very heart of liberalism is the conviction that the normal adult members of society are free and equal. That conviction emerged slowly, haltingly, and in complicated ways, out of the seedbed of Christianity in the West. Now suppose one shares—as probably most people nowadays do—the epistemological despair which underlies Rawls' project. I mean, the despair of ever grounding that conviction in the deliverances of our generic human nature. If one rejects appeal to religion and anything similar, it is hard indeed to see what other source there could be for that conviction than the consensus populi. We Americans—or as Richard Rorty candidly and bluntly puts it, we liberal bourgeois democrats—we, as it so happens, just do believe that we are free and equal. Not that everybody is. Just that *we* are.

I think it is more than dubious that we all do believe this; Rawls seems to me to have an extraordinarily idealized picture of the political culture of modern constitutional democracies. But let that pass on this occasion; and notice that the consensus populi is a most peculiar source. Throughout my discussion I have been assuming that the consensus populi, if there is one, and if it is rich and thick enough, does qualify as the independent source that the liberal needs; and indeed it does, in a way. But it's a very odd source in the following way: If someone asks, *why* should I believe that all normal adult members of my society are free and equal, *what reason* is there for believing it, no answer is forthcoming. The liberal can observe that, as it just so happens, we all do believe this. But this *We-ism* is not an answer to the *why believe* question. When someone begins to wonder whether we are all free and equal—perhaps the hypocrisy of our own society on the issue raises the question in his mind, perhaps critical comments by someone from an alternative society raises the question, perhaps his own internal reflections do so—when someone begins to wonder, the observation, "*But we all do happen so to believe*," is no answer.

Rorty's response is that no answer is needed. *We-ism* is sufficient. We all do happen to believe that the normal adult members of our society are free and equal; we like it this way; and that's the entirely satisfactory end of the matter. Rawls' strategy allows him more room to maneuver. It's open to him to say that if a person wants a reason, the place to look is to his or her own particular religion or comprehensive perspective. But if I'm right in my argument above, that the commitment of our society to the neutrality postulate has an inhibiting effect on serious reflection by religious communities on political issues, then it will be unlikely that the various religious communities will in fact develop their reasons with any depth and solidity. Liberalism saws off the branch on which it sits.

§9. Recently a group of Christians, organized as the Christian Environment Council, appeared in Washington D.C. Speaking to the national media and the congressional leadership, they spoke up in support of endangered species, declaring themselves opposed to "any Congressional action that would weaken, hamper, reduce or end the protection, recovery, and preservation of God's creatures, including their habitats, especially as accomplished under the Endangered Species Act." The heart of the reason they offered was that "according to the Scriptures, the earth is the Lord's and all that dwells within it (Psalm 24:1), and the Lord shows concern for every creature (Matthew 6:26)."

Liberalism, with its neutrality postulate, insists that such appeals as this must be silenced—or that those who present the appeal always have an additional, consensus populi, reason at the ready. To those organized as the Christian Environment Council it says: speak thus to each other in your own churches, if you wish; but when you come to Washington, speak, or be ready to speak, on an independent basis. I regard that silencing-injunction as without basis, and unfair to religion.[12] Besides which, I care about species; and I firmly believe that, over the long haul, endangered species are safer in the hands of those who ground their appeals in religion than in the hands of those who ground them in privatism, nationalism, or economism.

Instead of forbidding the Christian Environment Council to offer its religious reasons in the public space, why not invite them to continue saying with civility what they do believe for such reasons as they do in fact have for their beliefs—which in this case are religious reasons? Why not invite others to do the same? And why not invite and urge all of them then to listen to each other, genuinely to listen, changing their minds as they feel the force of the testimony and argumentation of others, in this way slowly coming to so much agreement as is necessary for the task at hand? In the case just mentioned, that will be a distinct service to the species endangered. And it will recognize, in the other human being, not only the worth of her humanity, and the worth of her membership in one's own people, but the worth of her convictional particularity. Why not let people say what they want, but insist that they say it with civility? Why not concern ourselves with the *virtues* of the conduct of the debate rather than with the *content* of the positions staked out in the debate? Why not let people act for whatever reasons they wish, provided their actions fall within the boundaries of the constitution?[13]

---

12   It appears that Rawls agrees on this specific point, on the ground that "the status of the natural world and our proper relation to it is not a constitutional essential or a basic question of justice" (*Political Liberalism*, 246).

13   And what justifies the constitution—that all citizens accept it on the basis of their common human reason? Hardly. At the American constitutional convention, votes were taken! It's not likely that, if votes were taken today among the populace as a whole, our present Constitution would result. But so far, most of us agree that overturning it would be the greater evil.

The agreement arrived at need not be agreement based on principles rich enough to settle *all substantial political issues whatsoever*. Sufficient if it be agreement *on the matter at hand*. It need not be agreement based on *principles shared by all alike*. Sufficient if all, each *on his or her own principles,* come to agreement on the matter at hand. It need not be agreement *for all time*. Sufficient if it be agreement for *today and tomorrow*. It need not be agreement that one can reasonably expect of *all human beings whatsoever*. Sufficient if it be agreement among *us*. It need not even be agreement among *each and every one* of us. Sufficient if it be the fairly-gained and fairly-executed agreement *of the majority* of us.

The Return of the Prodigal?
Liberal Theory and Religious Pluralism

Timothy P. Jackson

"And above all these put on love, which binds everything together in perfect harmony." (Colossians 3:14, RSV)

"God grant that what we here have written serve to increase His glory and to establish the common peace." (Herbert of Cherbury)

Introduction

Like USC and Notre Dame, liberalism and religion are often thought to be inherently adversarial. How you characterize the struggle, however, depends on which side you're on, if not which state you're in. From one sideline, liberalism is seen to uphold diversity and tolerance, the hard-won ethos of a democratic society. Liberal theory must cope with or compensate for religious faith as a threat to individual liberty and a potential disrupter of social harmony. Religions offer mythic metanarratives about the true and the good and the beautiful, the story goes, but the myths are both unverifiable and incommensurable. We are not sure what agreement would mean, and we can never arrive at even the semblance of agreement without coercion. Indeed, religious traditions tend to inspire nonrational, if not irrational, loyalties that liberalism must constantly neutralize in the name of "civility." On this view, then, liberalism is the champion of reasonable pluralism, including (ironically) religious pluralism.

From the other sideline, religious conviction appears the last bulwark against the corrosive effects of modernism and postmodernism. Religious faiths refuse to worship technology and autonomy, the idols of the Enlightenment, since these destroy community and identity. Liberals don't know who they are anymore, and they would make us all self-forgetful Californians. Liberalism would conceive of social discourse in nonmoral or minimally moral terms, for instance, but this leads to well-documented evils: individualism, relativism, MTV. Bourgeois capitalism substitutes a self-interested materialism for a sense of social responsibility, and cultural postmodernism can only venerate idiosyncrasy and power. Our heroine is no longer the Mother of Jesus, say, but rather the "real" Madonna, the "material girl" who gets pregnant by an immaterial boy (not the Holy Spirit). As Stanley Hauerwas puts it, "liberalism makes for shitty people." From this vantage point, then, religion is the solitary champion of personal virtues, both in theory and in practice.

Of course, there is *some* warrant for both of these perspectives. On the one hand, the religious wars of the sixteenth and seventeenth centuries still suggest to many that religions must be kept down, down, down. And more recent memories of Jonestown and the Waco Branch Davidians are vivid and troubling to almost all. Religious zeal seems, with disturbing frequency, to go hand-in-hand with homicide. On the other hand, the Holocaust was at least partially the product of scientific rationality and democratic governance. Even where it does not cause them, secularity seems incapable of coping with many of today's most distinctive problems. Ethnicity and national identity—realities the Enlightenment sought in principle to synthesize ("one people, one country")—now seem as intractable occasions for bloodshed as religious creeds. Think of Bosnia and ethnic cleansing.[1] Might it be that in the present age only religious motives and mores can check the genocidal tendencies of political conflicts by appealing to comprehensive norms?

There is some warrant for the adversarial picture, but I hope to show that it is finally based on caricatures. It is important to question, to unpack and qualify, the preceding accounts of both liberalism and religion. It has been tempting of late for religious believers simply to turn the tables on liberalisms and vilify them for the moral decay of Western culture. Given the historical genesis of much of Western democracy in Christian (especially Protestant) piety, however, this is a colossal irony.[2] It amounts to a disowning of a formerly beloved, however currently prodigal, child. Given its supernatural origin and end, the Christian faith must always preserve a critical distance from any temporal institution or social arrangement, but I would defend nonetheless a modest positive thesis: *a form of liberalism, properly understood, is (or at least can be) itself a religious commitment.* Freedom and equality are not the only values, but they can be the conscientious upshots of love of God and neighbor. The question of whether a viable liberalism *must* be religiously based, I leave largely open . . . though I have suspicions.

In Part I of this paper, I discuss two idealized types of liberal theory; in Part II, I outline two takes on two types of pluralism. These types and takes are presented not as exhaustive but as instructive. In Part III, I sketch a third understanding of both liberalism and pluralism that aims to overcome the problems with the previous two. When it misunderstands conscientious forms of pluralism, liberal "theory" concludes that it must be morally empty or basic; but, in fact, the best defense of liberalism is morally perfectionist, I believe.

---

1   Benzion Netanyahu has argued that even the Spanish Inquisition was more motivated by race than by religion. See Netanyahu, *The Origins of the Inquisition in Fifteenth Century Spain* (New York: Random House, 1995).

2   For three recent treatments of Christianity's role in producing and sustaining commitments to human rights, see Max Stackhouse, *Creeds, Society, and Human Rights* (Grand Rapids: Eerdmans, 1984); John Witte, Jr., "The Essential Rights and Liberties of Religion in the American Constitutional Experiment," *Notre Dame Law Review* 71, no. 3 (1996): 371–445; and Witte, ed., *Christianity and Democracy in Global Context* (Boulder, Colo.: Westview Press, 1993).

The best defense recognizes and defends those substantive virtues that make democratic equality possible. In contrast to John Rawls's political liberalism, for example, which relies on minimal moral powers for the balancing of diverse ends, perfectionist liberalism focuses on how people are enabled to acquire and sustain ends in the first place. This is a communal affair. Rather than appealing to rationality (Gewirth) or overlapping consensus (Rawls) or fear (Shklar) or irony (Rorty), perfectionist liberalism puts some form of benevolence first and appeals to empathy. We only acquire ends because others have graciously cared for us beyond what consistency or contract theories or personal prudence can require. And we disguise this fact by talking too devoutly of "appraisive reason" and "distributive justice."

Secular versions of perfectionist liberalism are possible, if problematic. When life and love are seen as gifts from a Higher Power, however, "religious pluralism" comes into its own. Accordingly, I try in Part IV to describe a distinctively Christian version of perfectionist liberalism, one that highlights the transcendent source of all goodness yet still embraces conscientious pluralism. The two defining features of Christian pluralism are: (1) its confidence in a fundamental, if elusive, unity amid the diversity of human goods and faculties, and (2) its readier openness to self-sacrifice, including various forms of forgiveness, than in most secular philosophies. Christianity does not endorse all forms of self-sacrifice or recommend suffering for its own sake. But it does insist that the self-giving that flows from charity is indispensable and that charity itself is a divine gift that preserves human existence from chaos.

To elaborate further the meaning of charity, I close Part IV by briefly contrasting Origen and Aquinas with Rawls on the goodness of incarnate lives. My thesis here is that Rawls's account of justice—especially its inclination to exclude prophetic voices from public debate—is less compatible with the two types of pluralism than many of the two theologians' views. Whereas Rawls presupposes free and equal persons with basic moral powers as part of the self-image of a democratic culture,[3] prophetic Christianity asks the prior question of how such persons are produced, recognized, and sustained. Suffering love, "primal goodness," is its answer. Without major reworking, I conclude, even Rawls's carefully crafted liberalism is an unwitting threat to genuine pluralism, not its champion; with such reworking, religion may be a supplement to reasonable theory, not a dangerous source of irrationality or discord. This is the constructive reversal, the reconciliation of parent and prodigal, that awaits us: "religious theory" that is more than theoretical sustaining a "liberal pluralism" that is more than political.

---

3   Robert Nozick criticized Rawls's A Theory of Justice for treating "the things people produce" as though they were "manna from heaven." (See Nozick, Anarchy, State, and Utopia [New York: Basic Books, 1974], 198.) To my mind, Rawls intentionally treats the things that produce people in much the same way.

I. Two Types of Liberalism: Subjectivity and Objectivity

A. The politics of subjectivity, or liberalism-as-morally-empty: My first type of liberalism begins and ends with the solidarity of a particular group. No appeal to a universally shared human nature or a categorically binding moral imperative is made or can be made. These ideas are judged remnants of a discredited Judeo-Christian theology or an all-but-discredited Enlightenment philosophy. The good life, privately understood, is a matter of imaginative invention; in more corporate contexts, one relies on pragmatic conventions. "This is how we agree to act together, this is what we do, given what we find commonly desirable, and what we find desirable is democratic freedom and equality." This is the postmodern experiment: the quest for Homeric *diké* without the aristocratic hierarchy . . . a world governed by egalitarian *Sittlichkeit* rather than Kantian *Moralität* . . . Nietzsche without the *Übermensch* . . . or, rather, Nietzsche with *all of us* as *Übermenschen*, poetically (re-) creating ourselves. I call this first type of liberalism, then, liberalism-as-morally-empty. We neither have nor need access to objective values or transcendental principles or the revealed will of God; we stay in Plato's cave and content ourselves with shared appearances of artificial objects (and subjects). "This works best *for us* as we forge our distinct identities."

This is *not* a liberal prescription for nihilism, I hasten to add; it is *not* a refusal to value any particular social arrangement over another. It is rather a political valuation that remains within aesthetic categories. Liberalism-as-morally-empty, what I playfully call the "l-a-m-e" version, would be liberalism-as-aesthetically-full: democratic society as a colony of strong poets. A species of social criticism is possible here, but the criticism is highly parochial and instrumentalist. The critic offers, at most, what Michael Walzer calls "prophetic interpretation," the calling of a community back to its typical script, its defining rituals and original self-understandings.[4] There is no higher standard of good and bad than our own voluntary practices, but our *de facto* practices may be fine-tuned to make them more effective or fetching or consistent on their own terms.

Liberalism-as-morally-empty, to summarize, is an ethos of local bestowal. There are no objective goods to be appraised, only subjective allegiances to be bestowed;[5] there are no moral truths to be discovered "out there," only social practices to be habituated "in here." Thus liberalism-as-morally-empty consciously rejects *theoria* as a means of arriving at knowledge. There are no general theoretical truths, at least not in ethics and politics. Political knowledge is at most a matter of *kennen* not *wissen*, *savoir-faire* not *connaître*.

---

4   Walzer, *Interpretation and Social Criticism* (Cambridge, Mass.: Harvard University Press, 1987), *passim*.

5   The terminology of *appraisal* and *bestowal*, I borrow from Irving Singer, *The Nature of Love*, 3 Vols. (Chicago: University of Chicago Press, 1966–87).

The attractiveness of this perspective is its humility, its acknowledgment of finitude and particularity, contingency and history. The fanaticism that can spring from supposedly "certain" knowledge of timeless Truth is ruled out of court at the outset. We intentionally hobble our self-image in order not to run over people. "Better not to believe in moral knowledge and truth if these lead to holy wars and final solutions; better not to talk of virtue and vice, guilt and innocence, if these lead to self-hatred and suicide. We can be maximally tolerant by being minimally metaphysical, most safe by being least credulous." So the argument goes, with some power.

Yet the problems with this picture are familiar: it would purchase tolerance at too high a price. Subjectivity, raised to a group level, does not thereby escape narcissism and ennui; it simply becomes corporate. Purely aesthetic or political categories are not enough to capture our actual self-understanding or to motivate our critical practices. Neither irony nor fear nor sheer power is enough to secure the respect for others necessary to sustain liberal society. *Motives matter*, and one cannot be motivated to care equally for others who are not judged equally valuable (either intrinsically or in the sight of God). Strong poets make dubious neighbors. (Think of the lame Lord Byron—"mad, bad, and dangerous to know"—and his craving for "a hero" like Don Juan.) We are born with concrete aptitudes and potentials that must be cultivated rather than assumed, even as we are born with concrete wants and needs that must be attended to rather than created. Human beings do not stand in solidarity with one another the way God dispenses grace: as an utterly unmerited gift. I accent below the ineliminable place of gratuitous care in a good society, but human care builds on finite potentials already in place. Creatures do not create *ex nihilo*; the integrity of others calls for recognition, not mere invention.

Liberalism-as-aesthetically-full would use irony and humor to deflate pretension, but there is no salt in its tears. Its empathy with others' real pain is ultimately an inconsistent laugh. To think that one generates human community *de novo* is not finally humility but something very close to the sin of pride. To be open to others as they are in themselves, in contrast, is to unlock the door to nonlocal discoveries. Lame poets must let themselves be touched by realities beyond their control.

The root problem with liberalism-as-morally-empty is that it leaves us without the resources to distinguish the means to virtue (a political community) from virtue itself (love and justice). Love and justice are social virtues, inseparable in their acquisition and practice from a good society, but no particular society is the *telos* of love or justice as such. These virtues invariably relativize whatever political community they emerge in.

B. The politics of objectivity, or liberalism-as-morally-basic: A second ideal type of liberalism models itself on the disinterested philosophical spectator rather than the traditional historical interpreter. To avoid the apparent conservatism and conventionalism of liberalism-as-morally-empty, it aims to specify a liberalism that is morally basic. Moral utterances are now judged to be more than group expressions of practical commitments; they are thought to have truth value. Moreover, moral utterances are to abstract *away* from the distinctive identity and historical community of the utterer. Rational judgers will limit themselves to apprehension of things like aggregate benefits or natural rights. One has left the cave of mere appearances to espy the true and the good and the beautiful from an impersonal vantage point beyond prejudice or passion.

If the politics of subjectivity offers local bestowal of value among "us," the politics of objectivity accents the general appraisal of value as though everybody, including oneself, is a "them." Liberalism-as-morally-basic focuses, that is, on justice as *suum cuique*, the unclouded appraisal of what individuals are due, the detached guarantee of basic human rights. Disinterestedness is key; therefore emotions are suspect. Emotions are thought to carry an ineliminably first-person flavor—we speak of having "the very same idea" as someone else more readily than of feeling "the very same emotion"—while moral judgments tend to be in the third person. "*One* ought to do this because it maximizes utility or is dictated by duty or is the will of God, etc." This is "liberal theory" in the technical sense of *theoria*: a general account aimed at truths rationally communicable to all. Utilitarian and deontological theories share an aspiration to such objective rationality.

The allure of this account of liberalism is its even-handedness, its fine self-transcendence for the sake of clear vision. Being capable of the long view and not making an exception in one's own case does seem a central part of moral wisdom. It is the wisdom of the "l-a-m-b" that surrenders its distinctive identity for the sake of universal truth; it is the sacrifice of egotism on the altar of impartiality and fairness. Liberalism-as-morally-basic would build securely on the foundation of a rational justice, and as such it is a powerfully moralizing influence on any social context.

The rub, however, as many have noted, is that the perfectly disinterested spectator tends to be insufficiently engaged in or committed to his or her own culture. And the merely *self*-interested contractor is similarly alienated from others. As much as they may differ concerning the priority of the right or the good, both the disinterested spectator and the self-interested contractor make moral education in personal virtues hard to imagine. Both tend to neglect the social recognition of the good and the interpersonal motivation for doing right. Michael Walzer has noted that in Rawls's original position, for instance, "it ceases to matter whether the constructive or legislative work is undertaken by a single person or by many people. . . . one person talking is enough."[6]

---

6   Walzer, *Interpretation and Social Criticism*, 11. In fact, Rawls appears ambivalent about subjectivity and objectivity. At times, he has seemed allied with Richard Rorty and constructivism, advocating a "political" conception of justice that is all but morally empty; at other times, he has spurned a mere *modus vivendi* in

An ethic of pure appraisal, unmotivated by richly individual desires and socially generated commitments, is not sustainable. The view from nowhere, to use Tom Nagel's phrase,[7] seeks to overcome the provincialism of liberalism-as-morally-empty, "the view from now-here." But pure objectivity is less than human: it brackets out of consideration many of the very things that make life in community worth living: friendships, family ties, erotic relations, patriotic emotions, etc. There is an odd, almost masochistic, impersonalism in the "l-a-m-b" version of liberalism: a too-willing sacrifice of moral affections like gratitude and devotion, pity and forgiveness. The danger is loss of the sense of embodied selfhood. It is essential in working with divisions to find the common denominator, but if the numerators are all zeros, one is left with nothing.

Basic justice is not enough. The "lamb" must be spared, so to speak, immolation of individuality abolished, if community is to take humane form. Justice defined as *suum cuique*, and elaborated in terms of rights and duties, lifts us out of purely aesthetic categories. It is, as such, a necessary condition for a moral polis of free and equal persons. Yet impersonal justice is derivative. *The prior question is how we generate caring people capable of free agency, respectful of rights and duties, to begin with.* This is first of all a matter of benevolent service rather than appraisive rationality. Moral personality is a strangely belated thing, neither self-creating nor self-fulfilling; we are all *"second* persons," in Annette Baier's terms,[8] dependent on others who have come before and who will go after. Benevolence must look to the needs of persons, potential persons as well as actual, before justice can turn to their deserts. And character formation into the way of caring is a primary personal need. Forming character well, in turn, requires mythic narratives (stories of heroes with whom we actively identify) rather more than abstract principles (general rules to which we impersonally conform).

But let this suffice for a brief look at two highly idealized liberalisms; I turn next to pluralisms.

II. Two Takes on Two Types of Pluralism: Expansion and Reduction

It is important to distinguish at the outset two types of pluralism.[9] The first,

---

favor of substantive (if basic) moral truth claims. The latter now seems closer to his considered view. I discuss Rawls at greater length below; for a still more detailed treatment, see my "To Bedlam and Part Way Back: John Rawls and Christian Justice," in *Faith and Philosophy* 8, no. 4 (October 1991): 423–47.

7   Thomas Nagel, *The View from Nowhere* (Oxford: Oxford University Press, 1986).

8   Annette Baier, *Postures of the Mind: Essays on Mind and Morals* (Minneapolis: University of Minnesota Press, 1985), 84.

9   I have been stimulated in what follows by Charles Larmore's "Pluralism and Reasonable Disagreement," in *Cultural Pluralism and Moral Knowledge*, ed. by

which I will call *epistemic pluralism*, is the view that there are many different ways of disclosing (or attempting to disclose) truths—whether the truths be empirical, moral, metaphysical, or theological. Each way has, moreover, its own particular logic and criteria. In specifically moral contexts, epistemic pluralism is often associated with the idea that reason, emotion, and will all have a role in the quest for knowledge of the good life, even as do appeals to tradition and culture. The means to ethical knowing, the faculties of moral psychology, are multiple. Thus practical wisdom is a matter of the discriminate balance or synthesis of various sources, or would-be sources, of insight.

The second type of pluralism might be called *ontological pluralism*. This is the view that the *objects* of knowledge, rather than the means to discovering them, are multiple. There are empirical, moral, metaphysical, and theological realities, the ontological pluralist typically holds, as well as different realities within each of these large disciplinary categories. In moral contexts, for example, ontological pluralism is often associated with the thesis that there are many genuine virtues, many binding rules or commandments, many valuable ends, etc. Hence the second form of pluralism, understood axiologically, is the opposite of any monism that would equate all worth with a single trait of character or principle of action or consequence of acting. Goodness is variegated, on this account.

As I have defined it, epistemic pluralism is distinct from both epistemic scepticism and epistemic despair. The first form of pluralism is distinct, that is, from both the conviction that the (putative) sources of insight are unreliable or prone to error and the conviction that they are deeply conflictual—whether across disciplines or within an individual discipline. To say that there are many ways to know (or to try to know) is not to comment on whether these ways are inclined to mistake or otherwise illegitimate, nor is it to say that they are at odds. One might be an epistemic pluralist yet also an epistemic foundationalist, for example, taking the deliverances of revelation, reason, will, and emotion, say, to be incorrigible and harmonious when properly understood. Such a position would no doubt be implausible, but it is not conceptually impossible. Short of foundationalism, one might unite epistemic pluralism with epistemic fallibilism and see the many human faculties as individually subject to error but generally reliable as a group.

Analogously, ontological pluralism differs on my definition from both ontological chaos and ontological agony. The second form of pluralism differs, in other words, from both the thesis that the various objects of knowledge

Ellen Frankel Paul, Fred D. Miller, Jr., and Jeffrey Paul (Cambridge: Cambridge University Press, 1994). Larmore does not use the terminology I do, preferring to reserve the label *pluralism* exclusively for what I call *ontological pluralism*, but he does draw similar distinctions. I differ from Larmore in thinking that ontological pluralism, as well as the expectation of reasonable disagreement, is naturally aligned with the heart of liberalism.

claims are incomparable—whether across disciplines of within an individual discipline—and the thesis that they are somehow intrinsically antithetical ("agonistic" in the classical Greek sense of implacably struggling). To say that there are many realities is not to say that these realities are incoherent or surd, nor is it to say that they contradict each other like matter and antimatter. One might be an ontological pluralist yet also an ontological optimist, for instance, taking the diverse things in the world to be finally intelligible and compatible. In metaphysical treatises, ontological optimists write of "the great chain of being," "the plenitude of existence," "the harmony of the spheres," etc.; in moral tracts, key phrases include "the unity of the virtues," "the consistency of practical reason," "the goodness of being with evil as its privation," etc. This position may also seem implausible to many, but most monotheists embrace such an optimism.

Against this backdrop, let me now clarify two possible takes on epistemic and ontological pluralism.

A. Expansive pluralism radicalizes epistemic pluralism to entail either epistemic scepticism or epistemic despair. It is chiefly prompted by perceived disagreement about fundamental values, beliefs, and practices—both within and across traditions. The expansive accent is on the irreconcilability of diverse faculties and disciplines (reason and emotion, philosophy and poetry) and on the incommensurability of diverse cultures and practices (the Trobriand Islanders and us, our public selves and private selves). Even in the West, the reality of paradigm shifts means for expansive pluralists that there is no abiding inquiry, much less consensus after inquiry, that can be called "*our* moral tradition.*" There are only fluctuating historical traditions of quite local character, with no adjudicating basic epistemic disputes between them. In the extreme, expansivists assert that we should stop talking of "discovering truth" altogether.

In the expansive lexicon, phrases like *religious pluralism* or *cultural pluralism* conjure up images of hopelessly conflicting camps that must be reined in rather than happily coexisting communities that may be cross-fertilized. Thus expansive pluralism often emerges as a *modus vivendi*, a tolerance of what is alien for the sake of getting on. At best, it represents a benign neglect of social patterns that one does not endorse and probably cannot understand; at worst, it amounts to a grudging truce between permanently warring factions. We whoop for our side as they whoop for theirs, but we refrain from throwing stones.

Expansive pluralism also radicalizes ontological pluralism to entail either ontological chaos or ontological agony. The types of realities (or supposed realities) are so complex and discontinuous that we live, quite literally, in many fragmented, even incompatible, worlds. In ethics, this often translates into the affirmation of moral dilemmas. Define a moral dilemma as a situation in which, through no antecedent fault of your own, you cannot but transgress against some sacred value or binding rule, cannot but become guilty. I refer not to inescapable *feelings* of guilt but to actual culpability, a scenario involving two equally binding but mutually exclusive ethical requirements. Neither do I have in mind moral ambiguity or weakness of will. No additional information or resolve will help when confronted by a genuine dilemma: You are literally damned if you do and damned if you don't. "It is the case that you ought to be or do X, and it is not the case that you ought to be or do X." Expansive pluralism often internalizes the fact of disagreement to the point of affirming such a contradictory scenario. One ought to be "liberal" enough about goods to "dirty one's hands," to do evil that good might come, some expansive pluralists maintain.[10]

I will have much more to say about expansive pluralism below, but I can anticipate by noting that some commentators find it overly pessimistic about communication across cultural boundaries as well as about the possible coherence of personal loyalties. Conflict and change are taken too much to heart by expansive pluralists, critics assert, and, rather than respecting differences, expansive pluralists leave us with blind tolerance on the cultural level and desperate sadness on the personal level. Hermetically sealed traditions and tragically dilemmatic choices are needlessly affirmed.

B. Reductive anti-pluralism rejects both epistemic and ontological pluralism, at least within ethics. It is an *intra*mural affair, beginning with the fact of agreement, *within a metatradition*, on a single moral value (e.g., happiness) apprehended by a single highest faculty (e.g., reason). Everything revolves around these centers. Reductionism may admit the diversity of human goods and powers, but it would grasp these in a coherent vision by privileging one *moral* datum and one means to *moral* knowledge. This is often done by looking for the common denominator in seemingly incompatible traditions and rituals. The good will or rational consistency or maximal pleasure, for instance, is isolated as the motive force behind all historical praxis. *De facto* traditions are then understood as variations on the same basic theme, as intelligible dialects of the same mother tongue. We can be pluralistic about mores, if you will, because we are monistic about morals. There is but one *fons et origio* of distinctively moral goodness, and when seen from the impersonal point of view, all enlightened cultures flow from it and aspire to it. Wisdom is simply

---

10   For a collection of contemporary philosophical essays on dilemmas, together with some historical background pieces, see *Moral Dilemmas*, ed. by Christopher W. Gowans (Oxford: Oxford University Press, 1987). For an intelligent rejection of moral dilemmas, see Edmund Santurri, *Perplexity in the Moral Life: Philosophical and Theological Considerations* (Charlottesville: University of Virginia Press, 1987). For an influential defense of same, see Martha Nussbaum, *The Fragility of Goodness*, esp. Chap. 11 and Interlude 2, and *Love's Knowledge: Essays on Philosophy and Literature* (Oxford: Oxford University Press, 1990), esp. Chaps. 2 and 4.

a matter of being able to see through the contingent forms to the abiding content, to rise above peripheral disputes to tap the core consensus. In spite of ethnographic complexity, the epistemological and ontological centers hold.

The objections to reductive anti-pluralism are the familiar ones to foundationalism. Critics doubt that any Urtradition can encompass the vast array of human goods (and ills)—aesthetic, economic, political, moral, religious—within a single coherent picture. More specifically, they object to the essentialism necessary to get everyone talking the same moral language. There is no single moral good on the basis of which to explain cultural diversity, the objection runs, no one touchstone for civil discourse. And neither is there a highest or most characteristic moral faculty. Ethical Esperanto based on the definitiveness of reason, say, is, at best, a pipe dream and, at worst, an invitation to tyranny. The fear is of yet another dogmatic Messiah slouching toward Bethlehem to be born.

You see where I am going. Liberalism-as-morally-empty moves hand-in-glove with expansive pluralism, while liberalism-as-morally-basic is built for or on reductive anti-pluralism. Liberalism-as-morally-empty is impressed by the fact of broad cultural disagreement and is inclined to talk of "many worlds," "untranslatable paradigms," "us against them," etc.; liberalism-as-morally-basic, on the other hand, opts for semantic ascent and a unified system that looks down on diversity from nowhere in particular and with no one person in mind. This (non)perspective is defined as "the moral point of view," whether elaborated in terms of total hedons or the categorical imperative. In short, the "l-a-m-e" version of liberalism expands "pluralism" to the breaking point by disallowing intrinsic worth altogether, even as the "l-a-m-b" version contracts "pluralism" to a vanishing point by treating all moral goods as one, or at least as measurable in terms of one thing apprehended by one means.

Is there any way to get beyond this twofold either/or? I want now to combine the previous two parts of my discussion and imagine a third kind of liberalism together with a third understanding of pluralism. I think of this exercise in roughly Hegelian terms: striving for an *Aufhebung* of the two contrary liberalisms based on a synthesis of the two contrary views of pluralism.

III. Two Third Alternatives: Conscience and the Care of Persons

A. Conscientious pluralism, my third take, aims to do justice to both the reality of cultural disagreement (epistemic concerns) and the plurality of legitimate goods (ontological commitments). It seeks to move beyond the brute diversity of traditions, associated with expansive pluralism, and the too-sanguine unity of an Urtradition, associated with reductive anti-pluralism. The central thesis of conscientious pluralism is that both human faculties and human goods are happily multiple. Most characteristically, conscientious pluralism is a joyful affirmation of the plenitude of the world and the self;

diversity and multiplicity are celebrated, not simply tolerated. When such pluralism takes a religious form, we have not the gallimaufry of conflicting faiths but grateful attention to the great chain of being. This chain leads back to a Creator to whom all are responsible, but responsibility involves respect for the consciences of others made in the Creator's Image.

Conscientious pluralism rejects all axiological reductionisms. Such views easily degenerate into a *global* monism, in which *all* worth (not just moral worth) is equated with one particular person or thing, and *all* truth (not just moral truth) is grasped by one particular faculty or sense. Human life then becomes a cliff-dive into a tidal inlet: one stops one's ears and holds one's breath and plunges to the bottom to retrieve "the pearl of great price" . . . only to drown in an undertow. Thus does an impoverished ontology drive one to an impoverished epistemology, and vice versa. In its hyperKantian form, reductive objectivity avers that the only truly good thing is the good will, which acts out of rational respect for duty; in its hyperutilitarian form, pleasure or happiness becomes the sole good, as this is maximized by an impersonal spectator. For conscientious pluralists, however, values and the means to appreciate them are irreducibly multiform. Passion and volition, for instance, are as important sources of moral and religious insight as reason.

Conscientious pluralism is similar to the expansive variety in acknowledging distinct and possibly conflicting goods; one may have to sacrifice physical safety to secure social justice, for example. Yet conscientious pluralism differs in holding that the distinctions and conflicts are still intelligible within a unified system. Aesthetic, moral, and religious diversity stops short of chaos and dilemma. There are many values and many sources of insight into them, but this does not rule out a true vision or a lexical ordering. We must recognize the breadth of life, but we must not overlook its depth. There is that much wisdom in reductive visions. The question is how complete the tension between various goods and faculties can be within a conscientious perspective. Again, both conscientious and expansive pluralists grant that there can be conflicts and tradeoffs between the moral and the nonmoral. But many expansive pluralists also argue that moral goods themselves are so fragmented, the agreed sources of ethical insight so at odds, that deep dilemma is sometimes unavoidable. Utility tells us one thing, say, and deontology something incompatible but equally compelling. The challenge to conscientious pluralism is to rebut the expansive case for moral dilemmas without denying tragedy altogether, as reductivists do.

For the conscientious pluralist, seeing moral realities as chaotic is bad enough, but seeing them as utterly agonistic is the death of *any* tradition claiming ethical knowledge. Because a self-contradiction is necessarily false, to affirm a moral dilemma appears to conscience not as pluralism but as schizophrenia. Moral knowledge self-destructs here, even intramurally, for the expansive pluralist. Hence the expansive pluralist's drive toward a liberalism that is highly aesthetic, based on solidarity to a group practice rather than the propositional truth of a moral vision. Moral truth claims run aground on practical paradox. In the face of a Walzerian "supreme emergency," say, our politics is unabashedly fatalistic, if not immoral. When faced with a severe and imminent threat to the nation, we must be willing to murder innocents in other countries to preserve our own. We can give no consistent moral argument, however, for why we should be willing to do so. The agony of ontological "necessity" simply compels us to violate our most basic moral principles and values in order to avoid political calamity.[11]

Expansive pluralists tend to emphasize the fragmentation of goods and powers (even unto admitting moral dilemmas), while reductive anti-pluralists deny the possibility of any real tragedy in the moral life (even unto going monistic). Conscientious pluralists find both alternatives implausible: The voice of the expansivist is Machiavellian, while that of the reductivist is Pollyannaish. But how does one argue for conscientious pluralism? The best I can do is to try to draw a compelling picture of one version of it. The version I have in mind maintains that literal dilemmas don't exist because aesthetic, moral, and religious goods are ordered by a metavalue. That metavalue is love. In the next section, I will try to spell out what is distinctive about Christian love (*agape*), but for now I want to keep the discussion general enough to cover what the Stoics called "*humanitas*" and "*misericordia*," Hutcheson and Smith dubbed "benevolence," and contemporary secular philosophers often refer to as "the care of persons" or "personal care."

Care, understood interpersonally, is characterized by two features: (1) practical commitment (emotional and intellectual) to the good of the other and (2) equal regard (local and universal) for the worth of the other. The expansive pluralist is, at most, a *weak* philanthropist who rates care as the first among a host of equals that may be directly at odds: health, happiness, political enfranchisement, personal courage, etc. More than likely, though, she is a *non*philanthropist who sees universal love of neighbor as unfair to those in special relation to oneself and impossible in any case: empathy should not and, in any event, cannot extend to everybody (Nietzsche and Freud). As I define her, the conscientious pluralist is, in contrast, a *strong* philanthropist. She sees personal care as that singular good without which we have no substantive access to other values. There *are* other genuine values—here is no love monism—but without love these values are but "glittering vices." Loving care is not simply to be numbered with courage, temperance, prudence, and justice as one more significant virtue. Care is, in Charles Taylor's parlance, *the* hypergood.[12]

---

11   See Michael Walzer, "Political Action: The Problem of Dirty Hands," in *Philosophy and Public Affairs* 2, no. 2 (Winter 1973): 160–80; *Just and Unjust Wars* (New York: Basic Books, 1977), Chapter 16; and "Emergency Ethics," The Joseph A. Reich, Sr., Distinguished Lecture, No. 1 (Colorado Springs, Colo.: United States Air Force Academy, 1988).

12   Charles Taylor, *Sources of the Self: The Making of the Modern Identity* (Cambridge,

To repeat, the reductivist may concede many goods and powers, but the distinctively *moral* candidates reduce to one. Thus, for the reductivist there can be no conflict between moral values or faculties. For the agonized expansivist, there can be an irremediable conflict between *any* two values or faculties: Love may sometimes have to sacrifice justice, for instance, and thus dirty its hands. For the conscientious pluralist, the variety of goods and powers does not preclude putting benevolence first. No way of life can attain all goods, so there are multiple and even incompatible ways of flourishing as a person. But all moral lives can, in principle, realize the metagood of care of persons. This is not to say that they will actually do so, only that, when they do not, "the fault is not in our stars, but in ourselves." It is never appropriate to surrender loving care for some other good, moreover, for without care the other good is unredeemable. Personal care always trumps other principles or sources of knowledge, but it does not deny or destroy them.[13]

B. The politics of care, or liberalism-as-morally-perfectionist: We are at last in a position to imagine a third kind of liberalism in some detail. Liberalism-as-morally-perfectionist, as I call it (borrowing from William Galston[14]), aims to transcend a simple dichotomy between subjectivity and objectivity, on the one hand, and expansion and reduction, on the other. The "l-a-m-p" version of liberalism begins with the proposition that there are distinctively liberal virtues that pivot around a robust fellow-feeling rather than a neutral justice. The question that divides secular and theological lamps, of course, is whether these virtues are natural or supernatural in origin. Do we need the love of God (either subjective or objective genitive) for love of neighbor? A secular theorist might argue on sociological grounds that benevolence is a universal human potential, a latent capacity as common to the species as its genius for hatred. A Christian theist will maintain, in contrast, that a properly ordered charity is a gift of grace and outstrips any requirements articulable by right reason, or even right emotion. Neither secular humanist nor Christian

---

Mass.: Harvard University Press, 1989), 63 ff.

13   On the possible competition between love and other goods, Saint Paul perhaps has the last conscientious word:

> If I speak in the tongues of men and of angels, but have not love, I am a noisy gong or a clanging cymbal. And if I have prophetic powers, and understand all mysteries and all knowledge, and if I have all faith, so as to remove mountains, but have not love, I am nothing. If I give away all I have, and if I deliver my body to be burned, but have not love, I gain nothing. (I Cor. 13:1–3, RSV)

14   Galston is picking up on a reference in Rawls. See William A. Galston, *Liberal Purposes: Goods, Virtues, and Diversity in the Liberal State* (Cambridge: Cambridge University Press, 1991), 79.

need think that actual persons ever become perfect to speak of "perfectionist *ideals*," however.

Benevolent care is more than the way of discovery; it is constructive. Care does not merely provide theoretical knowledge of another's condition; it carries with it, intrinsically, a practical impetus to action based on emotional identification. Care involves both appraisal and bestowal of value: it appreciates in vivid detail what another is going through but also moves to remedy what is bad and augment what is good. We would not call "caring" someone who had but an abstract understanding of another's pain, however complex that understanding might be. The point here is not merely that care must entail emotional empathy as well as intellectual judgment, for a sadist is emotionally sensitive to another's suffering yet disinclined to diminish it. The point is that care consistently wills and acts on the good for another (and oneself).

Many contemporary liberals are rightly impressed with the fallibility of human minds and the multiplicity of human ends, but in attending to these epistemological and ontological factors, they often fail to appreciate how persons come to be ends in themselves, capable of having and sustaining ends to begin with. John Rawls, for his part, combines a rather sceptical epistemology with a somewhat agonistic ontology. "The fact of reasonable pluralism" means, for him, ongoing and finally intractable disagreement about fundamental questions of meaning and value.[15] Being struck by the reality that reasonable people tend to differ, even after extensive dialogue, in their moral-cultural commitments is not itself sceptical. On the contrary, it is central to a liberal sensibility that would avoid coercing conscience whenever possible.[16] What *is* sceptical, however, is Rawls's epistemic prescription in the face of such disagreement.

Rawls would have us reflect on social justice in terms of a hypothetical appeal to political rationality: the veil of ignorance in the original position. As part of this appeal, Rawls is committed to an "ideal of public reason" in which citizens justify their constitutional commitments only in terms that are publicly accessible to all, independently of controversial appeals to religious faith or philosophical theory. A political conception of justice must be "freestanding," in the sense that "we leave aside how people's comprehensive doctrines connect with the content of the political conception of justice and regard that content as arising from the various fundamental ideas drawn from the political culture of a democratic society."[17] A comprehensive doctrine is any worldview that outstrips a basic sense of justice and a thin conception of the good, the sort of worldview that is denied one from behind Rawls's veil of ignorance. Only

---

15   See Rawls, *Political Liberalism*, (New York: Columbia University Press, 1993), 4.

16   As Larmore points out in "Pluralism and Reasonable Disagreement," 74 and 77–79.

17   Rawls, *Political Liberalism*, 25 n. 27.

by relying on an "overlapping consensus" that is compatible with, but does not explicitly rely on, comprehensive moral and metaphysical views can one avoid offending against "the duty of civility," according to Rawls.[18]

But why try to specify *a priori* what vocabularies can be deployed in the service of important social ends? Why not let a thousand languages bloom, comprehensive or otherwise, constrained only by prohibitions on force and fraud? This is not an abandonment of the general commitment to respect one's political interlocutors; it is rather an acknowledgment that bracketing one's comprehensive doctrines may simply make one incomprehensible to others, as well as to oneself. Sensitivity to rhetorical context is a virtue, but first of all and most of the time we owe others (and ourselves) our best explanation of what we believe and why we believe it, as well as our best motive for acting on this belief. It is an oddly sceptical epistemology that rules robust religious and philosophical visions out of court *ab initio*. Perfectionist liberals hold, *pace* Rawls, that ideals like equal dignity and liberty of conscience can win out in a fair epistemic fight. Or if such ideals can't at least "go the distance," they are not worthy of defense by conscientious persons.

It is an irony of civility that at times more sincere respect is shown to others by confronting them with revolutionary possibilities and transformative vocabularies than by assuming the status quo. Perfectionist liberals do not give up the ideal of mutually accept*able* justifications of political judgments, but they do let go of the idea that justifications and their idioms must be mutually accept*ed* prior to discourse. An early criticism of Rawls's *A Theory of Justice* was that it characterized justice too decidedly in terms of end-state principles that prejudice the outcome of free public exchange.[19] One need not be libertarian to worry that his *Political Liberalism* depicts public reason too emphatically in terms of nation-state duties that prejudice the outcome of free public dialogue. In both cases, one suspects an effort to evade embodied finitude by foreordaining the result of historical interaction. Rawls vetoes the use of controversial ways of knowing for key political purposes, thus imposing a peculiar (if passive) epistemic abstinence on citizens.

The questionable epistemology is coupled, in turn, with a questionable ontology. On the one hand, Rawls declines to consider how people become (or fail to become) free and equal; on the other hand, he interprets freedom and equality in a fashion weighted toward agony. His contractors are not actively antithetical to one another, but for deliberative purposes they are thought of as "rational and mutually disinterested," as "not taking an interest in one another's interests."[20] Rawlsian deliberators are not meant to model actual

---

18   See *Political Liberalism*, esp. Lectures IV and VI, 131–72 and 212–54.

19   See Robert Nozick, *Anarchy, State, and Utopia*, 198–204.

20   Rawls, *A Theory of Justice* (Cambridge, Mass.: Harvard University Press, 1971), 13.

moral agents, but their sense of justice and thin conception of the good nevertheless represent an emotionally detached, even implicitly adversarial, anthropology. Such an anthropology may be defensible, but to presume it as part of "political reason" is to beg a host of material questions. The reflection of Rawlsian contractors about how justly to balance ends systematically precludes weighing the fact that persons require more or less gratuitous care, public and private, to grow into rationality and to sustain moral agency itself.

It is crucial to realize that Rawls's justice as fairness is not egoistic in any crude sense: He does not wish to ban benevolence as part of an individual's "comprehensive" account of a well-lived life or part of a society's "background culture." (Indeed, his difference principle is sometimes likened, in its effects, to a Christian preferential option for the poor.) But Rawls declines to let love of neighbor do any real work (epistemic or ontological) with respect to the political. For his purposes, the primary sense of public goodness is "rationality."[21] This, by perfectionist lights, is too minimalist, *an impossible separation of the "political" and the "nonpolitical" that subverts proper moral motivation*. Rawlsian rationality is moved to egalitarian social principles by a prudent fear of being disadvantaged oneself, for example, rather than by an empathetic concern for the least well off that knows that it need never join them. One endorses principles of justice that guard against worst case scenarios (e.g., the difference principle) because, from behind the veil of ignorance, one does not know one's place in society and thus cannot be sure that one will not be among the least well off. Yet to limit moral motivation in this way is to preclude a perfectionist understanding of political virtue, as Rawls himself makes clear. The martyr who chooses to join the poor and afflicted voluntarily, to compel others' moral attention, is unintelligible. Less extremely yet more importantly, the civic republican who would structure society so as to protect the weak for their own sake is also beyond the pale of Rawlsian political reason.

Perfectionist liberalism does not *replace* justice with loving care or fall *below* giving persons their due; it holds instead that a good society should rise *above* both pure appraisal and pure bestowal to give individuals *more* than their due, narrowly defined. We all require a protection and empathy which we have not earned; we live together by supererogation. This does not mean that liberalism-as-morally-perfectionist simply demands the supererogatory of citizens; that would be a contradiction in terms. Say rather that, by the lamp of perfectionist liberalism, citizens publicly do two things: (1) redraw the usual bounds between obligation and supererogation, construing some of the actions and attitudes normally judged optional as duties of beneficence (cf. child welfare laws and national health insurance), and (2) safeguard and encourage genuine supererogation against expansive or reductive liberalisms that would

---

21   See Rawls, *A Theory of Justice*, esp. 147–49 and 476–85; and *Political Liberalism*, esp. 12–13 and 173–78.

effectively (if inadvertently) stifle charity as "unreasonable" or "merely private."

In sum, the perfectionist liberal foregrounds rather than backgrounds love. For the perfectionist liberal, the solidarity of need, in addition to desire and ability, ought to move us to recognize a range of faculties beyond science and common sense, as well as a plethora of goods beyond the idols of the tribe.[22] Again, neither group solidarity (pure subjectivity) nor impersonal rationality (pure objectivity) is sufficient for a stable society of decent citizens.

IV. The Distinctiveness of Christian Liberalism/Pluralism

A. Charity and self-sacrifice: I have suggested that a perfectionist liberalism based on personal care is an attractive synthesis of subjectivity and objectivity. At the end of the day, however, I find secular versions of this synthesis problematic. I cannot defend this impression in any detail here, but secular attempts to justify an ethic of benevolence often seem tainted by either despair or self-seeking. A vigorous love of neighbor frequently appears to them either too demanding or but a means to narrowly, if not resentfully, self-interested ends after all. Even the appeals to "sympathy" of some of the splendid British moralists of the eighteenth century grow flat or idiosyncratic as they float free of religious faith. Benevolence in Hume, for instance, is tied ineliminably to reciprocity.[23] Self-interest and reciprocity have their places, of course, but seldom is a prophet cast up by secular versions of these, for they eschew what George Steiner calls the "wager on transcendence."[24]

Prophetic Christianity is often associated with epistemic foundationalism as well as ontological (specifically, axiological) monism. The Protestant prescription, *"Sola Scriptura,"* is read as the inerrancy and sole legitimacy of the Bible as a source of truth. And the Bible is thought to teach that God is "all in all," exclusively valuable if not exclusively real. This twofold association is

---

22 For an adept secular defense of charity as "the enforcement of passive forbearance in the face of the needy person helping himself to resources," see Jeremy Waldron, "Welfare and the Images of Charity," Chapter 10 in *Liberal Rights: Collected Papers, 1981–1991* (Cambridge: Cambridge University Press, 1993), 246 and *passim*.

23 Hume writes: "All our obligations to do good to society seem to imply something reciprocal. I receive the benefits of society, and therefore ought to promote its interests." See "Of Suicide," in *Essays Moral, Political, and Literary*, ed. by Eugene Miller (Indianapolis: Liberty Classics, 1985): 577–89, cited in Beauchamp and Childress, *Principles of Biomedical Ethics* (Oxford: Oxford University Press, 1994), 269.

24 See Steiner, *Real Presences* (Chicago: University of Chicago Press, 1989), 4. As I hope to show, this willingness to gamble is (paradoxically) the last step in recovering from prodigality. It is often decisive for being "energized into creative responsibility" (p. 15).

unpersuasive, however. A distinctively Christian pluralism can readily endorse both epistemic and ontological pluralism, even while insisting that charity is the first virtue and God is the Creator of all that is. Let me first make the historical case for a rich Christian epistemology, then turn to the logic of a variegated Christian ontology.

Roman Catholicism commonly points to four avenues to knowledge, including moral and religious knowledge: scripture, tradition, reason, and culture. As the revealed word of God, the Bible has pride of place, but it is not the unique source of all insight, if only because the Bible itself must be interpreted according to the best literary-critical and historical lights we can command. In addition, the Bible does not provide explicit or exhaustive guidance on all questions, and even where it does address a given issue, individuals must determine how to apply a Biblical teaching to a concrete situation. Thus other forms of wisdom are required: psychological, sociological, etc. It is simply not possible to be thoroughgoing Campbellites, "silent where the Bible is silent."

Due to its wariness of introducing faddish or sinful elements into the sources of faithful response to God, Protestantism has tended greatly to deemphasize tradition, reason, and culture, at least in theological contexts. Yet there is no unanimity on the matter of degree. Calvin, for instance, allowed some possibility of "lightning flashes of insight" even to fallen human nature. And Roman Catholics are not alone in their fairly inclusive epistemology. The Methodist quadrilateral refers to scripture, tradition, experience, and reason. Even Karl Barth, that staunch foe of natural philosophy, cautioned against conflating the Word of God (the Trinitarian Son) with the word of man (the Bible). Quite generally, Christians speak of empirical facts apprehended by the five senses, natural laws grasped by practical reason, and supernatural truths appropriated by faith. Faith itself is now widely acknowledged to have rational, affective, and volitional elements.[25]

With respect to ontology, many Christians continue to take their lead from Genesis in calling a complex creation "good." Such Biblical pluralism still holds God to be the *Summum Bonum*, but this does not imply that God is the *Solum Bonum*. It is judged an expression of divine omnipotence and omnibenevolence that God creates real and valuable entities over against the Godhead. To distinguish the infinite Creator from finite creation in this way is already to distance both a mysticism that would collapse the world (without remainder) into God and a pantheism that would collapse God (without remainder) into the world. There is a common *source* of all being and worth, on this view, but this is not to assert that there is only one worthwhile being. As the creative font of everything that is, the God who is Love provides the

---

25   For debates about how to relate these elements, see Audi and Wainwright, eds., *Rationality, Religious Belief, and Moral Commitment*, especially the essays in Part I.

touchstone with which to evaluate all subjects, objects, actions, and events. To say that temporal goods are intelligible with reference to God, however, is not to say that they are reducible to or directly measurable in terms of God.[26]

Christians still justify their conscientious valuation of all creatures by gesturing, in faith, toward a Creator who is off the scale of value altogether. Christian pluralism depends, undeniably, on a singularity. But the eternal singularity of God makes possible, in turn, three crucial temporal realities: creation, incarnation, and redemption. These three are the foundation of Christian democratic equality. In creating a single couple (Adam and Eve) to be the first parents (monogenism), God is held to establish the consanguinity of all humanity. Social solidarity ought not merely be local, for the entire species is made in the Image of God and stems from a single common origin. Ultimately, all are family. It is hard to overstate what the loss of this self-understanding—to be sure, never adequately acted on—means to Western culture. Second, the fullness of God's love for humanity is believed by Christians to be manifest in the Incarnation. God meets fallen humanity where it is, in all its diversity, sin, and suffering, and the soul feels its worth by imitating the Christ. The eternal God is "pluralistic" enough, so to speak, to identify with temporal beings. Lastly, the divine condescension calls for a creative human response. Out of gratitude for the redemption extended to humanity on the cross, an integrating love is now judged both possible and mandatory for

---

26 In "Pluralism and Reasonable Disagreement," 73, Charles Larmore writes that liberalism is distinctive for "its refusal, ever more pronounced, to base the principles of political association upon a vision of God's plan or of an ordered cosmos." This may now be descriptively true, but it is not normatively so, I have maintained. Perfectionist liberalism is exactly a refusal of the refusal Larmore refers to. Larmore goes on, p. 74, to contend that "pluralism is a doctrine about the nature of value. It asserts that the forms of moral concern, as well as the forms of self-realization, are in the end not one, but many. It stands, therefore, in opposition to religious and metaphysical conceptions of a single source of value." I disagree. I have repeatedly argued that a Christian liberalism that sees God as the *origin* of all value—God as the "single source," in this sense—need not *equate* all value with God. One can believe the cosmos ordered and thus avoid ontological chaos and agony, in short, without being a reductionist about value.

I can further elaborate these ideas with reference to one of Larmore's own distinctions. Larmore argues for understanding the variety of moral goods as "comparable" but not "commensurable" (especially pp. 67–69). We can weigh heterogenous values and evaluate alternate courses of action, he contends, without thinking that these are quantifiable within a single metric based on a unique Good. This distinction is useful in explaining how strong agapism can hold to the primacy of love without reducing to love monism. Charity can be compared to other real goods without thinking that those goods are but competing instances of charity. *Agape* is the first virtue for many Christians because it is the most direct participation in the life of the Creator and a necessary condition for the other virtues, but there are other created goods and virtues.

believers. "And above all these put on love, which binds everything together in perfect harmony" (Colossians 3:14, RSV).

Let me concentrate on the love Christians call *"agape."* The two commandments of Matthew 22:37–40 indicate to Christians that the first form of this love is unconditional obedience to God. The second form, love of the neighbor, embodies the two aspects of care described above, but it combines them with a third that is more radical: *(3) service open to self-sacrifice for the sake of the other.* I use the phrase "open to self-sacrifice" advisedly. Feminist critiques have made clear the dangers, especially for women, in both an uncritical equation of *agape* and self-sacrifice and an uncritical contrast of *agape* and self-regard.[27] (Valorizing self-denial can lead to masochism; vilifying self-development can lead to sloth.) Even so, readiness to serve others remains an evangelical virtue near the heart of Christian ethics. To bear one another's burdens is "to fulfill the law of Christ" (Galatians 6:2).

Steadfast love is not nonresisting in the face of injustice, nor is it even always nonviolent, I believe.[28] But a forgiving mildness is often the only effective means to break the cycle of hatred and retaliation that results from sin. When this can be done freely and constructively, *agape* does surrender certain rights (e.g., to punishment) to restore mutual relation. It must be emphasized, however, that self-surrender is necessary not merely as a remedy for sin. *Agape* must sometimes forego genuine goods for another's benefit independently of antecedent injustice. Creative service is needed, that is, not simply to restore justice but to inaugurate justice. Mutuality, the joyful communion between free and equal individuals, remains an ideal for Christians. But the genesis of free and equal persons requires sacrifice on the part of individuals as well as groups. (Think of parents working to provide food for their infant children and nations voting to provide health care for their citizens who cannot pay.) This is the great moral truth that prodigal liberalisms have forgotten. Much liberalism, both the morally empty and the morally basic variety, has been so concerned to protect the exercise of autonomy that like an ungrateful child it has forgotten at what cost that autonomy has been acquired.

To be finite is to be in need of unearned assistance from others and to be called to give unearned assistance to others. *Pace* many secular philosophers

---

27   For a summary discussion, see Barbara Hilkert Andolsen, "*Agape* in Feminist Ethics," in *Feminist Theological Ethics*, ed. by Lois K. Daly (Louisville: Westminster John Knox Press, 1994). Andolsen (p. 156) writes: "Frequently for women the problem is too little self-assertion rather than too much. Neither self-sacrifice nor other-regard captures the total meaning of *agape*. The full expression of the Christian ideal is mutuality."

28   For a defense of the just war tradition as compatible with charity, see my "Christian Love and Political Violence," in *The Love Commandments*, ed. by Edmund Santurri and William Werpehowski (Washington, D.C.: Georgetown University Press, 1992).

and some feminist theologians, however, Christian faith wagers that there is no ultimate contradiction between caring for the neighbor and properly loving oneself. Both creation stories in Genesis, for example, suggest that humanity's interdependence is a part of God's initial intention for the world. It is good to need each other. *Agape* often entails genuine self-sacrifice, as I have repeatedly indicated, but it is not just a zero-sum game in which loving the neighbor means wronging oneself. Choices have to be made, priorities set, and these will relativize temporal ends and associations. To those without religious conviction this may seem like world-hatred or self-loathing, the opposite of pluralism; indeed, Christ himself proclaims: "If anyone comes to me and does not hate his own father and mother and wife and children and brothers and sisters, yes, and even his own life, he cannot be my disciple" (Luke 14:26, RSV). Yet Christ's own example makes clear the sense in which one is to "hate" personal ties: They are not to be allowed to interfere with obedience to God or concern for the stranger. Faith does not despise finite existence; it is neither masochistic nor slothful. It simply believes that charity is its own reward, a participation in the Holiness of God, even when real values like health and happiness and even public cooperation are freely given up out of fidelity to that love.[29]

A prophet must frequently surrender health, happiness, and civic harmony for the sake of a higher loyalty, but applauding this willingness presupposes axiological pluralism. A martyr is admirable exactly because she has sacrificed something really valuable. Less spectacular than martyrdom, forgiveness is an especially neglected form of self-sacrifice in liberal societies, yet it is essential to the prophetic reconciliation of subjectivity and objectivity. The Christian prophet is a more dynamic voice than that described by Walzer, for she is a strong agapist who criticizes the community's self-understanding, not merely interprets it. But her prophetic criticism links judgment with a call for forgiveness, an insistence on social justice (objectivity) with a sense of our common sinfulness (subjectivity). The prophet enjoins bearing one another's burdens, but she wagers on a divine presence in all creatures that makes mercy's burden light. Her steadfast love ("*hesed*" in Hebrew) is most distinctive in distancing prudential reason without despair. As participation in the life of God, *agape* is willing to serve where appropriate without human

---

29   *Agape* is not a zero-sum game, but for Christians it is a categorical command (in addition to Matthew 22:37–40, see John 13:34 and I Corinthians 14:1): It may not be surrendered as a motive, no matter how much this might contribute to other genuine values like public peace and cooperation. Furthermore, *agape* is, in most respects, *a nonaggregative good*: It aims to foster virtue in others, but it may not be abandoned by individuals for the sake of net increases in *agape* itself. That would be personal apostasy, a form of "self-sacrifice" to which a Christian is not open.

reciprocity. The fidelity *of* God on the cross is sufficient for empowering fidelity *to* God and creatures.

A much-noted threat to liberal culture is its tendency to degenerate into factionalism: special interests vying for scarce resources with little or no sense of the commonweal. This orientation is particularly destructive when calls for distributive and compensatory justice erode into the politics of resentment: past social wrongs forever alienating race from race, gender from gender, faith from faith, etc. *Agape's* capacity for forgiveness together with its sense of a shared human nature, god-like but fallible, comes into its own here. Zeal for justice alone, independent of *agape*, often becomes mere petulance, if not perpetual vendetta. Forgiveness must not be masochistic or uncritical; it must not acquiesce in tyranny or abet indifference. Blessed is she, however, who leavens judgment with understanding. Without a spirit of love that transcends resentment, including the adversarial resentments between caricatured liberalism and religion, I see little hope for truly liberal nations or universities.[30]

As a variety of perfectionist liberalism, civic agapism rises above political morality as exclusively concerned with justice and injustice, rage and counter-rage, to embrace the indispensability of love. *But now the love is of both God and neighbor.* God's love (subjective genitive) for humanity is the source of humanity's love of itself and of God (objective genitive). The politics of charity that result will emphasize how individuals are empowered to have or regain a range of viable ends rather than how they can be unencumbered for the pursuit of ends already entertained. *But now the empowerment is traced back to a super-*

---

30   Listening to the militant chants of many campus groups these days, one cannot help but compare them with the civil rights protesters led by Martin Luther King, Jr., in the 1950s and '60s. King's followers sang "We Shall Overcome" and projected a spirit of justice fundamentally tempered by Christian charity. To bigots of all stripes they declared, in effect: "Though you mistreat us, we will stand up for our rights; though you despise us, we will overcome you with nonviolent love. For we refuse to hate you no matter what you do; we aim at *mutual redemption* and so will not diminish ourselves, or you, by mirroring your inhumanity." In the 1990s, in contrast, the message is frequently one of intimidation: "Hey, hey, ho, ho, Xism has got to go!" The anger at racism, sexism, economic exploitation, cultural imperialism, etc., is understandable, even justifiable; righteous indignation is, frequently, the catalyst of moral revolution. But the troubling subtext of much campus anger is: "If you don't give us what we want, we will roll over you! We as a crowd will fight fire with fire, for we are victims and will become victimizers ourselves rather than remain so!" The tactics of intimidation and resentment are so popular because, in the short run, they "work": they get attention, and administrators are often cowed by them. In the long run, however, "liberal" anger alone is an even less reliable moral compass than "liberal" justice alone. Undiluted rage turns readily to a hatred that wills harm; even the noble idea of "multiculturalism" has become an occasion for ethnic groups to bait and loathe each other. And so we fail to show our students how to say a healing word.

natural origin not intrinsic to any finite good or any human faculty as such. In short, Christianity refers the mystery of human belatedness back to a timeless Trinity: We "second persons" must rely on a First, Second, and Third Person who loves us unconditionally. Unlike the Stoic citizen of the universe, the Christian agapist is in the world but not of it; his life is not his own but a gift, and his hoped-for destiny is an eternity that transcends any natural harmony or disharmony.[31]

This is not a denial of fragility, a refusal of humanity, but rather a "wager on transcendence" from within a fidelity to immanence. It is attention to both capacities and limits, the effort to be true to both heaven and earth, that gives Christian liberalism its distinctiveness. Christian faith checks modern and postmodern accents on the "fragmentation" and "agony" of values by insisting on the primacy of love, but that same faith augments Stoic and Enlightenment talk of the "harmony of nature" and the "perfectibility of man" with an emphasis on the supernatural origin and end of the prime virtue. Perfection*ist* liberalism is not to be confused with Pelagian perfection*ism*. At the Fall, humanity freely corrupted itself beyond human undoing; but out of the hand of God human beings were not agonistic, and in the hand of God they may cease to be so. Thus the proper response to present conflict is not to accept it as fated or permanent but to remind ourselves of our original possibilities and ongoing redemption by God. "With this faith" (King), Christianity offers a remedy for the degeneration of much secular "theory" into dilemmas incompatible with charity.[32] The Christian agapist is highly critical, e.g., of Seneca's

---

31 Whether one requires an afterlife to practice *agape* consistently is debated even in Christian circles; see my "The Disconsolation of Theology: Irony, Cruelty, and Putting Charity First," *The Journal of Religious Ethics* 20, no. 1 (Spring 1992): 1–35.

32 Some Christian ethicists endorse moral dilemmas as consistent with, even integral to, religious faith. Among the more skillful recent defenders of hard practical paradoxes is Philip Quinn. Quinn holds that "the possibility of a dilemma arising is built into Christian ethics at its foundations. . . . [I]t seems clear that it is possible for a situation to arise in which the two parts of the Great Commandment [to love God with total devotion and to love the neighbor as oneself] are in conflict." Quinn observes in a footnote that "the greatest and first commandment" is "You shall love the Lord your God with your whole heart, with your whole soul, and with all your mind" (Matthew 22:37), with the "second," which is "like it," being "You shall love your neighbor as yourself" (Mt. 22:38). I am not sure, however, why he then continues to refer to the two commandments together as "*the* Great Commandment." There can be tension between the two commandments, for they are not simply identical, but there are limits to the opposition. Referring to the commands in the singular blurs the fact, which Quinn grants, that they are lexically ordered. In any case, the thrust of the Gospels seems to rule out the commandments' being flatly contradictory: "[H]e who loves his neighbor has fulfilled the law" (Romans 13:8). I reply at length to Quinn, et al., in my *The Priority of Love: A Defense of Christian Charity* (forthcoming from Cambridge University Press). It must suffice here to note that, even for Quinn, "[i]t is . . . a

defense of suicide and Walzer's defense of emergency ethics: Both suggest a superlative mind and heart running up against the limits of a naturalistic philosophy. The result is an all-too-literal self-contradiction that cannot be squared with love of God and neighbor.

B. Origen, Aquinas, and Rawls on goodness and incarnation: I have maintained that agapic love outstrips anything that tribal custom or Greek rationality can render plausible, but that it is, nevertheless, the basis of Christian liberalism. To support this claim, if only anecdotally, let me cite two rich resources, Origen and Thomas Aquinas, and compare them briefly with John Rawls. I do not suggest that Origen and Aquinas are straightforwardly liberal in ways that all perfectionists, secular and religious, would validate. My aim is merely to highlight some surprising affinities between their orthodox faith and democratic scruples.

In *De Principiis*, Origen writes: ". . . it is one power which grasps and holds together all the diversity of the world, and leads the different movements towards one work, lest so immense an undertaking as that of the world should be dissolved by the dissensions of souls."[33] This belief in the unity of a diverse world, founded in Origen's case on a monotheistic faith, strikes fear in the hearts of many secular philosophers. It may even strike religious traditionalists as a bit quaint. Who thinks of the universe as a single, purposive "undertaking" anymore? Believers in liberal democracy in particular are taught to be wary of "universalist" claims and sweeping "metanarratives," even as are the sectarian critics of liberalism. Such claims and narratives are thought to foster tyranny. The theists among us will still affirm the workings of divine providence, but even theists may balk at Origen's optimism that "all things are [eventually] to be restored to their original condition" by God's ineffable wisdom.

It is easy enough to find proto-democratic sentiments in Aquinas's explicitly political writings.[34] I want, however, to lift up Thomas's comments on the

---

typically audacious Christian hope that even a tragic ethical dilemma need not spell tragedy for the whole of one's ethical life. Providence may provide a replacement for shattered goodness." See Quinn, "Tragic Dilemmas, Suffering Love, and Christian Life," in *The Journal of Religious Ethics* 17 (1989): 171, 179, and 181. See also his "Moral Obligation, Religious Demand, and Practical Conflict," in Robert Audi and William Wainwright, eds., *Rationality, Religious Belief, and Moral Commitment* (Ithaca and London: Cornell University Press, 1986).

33   Origen, *De Principiis*, in *The Ante-Nicene Fathers*, ed. by Alexander Roberts and James Donaldson, Vol. IV, trans. by Frederick Crombie (Grand Rapids, Mich.: Wm. B. Eerdmans, 1979), Bk. II, Chap. 1, p. 268.

34   "Nature has made all men equal in liberty," Saint Thomas informs us, and "the rule of the sovereign" is to be "for the good of the subjects whose servants the sovereigns may call themselves . . ." See *Commentary on the Sentences of Peter the Lombard*, II, 44, 1, 3, reply to Obj. 1, trans. by Vernon J. Bourke, in *The Pocket*

Word made flesh as a neglected liberal resource. In the *Summa Theologiae*, he allows that there may, in principle, be multiple Incarnations:

> . . . the uncreated cannot be comprehended by any creature. Hence it is plain that, whether we consider the Divine Person in regard to His power, which is the principle of the union, or in regard to His Personality, which is the term of the union, it has to be said that the Divine Person, over and beyond the human nature which He has assumed, can assume another distinct human nature.[35]

Unlike the Origen quote, this passage might well be greeted with muted applause by secular liberals. It suggests an admirable openness to Goodness appearing in different times and places. The Truth, it seems, may take a plurality of finite forms. For many religious traditionalists, in contrast, the quote from Thomas may seem disturbingly relativistic. How should there be another Incarnation if Jesus is singular, the fullness of God made manifest, "a full, perfect, and sufficient sacrifice" for humanity's sake, the only begotten Son? Isn't the glory of the Christian faith its trusting in the unique salvific significance of the one historic Jesus? (As one of my students put it, "Wouldn't the Third Person of the Trinity say: 'Been there, done that'?") Or are the Jesus*es* of history separable from the Christ of a common faith?

The quotes from Origen and Aquinas appear antithetical, but this is *prima facie*. Both Origen and Aquinas offer cues for Christian liberalism in together helping to reconcile expansive and reductive viewpoints. Origen's insistence on this being One World helps rather than hinders a commitment to cultural diversity and individual liberty. His brand of universalism is a study in the potential of reductive sensibilities to become conscientious. Correlatively, Aquinas's celebration of the Incarnation holds a key to revising expansive pluralism. Thomas does not simply endorse the goodness of embodied existence, as important as that is; remarkably, he is open to the possibility of numerous Christs. Each Christ remains a singularity, however, in that each embodies the same God, a God who identifies with humanity but remains opaque to creatures in time.[36]

Aquinas (New York: Simon and Schuster, 1960), p. 234. Moreover, "the best form of government is in a state or kingdom, wherein one is given the power to preside over all; while under him are others having governing powers; and yet a government of this kind is shared by all, both because all are eligible to govern, and because the rule[r]s [*sic*] are chosen by all." See *Summa Theologica*, Pt. I-II, Q. 105, Art. 1, trans. by the Fathers of the English Dominican Province (Westminster, Md.: Christian Classics/Benziger Brothers, 1981), Vol. II, p. 1092.

35   Thomas Aquinas, *Summa Theologica*, Pt. III, Q. 3, Art. 7, in Ibid., Vol. 4, p. 2043. (In my own writings, I refer to Thomas's major work as the "*Summa Theologiae*," historically a more accurate title, I believe.)

36   Although Thomas might be called an *eschatological* foundationalist—at the end

Rather than monotheism licensing tyranny and enforcing sameness, Origen allows that "under the influences of different motives, creatures nevertheless complete the fulness and perfection of one world, and the very variety of minds tends to one end of perfection."[37] If one is tempted to see a proto-Adam Smith here, it must be emphasized that the "invisible hand" at work is God's, and that the motive moving God's hand is what Origen calls God's "primal goodness." This goodness does not necessitate, moreover; it is a respecter of personal liberty. Origen writes:

> . . . every spirit, whether soul or rational existence, however called, should not be compelled by force, against the liberty of his own will, to any other course than that to which the motives of his own mind led him (lest by so doing the power of exercising free-will should seem to be taken away, which certainly would produce a change in the nature of the being itself)[38] . . .

Note that the Origenal defense of liberty is tied to a reverence for created individuality, not merely for autonomy as the expression of arbitrary or narrowly prudent choice. Origen is working out the implications of respect for creaturely finitude rather than questing after a limitless or merely self-referential freedom. One does not (normally) coerce, for this changes people's specific natures and thus tampers with God's creation.

God's primal goodness, it seems, is nothing less than a love of the diversity of the world; and even in directing that diversity to a discrete end, providence honors particularity. In short, Origen adumbrates a distinctive brand of liberalism: neither Enlightenment universalism based on foundationalist epistemology and justice-centered politics nor postmodernist pragmatism based on relativist anti-epistemology and bourgeois insouciance. The human end for Origen is Christlike love, which cannot be forced but can be freely, i.e., conscientiously, shared by all. It is precisely because Origen believes in God's primal goodness that he can celebrate the apparent chaos of the world. Because he holds to the primacy of love, God's own joy in creation, Origen can see the unity in diversity, the harmony in seeming cacophony, and thus not squelch the complexity.

If Thomas can be pluralist about the God-man in thirteenth-century Italy, we can be catholic about human nature in twentieth-century America. The task for liberalism-as-morally-perfectionist is twofold: (1) to honor the singularity

---

of time we will contemplate with certainty the full range and meaning of Truth—his epistemic humility about *this* life has much to teach liberal theorists about how to avoid both dogmatism and nihilism. On earth, creatures' rational knowledge of God is at a distance and *ab effectu*.

37   Origen, *De Principiis*, Bk. II, Chap. 1, p. 268.

38   Ibid.

of historical traditions while avoiding sectarianism, yet simultaneously (2) to affirm the universality of certain truths about human nature and social nurture without going hegemonic. Thomas on the Incarnation provides a clue to how this might be done in a characteristically Christian way. For Thomas, Jesus is a singular universal, eternal Goodness having assumed temporal form. The Biblical stories of Jesus' life, death, and resurrection are accessible to all believers yet stamped by the ethnic specificity of first-century Judaism. They are the defining narratives, the mythic histories or historical myths, of the early Christian church as well as of contemporary converts. More to the point, they do not exclude the possibility of ongoing revelation in other quarters.

Obviously, claims about incarnate Goodness will strike some contemporary liberals as the quintessence of religious ir- or a-rationality. But such claims, "the scandal of particularity," were controversial long before modernity, or even Aquinas. Jesus was put to death as an "insurrectionist," after all. It is crucial to realize, however, that Jesus was condemned not because he advocated armed rebellion against the Roman state or because he sought to overturn the Mosaic Law. Jesus was neither a political zealot nor a religious revolutionary; he was, to mix metaphors, a perfect liberal who refused to hide his lamp under a bushel. His message was disturbing precisely because he offered a vision and a vocabulary that highlighted the *limits* of local politics and traditional ritual. Jesus was *offensive* to Pilate and the Sanhedrin because he was mostly indifferent to their powers and ceremonies. He accepted taxes and went to temple, yet he associated with publicans and sinners; he was no ascetic despiser of the earth, yet he gestured toward an unconditional value he identified with a heavenly gift. His charisma did not pander to human subjectivity, nor did his reverence for life absolutize anything objective in the world. In recommending radical love of God and neighbor, Jesus was not directly seditious or blasphemous, but he was (by entrenched lights) uncivil. He trusted conscientiously in a higher Good than temporal authority or common rationality could admit, and for this "pluralism" he was killed.

This makes all the more chilling the fact that in *Political Liberalism*, John Rawls normally requires a bracketing of one's religious convictions in public debates about basic matters of justice.[39] It is unclear how Rawlsian public rationality and Christian social prophecy are compatible. Rawls as a rule limits public justification to "common sense . . . and the methods and conclusions of science when these are not controversial,"[40] while prophecy knows no such epistemic bounds. It is not religious voices alone that seem unduly muzzled by the duty of civility. In *Political Liberalism*, Rawls would banish *all* comprehensive doctrines, both religious-theological and secular-philosophical, from

---

39 Rawls, *Political Liberalism*, esp. 217–36; yet cf. the discussion of "free political speech" and "subversive advocacy," especially pp. 340–56.

40 Ibid., 224.

explicit advocacy concerning basic justice and constitutional essentials in a well-ordered society. But this evenhandedness is called into question by, among other things, his controversial footnote on abortion.

> Suppose . . . that we consider the question [of abortion] in terms of these three important political values: the due respect for human life, the ordered reproduction of political society over time, including the family in some form, and finally the equality of women as equal citizens. (There are, of course, other important political values besides these.) Now I believe any reasonable balance of these three values will give a woman a duly qualified right to decide whether or not to end her pregnancy during the first trimester. The reason for this is that at this early stage of pregnancy the political value of the equality of women is over-riding, and this right is required to give it substance and force.[41]

Rawls is quick to emphasize that his remarks are not an adequate argument for a moral position on abortion; they are an opinion. The disclaimer notwithstanding, however, many Christians will find these words insensitive to how the Image of God becomes incarnate among us. Human life is a vulnerable gift from God, they hold, and gratitude for one's own nurture ought normally to incline one to protect that life throughout its maturation. Even so, Rawls's opinion is not unreasonable. It is the expected upshot of protecting the autonomy of actual persons over respecting the life of potential persons, of basic liberalism's placing justice ahead of love. The point is that Rawls's words are not metaphysically neutral; he does appear, despite protests, to take a key-things-considered stand.[42] And why not grant this? A "public reason" that would prescind entirely from contested issues surrounding human nature and social purposes—call this "natural law by artificial means"—seems either vacuous or a misleading way of privileging a particular (often secular) agenda.[43]

41   Ibid., 243 n. 32.

42   Philip Quinn has pointed out that one need not disagree with the substance of Rawls's remarks on abortion to insist, nevertheless, that they flow from a debatable view about the meaning of life, love, birth, death, autonomy, equality, etc. See Quinn, "Political Liberalisms and Their Exclusions of the Religious," in *The Proceedings and Addresses of The American Philosophical Association* 69, no. 2 (November 1995): 35–56. Quinn's essay is included in this volume as Chapter 4.

43   Robert Audi argues for what he calls "the principle of secular motivation": "[O]ne should not advocate or promote any legal or public policy restrictions on human conduct unless one not only has and is willing to offer, but is also *motivated by*, adequate secular reason, where this reason (or set of reasons) is motivationally sufficient for the conduct in question." See Audi, "The Separation of Church and State and the Obligations of Citizenship," *Philosophy and Public Affairs* 18, no. 3 (Summer 1989): 284. Cf. also Audi's contribution to the present collection. One may have any number of religious inspirations for a political

An alternative to Rawlsian "civility" is an epistemic pluralism that allows much more readily for the prophetic. The prophetic moment in political discourse comes when a powerful, often suffering, voice challenges the entrenched assumptions of science and/or commonsense and moves fellow citizens to reevaluate these. Rawls's rather adversarial stance against the prophetic is in the name of democracy, rather than empire or synagogue—Kant, rather than Caesar or Herod—but it remains a recognizable syndrome. It is, I am tempted to say, a preference for the German Immanuel over the Israelite one. Christians should be wary of it as (unintentionally) prejudiced against their flesh, as well as their soul: In the name of publicity, communities of faith must disincarnate themselves and their distinctive voices. For Rawls, it seems, the priority of the right supersedes the primal goodness of faith. Thus would the prodigal son of political liberalism slay its original father.

The passages from Origen and Aquinas quoted earlier suggest that neither agnosticism nor atheism is necessary for a viable pluralism; on the contrary, the quotes convey distinctively religious reasons for liberality and civility. Beyond this, a charitable reading of more recent Christian history implies that Rawls's quest for a metaphysical impartiality that is neither agnostic nor atheistic but somehow comprehensively neutral is at best unnecessary. Annealed in the fire of Catholic-Protestant antagonism, Christianity knows all about respect for individual conscience: Out of love for the other as a free creature of God, no one should be compelled to speak or act against her will, normally.[44] Even in a highly liberal society, there must be *some* restraint of civic conversation for the sake of mutual respect and public legitimacy. But such restraint cuts both ways. If perfectionist accounts of benevolence risk becoming tyrannical or obscurantist, purely political accounts of justice may invite

---

stance, according to Audi, but one must *also* have and be moved by secular ones. Yet whence comes Audi's implicit faith that there will always be an "adequate" nonreligious rationale in crucial moral contexts? Can't much of a secular society, of any society for that matter, go morally bankrupt (one inevitably thinks of Nazi Germany)? "Adequacy" cannot be a function of rhetorical effectiveness alone, but then what does constitute "adequate secular reason"?

44 As the American evangelical leader John Leland argued in 1791

> Every man must give an account of himself to God and therefore every man ought to be at liberty to serve God in that way that he can best [*sic*] reconcile it to his conscience. . . . It would be sinful for a man to surrender to man which is to be kept sacred for God. A man's mind should be always open to conviction, and an honest man will receive that doctrine which appears the best demonstrated; and what is more common for the best of men to change their minds?

See Leland, *The Rights of Conscience Inalienable*, quoted by Witte in "The Essential Rights and Liberties of Religion," 390–91.

quietism or despair. There is no neutral way to adjudicate love/justice and theism/atheism debates, and we must be vigilant against the erosion of moral motive that comes from subscribing to views of reason, justice, and person-hood simply because they jibe with the considered opinions of the age, however procedurally democratic.

Conclusion

I have not argued that "America must be Christian,"[45] but rather that Chris-tians must not be *merely* American. (Call this the "uncivilizing" of charity.) Neither have I suggested that federal or state government is always to be the vehicle of benevolence. The principle of subsidiarity, allowing those local groups and institutions closest to a need to address it, is quite compatible with the liberalism I defend. Still, it might seem that, at most, I have suggested why nonperfectionist liberalisms may seem derelict *to Christians*. "You can preach love to the choir all you want," the objection might read, "but secular liberals aim at a wider audience and must appeal to a narrower consensus. For his part, Rawls must address atheists, agnostics, believers (of many faiths), ra-tional decision theorists, romantic poets, retired generals, conscientious objec-tors, et al. Why criticize him, moreover, for not doing what he does not claim to do? He does not offer a comprehensive account of the good life or the best society, and he does not mean to impugn private charity. Indeed, justice as fairness is intended to be endorsable by all reasonable doctrines, including Christianity."[46]

My response is that Rawls and others are themselves "preaching to the choir," instructing them not to sing their hymns out loud. If, as I suspect, some politically relevant truths can only be grasped in religiously sonorous terms, then for the choir to stifle itself in the name of "fairness" would be folly. (The parent must call out publicly to the prodigal in her own recognizable voice.) As a matter of sociological fact, I doubt that evacuating most public speech of perfectionist appeals to benevolence (religious or not) will enhance the pros-pects of civic harmony, much less of private charity. More likely it will lead to social callousness and the competitive individualism that alienates us from

---

45   This is the troubling title of a book by H. C. Goerner (Atlanta: Home Mission Board of the Southern Baptist Convention, 1947).

46   Several Christian authors have in fact defended justice as fairness as an expres-sion of, or at least as compatible with, *agape*. See, *inter alia*, Harlan Beckley, "A Christian Affirmation of Rawls's Idea of Justice as Fairness: Parts I and II," *The Journal of Religious Ethics* 13, no. 2 (Fall 1985) and 14, no. 2 (Fall 1986); and Paul Weithman, "Rawlsian Liberalism and the Privatization of Religion: Three Theo-logical Objections Considered," *The Journal of Religious Ethics* 22, no. 1 (Spring 1994): 3–28. For a response to the latter, see my "Love in a Liberal Society," *The Journal of Religious Ethics* (Spring 1994): 29–38.

our neighbors in a too-bourgeois culture. Charity needs all the explicit endorsement it can get, and for this the public example and collective diction of the religious may be vital. The important language of "rights" and "duties" must be augmented by reference to compassion for basic needs shared by all but not specifiable in terms of desert or contract.[47]

Admittedly, the language of "truth, goodness, and beauty"—especially when coupled with "the revealed will of God"—may seem to encourage dogmatism. Christianity has a great burden of historical guilt—sexism, racism (including anti-Semitism), triumphalism—but we must not assume that theology or any other perfectionist idiom is inevitably or uniquely the problematic partner in civil discourse. Minimalist liberal "theories" may themselves be stumbling blocks to a decent society, and we must constantly ask how to evaluate them. Once relativism prevails concerning notions like truth, goodness, and beauty, we cannot even talk about "liberal *theory*" in the classical sense of a general account of how things are, rather than how we want or imagine them to be. Rawls's views are clearly animated by a profound concern for his fellow citizens and the world at large. With no metaphysics of the person, however, it would seem his contractors treat people as free and equal not because they actually think them so but chiefly because doing so is part of the (mutable) political culture of their times. Ultimately, one must ask: Is Rawls's "theory" of justice falsifiable, or does it substitute *de facto* praxis for theory? Disturbing, if the latter.

What, specifically, might liberal theorists learn from the Origenal and Thomistic hints I have so briefly held up? I am under no illusion about the prospect of mass conversions among postmodern citizens: An effective atheism grips us all most of the time. Yet consider what a cultural self-understanding might look like if it began with the idea that human beings are capable, with grace, of at least an echo of what Origen calls "primal goodness." To wager on such goodness is to affirm that our moral faculties are not useless passions, to trust that the burdens of our care for one another are worth it. The tendency of some forms of liberalism to scepticism and agony might then be avoided by a genuine epistemological and ontological pluralism, one that recognizes that there are many ways to know the truth, though all are fallible, and that there are many good things to be known, though all stem from one source. Rather than beginning with an appeal to political rationality, we might then begin with imaginative empathy with fellow creatures; rather than seeing religious belief as a threat or cause for restraint, we might see it as an occasion for celebration.

Basing political action and reflection on distinctly theological virtues would remain, of course, a free choice of equal citizens. Religious liberalism *is* liberal. If the religion of faith, hope, and love were embraced, however, this would be

---

47   Elements of this paragraph are drawn from my "Love in a Liberal Society," 35.

primarily because it is believed true, not because it is commonly agreeable or practically expedient. Asking what is reasonably agreeable to all for the sake of public cooperation is an important liberal tactic. But when consensus (even democratic consensus) becomes the sole, or even the central, foundation of liberal respect itself, then political virtue in addition to religious faith is undermined. Political morality cannot wait on the *vox populi*, if only because agreement about public reasonableness itself is virtually as elusive as unanimity on God. This is not to say that religious liberalism is blind to the social origins and consequences of belief. On the contrary, a civic faith could be celebrated (secondarily) because it allows us to transcend cripplingly dilemmatic worldviews without denying the variety and vulnerability of embodied virtue. Taking Aquinas at his word, the faithful might even look for a new Incarnation of God's Word in distant persons (male or female) and places (pagan or Christian).

Were liberal "theory" to admit the possibility of such a rebirth, it would cease to be prodigal.

Postscript: Rawls and Religious Reasons

In the original hardback edition of *Political Liberalism* (1993), John Rawls rejects a fully "exclusive view" in which religious reasons are always illicit in the public sphere when basic or constitutional matters are at stake. Moved by the examples of nineteenth-century abolitionists and of Martin Luther King, Jr., Rawls concedes that his "inclusive view" properly "allow[s] citizens, in certain [disordered] situations, to present what they regard as the basis of political values rooted in their comprehensive doctrine, provided they do this in ways that strengthen the ideal of public reason itself" (p. 247; yet cf. p. 94). This concession can be interpreted in a number of ways, but its most natural reading has two problems: (1) it grants voice to religious sensibility as such only in a disordered society and (2) it requires that sensibility to be too motivated by concern for political consensus.

The consequence of both (1) and (2) is, for Christians, to make fidelity to God subordinate to political harmony. When civic disharmony reigns, Rawls suggests, one may appeal to comprehensive doctrine to urge the society in the direction of well-orderedness. In a well-ordered society, however, that appeal is unreasonable since it does not rely only on the existing overlapping consensus. In this way, obedience to God and love of neighbor lose their "regulative primacy," to borrow Rawls's phrase (p. 257); they are instrumental goods for political purposes, rather than fundamental values perpetually binding. With regard to (2), Paul Weithman has argued that Rawls's inclusive standard may imply a serious misdescription of religious activists' aims. It would be highly misleading to characterize Martin Luther King, Jr., for example, as invoking a comprehensive religious doctrine for the sake of political values and ideals. The motivation was obedience to God and love of the neighbor as fellow creature of God. Obviously, King had political goals, legislative agendas, etc.; but these were inspired by his antecedent religious faith, not the other way round.[48]

In his latest work, some unpublished at the time of my writing, Rawls relaxes still further the rigors of "civility." I cannot respond to all the changes in Rawls's highly nuanced position; I limit myself to three related observations, three connected questions, and a final speculation. *First observation*: Rawls now subscribes to what he calls "the wide view of public reason" in which "reasonable [comprehensive] doctrines may be introduced in public reason at any time, provided that in due course public reasons, given by a reasonable political conception, are presented sufficient to support whatever the comprehensive doctrines are introduced to support."[49] This is a significant advance on the past, I believe, one allowing a more conspicuous place for "witnessing" to one's comprehensive doctrine in protest of a social policy or practice (FC, pp. 15–16). Yet it remains an implication of the wide view that, if there are not sufficient public reasons to be adduced in addition to the comprehensive ones offered, then the latter are illegitimate.

This brings me to my *first question*: Why disqualify freestanding comprehensive doctrines? Simply to assume that this is required by a democratic polis is to beg the question about the indispensability of perfectionist sentiments, but to argue for it is to appeal to some comprehensive doctrine about the point of politics and thus to outrun the duty of civility. Public reasons are not sufficient for Rawls's political conception of justice itself. He grants that many reasonable people are not persuaded that justice as fairness is the *only* reasonable conception (IPL, pp. xlix and lii–liii), so presumably he ought not advocate his specific "theory" in basic or constitutional contexts. And given that some reasonably doubt that there is even a reasonable *family* of political conceptions, it appears Rawls should refrain from advocating the ideal of public reason entirely, especially if he ever becomes an elected official or Supreme Court justice. He may be willing to live with this conclusion (cf. FC, pp. 17–18), but it seems to approach a *reductio* of his ongoing labors.

Second observation: In "Further Considerations," p. 3, Rawls sides explicitly with those who maintain that judges cannot "put aside as irrelevant" or otherwise cease to rely on their comprehensive religious, philosophical, or moral doctrines when judging. That would be an impossible "bracketing" of their deepest identities. Indeed, Rawls imagines a nominee for the Supreme

---

48   See Weithman, "Taking Rites Seriously," in *Pacific Philosophical Quarterly* 75 (1994): esp. pp. 281–85.

49   Rawls, "Introduction to the Paperback Edition" of *Political Liberalism* (IPL), (New York: Columbia University Press, 1996), li–lii; see also his "The Idea of Public Reason: Further Considerations," (FC), *University of Chicago Law Review* (forthcoming), typescript, pp. 11–17. [Editor's note: The title of this essay has been changed to "The Idea of Public Reason Revisited."]

Court properly testifying that "my religion leads me to endorse a political conception of justice that supports the full range of constitutional values and the main political institutions of our society" (FC, p. 3). These essential themes have been struck by Rawls before, but I still find them hard to square with the notion that public reason is "freestanding" or "self-standing" (FC, p. 20).

Hence my *second question*: How are we to understand the logical relation between comprehensive doctrines and public reasons? There are, at most, seven possibilities here: (a) the reasons are merely compatible with the doctrines, (b) the reasons are rendered inductively probable by the doctrines, (c) the reasons are deductively entailed by the doctrines, (d) the reasons are rendered inductively improbable by the doctrines, (e) the reasons are deductively contradicted by the doctrines, (f) the reasons are incommensurable with the doctrines, or (g) the reasons are utterly incomparable with the doctrines. It would seem that if (e) is the case, then either the doctrines or the reasons or perhaps both may be deemed unreasonable: They cannot both be true, though both may be false. Yet when unreasonableness is an issue, Rawls talks almost exclusively about "unreasonable comprehensive doctrines" rather than "unreasonable public reasons." The burden of proof seems unfairly on the comprehensive side: Doctrines, not public reasons, must be purged of "distorting tendencies" (FC, p. 20).

Third observation: Rawls insists that political liberalism "is not attempting to say why a Christian, or a Kantian, or anyone else, should arrive at the political conception [of justice]" (FC, p. 23A). This is fair enough as a self-imposed limitation on scope, but it must be possible for the Christian, the Kantian, et al., to tell him- or herself why. In *Political Liberalism*, p. 11, Rawls writes that "citizens themselves, within the exercise of their liberty of thought and conscience, and looking to their comprehensive doctrines, view the political conception [of justice] as derived from, or congruent with, or at least not in conflict with, their other values." He echoes these thoughts in "Further Considerations," p. 5, noting that each comprehensive doctrine in an overlapping consensus "relies on its leading premises to support, or to arrive at, or to derive, or to approximate, as the case may be, the ideals and principles of the political conception of justice." But note how broad the range of options is here: Logical compatibility seems a sufficient condition for reasonableness.

Therefore, my *third question*: How does one reconcile such minimalism with the imaginative testimony I quoted above about being "le[]d" from comprehensive doctrine to political conception? Mere compatibility does not lead in any direction. If one's comprehensive doctrine tends to support public reasons, then taking "the veil" seems close to pointless; but if the doctrine does not so tend, then being "civil" seems artificial if not dishonest. In some instances, even compatibility is surrendered by Rawls. He holds that political and nonpolitical values "may not always line up in a concordant way," and he states explicitly that "[t]here can be a discrepancy in particular cases between the true [comprehensive] doctrine and a reasonable conception of justice" (FC,

p. 26). If and when this discrepancy emerges, it is evidently public reason that trumps "the whole truth" for Rawls, the ties of civility that have priority over individual conscience. This is a "troubling" prospect indeed (see FC, p. 27). If I read it correctly, it suggests the possibility of a "noble deception" at the core of public reason, a possibility that links ancient Greece's greatest political philosopher with present-day America's. Both Plato and Rawls, unlike most classical Christian theologians, allow for a fundamental slippage between true theory and just practice.

Final speculation: Perhaps Rawls's claim that judges are "under an obligation not to invoke certain kinds of reasons in making their decisions" (FC, p.3) connotes only that judges must use a certain vocabulary or set of principles in handing down official opinions. His second (appropriate) sense of "bracketing" comprehensive reasons might thus be a matter not of content but of form, rather like an interpreter at the United Nations agreeing to speak, while on the job, only in German. On this analogy, however, either the judge is literally translating into "public reasonese" what her comprehensive doctrine prescribes about some fundamental question—shades of liberalism-as-morally-basic's quest for an Ethical Esperanto—or else she is extemporizing in a foreign language without a script (or at least without a translation manual) from her mother tongue. In the former instance, the relation between comprehensive doctrine and public reasons seems far too close for Rawls: Something like a deductive relation would have to obtain for reasonableness. In the latter instance, the relation seems far too distant for both Rawls and conscientious liberals: Something like incommensurability (or even incomparability) would be enough for reasonableness.

In short, I still find in Rawls no answer to the problem of self-referential inconsistency. His contrast between two ways of "bracketing" comprehensive beliefs seems a distinction without a difference. And the nondistinction contributes, I fear, to an avoidance of love, the root cause of prodigality.

Liberal Theory, Human Freedom, and the Politics of Sexual Morality[1]

J. L. A. Garcia

Introduction: Liberalism and Its Freedoms

Liberalism as a historical political movement is distinguished by its exaltation of rights, individuals, and liberty. It is tempting, then, to combine these in a simple formula and see liberalism as characterized by its emphasis on the right to liberty of every individual. Important early texts of liberalism succumbed to this temptation, of course, as evidenced in the writings of Locke and our own Declaration of Independence. That, however, can mislead, for liberal theory has never treated liberty as an undifferentiated whole in need of uniform protection. Rather, historically liberals have selected only certain segments of liberty—that is, certain liber*ties*—for special recognition and protection. This way of putting things, of course, merely repeats Ronald Dworkin's insight that rights to these liberties, and not a general right to liberty itself, lie at the heart of liberalism.[2]

Recently, political philosophers have revived Benjamin Constant's classification of these into "'the liberties of the ancients': the political rights of participation and communication" by voting, petitioning, and otherwise engaging in political life, and the "liberties of the moderns" which include "liberty of belief and conscience, the protection of life, personal liberty and property—in sum, the core of subjective private rights," as Jürgen Habermas puts it.[3] Increasingly, however, many have come to see the rights to these ancient liberties of political participation and to modern liberties of religion, speech, and property as inadequate.

In the middle third of the twentieth century, many American liberals emphasized political measures to address economic deprivation and, more important for our purposes, sometimes sought to incorporate these initiatives as proper parts of the liberal agenda of liberty by conceiving them as moves

---

1   I am grateful to Paul Weithman for suggestions and comments on an earlier draft and to Howard McGary for discussion of these topics.

2   Ronald Dworkin, *Taking Rights Seriously* (Cambridge, Mass.: Harvard University Press, 1977).

3   Jürgen Habermas, "Reconciliation through the Public Use of Reason: Remarks on John Rawls' Political Liberalism," *Journal of Philosophy* 92 (1995): 127. He follows John Rawls, *Political Liberalism* (New York: Columbia University Press, 1993), 5, passim.

toward what Franklin Roosevelt memorably called "freedom from want." This occurred, at first, under pressure from the Depression and the rise of socialist states in Europe and Asia and, later, in the widespread growth, prosperity, and spirit of generosity that followed the Second World War. The legitimacy of this extension of the notion of liberty has been criticized, most notably, by libertarians and others who sometimes claim for themselves the title of 'classical liberals.' One reason they adopted this label was to stress their belief that the new emphasis on securing economic power distorted liberalism by diverting its focus from the liberties that the movement's classical thinkers, ancient and modern had emphasized. In this, they had a point. Roosevelt's terminology notwithstanding, entitlements to in-kind (or cash) economic assistance, healthcare, education, and so on appear quite unlike the liberties of either ancients or moderns. They seem to be less political liberties in themselves than claims to 'liberation' from poverty, disease, disability, ignorance, and other ills. Let us follow common practice and classify them 'welfare rights.'

The century's final third has brought new pressure to extend the agenda of liberalism—this time, to encompass within it rights to wide liberties in sexual 'lifestyle'—premarital and extramarital intercourse, divorce, heterosexual and homosexual sodomy, facilitated abortion and contraception, and the production, sale, and purchase of pornography, for example. The movement toward legalizing, legitimizing, and now privileging these activities as matters of moral and constitutional entitlement began to become socially and intellectually influential in the West during the 1960s; it has been argued with special fervor by thinkers whose intellectual formation was especially influenced by those years; and the matters of lifestyle on which it focuses are especially important to younger adults or those disposed—as by a youth-oriented culture—forcefully to reject forms of stabilization normally associated with the maturity and changed circumstances that age often brings. I will call these claimed lifestyle rights the 'liberties of the (Baby) Boomers.'

If liberalism commits us to recognizing and protecting certain rights, then how should we identify and delimit them, and how should we understand and justify the liberties to which it should accord special status? Some have suggested we divide liberties into 'freedoms for' or 'positive liberties' and 'freedoms from' or 'negative liberties.'[4] However, here Joel Feinberg seems to me right to insist that any full statement of one's liberties will specify both that which one is free to do (where, I think, doing can include saying, feeling, choosing, being, and even wanting) and that from which one is free to do it.[5] That you are free from bodily impediments to emigration does not imply that

---

4   Note that this is not the same as Berlin's idea that there are two concepts of liberty itself. Feinberg finds this distinction in Ralph Barton Perry and others. See Joel Feinberg, *Social Philosophy* (Englewood Cliffs, N.J.: Prentice-Hall, 1973), chap. 1.

5   Ibid.

you are free from financial impediments to your doing so, and vice versa. Moreover, we can and sometimes do use the notion of impediments broadly so that legal and moral standards count. These do not prevent you from doing something in the actual world, but they do prevent you from doing it legally or morally. Thus, we can say that you are subject to legal impediments to your killing your enemy, though free from them to hate her, and morally you are at liberty neither to kill nor even to hate her.

Perhaps the distinction these philosophers wanted to point out is better conceived as that between one source of impediments (from government and laws) and a different source (of natural, social, and mixed origins). At the extreme, thinkers almost exclusively concerned to eliminate obstacles of the first group become (right-)libertarian, and thinkers focused solely on obstacles of the second group, totalitarian.[6] This way of thinking of it allows us to say that, even if such a welfare right as an entitlement to healthcare against certain maladies is not itself really a liberty, nevertheless such a right does (to some extent) free the person who enjoys it from various fears and types of want. Once we replace the alleged difference between positive and negative liberties with a real difference between different sources of impediment, we are reminded of other differences among impediments and how thinkers divide according to which side of such divides they stress. Saint Augustine and Thomas Nagel, for example, both stress freedom from internal obstacles. Where the medieval theologian was especially troubled that people remain enslaved to desires, passions, appetites, and weakness of will, however, the modern philosopher portrays internal freedom as liberation from such very different internal impediments as inhibitions and guilt-feelings.

Because liberalism as a political movement has emphasized protecting some freedoms but not others, it faces the challenge of showing that the group of protected liberties possesses some significant internal unity and is not a mere grab-bag. Its intellectual defenders need to provide some rationale for which freedoms matter most, or even at all. If any freedom is to have the importance liberals assign some, then there must be some reason for distinguishing that freedom and protecting it specially. A philosophical account of

---

6   It remains to be seen whether the 'left-libertarianism' that some leftists, influenced by the lifestyle-oriented liberalism of the past few decades, have recently advocated, adequately safeguards against totalitarianism. The 'Old Left' emphasized securing people economic goods over freedom from political obstacles. Does securing them such goods under the rubric of enabling them by increasing their freedom from social obstacles constitute adequate change?

      Of course, one might instead cast the desired distinction as one between an emphasis upon some types of doing—such as voting, speech, writing—as against an emphasis on other types—such as eating, learning, being healthy, etc. However, it is difficult to see how to provide either stress a good grounding in the abstract.

liberalism is adequate just insofar as it succeeds in those tasks. One appealing route adapts Kant's idea that the freedoms liberals have valued in politics express the self in a special way, so that violating them not only violates one of the victim's preferences but violates the victim herself in her self-creation, her self-understanding, her ideals, or her identity. This approach may not only unite the liberties that liberals have traditionally emphasized, but also tie them in the right way to the new agenda of defending welfare rights and the liberties of the Boomers. However, this approach needs further grounding and elucidation if it is to do more than postpone the problem of providing an adequate rationale and is effectively to delimit the field of protected rights in such a way that it is not committed to ennobling and protecting all sorts of trivial acts and preferences should someone *deem* them important to her 'identity' (that is, her self-image).[7]

What grounds and unifies the special protections that liberals have traditionally defended? What exalts these over most other liberties? Does this unifying and grounding factor, whatever it is, require that, if we are to be consistent, the old catalog(s) of rights be expanded to incorporate claims to assistance in securing certain basic elements of individual welfare? Does it demand further extension so as to accord legitimacy to demands for special protection in those matters of sexual lifestyle—'the liberties of the Boomers'— that have become the heart of the new agenda some propose for liberalism? In this paper I will attempt some first steps toward answering these questions.

In Sections I and II below, I critically consider the position on these matters that Thomas Nagel presents in a recent article. Nagel wants to help illuminate the nature and grounding of human rights. He thinks his approach supports extension of liberal recognition of human rights beyond the 'liberties of the ancients' to political participation, beyond the 'liberties of the moderns' to free speech and religion, and beyond the economic entitlements embraced within President Roosevelt's 'freedom from want,' to a wide range of activities in pursuit of one's sexual fantasies. I argue that Nagel's argument is unconvincing and that an adequate view of the politics of human liberty and sexual morality profits from being placed in a fuller, substantive view of human sociality. In Section III, I briefly sketch some elements of one such alternative vision of the foundation of human rights, founded in certain assumed truths about the nature, origins, vocation, and prospects of human beings. Insofar as these assumptions are grounded in a particular religious tradition, its adoption as an basis for political action would require that some citizens and officials work from certain substantive metaphysical, moral, and religious convictions in their political deliberation and activity. In Section IV, I conclude by outlining responses to three versions of the objection that any such consid-

---

7   Also, of course, it is mere *hubris* to think we *create* ourselves, although a person's will can help shape her own, and others', characters.

eration violates crucial constraints on "public reason" and political action, constraints nowadays often held to be at the very heart of liberalism.

I. Nagel on Rights and Inviolability

Nagel begins with a telling story. He recounts his experience attending an international conference on human rights at which the American representatives made much of rights of access to pornography and abortion (as well as affirmative action and freedom for racist speech), while those from nations without secure democratic liberal regimes complained of the time and attention spent on what they saw as these frivolous and irrelevant matters instead of the real threats to free speech and political participation in other parts of the world. Nagel allows, with little sense of understatement, that "one could certainly understand their [the complainants'] point of view."[8]

To vindicate his conviction that both kinds of concerns, nevertheless, fell within "the same subject," Nagel concentrates on "the type of rights usually called negative—forms of freedom or discretion for each individual with which others, including the state, may not forcibly interfere." He claims that to see mistreating someone as violation of "universal human rights" is to see it as treatment whose victim "is wronged" whoever she is, wherever she lives, in such a way that the wrongness "is not a function of the balance of costs and benefits in this case.[9] He "favor[s]" understanding "the value of rights . . . as . . .intrinsic," and sees them as "a nonderivative and fundamental element in morality."[10] These are different claims, notice, for it may be both that rights have intrinsic value (that is, their value resides simply in what they are) and also that their existence derives from more basic moral concepts (that is, what they are is not beyond moral analysis). Nagel's question is, "How are we to understand the value that rights assign to certain kinds of human inviolability, which makes [it] . . . morally intelligible" that "it could be wrong to harm one person to prevent greater harm to others?"[11] His answer is that a morality without rights "fails to give any place to another very important value—the intrinsic value of inviolability itself" and, since "we would all be worse off if there were no rights . . . *ergo*, there are rights."[12] He sees his argument as similar to one of Warren Quinn's, whose summary statement Nagel approvingly quotes: People "have them [rights] because it is fitting that they should."[13]

---

8   Thomas Nagel, "Personal Rights and Public Space," *Philosophy and Public Affairs* 24 (1995): 83.

9   Ibid., 84.

10   Ibid., 86, 87.

11   Ibid., 89.

12   Ibid., 91–92.

13   Warren Quinn, *Morality and Action* (Cambridge: Cambridge University Press,

Nagel acknowledges two difficulties with his argument. First, it "has the form P is true because it would be better if P were true," which, he concedes, "in general [is] not a cogent form of argument." Second, if the status of inviolability has value only as an element in someone's sense of status, then Nagel's justification does treat rights as instruments for enhancing well-being after all, despite his approach's announced intentions. Nagel finds both criticisms wanting. Against the first, he maintains that argumentation of this form may be acceptable when "its conclusion is not factual but moral. It may be suitable to argue that one morality is more likely to be true than another, because the former makes for a better world than the latter—not instrumentally, but intrinsically."[14] Against the second objection, he claims that the *sense* of status is valued because of the prior value of inviolability, not the other way around. So, inviolability's value is not instrumental but intrinsic.

I think neither of these responses adequate and Nagel's argument fails. The response to the objection to the argument's form clearly relies on a strong version of the fact/value gap. This supposed logical gap has, at best, proven difficult to defend. However, Nagel is in especially poor position to avail himself of it, given his free talk of moral theories' "truth," as when he claims that his "argument is supposed to show that the morality which includes rights is *already true*."[15] (Original emphasis.) It is hard to see how one can maintain true moralities without moral truths, or moral truths without moral facts. What, then, can we make of his defense, which relies on the crucial claim that his conclusion is "not factual but moral"? The argument that morality has a certain structure because it would be better if it did more naturally fits a constructivist or more strongly relativist approach. There, it makes sense to reason that morality's structure is grounded in that structure's value, because the value people have found in the structure may have motivated them to *cause* morality to conform to it. Nagel, however, cuts off this avenue. A right, he insists, "can't even be created, though it can be recognized."[16]

Nagel's response to the charge that his position is in the end instrumentalist misses the larger point. Even if he does not argue that rights are valuable only as instruments to our sense of status, his argument for rights from the supposed intrinsic value of having them clearly opens itself to the charge that allowing rights into our moral theory, even if it realizes some intrinsic value, also brings with it such offsetting disvalues that it is better on the whole that there not be rights. This, in turn, would seem to warrant the inference '*ergo*, there are not any rights' by a line of argument parallel to Nagel's. Whether or not his argument depends upon rights' instrumental value, it crucially de-

1993), 173. Quoted at Nagel, "Personal Rights and Public Space," 90–91.

14   Nagel, "Personal Rights and Public Space," 92.

15   Ibid.

16   Ibid., 85.

pends upon the value—the *comparative* value—of having rights, and therefore upon the balance of values. This makes the question of the action's wrongness ultimately depend upon a balance of values and, even if that is consistent with his view that the wrongness of rights violations is independent of the balance "in this [particular] case," it raises an old problem. How does Nagel propose to execute the necessary commensuration or, at least, comparison, so that we know that the world with rights is "better"? Indeed, Nagel may need an account of commensuration for another reason as well, because he does not commit himself to absolute moral restrictions and allows that other concerns (other values?) may, at "a sufficiently high threshold of costs," override or limit inviolability. How is inviolability's value to be measured and compared on the scales unless it is comparable?

And what possesses this intrinsic value? Sometimes Nagel talks of it being better for everyone if we have rights, and even of each of us being better off in such a world: "we would all be worse off if there were no rights." Sometimes, instead, he assigns the value to the world itself: a morality with rights "makes for a better world."[17] These are different notions, notice, and Nagel needs to decide between them. A better world need not be one in which everyone is better off, and even a world in which everyone is better off need not be a better one.[18]

In any case, appeals to intrinsic value, though sometimes necessary, are too easy to make and too difficult to back up. We do well to avoid them when possible. It should also be noted that Nagel moves too quickly in going from human rights to inviolability. For many of our ordinary rights, such as the right to have the promises made one kept, it seems overly dramatic to understand them as expressions of individual inviolability. As inviolability may not be the best way to understand some rights, so rights-talk may not always well express inviolability. Increasingly, rights are understood, as Nagel understands them, as reserving certain matters to the rights-holder's "discretion."[19] Unless, however, some important rights are what Feinberg called "mandatory

---

17   Both quotations are from ibid., 92.

18   It may not be, for example, if intrinsic value resides in things other than how well off humans are, as G. E. Moore thought it did, or if the patterns within an individual's holdings (or across a set of individual holdings) matter in certain ways. (To illustrate the last possibility, consider a strict equalitarian principle of comparison, which denies that so-called 'Pareto improvements' really generate superior states of affairs. If such a principle is correct, then we should prefer a world in which everyone has the same amount of utility to one wherein the first person had one additional unit, the second two more units, etc. In the latter, inferior world, each person is better off.)

19   "The idea of rights exempts a core of individual discretion from the authority of others—removes it from the category of conduct that might be regulated if good public reasons so indicated." (Ibid., 95)

rights," that is, ones beyond the rights-holder's discretion so that even she may not waive them, then some forms of moral inviolability recognized in our moral tradition are not best expressed as rights.[20] The moral violation involved in assisting or performing suicide may be an example.

My own view is that inviolability can be expressed in rights-talk, but that such talk is derivative from deeper moral concepts, specifically, from the virtues. I cannot develop my view here. If I am right, however, that is an important result, for his neglect of the virtues seriously undermines Nagel's discussion of the new liberal agenda of sexual practices. We turn to that discussion next.

II. Liberties, the Self, and Sex

Nagel's treatment begins, unsurprisingly, with his presupposing an unanalyzed distinction between the private and the public. Nor does it surprise us to find that, for him, the private comprises an odd congeries of matters sublime and vulgar, of utmost importance and triviality. "The private domain includes the realm of choices of personal pleasures, sexual fantasy, nonpolitical self-expression, and the search for cosmic or religious meaning." (His strategy is to use the more respectable members of this group to legitimize the seedier tag alongs. I return to this below.) Nagel recognizes the air of the ridiculous about making such a big deal out of some of the individual liberties the state "destroys," such as that of smoking marijuana and indulging in pornography. "My objection to the censorship of pornography . . . is quite out of proportion to the actual harm done by such prohibitions." However, he thinks, "a sense of wrong disproportionate to the resulting loss is a good sign that a sentiment of justice, fairness, or right has been aroused." (Except, one wants to add, when it is just a sign that someone is rationalizing her overreaction to having a desire frustrated.) To Nagel, "the idea that state *may* be legitimately used in such ways . . . seems grossly wrong; instances of such use seem like gross injustices . . ."[21]

Why? Freedom of expression, Nagel thinks, merits the special protection liberals have usually accorded it, because "the sovereignty of each person's reason over his own beliefs and values requires that he be permitted to express them, expose them to the reactions of others, and defend them against objections. It also requires that he not be protected against exposure to views or arguments that might influence him in ways that others deem pernicious." In short, "mental autonomy is restricted by shutting down both inputs and outputs [i.e., blocking either restricts autonomy]."[22]

---

20   See "Euthanasia and the Unalienable Right to Life," in Joel Feinberg, *Rights, Justice, and the Bounds of Liberty* (Princeton, N.J.: Princeton University Press, 1980).

21   Nagel, "Personal Rights and Public Space," 95.

22   Ibid., 96.

These claims are attractive, of course, but this line of reasoning seems to demonstrate a good deal less than many liberals today want. Insofar as free expression is to be protected because of the role it plays in the responsible and rational person's efforts to formulate and test her beliefs by articulating them, listening to other people's responses to her expressions of them, and trying to develop and articulate defenses, then only such free expression as is part of this sort of process warrants protection. In contrast, today civil libertarians typically demand protection for flippant, thoughtless expressions, couched in language designed to offend rather than to invite rational and helpful critique, and often presented in such ways—emblazoned on T-shirts, say, or shouted with accompanying obscenities, scrawled anonymously on walls, printed on labels stuck on public advertising displays, and so on—as to wall the speaker off from opportunity to hear opposed views or to reconsider her ideas. They also demand comparable protection both for nonverbal forms of expression, though these normally lend themselves less easily to the conversational advantages central to Nagel's argument and even for forms of conduct (for example, forms of dress and, especially, of undress) tied to beliefs in ways so tangential that they remain quite distant from the rational give-and-take on which Nagel's defense of free expression rests. His argument, then, seems to support only a right to free expression for some, rational, civil speech and only then to the extent that it forms part of an individual's serious and sincere efforts to develop and test her ideas. Surely, a liberal should think these last are important rights and can welcome Nagel's argument as the beginnings of a philosophical defense. However, in doing that, she should recognize that she must either part company with the more thoroughgoing civil libertarian position or provide a separate, doubtless quite different defense for widening the scope of protection. Of course, it may well be a good thing for society to extend legal protection to a somewhat wider range of expression than we have described. However, such an extension would simply be a matter of political prudence, not human rights, contrary to the civil libertarian's wishes.

Nagel's defense of the moderns' liberty of free expression serves to introduce his spirited defense of what I have called the 'liberties of the Boomers.' Here, Nagel is unabashedly, even gleefully, liberationist and on this topic his academic judiciousness and philosophical caution sometimes seem almost entirely to abandon him. We can safely ignore most of this, but Nagel does offer some serious ideas about sexual freedom, ideas quite relevant for our questions about the grounding and extent of the rights liberals should recognize.[23]

---

23   Among the things I ignore are Nagel's diagnosis of our culture's current problem as insufficient "worldliness," his quasi-clinical judgment rendered of the-nation-on-the-couch that our "political culture" suffers from "generalized adolescent panic with regard to sex," and especially his odd remark, uttered in high dudgeon over the press and public's alleged mistreatment of Gary Hart, that, if

Nagel says his views throughout the discussion "are determined by a strong conviction of the personal importance and great variety of sexual feeling and sexual fantasy and of their expression." Given this importance, we should tolerate "sexual feelings . . . [in a way that] include[s] a certain of freedom for their expression," as part of "the form of moral equality that accords to each person a limited sovereignty over the core of his personal and expressive life." The sexual, Nagel concludes, is protected by "this sovereignty or inviolability [which] is in itself . . . the most distinctive value expressed by a morality of human rights." This protection of sexual expression takes precedence, "even if it [the expressive conduct] sometimes gives offense," for "the level of society's toleration for offense in this domain should be quite high, nearly as high as it should be for political and religious expression."[24]

Nagel's strategy in grounding and expanding the rights liberalism has traditionally recognized appears to be this. He maintains that rights in general matter because they acknowledge the value of the inviolability of persons. More specifically, the rights of religious and political expression, traditionally protected in liberalism, matter because they are within the "core" of the self, which should be inviolate. However, the sexual also lies within the core of the self, and various types of sexual behavior are also forms of sexual expression (that is, expressions of sexual fantasies, feeling, and desires). Therefore, sexual behavior should also be inviolate, that is, protected by rights in such a way that society cannot properly impinge on them without therein violating what political morality should regard as inviolate.[25] If that is Nagel's argument, what should we make of it?

Part of the reason Nagel insists that sex lies within the self's core is that the sexual realm is "central and fundamental in the lives" of both heterosexuals and homosexuals.[26] Let us begin our assessment there. Describing the impor-

---

every American adulterer and adulteress had sent Hart a dollar, his campaign would have been wealthy. (The campaigns of Burr, Grant, Blaine, and Nixon might also have prospered from contributions from those candidates' fellow murderers, drunkards, bigots, and liars as well, but what, one wonders, is this supposed to show?) All these are advanced without benefit of argument and with no effort to show sympathetic understanding of opposing viewpoints. (Indeed, Nagel does not treat disagreement on matters of sexual morality as intellectual conflict at all, which needs combatting with reasons, but as mere operation of pathological psychic processes, which need only be identified to be delegitimized. The view that homosexual practices are unnatural or even just "abnormal," for instance, is attributed to so-called 'homophobes' projecting their own horror at having homosexual feelings.) See Ibid., 99–104.

24   Ibid., 100, 106, 107.

25   This bears some resemblance to the strategy David Richards employs in *Toleration and the Constitution* (New York: Oxford University Press, 1986). I return to Richards in a note below.

26   Nagel, "Personal Rights and Public Space," 102.

tance and value of sex, he says that it is (a) the source of our "most intense pleasure," (b) "one of the few sources of human ecstasy," and (c) the "realm" wherein we dissolve "the defining and inhibiting structure of civilization" fully to express "our deepest presocial, animal, and infantile natures," offering therein "a form of physical and emotional completion not otherwise available." I think he is on to something in all three claims. Take the last first. Sexual thought and behavior can be a mode of entree to aspects of human nature usually buried beneath quotidian routine and responsibilities. A sex life untouched by spontaneity, playfulness, exuberance, impulsiveness, unconventionality, even the shocking, is likely to be a vapid, dessicated thing.[27] Those ingredients are, perhaps, especially necessary for parents, whose lives childrearing tends to render superficially placid, routinized, and tightly controlled. More impulsive, less conventional modes of sexuality provide a rare opportunity to release some element from the more primitive, less rational part of ourselves into lives ordinarily given over to plans, conventions, self-possession, and the face we show the world.

I have talked of the unconventional, spontaneous, and impulsive within the sexual; Nagel says that in sex "our deepest presocial, animal, and infantile natures can be fully released and expressed." His more extreme language helps remind us of a fact that he ignores and I have not yet addressed—this aspect of our sex lives presents dangers that call for more, not less, regulation—internal, if not external. Recall what Nagel seldom explicitly mentions, that paradigmatically sexual practices involve more than one person. Should not a person be granted some special social and legal protection precisely at those moments when she confronts another who has "dissolve[d]" civilization's inhibitions and now confronts her as a "presocial[ized] animal," governed by

---

27   It is, of course, necessary for reason and will to rein these elements in, lest they victimize others or degrade oneself. I discuss this shortly. Given the strength and importance of the sexual in human personality, however, this control is often best viewed as aspirational. Consistent success in it may prove itself less a sign of moral virtue than of stunted or warped desire. In any case, scrupulous attention to avoiding excesses in sexual behavior is often a mark of prudery and is, perhaps, less likely to hit the mark of perfect moderation than to rob the shared part of one's sexual life of the vivacity and light-heartedness through which it binds the partners and allows them to taste ecstasy.

That there can be such excess of rational control is, I think, a fact of moral life, and a profound one. However, I admit it is a paradoxical aspect of the virtues, and one not easily captured in the Aristotelian doctrine of moral virtue as a mean between excess and defect. Not every disposition (inclination) to act moderately stems from a properly moderated and virtuous desire. My concern here is that getting oneself so disposed that one always avoids all viciously excessive behavior in a realm (here, the sexual) may come through stunting rather than perfecting one's desires, even when the resultant behavior is not itself viciously defective either.

"infantile" imperatives, which are notoriously selfish and inconsiderate? On Barbara Herman's reading of Kant, his concern, mirrored by some of the more radical feminists of our day, is precisely that sex tempts an agent to treat another merely as a means to the agent's pleasure.[28]

We need not follow Kant into Pietist prudery nor follow Herman's fringe feminists into a repudiation of all heterosexual sex. However, I think it does show that Nagel's invocation of these aspects of sex does more to undermine than to support his call for broad personal discretion. Indeed, I should think we can trust people properly to exercise even the discretion traditionally accorded them in their sexual lives only if we are assured that in general they will restrain themselves from any temptation to victimize their partners.[29] A society where many follow a course of self-administered, inexpert psychotherapy in desire and self-restraint on some Augustinian (or, perhaps, Stoic or even Epicurean) model seems the safest bet for wide legal latitude in sexual matters. Indeed, one time-honored and sometimes effective way of keeping the preso-

---

28   See Herman's essay in Louise Antony and Charlotte Witt, *A Mind of One's Own: Liberal Theory, Human Freedom, and the Politics of Sexual Morality* (Boulder, Colo.: Westview, 1992).

29   The *locus classicus* for the vivid depiction of this possibility, of course, lies in the work of Sade. See, especially, the tutelage in sexual victimization that a *roue* offers the ingenue Eugenie in his classic, "Philosophy in the Bedroom," in Marquis Donatien de Sade, *Justine, Philosophy in the Bedroom, and Other Writings*, compiled and translated by Richard Seaver and Austryn Wainhouse (New York: Grove Press, 1965), 185–367. She learns her lesson well and concludes the work by cooperating with her tutor and his friends in torturing, raping, and sodomizing her own mother—as well as infecting her with venereal disease—for the crime of discouraging her daughter's sexual explorations. That all this occurs with the consent of the victim's husband illustrates Sade's view of the irrelevance of marriage and family once sexual activity is seen solely as a mode for the expression of fantasy and the pursuit of ever more inhuman modes of pleasure. (For an interesting history and critical reassessment of the recent exaltation of Sade, see Roger Shattuck, "Rehabilitating a Monster," *New York Times Book Review* (May 31, 1996): 31. Shattuck's points about the politics of scholarship and the personal interests behind scholarly revivals are, I think, well taken. Surely, some such explanation is needed for the wild claims sometimes made for Sade. Rosen, for example, thinks Sade "the first to perceive the sexual import of cruelty and torture for the specifically literature imagination" and, despite—or perhaps because of—this *aperçu*, thinks that once we assure ourselves that it won't set the kids to trading their Game Gears for implements of torture, "Sade's work might reasonably be made required reading for high-school students." (He does allow, parenthetically, that "he is perhaps a bit strong for the elementary level." See Charles Rosen, "Sade and Other Classics," *New York Review of Books* (May 9, 1996): 28, 29.) Nevertheless, I think Shattuck slights Sade's genuine importance as a precursor to Nietzsche in his stark understanding and evaluation of the metaphysics, morality, and social structure that awaits upon the victory of a thoroughly post-Christian culture.)

cial, animal, and infantile from turning sexual activity into victimization is to restrict that activity to the context of interpersonal relationships that are by mutual commitment expected to be both long-term and generative. In short, traditional marriage. There, the presocial, animal, and infantile aspects of sex—toned down now to what I called the unconventional, impulsive, and playful—are properly set within such a context that they are *humanized*. These primitive aspects of the self that sexual behavior should contain can be humanized by the marriage background because there they are integrated into a real and mutually respectful relationship, planned as a communal sharing, and properly committed to generating, socializing, and nurturing new members of society. Moreover, in such context sexual behavior is humanized because it is fully responsible in two important ways: first, it occurs in a context of assumed moral and legal responsibilities; and, second, each sexual partner agrees to be held accountable by tying it to a publicly recognized and protected institution. That marital sex is thus humanized does not mean that dehumanization cannot creep back in, of course, or that the unconventional, impulsive, and playful will not degenerate into what really is animalistic and infantile. But it does guarantee that some safeguards are in place and that there are redeeming aspects even when the risky elements in sexual behavior, as is to be expected, sometimes go too far in one or another morally significant way.[30] Sex and marriage are complementary in that marriage helps humanize the expression of sexual desire by domesticating it, while sexual behavior can introduce a necessary element of the wild and untamed into married life.[31]

---

30   Again, that sexual behavior contains dangers and requires limits and controls neither justifies a fearful approach to the sexual, which treats it primarily as a sphere of dangers, nor implies that an anxious concern always to observe limits should be a high priority in a person's sex life. Such an attitude, it seems to me, must either eliminate or give the lie to any playful, joyful, impulsive element within the sexual. That sin is the greatest evil does not entail that avoiding temptations to sin has lexical priority over avoiding other ills or over attaining various goods. That is a general moral truth, one not at all restricted to the sexual realm.

31   This injection of the untamed into married domesticity is, I think, desirable because marriage naturally tends to evolve into a multi-generational family. That threatens to reduce parents to decades of activities, entertainments, and conversations fitted to children and therein evacuated of the frankness, riskiness, and heightened emotions that adults sometimes need. The harm traditional family life often does children is, of course, much deeper and has become a staple of postwar memoirs, fiction, drama, and social studies. In the 1950s, some American men began to articulate a self-image as victims of family life (for whose support they were assigned the task of 'winning bread'), followed in a few decades by the stronger, feminist critique that it was women whose lives traditional family roles impoverished. There is, I suspect, considerable merit to all these claims of suffering. However, an institution that exacts such costs from all participants is, at least, not biased in the way the critics maintain, and the network may be better

In such a context as traditional marriage, sexual intercourse is likely to be something real, physical, and interpersonal. By that I mean it should escape the realm of fantasies on which Nagel's discussion lavishes such disproportionate attention. Nagel's continued return to and emphasis upon fantasy in his discussion of sexual matters is striking and distorting. What is most striking in his discussion of the sexual is its near-solipsism. Sex is the private domain; it occupies the inner life; it consists primarily in desires, feelings, and fantasy; and it matters in that someone cares about it.[32] There is no hint here that sex is normally oriented toward another person (preferably not just in thought) and always raises questions of charity, respect, justice, for that person as well as for others who may be affected by what happens between those sexually involved. This is quite disappointing coming from a philosopher who a few decades ago could write about sexual perversion, with some insight, as rejecting or ignoring the personhood and responsiveness of the other.[33]

The damage done by this neglect of the crucial interpersonal aspect of sex and its need for governance by traditional moral virtues is evident in Nagel's treatments of pornography and sexual harassment. Here his worry is exclusively over the damage to be done by restraint. He condemns efforts to improve the situation of women by "interfering with the sexual fantasy life and sexual expression of heterosexual men, so long as they do not harm specific women. . ." and insists even offensive expressions must be tolerated to a considerable extent.[34] Nagel seems unwilling to criticize any sexual fantasy. If its delight in violence and degradation disturbs someone, then Nagel's hermeneutic principle dictates that the person does not understand it. After all, "No one is sufficiently polymorphous perverse to be able to enter with imaginative sympathy into the sexuality of all his fellow citizens." So, if my neighbors' fantasy of sexual torture revolts me but pleases them, we must

understood as one of mutual sacrifice for a common good that really does benefit each, though not necessarily by giving them what they prefer. To the extent that intellectuals have until recently ignored or scorned the benefits of traditional family life, they have devalued it and the institution itself has lately become to deform. A younger generation of scholars has now begun to investigate the social costs, disproportionately borne by children, of this decline. (A recent address by David Popenoe to a May 1996 Rutgers University conference, "The Politics of 'Fatherlessness,'" offers a good example of this new scholarship.) Still, even those sympathetic to this new 'pro-family' line should bear in mind that, the most human and natural of institutions, traditional family life constantly carries both promise of personal development and menace of deformation to all its members and generations.

32   By "sexual relations" Nagel here seems to mean merely a kind of sex act, not relation*ships* between persons.

33   See Thomas Nagel, "Sexual Perversion." 66 *Journal of Philosophy* (1969). Reprinted in *Mortal Questions* (Cambridge: Cambridge University Press, 1979).

34   Nagel, "Personal Rights and Public Space," 104.

be reacting to different fantasies: "it's not that they are delighted by *the same thing* that revolts me; it is something else that I don't understand."[35] In the end, "If some men get their kicks by watching movies of women with big breasts engaged in fellatio . . . [or] depictions of gang rape, or flogging, or mutilation, this really should not give rise to a claim on anyone's part not to be surrounded by, or even included in, such fantasies."[36]

It is probably true that, even in an enduring marriage, the couple's shared sexual activity is only a small part of each spouse's larger sex life, which in each comprises memories, longings, faded dreams, lost hopes, etc. There is a limit to how much is shared. If the two are only metaphorically one flesh, they are still less one libido. Still, even if Nagel is right that something always remains uncommunicated, I cannot find much in his discussion to justify his claim that the liberal protection of basic liberties should extend to broad areas of sexual life. I will content myself with raising some questions and pointing out a few difficulties. Why should we not privilege other fantasies (of revenge or power, say) the way Nagel privileges sexual ones? Suppose one finds ecstasy in them? Why should we agree with Nagel that none of your rights are violated when someone includes you in her fantasies? Suppose you are the fantasist's daughter, son, grandchild, ward, employee, or student. Does not even the danger of bad and harmful actions latent in bad attitudes count?

Nagel's discussion of this point manifests the poverty of restricting moral language to rights-talk. Discussion here of *virtues* of self-restraint and of appropriate modes of response to the value inherent in other persons would bring a much-needed element of reality to these discussions. It should introduce the concept of respect, for instance, which includes attitudes—cognitive, volitional, affective, desiderative—of valuing and deferring. Why think that degrading attitudes do not violate justice when they violate the very respect that characterizes acts of justice? Why think the respect I owe someone, and its attendant virtue of justice, are not violated by including her in my degrading fantasies? Vices of interpersonal mental state and activity are common enough: hate, contempt, ingratitude, and so on. Deliberate fantasies will also be vicious if they are characterized by hatred or contempt, whether or not the fantasies are sexual.

What supports Nagel's odd insistence that if one rejects another's sexual fantasies, then that shows one did not understand them in the first place? There is little general plausibility to the thesis that to understand something is to accept it, though postmodernists sometimes talk like that.[37] What makes this

35   Ibid, 105.

36   Ibid., 106.

37   Stanley Fish writes, "When you think a view wrong, you don't see what is seen by those who think it right," and "to say of an assertion that it is 'not true' is to say that you don't understand it." (Fish, "A Reply to Richard John Neuhaus," *First Things* (March 1996): 37, 38) Of course, doxastically to accept proposition P

perversion of the principle of charity any more plausible in the realm of fantasies? Again, does it extend also to sexless fantasies of revenge, or racist subjugation, or vulgar wealth, or just to sexual fantasies? Even if one thought others had the 'right' to give themselves up to dreams of humiliating and subjugating one and one's entire racial group, does not that merely show the inadequacy of rights-talk here, where clearly we need to attend to the formation of decent character, perhaps including creation of the kind of social environment where it can be properly shaped? But then why think the sexual so different?

That sexual fantasy can be quite ugly, vicious, unjust, and self-destructive is a fact from which Nagel shies. Attending to it can help us see that sexual fantasy and desire cannot properly be the starting points for useful reflection on sexual morality or its politics. In prison, Sade composed elaborate fantasies of sexual torture and murder stunning even in our own jaded time.[38] Nor were these produced merely by the repression that incarceration forced him to endure. It was the smaller-scale abuses he executed in life against prostitutes and other poor women that led to his lengthy imprisonment.[39] Two centuries later, in a recent press interview, a young woman who styles herself a "professional submissive" adds to her tales of run-of-the-mill clients (of both sexes), who have tied, whipped, pierced, and urinated on her, the stories of "Jerry the Clitorectomy Freak," whose fantasies of sexual mutilation she must simulate "so it's realistic enough for Jerry to be stimulated" and "the Cannibal Man" in whose fantasy, she says, "I'm the main course. Stewed and chopped up."[40]

(e.g., to "think it right") commits me to rejecting (as "not true") its contradictory proposition not-P, even as understanding an assertion of P is impossible unless I would also understand an assertion of not-P. So, Fish's claim, if true, would render impossible all understanding and belief. I admit I do not see what Fish sees in his claim, but I think that is because what he sees is not there.

38 Consult, for example, the astonishing catalogue of tortures and sexualized abuse recounted in the final sections of *120 Days of Sodom*. One sample of the unrestrained sexual imagination, by no means the worst: "They require a woman whose pregnancy is in its eighth or begun its ninth month, they open her belly, snatch out the child, burn it before the mother's eyes, and in its place substitute a package containing sulfur and quicksilver, which they set afire, they stitch the belly up again, leaving the mother thus to perish in the midst of terrible agonies, while they look on and have themselves frigged [sic] by the girl they have with them." (Sade, *The 120 Days of Sodom and Other Writings*, compiled and translated by Richard Seaver and Austryn Wainhouse (New York: Grove Press, 1966), 639).

39 See the summary of some of Sade's crimes recounted in the editor's "Chronology" of the Marquis's life contained in Sade, *Justine, Philosophy in the Bedroom, and Other Writings*, 73–119.

40 See Jessica Willis, "Q & A: Bleu," *New York Press* (5–11 June 1996): 22. The woman interviewed is a filmmaker named Maria Beatty, but who uses the name 'Bleu' for her work in the sex industry. Lest it be thought I am digging too deeply into

Although the woman says she entered sex work for money, she also considers herself a born masochist, "turn[ed] on" by fear, who regards her sessions play-acting roles in others' fantasies as "about how far I can push my [own] fantasies." These are modern glimpses of the sexual imagination run amok, regarded as in need only of the liberation from inhibition that Nagel praises. Indeed, in the context of "Jerry" and "Cannibal Man," Nagel's glib, almost smirking remark that we live surrounded by others' fantasies in such fashion that a person never knows what sexual roles she is playing in the imagination of her butcher takes on a truly frightening aspect.[41]

Not many follow Sade's route from fantasy to criminality, and few have sexual imaginations as wild as his, "Jerry's," or "Cannibal Man's." However, even those with milder imaginative lives sometimes tend toward degradation when their sex lives are taken over by fantasy and disengaged from the humanizing context of interpersonal commitment. Nancy Friday, whose compilation of several volumes of women's fantasies (and one of men's) makes her a leading authority on the subject, reminds us that fantasy is often divorced from sexual relationships and used as an accompaniment to sexual self-stimulation.[42] Indeed, the very title and subtitle she gives a section in one book show the implications of this loving attention lavished on fantasy: "Separating Sex and Love: In Praise of Masturbation."[43] Her books bear out this separation with

the sexual netherworld to make my point, I should point out that the periodical in which the interview appears, while certainly not the mainstream press, is a respected and popular alternative weekly newspaper in New York City, read mainly for its entertainment coverage and listings, comparable to *The Village Voice* (with which it has recently and successfully competed).

41   "Who knows what unspeakable acts you are performing in the imagination of the mortgage officer as he explains to you the relative advantages of fixed and variable interest rates, or the policewoman who is giving you a traffic ticket, or the butcher who is wrapping your pork chops?" (Nagel, "Personal Rights and Public Space," 105–6.)

42   Friday, *Women on Top: How Real Life Has Changed Women's Sexual Fantasies* (New York: Simon & Schuster/Pocket Books, 1991): 27–29.

43   In this, one detects in Friday the spirit of a soulmate to Nagel's unequivocal enthusiasm for sexual liberation as a key to comprehensive liberation through sex. In a subsection called "What We Win from Masturbation," Friday lists this very separation among the benefits she sings. (Ibid., 33–42.) This is a long-time theme of Friday's from her early compilations in the 1970s through her most recent work. One reviewer of her 1996 book, *The Power of Beauty*, writes that Friday's view "is both hopelessly 60's and quintessentially American: sex can make us happy, and because it makes us happy as individuals it can change society as a whole. . . . [For Friday,] if we could only learn to love our genitals, most of the world's problems would be solved." In this belief in comprehensive liberation through sexual liberation, she resembles Sade who "insisted that the political liberty won the French revolution was incomplete and even meaningless without sexual freedom." (Rosen, "Sade and Other Classics," 28.) Of course,

pages and even whole chapters given over to fantasies of active or passive sexual contacts with animals, of rape, of incest (intra- and cross-generational), of sexual humiliation and bondage, of adultery and promiscuity, of sacrilege, of sadism and masochism, and on and on and on.

My focus here is not on the morality of the sexual self-stimulation that fantasy often feeds, nor in particular instances of the various practices just listed. Instead, I mean to draw attention to the need for the expression of sexual desire to occur within a humanizing context such as that which a committed, long-term, and generative love-relationship provides. Such a relationship tends to humanize by making sexual behavior the expression of something more than mere fantasies and other quirks. Rather, sexual conduct can there become the expression of a communion of persons in the depths of their emotional and volitional lives, persons in the act of giving themselves to each other in what is, first, in itself a communion of souls and, second, in its potency, an opportunity for communion to evolve into a multi-generational community through the generation and rearing of new persons. Sexual imagination, like many other forms, is of course good, and, properly cultivated, it can add something valuable to a loving sexual relationship. Still, its value is as a part of that larger human good, and divorced from it, like sex divorced from love and spousal love divorced from the sort of long-term, committed, generative relationship that is traditionally consecrated as marriage, there is little to prevent fantasy and its expression from turning vicious when removed from the environment it needs.[44] Contra Nagel, then, fantasy and desire cannot serve

Friday's optimistic, 1960s mentality does not accept the dark understanding of this freedom found in Sade, whose "inspired originality," according to Rosen, "was to introduce the excesses of cruelty systematically into the vast corpus of erotic literature.") Like Nagel, Friday faults some recent feminists for being insufficiently enthusiastic about sex play. The reviewer concludes her "catalogue of everything Ms. Friday believes has gone wrong with America because of feminism" with "Strippers don't enjoy their work like they used to. And *nobody* is masturbating enough." (Larissa MacFarquhar, "More than Meets the Eye: Review of 'The Power of Beauty' by Nancy Friday," *New York Times Book Review* (23 June 1996): 7. Emphasis retained.)

44   Again, I should add that the fact that sexual fantasy holds dangers and can turn bad does not require the view, sometimes taught by religious moralists, that people should assign high priority to maintaining 'custody of imagination' (and memory and the eye) lest we slip into sin. Such courses of treatment pose risk of encouraging a fearful and suspicious attitude toward one's sexuality. I am inclined to think that anyone's sexuality—whether or not she is sexually active— should be an occasion for her at least to glimpse some of this life's most striking delights and beauties. So, I think skepticism warranted about the general desirability of a strict discipline that wars against such enjoyment.

I am aware that some of the doubts I tentatively express here about disciplines suggested for avoiding what have been considered 'impure thoughts' may be in some tension with the emphasis of some Christian traditions on the "apprentice-

as the starting points for a sensible exploration or insightful understanding of our sex lives. Rather, the wild, primitive element with which fantasy enriches sexual behavior needs the tempering that comes from sex's other key aspects: communion and generation.

I have cautioned that the wild element in sex calls for the kind of context of social responsibility that traditional marriage is designed to provide and that sexual fantasy can become vicious and even unjust if not properly disciplined and directed. This, in turn, suggests that Nagel's agenda of sexual liberation in law may require replacement of his liberationist view of internal freedom with a more Augustinian one that stresses liberation *from* raw sexual appetites rather than liberation *of* them. Broad legal rights in sexual matters, if they are ever a good thing, will require the context of a strong culture of virtue. Virtue, however, is a notion entirely absent from Nagel's treatment. Even Freud, whose thinking Nagel regards as insightful, saw a measure of discontent, based in the disciplining and sublimation of libido, as intrinsic to civilization.[45] Nagel's liberationist position seems closer to the glibber, cheerier social psychologies that Herbert Marcuse and Wilhelm Reich dispensed at mid-century.

The important question for us is whether Nagel succeeds in showing that sexual lifestyles warrant the same legal protection as liberals traditionally

---

ship of self-mastery," the doctrine that no sexual pleasure may licitly be sought outside marriage, and the wickedness of libidinous materials. (See, for example, the discussion in the 1994 English edition of *Catechism of the Catholic Church*, secs. 2338–55.) Personally, I should want to see an argument proving them contradictory. Much in that argument will be depend on what sorts of pleasure are meant, what thoughts 'custody of imagination' is supposed to lead us to shun, the ranking of the good of self-mastery as against such other goods as that of nurturing and developing one's erotic imagination and appreciation, and so on. As for pornography, I do not deny it is a bad business, but everything will depend on what lies within its scope and how it is distinguished from other erotic material. I suspect that one of many benefits of the increased eroticism that the past few decades have effected in advertising, *couture*, popular music and film, literature, etc., is ultimately to help reduce demand for unequivocally depraved and degrading material. However, I recognize some reasonably read the recent history as supporting the opposite thesis. In any case, this is not the place, and I am not the scholar, to undertake the sociological research to defend that view, let alone the theological work needed for a persuasive reconciliation of the views to which I lean with various texts within Christian tradition. My inclination— probably born of some mix of generational and traditional loyalties—is to reject the doctrines of recent sexual liberationists, which transvaluate sexual immoderation and perversion into elements of mental, social, moral health; at the same time, I see little to recommend the emphasis sometimes assigned avoiding all sexual temptation and tightly restricting even the mildest erotic enjoyment to marital intercourse.

45   See Thomas Nagel, "Freud's Permanent Revolution," *New York Review of Books* (12 May 1994).

accord free speech because they are protected by the same moral rights. What is so important about sex acts? In his discussion of the importance of sex, recall, Nagel pointed to three things: sex as pleasure, sex as ecstasy, and sex as self-completing through escape from civilization to our "presocial, animal, infantile natures." Can these do the job? That is doubtful.

If whatever gives pleasure is to be accorded special protection or if the level of protection accorded something is to be determined by the intensity of the pleasure it affords, then all the high-minded Kantian talk of autonomy and the religiously tinged talk of 'meaning' may as well be abandoned. We are back to Benthamite liberalism, with all the embarrassment and trivialization such theory brings to politics and morality. What, then, of ecstasy? Here, I think, Nagel's position must again trade on the vaguely religious associations of the term. Literally and etymologically, ecstasy is little more than a kind of conscious loss of one's senses. Religious mystics valued this experience as transcendence—a slipping of this world that provided occasion for some sort of union with or insight into God. Though the ecstatic dimension of sex is probably underemphasized in theological writing, within those Christian traditions that understand marriage as a sign of Christ's relation to His Church sexual ecstasy within marital intercourse should be appreciated as a unique foretaste of the saved soul's beatifying vision of God in the afterlife. Without the dimension this possibility of divine union offers, it is hard to discern the great value Nagel sees in sexual ecstasy. What is it beyond one of the pleasures sex offers? This second value, then, appears to collapse into the first.

"Self-completion," the last of the three types of "personal importance" Nagel finds in sex, certainly sounds like a serious business, perhaps important enough to warrant his claim that the "roots" of sexual relations "in individual sexuality are so deep that the protection of individual freedom within the public sexual space is an overwhelmingly important aspect of the design of a system of individual rights." Yet, what is this self-completion? Why think this sort of completion so desirable? Would many selves remain incomplete without the broad legal latitude in sexual matters that Nagel advocates? Why think the sort of brief, isolated, small-scale release of the "presocial" and "animal[istic]" that a person can get in responsible, humane sexual activity is not too little to achieve anything so grand as 'self-completion'? (Recall that, according to much-discussed surveys, married Americans today average only two episodes of sex per week and the unmarried still less.)

More important for us, why think this possibility of self-completion, if it is real, indicates that there is a wide area of discretion and choice in sexual matters protected by moral rights and calling for comparable legal protection? To these questions, as far as I can see, Nagel provides few answers. Indeed, as we saw, by tying self-completion to the dissolution of civilized compunction and the release of deep presocial, animal, and infantile natures, he depicts sex in such a way that makes it sound like a social danger very much in need of constraint. Nagel simply assumes that political/legal liberation of our sex lives is only a step to a more comprehensive rejection of sexual inhibitions and self-restraint, a rejection he enthusiastically endorses. This ties liberation from legal and other external impediments with liberation to one set of internal impediments (inhibitions). However, it radically devalues, with no express justification, a different model of internal freedom—Augustinian liberation from desires, appetites, and fantasies themselves.

In Nagel's mind, recent sexual history is a story of "great progress" now threatened because "the reduction of censorship and the decriminalization of many forms of nonmarital sex" have made people aware of things "some people find disturbing and an affront to their own sexual feelings." Still, he affirms, "as with differences of religion, it is essential that we learn to live together without trying to stifle one another's deepest feelings."[46]

Sexual differences are, then, to be protected like religious differences. But how different these two kinds of difference are! Religious differences, if they are serious, should ultimately come down to differences of faith, that is, differences in belief about the origins and character of human beings in their world. Not so sexual differences, which comprise divergent preferences and sensitivities about how one acts and is acted upon. Nagel's implicit reduction of religion to "deep . . . feelings" may put it on a par with sex, but this parity by itself leaves it open whether we should treat sex with more seriousness and deference or this denatured religion with less. Nagel seems here to be misled by the common modern view that religion is especially private. Since sex is also commonly thought to be something properly kept private, religion and sex appear quite similar and both seem to fall within a zone of privacy that is properly accorded special protection. I say that Nagel is misled on this because the similarity is slight, little more than verbal. Sex was originally thought private in that we do or should feel ashamed about making public display of our sexual parts or activities or witnessing display of others'. ('*Pudenda*', etymologically, are those things of which one should be ashamed.) Religion is not something private in that sense, if it is private in any. Sensible religious people do not feel embarrassed on being witnessed in devotions nor about witnessing others. Rather, they often build huge temples, mosques, and cathedrals to accommodate thousands making devotions together.

To Nagel, a refusal to let the disturbing or frightening content of others' "means of sexual gratification" provide "any ground for interference whatever, should be a fundamental aspect of the kind of recognition of inviolability that makes up a commitment to human rights."[47] Expressions of sexual interest, sexual compliments, and "evident sexual appreciation," he says, should be tolerated even when they give offense. All such matters properly belong to the protected "core of . . . personal and expressive life."[48] It is significant that

46   Nagel, "Personal Rights and Public Space," 100.
47   Ibid., 106.

Nagel's defense of a right to perform homosexual acts rests merely on the claim that homosexual relations are as "central and fundamental" in homosexuals' lives as are heterosexual relations in the latter's lives. This brings us to the fundamental questions about Nagel's account. Why think sex is within the self's "core"? Is it in everyone's core or just those who care a lot about sex? What puts it into the core of your or my self? Personal decision? Social formation? The nature of sex itself? Human nature? Are a person's judgments about her own identity and core infallible? self-justifying? performative? privileged? (If the last, how much?) When sex is within someone's core, what parts or aspects of her sexuality are there? Her orientation (as heterosexual, homosexual, or bisexual, or whatever)? Her preferred positions? Her quirks, kinks, and fetishes? Her ability freely to form a family with opportunity and potential for generating a rearing children?

Only the last touches something of fundamental human importance. However, even if all sexual preferences are within the core, which restrictions on them are such as to constitute 'violations'? Nagel offers little guidance on these crucial questions. I think his central metaphor of a personal 'core' so murky as to be useless without further clarification. What is a person's core except the deepest, most important truths about her, the truths that track her across times and possible worlds, perhaps, or that contain the truth about her origins, nature, destiny, and vocation? I turn next to an approach that forthrightly attempts to ground human rights precisely on what it claims to be such truths. I will not here assess those truth-claims themselves but will investigate their implications for the rights liberalism traditionally advocates and for the demands heard in this century that those liberties be extended to what I have here called welfare rights and the 'liberties of the Boomers.'

III. An Alternative View of the Value of Liberty

Karol Wojtyla wrote, some decades ago and well before his accession to the Papacy, that "freedom is on the one hand for the sake of truth and on the other hand it cannot be perfected except by means of truth."[49] I wish to explore an alternative view of the foundations of human rights, which he presents, and point out some aspects relevant to our inquiry.

John Paul II thinks that we are made for freedom, but for the free choice of our genuine good.[50] Freedom dignifies us, in this view, because it is a principal way in which we reflect God, who is free, and also (as Kant saw) rise above

---

48   Ibid., 107.

49   Quoted in Avery Dulles, "John Paul II and the Truth about Freedom," *First Things* (August/September 1995): 36.

50   "[H]uman freedom itself, the authentic meaning and purpose of which are found in its orientation to the true and the good . . ." (John Paul II, *Gospel of Life*, Vatican trans. [New York: Times Books, 1995], sec. 74).

the rest of earthly creation, which is not.[51] However, this freedom is ill-used unless it operates to select in accord with what we really are and need. That is, genuinely free choice is realistic, facing up to our status as creatures and our need for God. Without God, we can get things we want but never be satisfied with them, for, as he later wrote as Pope, we then "detach . . . human freedom from its essential and constitutive relationship to truth."[52]

Autonomy is often counterposed to paternalism in both political philosophy and medical ethics. Paternalism is, in the abstract, an unsettling notion simply because of its etymology. Society does not stand to me as father to child. However, autonomy is also disturbing in its root meanings, for the idea of everyone making the law and thus being a law unto herself is unsettling in the extreme. John Paul II tames autonomy, insisting that the autonomous person understands her autonomy as a "participated theonomy," that is, not as humankind inventing a law for itself but someone making the natural law (i.e., the law of our nature as creatures) her own when she internalizes it and adopts it as her personal rule of behavior.[53]

"[I]n him [Jesus] we are enabled to interiorize the law, to receive it and to live it as the motivating force of true personal freedom . . ." (John Paul II, *Splendor of Truth*, sec. 83)

According to John Paul II, "freedom is ordered to truth. . . . [R]eference to the truth about the human person . . . is, in fact, the guarantor of freedom's future."[54] The crucial truth about humanity is that we are inherently: (a) *inter*personal, (b) fulfilled in (and called to) loving service, and (c) creatures in need of God's guidance.[55] These truths—together with the fact that, unique within earthly creation, we possess metaphysical freedom beyond order of causal determination—ground our distinctive human dignity and thus ground universal human rights. There are notable advantages to this way of conceiving and grounding human freedom. First, it provides normative grounding for *some* freedom. Second, it limits the importance of preference

---

51   "Genuine freedom is an outstanding manifestation of the divine image in man." (*Gaudium et Spes*, 11; quoted in John Paul II, *Splendor of Truth*, Vatican trans. [Boston: St. Paul Books and Media, 1993], sec. 34.)
      "Freedom is the measure of man's dignity." (John Paul II, *Make Room for the Mystery of God* [Boston: Pauline Books and Media, 1995], 30).

52   John Paul II, *Splendor of Truth*, sec. 4.

53   "The rightful autonomy of the practical reason means that man possesses in himself his own law, received from the Creator. . . . [People] speak, and rightly so, of . . . participated theonomy, since man's free obedience to God's law effectively implies that human reason and human will participate in God's wisdom and providence." (Ibid., secs. 40, 41).

54   John Paul II, *Make Room for the Mystery of God*, 31.

55   "When God is forgotten the creature itself grows unintelligible." (*Gaudium et Spes*, 36, quoted in John Paul II, *Gospel of Life*, sec. 22.)

and its ability to bestow significance on trivial acts. Third, it ties a person's freedom to her flourishing and happiness. Fourth, it derives humanity's special normative status (in part) from our special metaphysical status and identity as possessing freedom as initiators. Fifth, it works from a conception of identity (who I am) that is universal(ist), necessary, important beyond social construction, morally loaded (normative). Sixth, it roots freedom not in individual alienation but precisely in our sociality and need (in order fully to be persons) for relationship with others. In these ways, it is quite unlike today's gender, race-, ethnicity- based conceptions of identity.

Moreover, this way of thinking about freedom sees it as important because it is internal to the moral importance of some other kinds of human actions and omissions. For example, religious worship is valuable and morally virtuous only insofar as it is freely offered. This last point fits the important insight of Ronald Dworkin's Tanner Lectures that paternalism is self-defeating to the extent that, by coercing the behavior it wants, it deprives that behavior of moral credit and thus fails effectively to force people to become good.[56] However, it does not vindicate Dworkin's wider anti-paternalist conclusion, since some measure of paternalism may be justified for other reasons. For example, it may help a person avoid vicious conduct and her being a(n even more) vicious person, even if they are insufficient to make her virtuous.

This understanding of freedom has implications for our questions about political policy and principles about liberties. Prefiguring Nagel's language, but grounding it quite differently, John Paul II affirms that "The sacredness of life gives rise to its inviolability. . . . Thus the deepest element of God's commandment to protect human life is the requirement to show reverence and love for every person and the life of every person."[57] He told the UN in October, 1995 that every culture is a response to mystery of life.[58] That may be overstated, but religious conviction normally (if not always the whole of culture) *is* such a response. Since such freely given response is the point of life, as correctly understood, religious freedom is needed in the first place.[59] Free exercise of religion will be a matter of rights. Strictures on state endorsement of religion will be matters of rights only insofar as the endorsement of one constellation of religious beliefs and practices is so extreme that it involves the

---

56   Dworkin, "Foundations of Liberal Equality." In *Tanner Lectures on Human Values XI*. Edited by Grethe Petersen (Salt Lake City: University of Utah Press, 1990).

57   John Paul II, *Gospel of Life*, secs. 40, 41.

58   "Every culture is an effort to ponder the mystery of the world and in particular of the human person." (John Paul II, "Address to the U.N. General Assembly," John Paul II, *Make Room for the Mystery of God*, 29.)

59   "[T]he right to religious freedom and to respect for conscience on its journey towards the truth is increasingly perceived as the foundation of the cumulative rights of the person." (John Paul II, *Splendor of Truth*, sec. 31.)

citizenry in that endorsement in such a way as to constitute an infringement of their ability freely to exercise their own religious convictions. (For example, religious tests for public office.) Other related and derivative forms of expression, such as political (and, maybe, artistic) speech and writing, assembly, moral protest, and so on, should also be specially protected *as a matter of right* against unwarranted state restriction insofar as they really are undertaken as opportunities to carry out the duty to search for God's truth.[60] Thus, the liberties of the moderns to freedom of religion, speech, and press are presented as more basic than those of the ancients to political participation, in accord with an important strand of recent liberal thought.[61] Notice that this way of grounding religious freedom cannot easily be extended to the sexual. For religious inquiry, belief, and practice are specially privileged, on this view, as a way of finding the origin, nature, and meaning of human life and of accepting the discipline of living up to the demands of what one finds. Nagel, as we saw, begins like this too, but ignores the depth of the religious when he argues that the same reasons that ground religious freedom also ground broad sexual license. Unfortunately, his intellectual allies make a similar mistake.[62] Even on

60   "In particular, the right to religious freedom and to respect for conscience on its journey towards the truth is increasingly perceived as the foundation of the cumulative rights of the person." (Ibid., sec. 31.)

61   Rawls writes, "Thus one strand of the liberal tradition regards the political liberties as of less intrinsic value than freedom of thought and liberty of conscience. . . . The role of the political liberties is perhaps largely instrumental in preserving the other liberties." (*Political Liberalism*, 299) Rawls himself does not explicitly endorse this view, but he does attribute it to Isaiah Berlin, nowadays considered one of this century's leading liberal thinkers.

John Dewey seems to have opposed this view. His liberalism subordinated rights to social needs. "For Dewey, the 'first object of a renascent liberalism' was not justice or rights but education, the task of 'producing the habits of mind and character the intellectual and moral patterns,' that suited citizens to the mutual responsibilities of a shared public life." In his view, the virtues of democracy are "like those of science: It excluded the fewest alternatives, allowed all ideas a fair shot at being tried out, encouraged progress, and did not rely on authority." (Michael Sandel, "Dewey Rides Again," *New York Review of Books* [9 May 1996]: 36.) The second passage is quoted from Alan Ryan.) Such a view elevates merely procedural matters (the liberties of the ancients to political participation) over the deeper, substantive ones (the liberties of the moderns to religious practice and to speech) that give them point. It is ironic that Dewey's self-consciously modernist liberalism is less forward-looking here than the sort that can be seen to emerge from the Pope's position, notwithstanding the latter's Aristotelian and scriptural roots. It is sad that some liberals, sensing the movement's crisis, look to Dewey rather than the more enlightened (though less Enlightenment) position I think can be found in religious sources.

62   I especially have in mind Richards as an ally of Nagel. He argues that religious liberty is grounded in a "background right of moral independence," which he identifies as "equal respect for the moral powers of human personality."

the most generous interpretation, the matters of sexual tastes, orientation, quirks, and satisfaction cannot rise to this level of significance, one, which truly encompasses the whole of human life.[63] Indeed, someone whose sexual preferences were assigned such weight would find herself leading a grotesquely misshapen existence.

Moreover, the welfare rights are well grounded in this account of humanity and justice. The papal voice repeatedly raises "the evangelical cry in defence of the world's poor," in condemnation of the "ancient scourges of poverty, hunger, [and] endemic diseases," and "the violence against life done to millions of human beings, especially children, who are forced into poverty, malnutrition and hunger because of an unjust distribution of resources between peoples and between social classes."[64] Indeed, this protection will extend further than many liberals nowadays want it to, for the Pope is explicit that dignity extends to all human beings, including those (the severely brain-damaged, the unborn, the terminally ill, the despairing) whom elite opinion increasingly relegates to the margins of human personhood and strips of moral and legal protection.

In contrast to the support thus given the liberties of the moderns and welfare rights as basic and the liberties of the ancients as derivative, however, the new agenda of lifestyle freedoms does not appear to be closely enough linked to the free quest for God, in this view, to warrant comparable protection. What of efforts like that of Nagel to model sex on religion and thus win it comparable protection? John Paul II recognizes that sex contributes to human dignity. He calls "sexuality . . . the sign, place, and language of love, that is, the gift of self and acceptance of another, in all the other's richness as a person."

(Richards, *Toleration and the Constitution*, 252.) This right of equal respect, in turn, will also generate privacy rights to abort pregnancies, use contraceptives irrespective of marital status, engage in homosexual acts, and so on down the checklist of what I have here called 'liberties of the Boomers.' Without going into the details of Richards' exposition here, permit me to say that I see no principled way of keeping such a right from specially protecting almost anything as part of one's privacy, that it is hard to see why equal respect for persons requires blessing all their sexual quirks, and that this sort of right fails even in its initial task of capturing the special importance of religion in human life. (Compare Richards, *Toleration and the Constitution*, chap. 9.)

63   Paul Weithman has reminded me that I should make it explicit that I do not mean to deny that some sexual matters can take on special significance as part of a religious quest, e.g., one might feel called by God to such vocations as marriage or consecrated celibacy. I will not here enter the vexed constitutional issue of how far religious liberty should extend to socially objectionable behavior (e.g., using peyote) that one believes required or strongly indicated by religious conviction.

64   John Paul II, *Gospel of Life*, secs. 3, 5, 10.

The value, the glory of sexuality in this vision is that it symbolizes the gift of self that humanizes us by imitating the sacrifice of Christ.[65]

John Paul II warns, however, in a passage addressing just the private fantasy-driven picture of sex we examined, that sexuality can become "the occasion and instrument for self-assertion and the selfishness of personal desires and instinct. Thus the original meaning of human sexuality is distorted and falsified. . ."[66] In contrast, he maintains that the relationality essential to our natures and by which we image the Divine Trinity is first and most universally manifested in the family, for we are all born sons or daughters. "The family, as a community of persons, is thus the first human 'society.'" It is in the family that we first realize our separateness and begin to transcend it through our relatedness. "In prayer, the family discovers itself as the first 'us,' in which each member is 'I' and 'thou'; each member is for the others either husband or wife, father or mother, [etc.]" It is in virtue of our innate capacity to develop into such interpersonal relationships that we are persons.[67] "Love causes man to find fulfillment through the sincere gift of self."[68] This provides the context for an understanding of sex because sexual behavior is for Wojtyla, as for Nagel, significant primarily as expressive. However, where to Nagel it matters as expression of an individual's fantasies, feelings, and desires, to Wojtyla it matters chiefly as an expression of love. The latter is a deeper view, as it is more fully human. Love, especially the committed spousal love that the Pope intends, is unlike mere desire in that it encompasses the person not merely in her imagination and tastes, but in her will, rationality, and social dimensions as well.[69]

---

65   "[T]he deepest and most authentic meaning of [human] life: namely that of being a gift which is fully realized in the giving of self." (Ibid., sec. 49.) In the pope's Christocentric anthropology, it is Christ's life that serves as our deepest source of insight into *human* nature.

66   Ibid., sec. 23.

67   A given person may not live out or experience any such relationships—due to physical isolation, emotional arrest, or mental incompetence—but we cannot grasp the concept of personhood save by reference to the interpersonal.

68   John Paul II, *Letter to Families*, secs. 7–11.

69   My aim in this section is to present a view developed in papal writings and to show some of its advantages. Although I do not here pursue shortcomings in the approach discussed, that is not to imply that I think it free of imperfections. One problematic area lies in the approach's single-minded concentration on restricting sexual imagination and desire to marriage. This exclusive emphasis tends to undervalue ways in which periods of sexual abstinence can heighten awareness of ambient erotic stimuli and generate a less focused, free-floating, and passive appreciation of erotic elements in both natural and artificial creation. (Think of how one sees the world in Georgia O'Keefe's paintings of flowers in almost microscopic detail or in Robert Mapplethorpe's close-up photographs with similar images.) One could maintain that, in contrast to the papal approach's

This vindicates liberals' traditional view that some freedoms from political obstacles to certain activities are especially important. These are liberties essential for the exercise of our duties to respond to the human vocation, if I may adapt Fichte's language to my own purpose, to seek understanding of our common human nature and destiny and to express it in love. The rights to these fundamental liberties are rooted in our station as creatures in God's image as free, beyond nature, and entrusted to share in God's governance by choosing to (do God's will that) we fulfill our own deepest needs, nature, and identity. Our nature and identity (as creatures, but creatures of a special kind) ground our dignity, and our dignity grounds our rights.[70] Liberals are marked by the special value they place on certain freedoms.[71] It follows that liberals, from their commitments as liberals, should: (a) not try to curtail licit and important freedoms (even in order to advance further freedom), and should, indeed, (b) try *not* to curtail them, seeking means less restrictive of important freedoms in legitimate efforts to protect society and encourage virtue. Such would be the commitment of a conception of liberalism that grounded its conviction that certain liberties are matters of universal human entitlement in a comprehensive picture of humanity's origin, nature, and calling of the sort developed in recent papal writings. The important question about government action for liberals is not whether, in its reasoning, the state acts from a religious conception but whether in its substance what it does duly respects each individual, especially in the legitimate range of her own freedom.[72] It is

---

emphases, a joyful sensitization to the erotic element in the splendors both of nature and our social surroundings has great and legitimate advantages in allowing us to see God and His world as good, as sources of bliss and exhilaration, notwithstanding the soul-crushing horrors of life that are never far from consciousness at any moment in our earthly journey. In any case, I leave the theological questions of whether there is room for revision and development in this area to those better equipped to answer them.

70   "The dignity of this life is linked not only to its beginning, to the fact that it comes from God, but also to its final end, to its destiny of fellowship with God . . ." (John Paul II, *Gospel of Life*, sec. 38.)

71   Acts *intended* to curtail these freedoms (as means or end) egregiously breach this value and are therein particularly objectionable. Deliberate government restrictions are odious (whether *de jure* or covert). *De facto* negative impact of state action on these freedoms is also quite bad; natural restrictions and other unintended social restrictions take on special moral importance. Otherwise, they are merely among the many undesirable things of life we should try to help each other avoid, whether or not we use the mechanisms of the state in doing so.

72   For an intriguing argument that this, surprisingly, is the view even of such a quintessentially pre-liberal thinker as Thomas Aquinas, see John Finnis, "Public Good: the Specifically Political Common Good in Aquinas." Paper read at a Fall 1995 Princeton University conference on the moral philosophy of Germain Grisez.

the chief mistake of much recent, neutralist liberal theory to think that a negative answer to the latter question can be directly inferred from a positive answer to the former. In the final section, I raise some questions about this version of liberalism.

IV. Religious Pluralism and Public Reason

My suggestion is that a certain religious and metaphysical understanding of the human nature and destiny offers a better and more sensible grounding for rights to the liberties that liberals' have historically favored. But even if so, so what? In a pluralistic society, can it be appropriate for the state or its citizens to appeal to or rely upon such a religiously informed understanding? Not according to the mainstream of recent discussions in liberal political philosophy, which demand that state agencies—and even individuals in their capacities as citizens—maintain secular neutrality and "epistemic abstinence" from advocating or acting on religious views in political debate.[73]

I will close with a few words on how my suggestion, that the liberal state understand the protection of certain liberties along the lines indicated by John Paul II, might deserve consideration in the face of the 'gag rule' urged by liberal neutralists and their allies against any the employment of religious views as bases for public policy.

First, Robert Audi thinks it a matter of civic virtue and a prima facie duty that everyone eschew religious rationales and motivation in her political advocacy and action.[74] Quinn and others have argued with some cogency that this demand is not fair in its application, since secularists are permitted to act from controversial philosophical bases, but not religious people from controversial religious ones.[75] I wish here only to ask whether a position like Audi's does not also threaten effectively to disenfranchise and politically silence those, like followers of many of the great Protestant Reformers, who view all moral demands as wholly derivative from God's commands. Of course, they would not be altogether silenced, since they could still advocate policies on

---

73   See Bruce Ackerman, *Social Justice in the Liberal State* (New Haven, Conn.: Yale University Press, 1980); Robert Audi, "Separation of Church and State and the Obligations of Citizenship." *Philosophy and Public Affairs* 18 (1989); Robert Audi, "Religious Commitment and Secular Reason: A Reply to Professor Weithman," *Philosophy and Public Affairs* 20 (1991); Paul Weithman, "Separation of Church and State: Some Questions for Professor Audi." *Philosophy and Public Affairs* 20 (1991); and the pieces in this volume by Audi, Quinn, and Wolterstorff, among other sources, for advocacy or critique of this liberal neutralist position.

74   Audi, "Separation of Church and State and the Obligations of Citizenship," and "Religious Commitment and Secular Reason."

75   Philip Quinn, "Political Liberalisms and their Exclusions of the Religious," *Proceedings and Addresses of the American Philosophical Association* 69 (1995).

nonmoral grounds. But how could they legitimately advance any moral basis for political action when no such reason will count as a secular one for them? Of course, one who takes Audi's side might insist that moral reasons (at least, many of them) really *are* secular reasons whether or not these theological voluntarists realize it. However, I fear that this threatens to be untrue to these people's own reasoning insofar as they view moral claims as true, justified, refuted, and so on solely on the basis of how they stand vis-à-vis what are taken to be God's commands.[76]

Second, Rawls introduces strictures on what he calls "public reason," which my suggestion clearly violates. Even on what he calls "the wide view," reasons for state action derived from a religious or other "comprehensive doctrine" may only enter public discourse if the doctrine is "reasonable" and if "in due course sufficient public reasons are presented that fall under a reasonable political conception of justice."[77] Why must our reasons for state action pass these criteria for public reason? Rawls' answer to this crucial question is not clear to me and seems to have changed. In *Political Liberalism*, he appears to think that passing the tests is necessary as part of an elaborate mechanism (including the constructed overlapping consensus, the political conceptions of the person and of justice, etc.). At the beginning of that work, he offers the mechanism as his answer to the question of how to bring a pluralistic society not just justice but stable justice and, later in it, he says the machinery (of the overlapping consensus, and so on) helps enable us "to see how a well-ordered society can be unified and stable."[78] In a later paper, however, he claims that this focus on the question of how to achieve stability (despite pluralism) was misleading and maintains, instead, that the goal of his mechanism is "to answer the question of the most reasonable basis for social unity" in the face of pluralism.[79]

These two accounts of the point and importance of meeting the tests of public reason (and the rest of Rawls' mechanism) are quite different. The second is not simply a better way of putting the same point, as his claim that the former passages did not state the aim of the enterprise "in the best way"

---

76 To insist that these theological voluntarists' moral reasoning is really secular though they think it is not, is rather like the suggestion of Amy Gutmann and Dennis Thompson that the appeal to virtue and responsibility in fundamentalists' arguments about abortion, homosexuality and other issues is not really moral reasoning though they think it is. (See Amy Gutmann and Dennis Thompson, "Moral Conflict and Political Consensus." *Ethics* 101 (1990).) A better alternative to both views, I think, is to allow what seems true anyway: There are religious moral arguments as well as secular ones, even as there are both secular and religious theories of morality.

77 Rawls, forthcoming.

78 Rawls, *Political Liberalism*, 4, 134.

79 Rawls, "Reply to Habermas," *Journal of Philosophy* 92 (March 1995): 146, n. 27.

suggests. Whether public reason and the rest of Rawls' paraphernalia would generate a stable acceptance of his (or another) theory of social justice is not itself a normative issue. Whether it is the most reasonable basis of social unity, however, is paradigmatically normative for Rawls.

Consider the question about stability. While this is not a normative issue, it is a problematic one. Rawls criticizes other ways of maintaining social peace in the midst of pluralism—what he calls *modus vivendi*—for being unreliable in the long run. They are insufficiently stable. But how much stability is desired, and why? Maybe some instability is a good thing. Perhaps it is not a bad thing for a culture to try out different conceptions of justice from time to time rather than sticking consistently with the same one. More seriously, why think that reliance upon public reason and the "free-standing" conception of political justice to which it is tied is either the *only* or the *best* way of achieving stability? Consider one possible alternative. For all Rawls' emphasis on the plurality of comprehensive doctrines in our society, the great majority of people hold religious beliefs within the Jewish and Christian traditions.[80] There is, therefore, considerable unity within the diversity. Might not reliance upon this underlying agreement, a passive and latent consensus in contrast to the constructed and explicit one Rawls imagines, achieve a broad and lasting base of support for a widely shared conception of justice based on a human dignity that is rooted in our status as image of God? Of course, someone might deny this could bring (long enough) lasting stability because she assumes that the inexorable tendency of modern culture is to break down religious convictions. However, this seems to be just the sort of controversial social and historical claim on which Rawls thinks we should not rely. It sounds like secularist wishful thinking. In any case, it is not obvious we have the overlapping consensus Rawls thinks we do on matters of social justice, especially, welfare policy and taking care of the worst off.[81] So, there may be alternative bases for social unity that are good in some important ways. We need to know why appeal to a certain cross-denominationally appealing conception of God and divine creation, as my suggestion about freedom involves, might not be as good or better than Rawls' method.

These evaluative questions bring us to Rawls' later, more difficult, and explicitly normative understanding of the aim of his theoretical apparatus. If I understand him correctly, when Rawls calls this "the most reasonable basis

---

80   Stephen Carter cites press reports of poll data in the early 1990s indicating that 82 percent of Americans identify themselves as Christians (with about two Protestants for every Catholic) and another 2 percent as Jews. (See Carter, *The Culture of Disbelief* (New York: Doubleday, 1993), 4, 279.) Of course, not all these will accept the view of things I sketched from Wojtyla's writings, but I doubt many hold beliefs strictly incompatible with the relevant parts about the origin, nature, destiny, and vocation of human life.

81   See Philip Quinn, "Political Liberalisms and their Exclusions of the Religious."

for social unity," he means 'reasonable' not merely to embrace some form of practical reason but to have a moral dimension as well. The limits on the reasons admissible within public reason express and maintain a relation of "civic friendship" which is captured by the "ideal that citizens are to conduct their fundamental political discussions . . . within the framework of what each sincerely regards as a reasonable political conception of justice, a conception that expresses political values that others as free and equal also might reasonably be expected reasonably to endorse."[82] Here several questions come quickly to mind. Why is accepting these restrictions the only or the best mode of expressing and institutionalizing civic friendship? What is it for a person as free and equal to accept something, and how can this condition be violated? More important, how specifically would a society's following my suggestion that the state employ a religiously informed picture of human freedom violate it? Would an unbeliever who did accept such a reason—perhaps for pragmatic reasons or as part of an explicit deal—or who agreed to let us act on it, therein render herself less than equal to believers? Less free than they? How so?[83] Is it reasonable of Rawlsians to demand that the state do nothing unless it has a rationale for action a person would have to be unreasonable not to endorse? How much even in scientific theory, let alone in any sphere of practice, can meet that standard?

Third and last, let us briefly consider a third way of defending what I have called the 'gag rule,' one not developed in the literature but intriguing nonetheless. The suggestion I will examine briefly is that it is permissible for the state to coerce someone only when the moral principle from which it acts is one it would be blameworthy to reject.[84] This suggestion has a certain intuitive

---

82   Rawls, *Political Liberalism*, 226.

83   Notice the similarity of my question to one Wolterstorff puts to Rawls in this volume: Why does appealing to or acting from religious convictions in a public matter violate the respect owed others as free and equal citizens? My remarks in the previous section also address another hard question Wolterstorff asks the Rawlsian: On what basis are we so confident that each is free and equal? This is part of the overlapping consensus, perhaps, but will it really remain either reasonable or stable once the underlying religious consensus evaporates? Why think so? Even our Declaration says we are equal because created so and free because divinely endowed with a right to liberty. Rawls thinks the moral convictions will survive unscathed the passing of the religious. However, there is little evidence for this. Most Americans apparently still hold the religious convictions. Academic elites tend not to, but then they are also the group among whom firm moral convictions seem shakiest, waxing and waning as intellectual fashion changes and anti-moralisms (cultural relativism, superego theory, Nietzschean immoralism) come and go.

84   James Sterba introduced a principle along these lines in the general discussion concluding Notre Dame's conference on Religion and Contemporary Liberalism. It was his interesting comment that stimulated me to reflect here on the possi-

appeal. For instance, it offers one way of capturing the attractive Kantian idea that one must regard others with a certain deference that goes beyond merely having good reason for doing things that harm them. It also holds some advantages over alternative grounds that have been offered for the proscription on religious arguments in public policy debates. Because it is framed in terms of the common-sense and straightforwardly moral concept of blameworthiness, this way of defending a certain form of rights-oriented liberalism avoids the difficulty we saw in Rawls of trying to identify with adequate precision the moral element within the murky concept of the 'reasonable' and distinguishing it both from the weaker notion of properly using practical reason and from the technical notion of rationality employed by decision-theorists. Unlike Audi's view, it does not seem biased specifically against the religious. Not only scripturally-based beliefs but philosophical and ideological convictions would also be debarred from public advocacy, if they could be rejected without deserving blame.

This suggestion has merits, then, but, before it can properly be embraced, it should need to be developed in such a way that it overcomes some internal difficulties. One of these is the need to determine whether the principle will require that *every* principle from which the state acts in doing something be one it would be blameworthy to reject or only that *some* of them be. The stronger principle is too strong, for if every principle has to be one it will be blameworthy to reject, then the state would probably be debarred from acting on reasonable but contestable derivative principles. For example, for it permissibly to tax me it would to have to be true that one would deserve blame not only for rejecting the principle that one should contribute adequately to the support of state functions, but also for rejecting the principle that someone in my situation should contribute exactly (or, at least, no less than) N dollars. There is simply too much room for judgment, error, and reasonable disagreement about that sort of detail for such a principle to apply without depriving the state of the right to exact *any* sum from me. The weaker principle, however, is too weak. Almost any act of vicious ideological fanaticism (e.g., exterminating some racial groups in hopes of thereby somehow improving the human race) will be done from *some* principle (e.g., bettering humanity) that only the vicious could condemn.

Another difficulty with this approach is that it needs to be fixed just who would have to be blamed if she rejected the principle. Is a principle unsuitable for state action if there is anyone who could innocently reject it? anyone in the community? anyone in the world? anyone in any (duly accessible) possible

bility. However, because Sterba's conference remarks were off-the-cuff, informal, and offered only for purposes of discussion, I develop and critique the suggestion in these paragraphs simply as a possible line for defending the 'gag-rule,' not as his own position.

world? anyone affected by the action the principle motivates? There are problems no matter which answer is selected. Consider just two. Suppose, first, that I am unjustly attacked. According to the principle under discussion, what must be the case for my coercive acts of self-defense—say, forcing my attacker to drop her weapon—to be permissible? Must it really be the case that anyone who rejects a principle of self-defense therein deserves blame? If so, it has to be the case that coercive self-defense is unjustified unless accepting pacifism is a culpable offense. That is too high a standard, and it seems morally absurd to maintain that disabling or even homicidal self-defense is permissible but not coercive. Of course, a parallel argument could be made for the even more intuitively unobjectionable possibility of altruistic defense of others.

Now imagine, second, that my (or some third party's) attacker is herself a pacifist—apparently a rather akrastic one—now bent on murderous revenge against me. (Perhaps I said that pacifism was not only wrongheaded but blameworthy, and that set her off.) To justify my defensive coercion must the attacker herself be someone who is (or would be) to blame for rejecting the principle of defense? Again, intuitively, that simply demands too much. In any case, if even this kind of coercion cannot be justified, the prospects for justifying as coercive an institution as the state seem dim indeed. So, the whole project of determining criteria for permissible state coercion appears to become nugatory on this principle. It is self-defeating.

Finally, it will be controversial whether this principle even succeeds in its intended work of justifying the exclusion of religious bases for state action and its advocacy. That is because for it to have that implication we must first assume that rejecting a religious moral principle (say, one based in the Bible or some other text assigned divine authority) is never blameworthy. Suppose we interpret this to mean that the principle is an unacceptable basis for state coercion if anyone could innocently reject it. Unbelievers, we may expect, will think their unbelief innocent and, in this easy-going age when even religious people are loathe to avoid any hint of dogmatism or self-righteousness, many believers may agree with them on this. However, it is not an open-and-shut case. According to ancient Christian doctrine, some people are damned for rejecting some Christian beliefs, and there is no uncontroversial reason to exclude religious moral principles from this set. This doctrine is unpopular these days, but it is not dead, not even among intellectuals. Robert Adams has recently developed a sophisticated account of how sins against faith can properly be culpable under some circumstances.[85] Again, what if some of God's command's really are, as Christian scripture maintains, written in our hearts? Then, it may be that everyone has basis enough to see their truth and, when someone does not find the evidence of the divine will (or even God's

---

85   See the title essay in Robert Merrihew Adams, *The Virtue of Faith and Other Essays* (Oxford: Oxford University Press, 1987) 9–24.

existence) compelling, that may be her own fault—a matter of some self-deception, of somehow convincing herself that she does not really see what her mind's eye reveals to her. Of course, all that may be benighted superstition. And it may not be. What matters for our purposes is that a decision on that is not a neutral one, but itself depends on one's religious views. Thus, even if the difficulties I have found in this view can all be overcome, religious believers of a certain stripe could accept the principle without thereby committing themselves to any principled exclusion of explicitly religious advocacy, reasoning, or motives in matters of public policy.

I have here tried to raise a problem about the basis and range of liberties that liberalism properly recognizes as those to which everyone is entitled, and to detail the failure of a prominent philosopher's method of addressing it. I have also sketched an alternative position derived from papal writings, pointed out some of its advantages, acknowledged one line of criticism against my suggestion, and pointed out a few difficulties within that critique. Nagel once joked that recent social changes could be seen as society coming to take a stand against religion and for sex.[86] Here I have argued against the way in which he and others have inadvertently lent this change plausibility by illegitimately claiming for sex, including demeaning forms of it, the virtues, dignity, and importance of religious search and conviction. Liberalism has gotten lost in the mire of fantasy. It may only relocate its way in the splendor of truth.

---

86   Nagel, "Moral Conflict and Political Legitimacy," *Philosophy and Public Affairs* 17 (1987). He rejects that view, though I do not think the arguments his article offers succeed in establishing a persuasive alternative reading.

The Question Concerning Authority

Jean Elshtain

Much of America's political ferment and diversity, past and present, stems from intense religious commitments. A particular religious faith was the carrier of universal value—of this religious abolitionists, civil rights protestors, and thousands of others who have helped to forge and to shape and to sustain this union had no doubt. We now have such doubts for some very good reasons—we honor and recognize religious and political plurality. Although such plurality was characteristic of American society from the beginning within the broad Christian Protestant dispensation, that recognition now extends, as it did not at the beginning, to Catholics, Jews, and Muslims. But we have doubts for other, less convincing reasons, including the notion that it is okay to have religious beliefs so long as one keeps them to oneself. But this is precisely what a devout person cannot do. For religious faith isn't primarily a private affair: It is constitutive of a form of public membership in a particular body—the church, the temple, the mosque, the synagogue. Out of the house and into not only the *polis* but *ecclesia*.

There is, then, some irony in our current situation. We are fretting simultaneously about too ardent religious belief and the loss of belief, specifically, the loss of the democratic faith. An anemic and faltering democratic faith—a decline of confidence in our basic institutions—threatens to render us incapable of sustaining these institutions over the long haul. This decline of confidence flows, in part, from a general crisis of authority—or so I shall argue.

But a few additional preliminary remarks to help frame my concern with authority are here in order. In the debate between those who might be called Rawlsians and the rest of us, I think it is worth noting that it is not only the conditions or terms of *exclusion* of religious commitments from the public square that are worth critical scrutiny but, as well, those terms of *inclusion* that have the practical effect of decomposing any and all authoritative religious claims, meaning the claims of particular communities.

Must we really refuse to admit to public debate or debate about matters public strong claims that trace their points of origin to authoritative religious traditions whose creeds are couched in language that falls outside the liberal (meaning here "philosophical liberalism," not rough and ready political liberalism) dispensation? If we push too far the notion that, in order to be acceptable public fare, we must absorb all religious claims and categories into a certain sort of philosophic language of justification without remainder, we depluralize in the name of democratizing. That is, if we operate under an epistemological urgency that dictates translating religious language into one dominant philosophic language and go on to insist that one can effect this translation without remainder—nothing important is left out—we erode over time the authoritative grounding of the American democracy itself, one committed to plural communities, to a freedom that is in some ways communal—or to that possibility—and not just to the liberty of a sovereign self.

This, in fact, is what has happened given a pervasive analytic conceit that demands an elaborate justification of a certain sort if one is to go public with an argument in a way that insulates that argument against charges of sectarianism, divisiveness, or the mapping of "private" preferences onto public life. What has been lost along the way is the recognition that a variety of norms and rules are constitutive of plural communities and that a democratic polity has an enormous stake in keeping such plurality alive. For this is the only way to keep democratic politics alive. As political theorist Sheldon Wolin points out: "Rawls's 'well-ordered society' stipulates that 'the most divisive, serious contention about which must undermine the basis of social cooperation,' will be removed from the public agenda."[1] Rawls's philosophy, Wolin continues, is the "yearnings of an ideology seeking repose." With religious disputation as a negative paradigm, providing the "object lesson" for "profound doctrinal conflict," Rawls sees either "stability, cooperation, duration, and unified system" or "endless and destructive civil strife" as exhausting the repertoire of our current possibilities.[2] The upshot within his perspective is depoliticization in the interest of sustaining an order buttressed by a set of principles that are themselves removed from disputation. A rather ascetic rationalism supplants the strenuousness and rambunctiousness of all those past, present, and continuing arguments generated by the deep entanglement of politics and religion in American life.

What do these rather summarily couched debating points have to do with authority, political and religious? Let's begin by considering the "crisis of authority" in modernity more generally. Among the many strong claims lodged by Hannah Arendt, one must include the following: Authority, she claimed, "has vanished from the modern world. Since we can no longer fall back upon authentic and undisputable experiences common to all, the very term has become clouded by controversy and confusion."[3] We late moderns no longer "know what authority really *is*." What we have lost, Arendt continues rather elliptically, is not authority in general "but rather a very specific form which had been valid throughout the Western World over a long period of time."[4]

---

1   Sheldon Wolin, "The Liberal/Democratic Divide. On Rawls's Political Liberalism," *Political Theory* 24, no. 1 (February 1996): 107.

2   Ibid., 108.

3   Hannah Arendt, "What is Authority?" in *Between Past and Future* (Baltimore: Penguin, 1980), 91.

The effect of this inability generates and perpetuates a terrible mistake; indeed, a base confusion, namely, the tendency to conflate power, coercion, even violence with authority. Failing to distinguish between these different modalities and ways of being, we fall into something akin to the abyss conceptually and even politically. We lose the past as the "permanence and durability" of the world melts away. This loss "is tantamount to the loss of the groundwork of the world, which indeed since then has begun to shift, to change and transform itself with ever-increasing rapidity from one shape to another, as though we were living and struggling with a Protean universe where everything at any moment can become almost anything else."[5] Arendt singles out for critical fire tendencies within philosophic liberalism, by which she refers to that mode of thought most deeply implicated in the conflation of coercion and authority. This, in turn, spawns political actors who similarly disdain any distinction authoritarianism, on the one hand, and authoritative rule or governance, on the other. But authority is not tyranny; indeed, the resort to tyranny is a sign that legitimate authority has broken down and given way to violence.

The legitimate authoritative figure historically was one who was bound. He or she was bound by law, bound by tradition, and by the force of past example and experience. Being bound in particular ways guaranteed a framework for action and helped to create and to sustain particular public spaces—whether of church, polity, other institutions of social life. The bound authority figure was, therefore, not free to do just anything; to make just any claim and to make it stick. That was the lawlessness of the tyrant, whether the king who has become tyrannical and might, therefore, be killed as a scourge to his people and a rebel against God (here John of Salisbury's *Policraticus* is my touchstone); or the twentieth-century tyrant, a Hitler or a Stalin, who knows and recognizes neither the laws of God, nor of nature, nor of human decency (a "common sense," in Arendt's formulation) and makes himself a law unto himself, hence an enactor of capricious terror and violence. To see this latter as an instance of, say, unusually harsh authority is, for Arendt, to vulgarize; it is to do violence to the truth, to what she unabashedly called the stubborn fact of the matter. Authority and obedience or faithfulness are twins. But in obeying—in offering fealty to a tradition that is shared, constitutive of the self and of a world—one remains free, free yet bound. This bounded freedom is the only way to guarantee creation of a common space, to simultaneously constrain yet nurture and make possible human action.

As a political theorist, Arendt was most concerned with a political world constituted by authority, a world, therefore, that rejected despots as unfit to rule. For the power to coerce is incompatible with the freedom of others and

4   Ibid., 92.

5   Ibid., 95.

"his [the tyrant's] own freedom as well. Wherever he ruled there was only one relation, that between masters and slaves."[6] Between masters and slaves (or so the Greeks thought) there was no possibility of commonality or a common tradition; the gulf was impassable. All of subsequent political thought, at least until late modernity, is an attempt to establish "a concept of authority in terms of rulers and ruled . . . and there is no philosopher-king to regulate human affairs once and for all."[7] This is the Aristotelian move away from Plato, of course, but it is also much more: a search for a community of equals who share ruling and being ruled and share as well a mutual commitment to authoritative rules and norms.

For the life of the *polis* is not just about life but about the "good life." This good life plays a formative and educative role; it inducts the next generation into a way of being in the world made possible only through mutual submission to authority, the authority created when human beings pledge themselves to something, hold one another accountable, keep their promises. As well, authority is natural, Arendt averred, in the pre-political realm of necessity (this is where she located the family, for example). But authority takes on something—only something—of a volitional dimension in that sphere of action we call politics. The word *auctoritas*, deeded to us by those most indefatigable of antique lawgivers, the Romans, derives from *augere*, to augment, to deepen. What is augmented is an authoritative moment of political birth or founding. Without such an authoritative moment, there is only violence or a rampant antinomianism.

Interestingly, Arendt credits the powerful and long-lived legitimacy of the Christian Church precisely to its 'Romanization,' to the way Christ's death and resurrection constituted a moment of authoritative founding. The early Church understood the distinction between authority and brute force or dominion. But this distinction is now blurred, tattered, perhaps torn beyond recognition. Luther, Arendt concludes, was in error in this matter, and his error was this. He believed he could challenge the "temporal authority of the Church and his appeal to unguided individual judgment would leave tradition and religion intact," just as Hobbes hoped "that authority and religion could be saved without tradition."[8] Both were wrong.

Fast forward several centuries and we arrive at a point—the present—where our options get cast either as a desperate attempt to reaffirm and reassert traditional modes of authoritative determination of the sort Arendt argues modernity has shattered, or as a kind of political and epistemological free-for-all. We are, then, stuck increasingly in a political realm in which, lacking either recognition of, or commitment to, an awareness that "the source

6   Ibid., 105.

7   Ibid., 116.

8   Ibid., 128.

of authority transcends power," we are confronted daily "by the elementary problems of human living-together."[9] Because we place so little confidence in authoritative norms and claims, nearly everything at every moment is up for grabs. By Arendt's reckoning we aren't doing a very good job of confronting this crisis of authority. If we see the world as a series of volitional acts, as if anything that "I" affirm marks a new beginning, we are in a world of radical antinomianism and romantic flailing that all too easily fuel cries of "oppression" whenever any constraint is put on the self; whenever the self is called upon to bend the knee or bow the head before the authority of God or God's laws or the traditions of a community of faith or, in politics, to aver the legitimacy of a constitutional or juridical regime even if we disagree with it in particulars. One effect of the crisis of authority, then, is that all abstract institutional rules get taken for tyranny. It's an unhappy business if our only options are a brittle attempt to reconstruct tradition, on the one hand, or antinomianism, on the other.

To Arendt's discussion one might add a second complicated philosophic backdrop that vexes modernity, namely, the "problem of other minds," a problem that *became* a problem within a particular set of epistemological presuppositions. If the very existence of some other mind is up for grabs, how much more so the possibility of a world of commonalities, a world that gives birth to us and to which we owe our social being, a world that is itself made possible because there is a God above it or a transcendental horizon framing it: a perhaps awkward way to cast a world in which authority could still be understood and even taken for granted. For one version of what can roughly be called "liberal epistemology" is radical skepticism, including a variant so disassociated that the body itself no longer serves as a groundwork of being. It is this very disembodiedness—this assault on finitude—that characterizes late modernity. One might call it an anti-incarnational reading of the human condition. Mind you, Cartesianism is a way to reconstruct "certain knowledge" while jettisoning traditional belief. Jeffrey Stout puts it this way: "hyperbolic doubt is accepted as innocent until proven guilty. . . . It is this step that infects Cartesian philosophy with implicitly skeptical standards for knowledge and in effect guarantees a skeptical result."[10] I don't want to belabor Cartesian epistemology here but simply to suggest that its analogue crops up in more properly political philosophy—I mean the search for justification with all the traditional moorings unloosed.

Having jettisoned much of traditional belief, yet requiring a standard to repair to, we have attempted to deal with the question of authority politically through constitutionalism and adherence to certain fundamental laws and

---

9   Ibid., 141.

10   Jeffrey Stout, *The Flight from Authority* (Notre Dame, Ind.: University of Notre Dame Press, 1981), 27.

rules. These are now under assault from radical skeptics who view the "law of the land" as nothing but window dressing for the power machinations of a narrow-minded elite, finding little but coercion and arbitrariness in the proclamations of self-evident truths in the Declaration of Independence. None of this would surprise—or did surprise—Arendt, for there is nowhere to repair to if all is power and violence save to grab as much power for yourself as you can. This helps to account for the fear and worry, even despair, surrounding American democratic life at century's end. We are unable to justify authority in a robust sense but without justifiable authority we flounder and flail politically. Why should anyone be obliged to adhere to law if all that one is confronted with is so many arbitrary injunctions dressed up as a natural law or right or the good opinion of humankind?

This political crisis of authority and our concern about religion and politics are cut from the same cloth. Thus, in recent years we have witnessed mainline Protestantism giving itself over to nearly every enthusiasm of the day in tune with the skeptical project rather than putting tough questions to that project and its cultural manifestations, namely, a more voluntaristic, hence more conformist and potentially more authoritarian culture. For the end point of voluntaristic absolutism, by which I mean the loss of any way to justify limits and constraints on the actions of individuals, is more coercion, not less, as the institutional loci that protect plurality collapse. Institutions cannot survive without authoritative forms and norms, and these are dissolved if the self is made sovereign in all things and if claims on the self are construed as arbitrary impositions. This is the worst-case scenario unpacked by Alexis de Tocqueville when he fretted about the future and fate of the American democracy. It seems just possible that democratic authority—if it is lodged in a radically skeptical epistemology—cannot sustain itself over time. If I am right, it would be the case that not only can religious authority *not* be democratic, in this sense, but that democracy itself cannot be sustained by this sort of authority principle either.

Let's dig a bit deeper. Democracy requires laws, constitutions, authoritative institutions. It also depends on democratic dispositions, those habits of the heart that are formed and forged *within* the framework such institutions provide. The ever-prescient Tocqueville, in *Democracy in America*, offered foreboding thoughts along these lines. He warned of a world different from the robust democracy he surveyed. He urged Americans to take to heart a possible corruption of their way of life. In his worst-case scenario, narrowly self-involved individualists—radically voluntaristic—disarticulated from the saving constraints and nurture of overlapping associations of social life and the horizon of an authoritative set of laws with "higher" justification, would require more and more controls from above to muffle at least somewhat the disintegrative effects of egoism. Should the rich world of American associational life, a world in which citizens were both free and bound, weaken, the "bad egoism" and isolation that resulted would, in turn, generate new forms of domination from above. The social webs that once held persons intact having disintegrated, the individual would find himself or herself isolated, impotent, exposed, and unprotected. Into this power vacuum would move a centralized, top-heavy state or other centralized and organized forces (the maw of consumerist society comes to mind) that would, so to speak, push social life to its lowest common denominator. For Tocqueville, religious belief "was inseparable from free government and free public life because it was the channel of a self-imposed moral restraint that shaped and, in so doing, liberated the individual for participation in the republic."[11] The collapse of religious authority necessary to sustain those institutions that engage in ethical formation fuels a political crisis in turn.[12]

Arendt, too, saw this coming, or some version of it. She detected it in the assault on authority in every arena—including the family and the school. She saw it in the attack on truth, the "blurring of the dividing line between factual truth and opinion."[13] Factual statements—her example is "Germany invaded Belgium in August 1914"—are the last redoubt of political possibility, the need to have a record, to begin from some common understanding. But now we find many who would dissolve even these sorts of truths. All is froth and foam on the disappearing sea wave. All is up for grabs—even, as we have learned to our dismay in recent years, the Holocaust. For every historical event there are revisionists who go much beyond debating the interpretation and meaning of events to denial that certain events even occurred. Sadly, Arendt argues, since "the liar is free to fashion his 'facts' to fit the profit and pleasure, or even the mere expectations of his audience, the chances are that he will be more persuasive than the truthteller. Indeed, he will usually have plausibility on his side; his exposition will sound more logical, as it were, since the element of unexpectedness—one of the outstanding characteristics of all events—has mercifully disappeared."[14]

Facts are stubborn. They *bind* us. We would be free. So "factual reality"— that certain states of affairs exist independently, so to speak, and that our "constructions" don't bring them into being *tout court*—must give way. Arendt fears that whole societies may place themselves in a position in which they require no bureaucrats under Big Brother flush away embarrassing facts in the

---

11 George Armstrong Kelly, *Politics and Religious Consciousness in America* (New Brunswick, N.J.: Transaction Publishers, 1974).

12 Let me add that there is a flaw at the heart of the Fundamentalist project as currently being played out, namely, its anti-institutional bias. Stressing individual conversion and adherence to Holy Writ, short shrift is given to formative institutions or, alternatively, the version of institutions endorsed is too truncated to help to sustain the complexities of modern identity.

13 Hannah Arendt, "Truth and Politics," in *Between Past and Future*, 250.

14 Ibid., 251.

"memory hole." Our own minds and lives will be such a memory hole, a funnel down which facts go and out of which rushes opinion, but opinion of a particular sort: opinion that claims first-person privilege, that isn't amenable to correction, reproof, or authentic dialogue. "It's just your opinion; I have mine." This is a world in which nothing holds authority, in which the world itself is dead, never a source of meaning or limits, but entirely up for grabs, entirely "constructed" in the current lingo. Because "our apprehension of reality is dependent upon our sharing the world with our fellow-men," to the extent there is no world to share; to the extent that we have even severed ourselves from other minds, we witness the complete collapse of authority, including democratic authority.

Arendt seems to me right in insisting that facts are stubborn; they are superior to power. But they require authority to be known. Violence may destroy truth, she writes, but "cannot replace it."[15] What moves can we possibly make, then, to restore some of the texture of a world in which authority makes claims on us and we, in turn, on it, for authority helps to solidify the world; indeed, it helps to make a world out of what would otherwise be William James's "blooming, buzzing confusion." Let's spend a moment with Luther, both liberator and father of our travail, on Arendt's reading. I want to zero in on Luther on translation for here we find a Luther insistent upon authority, the authority of Holy Writ, and equally insistent that not just anything goes by way of interpretation, this despite the fact that, in his "Preface to the Revelation of Saint John," he writes: "About this book of the revelation of John, I leave everyone free to hold his own ideas, and would bind no man to my opinion or judgement; I say what I feel."[16] Luther pitted *his* interpretation, and the authority of Scripture itself, against the Church, whose emissary, Cajetan, was in sympathy with critics of Church corruption but insisted that the Church's authority—its authoritative teachings—must be upheld. Luther's dramatic challenge is that of an individual against an institution. What drops out is an insistence on concrete mediating forms—with concrete authority—through which theology receives its subject matter and which are normative for members of the body of the church.[17]

For what authority inheres in a founding text if one can read it and say what one "feels"? In a brilliant discussion of translation that prefigures Wittgenstein, Luther indicated that he had translated the New Testament "to the best of my ability and according to my conscience. . . . No one is forbidden to do a better piece of work." He knew better than the Papists how to translate, "how much

---

15   Ibid., 259.

16   "Preface to the Revelation of Saint John, 1522," in *Martin Luther*, ed. E. G. Rupp and Benjamin Drewery (London: Edward Arnold, 1970), 98.

17   See Reinhard Hutter, "The Church as Public: Dogma, Practice, and the Holy Spirit," *Pro Ecclesia* 3, no. 3 (Summer 1994).

knowledge, work, reason and understanding is required in a good translator; they have never tried it," being too slavishly tied to received authoritative readings and rulings.[18] For help in translating authoritatively one must look to "daily use," to the linguistic field in which one is immersed. One asks the mother in the home, the children on the street, the common man in the market.

But matters are never so simple. If *an* authoritative interpreter is denied, who then has the interpretive right or freedom? Despite his apparent interpretive pluralism in this matter, authority remains—the authority of internal textual evidence. You cannot turn it to just any purpose. You cannot make it do anything you want. In light of the noetic effect of sin, humility and charity is required in interpretation. The discursive universe exists apart from us; the world and the Word must, so to speak, have their ways with us. We are free but bound. The enthusiast who would sever all the ties that bind must be spit out from among us, Luther proclaimed in his typically volcanic prose.

Yet Luther had unleashed much more than he knew or wanted. Those authoritative teachings necessary if anything like a tradition is to be upheld and to be formative were—post-Luther—on shakier and shakier ground. When you add a radically skeptical epistemology into the mix—especially in its late modern form in which anything goes, more or less, and I am to be untrammeled in my expression of myself (as the self is claimed as the ground of its own being)—you are in a world in which all that is solid melts into air, the world Hannah Arendt imagined some thirty years ago. Oddly enough, given this dilemma, we seem to seek more of what ails us by hobbling ourselves in advance when it comes to robust arguments about important matters. If we talk rights talk we can say pretty much anything we want. But we if talk God talk or moral norm talk we are threatening to start a very uncivil civil war. We are urged to retreat where we should advance and we advance where we would be well advised to retreat.

Can we perform any sort of rescue attempt that preserves our commitment to the dignity of the human person, to democracy under law, and to traditions of faith in a world in which each is under assault? I am not sure what the shape and scope of such a project can, or should, be. But I believe it must be framed by certain recognitions and for help I will draw upon St. Augustine's brilliant unpacking of the sin of false pride.[19] For that seems to me to lie at the heart of our current troubles. It is pridefulness that holds up as normative a view of a self constructed in such a way that she is immunized from the claims made on her by others. False pride is the presumption that we are the sole and only ground of our own being, and it lies behind much of the contemporary assault

---

18   "On Translating: An Open Letter, 1530," in *Martin Luther*, 87.

19   I here lift passages from my book, *Augustine and the Limits of Politics* (Notre Dame, Ind.: Notre Dame University Press, 1996.)

on all authoritative claims and traditions. We deny our birth from the body of a woman. We deny our dependence on her and others to nurture and to tend to us. We deny our dependence on friends and family to sustain us. We most certainly deny that the nations are under God's judgment—that any authority beyond our construction of various immanent sovereignties exists. This false pride is the name Augustine gives to a particular form of corruption and human deformation.

Pridefulness denies our multiple and manifold dependencies and would have us believe that human beings can be masters of their fates. Those who refuse to recognize dependence are those most overtaken by an urge to dominate, or "the need to secure the dependence of others," an observation from Peter Brown, who goes on to argue that "first the Devil, then Adam, chose to live on their own resources; they preferred their own *fortitudo*, their own created strength, to dependence upon the strength of God. For this reason the deranged relationships between fallen angels and men show themselves in a constant effort to assert their incomplete power by subjecting others to their will."[20] Every "proud man heeds himself, and he who pleases himself seems great to himself. But he who pleases himself pleases a fool, for he himself is a fool when he is pleasing to himself," Augustine writes.[21] In late modernity we have all become self-pleasers, and self-pleasers cannot sustain institutional forms for that seems nothing but the imposition of unacceptable constraint on a subject deemed sovereign. So we are in the soup. We lament that the center does not hold. But we will not permit ourselves to be 'held,' so to speak. Our political commitments are thin. And our religious commitments increasingly chafe under any restraint. Thus we daily surrender a bit more of the pluralistic, communal, formative dimensions of that world known as the American democracy—one that requires institutional robustness of considerable variety.

What is required if supple yet sturdy authority is to survive is a recognition that it is the opposite of violence and coercive force; recognition of the extent to which our control over the world is limited; recognition of the fact that human beings live indeterminate and incomplete lives; recognition of the power exerted over and upon us by our own habits and memories; recognition of the ways in which the world presses in on all of us, for it is an intractable place where many things go awry and go astray, where one may all-too-easily lose one's very self. To the extent that a prideful philosophy hates these, Augustine would argue, to that extent philosophy hates the human condition itself. To the extent that a radical antinominianism repudiates these, to that extent the world itself—a world to which and by which we are bound but

---

20   Peter Brown, "Political Society," in Robert Markus, ed., *Augustine: A Collection of Critical Essays* (Garden City, N.Y.: Doubleday Anchor Books, 1972), 320–21.

21   Augustine, *Selected Writings*, Homilies on the Psalms, "Psalm 122: God is True Wealth," (Mahwah, N.J.: Paulist Press, 1984), 250.

within which we are free to act—has vaporized. We are all alone with our freedom and coerced in ways beyond our imaginings. The dominant philosophic liberalism of our time has little to offer if these are the recognitions we require and, alas, much of the ongoing debate that poses religion against liberalism is a distraction from, rather than a contribution to, our grappling with the crisis of authority in late modernity.

Deprivatizing Religion and Revitalizing Citizenship

John A. Coleman, S.J.

I invite you to eavesdrop. We find ourselves in Eagle Butte, South Dakota. The Annual *Habitat for Humanity* Jimmy Carter Jamboree has just finished in the hot July sun. Nearly 2,000 Americans, young and old, have come from around the country to build low-cost homes in a marathon house building cooperative venture. Thirty new homeowners, doing what Habitat calls their "sweat equity," work side-by-side with the professional and middle- class volunteers in helping to erect what will be their own home. Later, these homeowners will expand that self-interested sweat equity to join Habitat to build a house for other homeowners.

Each morning this week on the Indian reservation, the day's work begins with morning prayer and devotion. Hymns are sung and prayers intoned to start off a day of engaging in what Millard Fuller, the founder of Habitat, likes to call "the theology of the hammer." At the end of the process, each new home will be officially dedicated and the homeowner given a Bible. One of the Habitat executives from headquarters in Americus, Georgia, reflects on what he sees taking place, "I am looking at the way I carry out my Christianity as a way of expressing my citizenship. The liberal press today tries to say to us 'wait a minute, you have to put your religion over here.' We don't have freedom of religion today; we have freedom from religion. They put freedom over here in such a box that, if anything even approaches religion, then it can't be citizenship."[1]

I am going to be wrestling with some conceptual clarifications about the meaning of civil society and citizenship and their mutual inter-relationship. I will also try to uncover how these two realities of civil society and citizenship get intertwined with, even anchored by, religion. We will be concerned with both how the process of de-privatizing faith nurtures and feeds into a revital- ized citizenship and how working to achieve a revitalized citizenship presents challenges to contemporary American faith life.

Defining civil society and citizenship is no easy task since both realities include both descriptive and normative aspects and each is an essentially sharply controverted concept.[2] Thus, we need to ask about *which* version of

---

1   Tapes and transcripts of all interviews cited are available to interested scholars at The Center for Ethics and Social Policy, The Graduate Theological Union, Berkeley, California.

2   In the social sciences, an inherently contested concept (e.g., power, justice, citizenship, civil society) derives from the inescapable normative elements in it. I am following the notion of an inherently contested concept as it is found in

civil society and *which* account of citizenship we want to move forward. We are also entering onto no less strongly contested ground as we try to link civil society and citizenship to a religious source in discipleship. Besides conceptual clarification, I want to construe an argument which: (a) privileges civil society as the foremost terrain of a renewed democratic citizenship; (b) locates citizenship primarily in the sector of civil society rather than the state (and, more, not even exclusively in the directly political domain as such); and (c) contends that civil society is the appropriate sector for the citizenship activity of the public church. Even more strongly, I will contend that the fate of the public church and a vital and public civil society rise and fall together.

My basis for answering these questions will not be simply theoretical or abstract. For the past four years, I have been engaged with a research team in interviewing hundreds of Americans involved in paradenominational groups which promote citizen activism or education. Nearly four hundred reflective and thoughtful citizens have conversed with us about how they see the contours of citizenship in this country, what they are doing to improve the communal climate of our culture, how they see the tensions and complementarity between their Christian identities (what we call in the research project *discipleship*), and their common identities in a pluralistic society.

I was first led to focus on paradenominational groups because of the research of Princeton sociologist Robert Wuthnow. Wuthnow notes how such groups have been growing apace and seem to reflect the churches' response to a greater role of the regulatory state in American society since the end of World War II. Wuthnow alleges that the new paradenominational groups may "be the ones that increasingly define the public role of American religion."[3]

We determined to study the following six groups:

(1) *Habitat for Humanity*—founded by an evangelical but drawing widely from the whole range of religious and secular America. Habitat builds low-cost housing as a non-profit. It is the seventeenth largest homebuilder in America. But for most of its adherents, Habitat's real work is building civic community around civic voluntarism: "I tend to think of myself living my life as a disciple and that being how I am also a citizen," a Sioux Falls Habitat volunteer told us.[4]

(2) *The Pacific Institute for Community Organizing*—Pico (now a misnomer since Pico has affiliates geographically spread all over the country) is the second oldest and largest (after *The Industrial Areas Foundation*) non-partisan

Steven Lukes, *Power: A Radical View* (New York: Macmillan, 1974).

3   Robert Wuthnow, *The Restructuring of American Religion* (Princeton, N.J.: Princeton University Press, 1987), 121.

4   For Habitat cf. Millard Fuller, *The Theology of the Hammer* (Macon, Ga.: Smyth and Helwys Publishing, 1994); Millard Fuller and Dianne Scott, *Love in the Mortar Joints* (Clinton, N.J.: New Win Publishing, Inc., 1980).

church-based community-organizing group in America. Founded in 1972 by a Jesuit, John Baumann S.J., Pico helps give ordinary Americans voice by mobilizing them, equipping them with citizen skills to hold governmental officials accountable and bringing together the moral vision of the churches with participant democracy to revitalize urban neighborhoods and demand better police protection, improved schools, and economic development. Pico takes a participant democratic view of citizenship, first devised by Saul Alinsky, and weds it to a moral stance coming from the churches. Judy Reyes-Ortiz, a Pico organizer in Oakland, California, told us: "I really believe it's the relationship building and the community building and the grounding in faith that keeps us from getting too wild or too way out there. In other words, it keeps us from trashing people, our opponents, which is real important to me that we don't. We have to respect their dignity and I think, that comes from the faith base."[5]

(3) *Bread for the World*: This is a Christian-based lobby group which engages in education and research on hunger issues and lobbies congress on legislation related to hunger in the United States (e.g., food stamps) or abroad (e.g., establishing a grain reserve explicitly devoted for foreign aid to countries undergoing famine).[6]

(4) *Pax Christi U.S.A.*: Pax is a Catholic peace-education and activist organization which tries to affect both the Catholic church and the government on issues related to violence, wars, nuclear weapons. Ron Cioffi, the founder of the New Jersey metro Pax chapter told us: "A good Christian can't be a bad citizen, and a bad citizen can't be a good Christian." Tom Burke, a Pax member from Virginia (who used to work designing nuclear weapons) notes, "I am not a citizen exclusive of who I am as a member of my faith community." Michigan grandmother Helen Casey of Pax Christi links her citizenship to her faith commitments this way as she speaks about civil disobedience: "If there are B52's at Ritsmouth Air Force base equipped with nuclear weapons and they are told to take off and go bomb someplace, that's being done in my name, because it's a United States aircraft, United States soldiers on it and I'm a citizen of the United States. And from that point of view they are acting in my name. And I just wanted to state [through her civil disobedience at Ritsmouth] that I don't want to be any part of it—not in my name, don't do this in my name."[7]

5   Saul Alinsky, *Reveille for Radicals* (New York: Vintage Books, 1969); Saul Alinsky, *Rules for Radicals* (New York: Random House, 1971).

6   For the story of Bread for the World by its founder, a Lutheran minister, Arthur Simon (the brother of Senator Paul Simon of Illinois), see Arthur Simon, *Bread for the World* (Grand Rapids, Mich.: Wm. B. Eerdmans Publishing Co., 1975).

7   Pax Christi is discussed in Patricia McNeal, *Harder than War: Catholic Peacemaking in Twentieth Century America* (New Brunswick, N.J.: Rutgers University Press, 1992), 230 ff.

(5) *Focus on the Family*: This Colorado Springs–based evangelical ministry was founded by the well-known radio family pundit and best-selling author, Dr. James Dobson. Focus itself engages in public policy and is affiliated with public interest family councils at the state and national level which lobby for family-related legislation, e.g., taxation, vouchers, home schooling, protection of heterosexual marriage, divorce legislation. The best known of these affiliates is *The Family Research Council* in Washington, D.C., headed by Gary Bauer, who served in the Reagan and Bush administrations. Focus and its affiliates also galvanize local church members into greater political involvement through its grass-roots *Community Impact Forum*. While a number of Focus affiliates have loose alliances with the Christian Right, Focus spokespersons distance themselves from the hard Christian Right and foster a moderate image. None of the Focus members we interviewed wanted to impose a Christian hegemony on our pluralistic society, preferring what they called "winsome persuasion" to any appeals to coercive measures.

(6) *The African Methodist Episcopal Church.* We sampled four large megachurches of the AME, the oldest historic black church in America. For example, the site we studied in Baltimore, Bethel, manages the high school equivalency program for the city of Baltimore. The Congregation we focused on in Los Angeles spearheaded the community-development renaissance after the communal uprisings at the time of the Rodney King trial and has spawned dozens of non-profit spin-offs.[8]

My research focuses, then, on groups which are national in character and which have, as well, local grass-roots memberships. We did not want purely paper groups or national lobby organizations which lack local units. We also wanted our analysis to represent the range of Christian America: mainline Protestant, Catholic, evangelical, black Protestants (and two of our groups, Habitat and Pico, include Jewish respondents in the sample). The aim of the study is to dispel, somewhat, the stereotypes about Christians in politics which flow from the media's one-sided focus on the Christian Right. Many mainline groups engage in citizenship education without becoming partisan or, in any real way, violating the separation of church and state. Many (e.g., church-based community organizing which numbers approximately 3 million Americans in its local organizing units) of these groups have held their numbers or even grown in the last years, although the media does not much focus on them and their style of combining discipleship with citizenship.

I. Re-Discovering Civil Society

A high level, if little noticed or commented on, academic gathering took place

---

8   A social history of the Bethel AME Baltimore church is found in Lawrence Mimaya, "A Social History of the Bethel African Episcopal Church in Baltimore," in James Wind and James Lewis, eds., *American Congregations*, vol. 1. (Chicago: University of Chicago Press, 1994), 221–92.

in the fall of 1989 in Rome. Prominent political philosophers, social scientists, and theologians from both Western and Eastern Europe—including such well-known intellectuals as Germany's Jürgen Habermas and John Baptiste Metz and Poland's Adam Michnik—came together in a special convocation by the Vatican Council on Culture to discuss the topic, civil society. The former university professor, now pope, Karl Wojtyla, despite a punishing schedule, made certain that he was in continuous attendance at all of the several days' sessions. One of the very few North American commentators to even notice this meeting, the *New York Times'* columnist, William Safire, stated in a column he wrote at the time that this scholarly gathering just might be the most important academic symposium of that or many a year.

No one familiar with the democratic opposition movements in Eastern Europe, just then coming into ascendancy, should have been surprised that this pope from the east was deeply interested in the topic of civil society. For as his fellow countryman, Adam Michnik, had noted when writing about *Solidarity* in Poland: "The essence of the spontaneously growing independent and self-governing labor union, Solidarity, lay in the restoration of social ties, self-organization aimed at guaranteeing the defense of labor, civil and national rights. For the first time in the history of communist rule in Poland, 'civil society' was being restored and it was reaching a compromise with the state."[9] While still in opposition, Michnik had argued in an important essay, entitled, "A New Evolutionism," that the opposition in Eastern Europe differed from party revisionist reformers and neo-positivist technocrats. "I believe what sets today's opposition apart from [these other groups] is the belief that a program for evolution ought to be addressed to an independent public, not to power. Such a program should give directives to people on how to behave, not to the powers on how to reform themselves. Nothing instructs the authorities better than pressure from below."[10]

We find here, in germ, a preliminary definition of civil society: It involves self-organization, addresses an independent public not totally subservient to the state or in the pocket of comprehensive catch-all political parties. Harry Boyte who has written so meaningfully on a citizen-politics in the United States, offers this definition: "A citizen-centered politics recreates the concept of a public realm [different from the institutionalized forms of directly political life], in which diverse groups learn to work together effectively to address public problems, whether or not they like one another personally or agree on other issues."[11] This public societal realm of discourse and community deci-

---

9   Adam Michnik, *Letters from Prison* (Berkeley: University of California Press, 1985), 124.

10   Ibid., 144.

11   Harry Boyte, "Turning on Youth to Politics," *The Nation* (May 13, 1991): 627.

sion is conceived of as a kind of "second culture," to borrow a phrase from Vaclav Havel.

Havel has asserted that "the original and most independent sphere of activity, one that predetermines all the others, is simply an attempt to create and support the independent life of society."[12] Only in this independent sector, wedged between the logic of the market (which is driven by profitability and competition) and the logic of the state (with its essential thrust toward administrative bureaucracy), could the essential aims of plurality, diversity, independent self-constitution, and self-organization, moving toward the fulfillment of freedom, counteract the economic and political systems' demands for conformity, uniformity, and technical-rational discipline steered by the twin "bottom lines" of money and power. Like many of the Eastern European democratic opposition, Havel envisioned a notion of citizenship exercised in the name of civil society, if need be *against* the state. This view of citizenship aims at rediscovering and restoring civil society since, it is argued, only in this realm can citizens hope for a rehabilitation, *in everyday and tangibly accessible life*, of values such as trust, openness, responsibility, love and solidarity to replace the cynicism of the narrow ideals of a manipulative or passive citizenship sponsored by the state or elite experts.

In his now classic *samizdat* essay, "The Power of the Powerless," Havel looked to this independent sector as crucial to de-centering the totalitarian pretensions of the omnicompetent state. "Every society," claims Havel, "requires some degree of organization, of course. Yet, if that organization is to serve people and not the other way around, then people will have to be liberated and space created so that they may organize themselves in meaningful ways."[13] The democratic opposition, Havel contended, turns away from "abstract political visions of the future toward concrete human beings and ways of defending them effectively in the here and now."[14] For this to happen, we need to emphasize a politics of scale, the voluntary sector of civil society: "There can and must be structures that are open, dynamic and small: beyond a certain point, human ties, like personal trust and personal responsibility cannot work . . . The authority [of these structures] cannot be based on long-empty traditions, like the tradition of mass political parties, but rather on how, in concrete terms, they enter into a given situation. . . . These structures should naturally arise from below as a consequence of authentic 'self-organization.' They should gain their vital energy from a living dialogue with the genuine needs from which they arise."[15] In Havel's words we hear something

---

12   Vaclav Havel, *The Power of the Powerless: Citizens Against the State in Central Eastern Europe* (London: Hutchinson, 1985), 67.

13   Ibid., 69.

14   Ibid., 71.

15   Ibid., 93.

like the vision of Harry Boyte and Sarah Evans when they point to what they call "free public spaces" of community action and decision.[16]

Latin America's Civil Society Project

Nor is the rediscovery of civil society restricted to the Eastern European bloc. In Latin America, the church has been engaging for several decades in a new form of ecclesial organization, the so-called base-community movement. These small groups of Christians combine prayer, scripture, and what we in North America call community-organizing techniques to get essential services such as water, sewerage, and bus service delivered to the favellas of Lima, Caracas, and Sao Paulo. In Latin America too, the essential goal is the creation of intermediate and mediating organizations for health, education, and day care, popular organizations for workers and mothers, with the aim of building an embryonic civil society in nations which have heretofore known only the power of the state and of elite and oligarchical political parties tied narrowly to the state and corporate business. Embodying a democratic ethos, these intermediate organizations advocate an enhanced democracy for their whole societies. As one of the *Las Madres* in Argentina, who daily keened forth justice for their disappeared children in the central plaza of Buenos Aires, put it to Jean Bethke Elshtain in interviews she held with them, "We, too, must behave democratically in our movement if we are to advocate democracy for our society."[17]

Scott Mainwaring, one of the most astute observers of this changing church in Latin America, puts it this way in his study, *The Catholic Church and Politics in Brazil*: "It has been the church's role in empowering civil society (especially in the popular movements) rather than its negotiations with the local political elite that has been most significant."[18] The church empowers civil society, first, by training ordinary, even poor, people in transferable leadership skills in the basic community: skills of speaking, convoking a meeting, gathering people together, pursuing public discussions about issues of concern and moment in their society. Secondly, by outreach through the popular organizations, it teaches people that, through community-organizing skills, they can have voice and influence in the decisions about their life in their neighborhoods and places of work. Not surprisingly, many secular political analysts in Latin America have begun to highlight the need to rebuild (or construct for the first time) a viable civil society.[19]

---

16   Sara Evans and Harry Boyte, *Free Spaces: The Sources of Democratic Change in America* (New York: Harper and Row, 1986).

17   Jean Bethke Elshtain, *Democracy on Trial* (New York: Basic Books, 1995), 131.

18   Scott Mainwaring, *The Catholic Church and Politics in Brazil* (Palo Alto, Calif.: Stanford University Press, 1986), 183.

19   Guillermo O'Donell and Philippe Schmitter, eds., *Transitions from Authoritarian*

Rediscovering Civil Society in North America

Finally, in North America and Europe, where the voluntary sector, especially in the American case, has been the historic seedbed of a republican citizenry, new threats to the viability of civil society have raised serious questions about the future of the kind of civil society on which our politics has been traditionally premised. Jeffrey Goldfarb, for example, wrote a book with the chilling title, *The Cynical Society*, in which he sketches the anatomy of a new American cynicism about the political system at least analogous to that cynicism which eventually led to the precipitous collapse of the Eastern European authoritarian regimes.[20]

A recent sociological study, based on focus-group discussions among involved American citizens, found that people depend on "little-noticed meeting places—places of worship, libraries, community halls, where they can interact with others, offer their own thinking and become committed to, and sometimes engaged in the solution [to a political question or problem]. These places are becoming fewer, the researchers said."[21] The fewer such civic sites, the more likely the kind of increasingly cynical politics and the dimunution of the sense of citizenship.

Harvard University political scientist Robert Putnam presents us with some dramatic evidence of declines in the sites for the associations of civil society in America. The PTA, the League of Women Voters, fraternal and sororal organizations such as the Lions, Elks, Shriners, The Eastern Star, members of unions, and business groups such as the Jaycees—all show intense declension in membership, ranging from a 20 to almost a 50 percent drop in the past two decades. The number of Americans who say that they have attended a public meeting on city issues or school affairs has fallen by more than a third since 1973. Not only do Americans exhibit genuine distrust of actions of their national government (rising from 30 percent in 1966 to 75 percent in 1992) but a majority of them also increasingly claim that they can not even trust their fellow citizens.[22]

We have come a long way since Tocqueville's picture of us a century and half ago as a vigorous voluntary society and democracy. A modern-day French political scientist, Michael Crozier, in his book, *The Trouble with America: Why*

Rule, 4 vols. (Baltimore: The Johns Hopkins Press, 1986); Alfred Stepan, "State, Power and The Strength of Civil Society in the Southern Cone of Latin America," in *Bringing the State Back In*, eds. Peter Evans, et. al., (Cambridge: Cambridge University Press, 1985).

20 Jeffrey Goldfarb, *The Cynical Society: The Culture of Politics and the Politics of Culture in America* (Chicago: University of Chicago Press, 1991).

21 Reported in Mike Feinsilber, "General Public Knows What Should be Done," *Los Angeles Times* (10 November 1993): A-16.

22 Robert Putnam, "Bowling Alone Revisited," *The Responsive Community* (Spring 1995): 18–33.

the System is Breaking Down, could write that, despite his great respect for the United States, he was frightened by the changes that had taken place in this country between his first extended stay in 1946 and a subsequent sojourn in the 1980s. In Crozier's words, the United States had abandoned Tocqueville's hoped for "free schools of civic virtue" in American associational life and, perhaps, had degenerated into that 'soft despotism' which Tocqueville feared could infect a democracy which lost its moorings in civil society and virtue: "The United States today is no longer the America Tocqueville described. Its voluntary associations have ceased to be the mainstay of a democracy constantly on the move but are now simply means of self-defense for various parochial interests. . . . This breakdown of community structures is what has made America a country full of anxiety and periodically shaken by reactionary crusades."[23] No less than the Czechoslovakian dissidents Havel wrote about, Americans too increasingly long for some rebirth of civility and the decent virtues of personal trust, openness, personal responsibility, solidarity, compassionate care for the fragile and broken in our midst, love.

Variant Conceptions of Civil Society

Perhaps just because of these growing anxieties and the discontents of American citizenship, the literature on civil society has grown apace—indeed, has become a kind of cottage industry—since that papal symposium on civil society in 1989. It soon becomes apparent, however, to careful students of this scholarly literature that in it they encounter competing, even irreconcilable, definitions of civil society. On the right, from those who mainly fear the danger of an overly administered state, we hear cries for a new volunteerism such as William Buckley's plea for a national-service obligation for the young or President Bush's paean to "a thousand points of light." I miss, in this discourse from the right, sufficient attention to the reality that the government, while it may not have a monopoly on this care, nevertheless has a primary and indispensable care for the common good. I also miss any sensitivity to the extent to which many of the associations of civil society (from arts organizations to non-profit health groups and private universities to welfare agencies such as The Salvation Army or Catholic Charities which deliver services to the poor) depend deeply on governmental support for their budgets and resources. Few knowledgeable agents of such voluntary associations think that it is very realistic that, absent government subsidies, they can continue to provide the level and quality of services they presently deliver, let alone expand them to meet the growing welfare needs of the American population.[24]

23 Michael Crozier, *The Trouble with America: Why the System Is Breaking Down* (Berkeley: University of California Press, 1984), 85.

24 Sara Jay, "Charities Worry," *New York Times* (23 February 1996): B-2. For some sense of the amount of money charities get from governmental funds cf. Michael O'Neil, *The Third America: The Emergence of the Non-Profit Sector in the United States*

On the left, we hear social democrats such as Gar Alperovitz calling for renewed civil society as a space of community organization against the omni-competent power of corporations, in fighting plant closings, etc. I miss in many of these discussions a tutored sense of the inherent limits to the full-scale introduction of political modalities or democratic procedures into the economy or the business firm. At times, the programs of some of these social democrats seem to approximate the now-discredited and failed notions of worker democracies in running industrial plants and industries which even a socialism with a human face came to see were economically unfeasible.[25] In any case, often, these social democratic views of civil society still seem to imagine an overly mobilized and politicized civil society which might render governments unable sufficiently to govern and leave economies crippled in their efforts to innovate and become efficient.

The Competing Models

A rough typology of the several competing models of civil society would need to distinguish the liberal, neo-conservative, anarchist, undifferentiated, and strong democracy versions of civil society as an idea and social project. Thus, for example, the liberal version tends to rely on an overly individualistic concept of civil society. Civil society remains 'the private' sector in the strict sense of the term and is even named as such. Most liberal accounts of civil society leave it fully de-politicized, defenseless against the eroding forces of a market economy. Civil society, in the liberal version, secures individual rights but remains essentially without resources to address the fragility of the individual before the onslaught of giant industrial firms and governmental bureaucracy. Nor can liberalism make room, in its theory, for the important role of social movements as a protest against the 'colonization' of civil society by states and markets. Neither does it support any aggressive attempts, through social movements of protest and reconfiguration, to not only defend 'the private' sphere but move it into a more public arena where it confronts state and economy to make them more publicly accountable, inclusive, and participatory. Yet, when all is said, the liberal version does remind us that civil society remains also, in part, a private realm. In Jean Bethke Elshtain's fine phrase, it is the place which leaves social space for "difference, dissent, refusal and indifference."[26]

The neo-conservative model of civil society—as it is found, for example, in Peter Berger and Richard Neuhaus's influential book on mediating institu-

---

(San Francisco: Jossey-Bass Publishers, 1989), 98.

25   Gar Alperovitz and Jeff Faux, *Rebuilding America: A Blueprint for the New Economy* (New York: Pantheon Books, 1984). Worker ownership of companies, of course, is no anomaly. But the successful ones all follow ordinary management schemes.

26   Elshstain, *Democracy on Trial*, 49.

tions—sees civil society almost entirely as a defense against the state. The neo-conservatives tend to identify the freedom of civil society with the market. What remains outside the market sphere—what neo-conservatives see as the essentially non-political cultural domain—must be shored up and reintegrated through a conservative retraditionalizing cultural model that will help to reinvigorate the market, now suffering cultural deficit. Concretely, hedonism, the loss of a Protestant work ethic and a sense of economic responsibility as well as the decline of respect for traditional authorities in state, church, and elite culture become major targets—in the neo-conservative view—for the cultural work in civil society. Both liberals and neo-conservatives exhibit systematic bias against seeing the dangers of an imperialism of the market or the concomitant trivialization of genuine human choice and deliberation when it becomes reduced to mere consumer preference.[27]

While the neo-conservatives are frequently right in rubbing our noses in the genuine dysfunctions of the regulatory welfare state and the way it can erode human responsibility by turning citizens into passive clients, they remain less sensitive to the equal danger to a democratic citizenship when the untrammeled economy turns citizens into consumers. Worse still, some of them suggest a vulgar consumer metaphor for the very meaning of citizenship, as in Ross Perot's promoting of an electronic town meeting where citizens would press preference buttons on cue in the midst of a televised discussion, but where there is very little space for authentic public debate, genuine change of mind because of arguments proffered and true formation of collective will.)[28] We meed to rightly protest against this degeneration of authentic public opinion into a mere cumulative sorting of individual preferences without the mediation of public argument about what social goods we really should prefer.

Anarchist models of civil society forget that a differentiated state apparatus remains indispensable in modern complex societies as a steering mechanism to give directionality to society. Some authoritative institution must serve society both to aggregate demands and forge compromise solutions to multiple and conflicting demands. Some such institution must initiate and take responsibility for the institutionalization and monitoring of public policy. Anarchists tend to be much too optimistic about human goodness and lack an appropriate vision of the human as fragile, flawed, susceptible to corruption

---

27   Peter Berger and Richard Neuhaus, *To Empower People: The Role of Mediating Structures in Public Policy* (Washington, D.C.: The American Enterprise Institute, 1977). For this critique of the neo-conservative model of civil society see Jean Cohen and Andrew Arato, *Civil Society and Political Theory* (Cambridge, Mass.: MIT Press, 1994), 43. Cohen and Arato are political scientists at The New School of Social Research and their book, in my estimation, represents the best single work on civil society.

28   Elshtain, *Democracy on Trial*, 28.

yet capable of finite flashes of goodness.[29] Theories of civil society should not scout or diminish the state.

Undifferentiated models of civil society of a nostalgic type—what I like to call "the longing for good old *Gemeinschaft*"—forget that "abolishing the state, which is impossible in fact but certainly imaginable, would lead not to an autonomous plural civil society in other ways resembling its modern forerunner but to a restoration of traditional political-civil society without modern administration but also without a modern structure of rights and liberties carving out autonomous spaces from the world of politics."[30]

II. Defining Civil Society

I am going to draw primarily on three sources to anchor my discussion and definition of civil society: Michael Walzer, Jean Cohen and Andrew Arato and Robert Putnam.

The Idea of Civil Society

In his 1990 Gunnar Myrdal lecture, "The Idea of Civil Society," Michael Walzer defines it as "the space of uncoerced human association and also the set of relational networks—formed for the sake of family, faith, interest and ideology—that fill this space."[31] Walzer laments that "we have been thinking too much about social formations different from, in competition with, civil society and so we have neglected the networks through which civility is produced and reproduced."[32]

Walzer contrasts his own emphasis on rebuilding civil society as a path of social reconstruction with four other nineteenth- and twentieth-century answers to the generating question: "What is the preferred setting, the most supportive environment, for the good life?" From the left, as one answer, comes the ideal of a direct, unitary, and participatory democracy. In a variant of Oscar Wilde's famous retort that he was not a socialist because—as the modernist dandy Wilde saw it—"it would simply occupy too many of my evenings," Walzer argues that "despite the singlemindedness of republican ideology, politics rarely engages the full attention of the citizens who are supposed to be its chief protagonists."[33] Citizens have far too many other things besides direct engagement in politics occupying their time and energy: making a living, raising a family, pursuing relationships and hobbies, engag-

---

29   For this view of the human as fallible yet reformable see Philip Selznick, *The Moral Commonwealth* (Berkeley: University of California Press, 1992), 175–82.

30   Cohen and Arato, *Civil Society and Political Theory*, 158.

31   Michael Walzer, "The Idea of Civil Society," *Dissent* (Spring 1991): 293.

32   Ibid., 294.

33   Ibid., 295.

ing a private life. Thus, it is not so much that the Athenian ideal of a direct participatory democracy is not a good life as "that it isn't the 'real life' of very many people in the modern world."[34] Moreover, the decisions made by a modern complex state can never be placed fully into the directly democratic hands of citizens. The large scale of modern social life, the increasing (and necessary) bureaucratization of the state apparatus, and the growing technicality of the decisions it is necessary to make in determining complex public policy dictate that "the participation of ordinary men and women in the activities of the state (unless they are state employees) is largely vicarious."[35]

A second left response to the query about the preferred setting for the good life focuses less on republican politics than on economic activity. The classic Marxist rejoinder, when asked about the ideal *locus* of the good life, points to a cooperative economy, where we are all *bona fide* producers and labor is immune from alienation, uncoerced and creative. Walzer puts his finger on the characteristic Achilles' wound in the classic Marxist position when he states, "But this version of the cooperative economy is set against an unbelievable background—a non-political state, regulation without conflict, 'the administration of things.' In every actual experience of socialist politics, the state has moved rapidly into the foreground."[36]

A third response, this time from the capitalist camp, proposes the marketplace as both mechanism and prime metaphor when thinking about the preferred setting for the good life. The problem with the market, however, when it gets set up as an all-encompassing ideal and model of social life—it is a mistake to make it so even for the *whole* of the economy, let alone to extrapolate this market model to civil society as a whole—is that "the marketplace provides no support for social solidarity."[37] In point of fact, people come to the arena of the marketplace with radically unequal resources. The vaunted equal opportunity utopia and the untrammeled freedom supposedly ingredient in the market is illusory for those in penury or of marginal and meager resources. As Walzer comments: "Capitalism in its ideal form, like socialism again, does not make for citizenship. . . . Citizens are transformed [by an exaggerated market logic] into autonomous consumers." Capitalism does not make for citizenship because capitalists themselves make lackluster citizens. "Because the market has no political boundaries, entrepreneurs also evade social control. They need the state but have no loyalty to it."[38]

Nationalism is the final proposed candidate as the ideal answer to the question of the preferred setting for the good life. Loyal members of the nation,

34   Ibid., 294.
35   Ibid., 294–95.
36   Ibid., 296.
37   Ibid.
38   Ibid., 297.

bound together by ties of blood and history, should find the good life in their shared heritage and communalism. Yet any nationalism, unanchored, first, in a broader vision of universal human rights and, secondly, in the modern sense of being a nation of citizens (each of which tempers and relativizes nationalism), becomes devoid of real content and directionality.[39] "Every nationalist will, of course, find value in his or her own heritage but . . . unlike religious believers who are their close kin and (often) bitter rivals, nationalists are not bound by a body of authoritative law or a set of sacred texts. Beyond [national] liberation, they have no program, only a vague commitment to continue their history, to sustain a way of life."[40] In the testing times of crisis, nationalism—as we see currently in the Balkans—too easily gets turned against other nations, against internal minorities, aliens and strangers.

Almost by default, Walzer turns to civil society as the preferred option for the good life, both despite and because of its being "the realm of fragmentation and struggle but also of concrete and authentic solidarities."[41] The other proffered sites for the good life in modernity are each too all-encompassing, too totalistic, in their solutions. Each needs a taming of their absolute pretensions by positioning them within the orbit of civil society. Thus, the market, when it is truly entangled in a denser network of larger associational life, when it conceives of multiple forms of property and ownership including worker- or community-owned firms, is both consistent with and indeed should bolster civil society. In any event, some variant of a free market seems essential to liberal and democratic societies as we have known them.

In an important paradox, the state and civil society need each other. "No state can survive for long if it is wholly alienated from civil society. . . . The production and reproduction of loyalty, civility, political competence and trust in authority are never the work of the state alone and the effort to go it alone . . . is doomed to failure."[42] Yet, the state is no less necessary to civil society. Only a self-limiting state which both recognizes and legally guarantees the range of civil, political, and social rights can anchor the full legitimacy of a separate civil sphere. Moreover, as Walzer notes, "the state itself is unlike other associations. It both frames civil society and occupies space in it."[43] Walzer rejects any anarchist version of civil society. Indeed, state, economy, and civil society in the modern world inevitably both interpenetrate each other and remain, at least analytically, independent. That civil society actually becomes

---

39 See John A. Coleman s.j., "A Nation of Citizens," in *Religion and Nationalism* (*Concilium* series 1995, vol. 6), eds. John Coleman and Miklos Tomka, (Maryknoll, N.Y.: Orbis Press, 1995), 48–57.

40 Walzer, "The Idea of Civil Society," p. 297.

41 Ibid., 298.

42 Ibid., 301.

43 Ibid., 302.

more than merely analytically independent rests on its secure institutionalization and the vigor of the social movements in its defense. In this regard, Cohen and Arato helpfully remind us that "the norms of civil society—individual rights, privacy, voluntary association, formal legality, plurality, publicity, free enterprise—were . . . institutionalized heterogeneously and in a contradictory manner in western societies."[44] From this perspective, securing the stable institutionalization of civil society remains less the settled achievement of any societies (including the Western democracies) than a continuing project.

The civility that makes democratic politics possible gets learned in the associational networks of civil society. The almost heroic citizenship ideal of the proponents of a direct participatory democracy becomes, in a citizenship primarily anchored in civil society, more modest in its claims and more diffuse in its institutionalizations. As Walzer argues the point: "But in the associational networks of civil society—in unions, parties, movements, interest groups and so on—these same people make smaller decisions and shape to some degree the more distant determinations of state and economy. . . . These socially engaged men and women—part-time union officers, movement activists, party regulars, consumer advocates, welfare volunteers, church members, family heads—stand outside the republic of citizenship as it is commonly conceived. They are only intermittently virtuous; they are too caught up in particularity."[45]

Yet, "States are tested by their capacity to sustain this kind of participation—which is very different from the heroic intensity of Rousseauian citizenship and civil society is tested by its capacity to produce citizens whose interests, at least sometimes, reach farther than themselves and their comrades, [citizens] who look after the political community that fosters and protects the associational networks."[46]

In the end, Walzer suggests that a notion of citizenship anchored in civil society might look "more like union organizing than political mobilization, more like teaching in a school than arguing in an assembly, more like volunteering in a hospital than joining a political party, more like working in an ethnic alliance or a feminist group than canvassing an election, more like shaping a co-op budget than deciding a national fiscal policy."[47]

Civil Society and Political Theory

Jean Cohen and Andrew Arato's densely argued theoretical study, *Civil Society and Political Theory*, stands out as one of the very few contemporary works to essay thoroughly a complete and sophisticated *theory* of civil society in condi-

44   Cohen and Arato, *Civil Society and Political Theory*, xiii.

45   Walzer, "The Idea of Civil Society," 299.

46   Ibid., 303.

47   Ibid., 303.

tions of modernity. I want to draw from it principally to present an ideal-type of a strong democracy version of civil society. Cohen and Arato look upon civil society as the privileged locale for the furtherance of democracy. They insist that we view civil society through a four-part scheme or lens which distinguishes between: (a) the state, (b) the economy, (c) political society, and (d) civil society. However, these essentially analytic distinctions (based, to be sure, on genuine institutional differentiations which point to quasi-autonomous spheres), should not blind us to the deep, pervasive mutual interpenetration of these four structural domains of society.

Drawing on Cohen and Arato, I want to contend that any real and serious project for the reconstruction of civil society will:

(1) pay attention to the threats of a colonization of civil society by the invading of its domain *both* by the over-regulatory state *and* a promiscuous expansion of the market metaphor beyond its legitimate sphere within the economy. "The task is to guarantee the autonomy of the modern state and economy while simultaneously protecting civil society from destructive penetration and functionalization by the imperatives of these two spheres."[48]

(2) recognize the need for each of these four differentiated spheres to acknowledge and institutionalize its own self-limitation. Indeed, the very existence of an institutionally anchored civil society depends on the self-limitation of the state, its recognition of a legitimate autonomous domain of free public spaces. The state guarantees the existence of civil society by a legal securing of the rights to privacy, communication, and assembly (and also social rights such as access to those necessary minimal material goods which enable human agency). Clearly, the institutions and movements of civil society will frequently turn to the law, secured by the state, as a defense of their space. Such a self-limiting state acknowledges its circumscribed autonomy in fully shaping citizenship norms and decisions. At the extreme, self-limitation of the state will even accommodate civil disobedience.[49] Conversely, the self-limitation of civil society, on its part, entails that it restrict itself, in normal circumstances, to projects of non-violent reform from below rather than revolution and that it accept an indispensable role for both the modern state and economy.

Indeed, as the successful non-violent revolutions in Eastern Europe demonstrate, it took a confluence of both a mobilized civil society and a sufficient

---

48   Cohen and Arato, *Civil Society and Political Theory*, 25. Besides Cohen and Arato's magisterial study, another good source to think through the meaning of civil society is Adam Seligman, *The Idea of Civil Society* (New York: The Free Press, 1992).

49   Cohen and Arato, *Civil Society and Political Theory*, 564–604, presents a theory of civil disobedience. One reason for choosing Pax Christi for our sample was its practice, among some of its adherents, of civil disobedience.

cadre of sympathetic office holders in the party apparatus and the state who were open to reform for the successful transition to democracy. Again, any pure fusion of civil society and the economy (which exists only as an imagined project in modernity; we have not really seen any real forms of it) seems both undesirable and incompatible with a differentiated modern world. Cohen and Arato coin the neologism, 'sensors,' to refer to elite allies in the state and economic systems supportive of the programs of democratization or cultural revision initiated by social movements or institutions within civil society. Thus, for example, some people from within the formal political and economic institutions must be receptive i.e., act as 'sensors') to the feminist, civil rights, or ecological social movements to allow their agendas to move into the economy and the state apparatus: fighting glass ceilings, supporting affirmative action programs, changing modes of communication from competition to cooperation, championing greater energy efficiency, recycling and conservation.

In a similar vein, Cohen and Arato address the self-limitation of civil society vis-à-vis *political* society:

> From an analytic point of view, the distinction between civil and political society helps to avoid the sort of reductionism that assumes that political activities with a strategic dimension are easily generated by societal associations and movements or are somehow unnecessary. Paradoxically, an undifferentiated concept of civil society gives us the stark choice between the depoliticization of society (where the political is assigned to the state) and its overpoliticization (where all dimensions of civil society are held to be political).[50]

In sum, civil society's social movements and voluntary associations do not replace the need for a bureaucratic state nor for political parties, political action, and lobby groups, and policy think tanks explicitly oriented strategically toward the polity and state. Political and civil society shade into one another and, necessarily, have two way bridges of influence and mediation. Nevertheless, they do not simply fuse, the one with the other.

(3) social movements, in a strong-democracy scheme, are not aberrant vehicles of political mobilization which short-circuit rational political action. They represent rational action every bit as much as does lobbying or crafting of legislation. "Social movements are a normal, albeit extrainstitutional, dimension of political action in modern civil societies."[51] Indeed, the provocation of protest movements frequently places precise agendas before political legislatures which otherwise would never be there. The peace movement of the

50   Ibid., 79.
51   Ibid., 565.

1980s, to take one example, did further government movement toward disarmament. Without the civil rights movement of the 1960s, there would not have been the Civil Rights Legislation of 1964–65. Yet, one should not overestimate the power of social movements alone to anchor a secure civil society as, once more, the Eastern European experiences teach us in their transition to 'democracy.' We forget to our peril that "it is easier to suppress a society without deep organizational roots than a highly articulated one, even if the former is . . . mobilized."[52] Whatever happened, we might ask, to the highly mobilized Polish Solidarity? Or to Cory Aquino's mobilized opposition to Marcos?

(4) recognize that civil society is not itself a purely neutral or virtuous terrain. It contains its own negativities and generates its own deformations. Surely, Michel Foucault's image of civil society as a kind of carceral socciety, turning modern life into a panopticon of surveillance by *civilian* professionals (e.g., psychologists, criminologists, doctors) who decide who is creditworthy, what is healthy, psychologically sound, or normal behavior should be sufficient to aid us in avoiding any easy canonizations of civil society or viewing it as an essentially innocent 'victim' being beaten up by those imperialistic bullies, state and market.[53] Civil society can degenerate, on its own steam, into mass society, driven by private interests and factions. Feeding on its own home-grown individualism, it can evacuate the larger social world of any sense of truly public or common goods. Both the Ku Klux Klan from an earlier period and the citizen militias of today, need we remind ourselves, were indigenous spawnings from the womb of civil society.

(5) insist that civil society, that amalgam of public and private realms, is a privileged locale for public deliberation and the formation of collective consensus and will. Jean Bethke Elshtain pithily captures this often forgotten truism: "A compilation of opinions does not make a civic culture; such a culture emerges only from a deliberative process."[54]

(6) know that civil society is the bedrock for social morality. Civil society represents much more than an ideal institutional bulwark to ward off threats from state and economy. We should look to it for something far more important and central than mere countervailing organizational power. It is the crucial seedbed for the moral life. "It is on this terrain that we learn how to compromise, take reflective distance from our own perspective so as to entertain

---

52 Ibid., 51.

53 For the carceral image of civil society, Michel Foucault, *Discipline and Punish* (New York: Pantheon, 1977). See also Foucault's *Power/Knowledge* New York: Pantheon, 1972.

54 Elshtain, *Democracy on Trial*, 29.

others, learn to value difference, recognize or create anew what we have in common and come to see which dimensions of our tradition are worth preserving and which ought to be abandoned or changed."[55]

Gianfranco Poggi takes this essentially Tocquevillean view of civil society as the primary school of virtue. Poggi reminds us: "Interpersonal trust is probably the moral orientation that most needs to be diffused among the people if republican society is to be maintained."[56] Our abstract duties to distant others when we are called upon to obey the state-made laws which coordinate a complex society (e.g., tax, traffic, food and drug, environmental laws) or exhibit fidelity to promise-keeping in the fiduciary contracts of the economy which anchor its flow of goods and services—these duties to state and market are sycophantic on our experiencing richly in the associational life of civil society, a true sense for mutuality, trust, interdependent ties which bind, openness, reciprocity. This moral mentoring by civil society represents what the sociologist Alan Wolfe has called the "gift of society," without which any economy or polity loses its moorings.[57] As we will see in a moment, when we consider the work of Robert Putnam, "even seemingly self-interested transactions take on a different character when they are embedded in social networks that foster mutual trust."[58]

(7) Finally, a strong democracy version of civil society sees it as simultaneously both a terrain and a target of democratization. Not all agencies of civil

---

55   Cohen and Arato, *Civil Society and Political Theory*, 23.

56   Gianfranco Poggi, *Images of Society: Essays on the Sociological Theories of Tocqueville, Marx and Durkheim* (Palo Alto, Calif.: Stanford University Press, 1972).

57   Alan Wolfe, *Whose Keeper? Social Science and Moral Obligation* (Berkeley: University of California Press, 1989), 237–61.

58   Will Kymlicka and Wayne Norman, "Return of the Citizen: A Survey of Recent Work on Citizenship Theory," *Ethics* 104 (January 1994): 369, speak of a risk of deforming the institutions of civil society if the democracy metaphor is over-played. "While these associations may teach civic virtue, that is not their *raison d'etre*. The reason why people join churches, families, or ethnic organizations is not to learn civic virtue. It is, rather, to honor certain values and enjoy certain human goods, and these motives may have little to do with the promotion of citizenship." For this reason I speak in the text of democratizing rather than democracy. For an attempt to show that there is democratizing potential in the Catholic Church, which is decidedly not a democracy, by an appeal to Catholic internal theological notions of collegiality, subsidiarity, and justice as participation see John A. Coleman S.J., "Not Democracy but Democratization," in *A Democratic Catholic Church: The Reconstruction of Roman Catholicism*, eds. Eugene Bianchi and Rosemary Reuther (New York: Crossroad Publishing, 1992), 226–47. The point is to find communitarian and participative structures within the institutions of civil society, not to turn these institutions into overly politicized formal democracies.

society are themselves internally democratic or embody a democratic *ethos*. Instead of an illusory ideal of direct participatory democracy, we need to argue for support for vigorous associations, networks, and social movements which carry egalitarian and inclusive democratic potential for the whole system. Democratization of civil society, in this view, opens up a grounding framework to push for more participatory forms within political parties and representative state and economic institutions. So, the project of civil society is not merely defensive, protecting what Jürgen Habermas calls the life-world against the systems of state and economy. It is also proactive and aggressive, moving out of social movements or settled organizations, working for alternative views of ecology, human relations, or a normative sense of modernity which bring moral norms (even religious values) back in to the very heart of the economy and state to make them more responsive, more accountable, more inclusive in the voices they consult and truly hear. In effect, a true citizen democracy encompasses much more than a mere procedure of suffrage, vote, and representation. It depends on a cultural *ethos* of democracy primarily anchored in civil society.[59]

Making Democracy Work

Robert Putnam's *Making Democracy Work* takes up just this issue of a cultural *ethos* of democratic civility. His larger questions reads: "What are the conditions for creating strong, responsive, effective representative institutions?" This is the sort of question being asked insistently in America today. To get tangible answers to this question, Putnam studied (and regularly monitored through interviews and questionnaires over a twenty year period) the emergence of the twenty new regional governments in Italy since the early 1970s. He compares the various Italian regional governments, testing their administrative effectiveness, bureaucratic responsiveness to citizens' requests or complaints, legislative innovation, institutional performances in generating social outputs and citizen satisfaction with their respective governments—each appropriately operationalized to generate a comparative quantitative measure. Putnam shows, in his stunningly elegant research design, that effective government varies, quite predictably and systematically, with the quantum of what he calls, 'social capital,' i.e., civic trust, thick networks of association, the vigor of norms of equality, civic engagement, and tolerance.

Making Democracy Work attempts an empirical test of the claims ingredient in Tocqueville's classic interpretation of American democracy which postulated that "the civic community is marked by an active public-spirited citizenry, by egalitarian political relations, by a social fabric of trust and cooperation."[60] Putnam's comparative research demonstrates clear and com-

---

59   Robert Putnam, *Making Democracy Work: Civic Traditions in Modern Italy* (Princeton, N.J.: Princeton University Press, 1993), 89.

pelling statistical correlations between the volume and vigor of civic associations and the percentage of active membership in civic organization in any given Italian region and:

(1) The stability of democratic government in the region, in avoiding precipitous turn-over or cabinet crisis;

(2) the extent to which political elites of varying political parties in the region were willing to cooperate, beyond political ideology, to find pragmatic solutions to social needs—in short, to make government work for their constituencies;

(3) citizen satisfaction with the performance of their regional governments;

(4) the usual measures of modern citizenship ideals of political equality and active participation (e.g., rates of voting, involvement in city or school affairs);

(5) Citizen demand for more active police interventions or prisons. The higher the degree of civic associationalism, the lower such demands.

It is worth noting that it seemed to make little difference whether these civic memberships were directly political or oriented toward politics. Thus, Putnam observes that choral societies, bird watcher groups, fraternal organizations, and soccer teams each teach self-discipline and collaboration. His clear conclusion reads: "A dense network of secondary association both embodies and contributes to social collaboration."[61]

Putnam's general conclusion informs my own contention about the location of citizenship primarily in civil society: "Norms of generalized reciprocity and networks of civic engagement encourage social trust and cooperation because . . . they reduce uncertainty. Trust is an emergent property of the social system as much as a personal attribute."[62] As this last sentence should make clear, it is not so much the case that citizens get the kind of governments they want or deserve (since, notoriously, people complain *everywhere* about unresponsive or corrupt governments) as that they get the kind of politics and government that their structure of civic institutions warrants and empowers. Paradoxically, we would more effectively foster a democratic citizenship if we focused our attention more on urging citizens to join and actively support the voluntary association of their choice (even if it is not directly political) than on efforts to get out the vote (important as this is for democracies.) The rate of voting would automatically increase with the increase in the volume of civic associations.

Much more could be said about a full blown definition of citizenship. Citizenship can be fruitfully parsed by following T. H. Marshall's classic triad

---

60   Ibid., 15.

61   Ibid., 90.

62   Ibid., 177.

of the essential civil, political and social rights of citizens.[63] It can be usefully sketched, as Michael Walzer has done, by honing in on citizenship as the constellation of membership rights and duties in the nation state.[64] Following Judith Shklar in her small book, *American Citizenship*, we could dissect the ways citizenship enhances dignity and participation by bestowing—especially on excluded groups such as blacks and women who were historically denied the suffrage—a sense of social standing and a right to inclusion in the world of working.[65] The key to the renewal of democratic citizenship will be found less in counting the number of people who vote than in the number of contexts, even outside of politics, where the right to vote—or its equivalent in the right to voice, dignity as social standing and influence—gets exercised.

III. The Church and Civil Society

We come to the last piece of our argument: Civil society is the appropriate setting for the citizenship activity of the public church. The fate of the public church and a vital and public civil society rise and fall together. We should not be surprised that religious leaders such as the pope cast a careful eye on the future prospects for civil society. The 'secular' freedoms of speech, association, free communication, after all, are but the correlates in the secular realm to the originating religious freedoms to preach, to assemble for worship, to disseminate the message. The central and privileged church-society strategy for the churches should attend to the vigor and democratic civility of civil society, their social home. Undoubtedly, some of the cultural privatization of religion in modern society derives from defining civil society (the realm where religion finds its rightful niche) as, itself, essentially a 'private' sector.

Clearly, in modern societies the state is no longer the appropriate sector for the public church. Juridical separation of church and state, almost everywhere a touchstone of most modern state constitutions, is not only good for society and individual freedom of conscience, it is good for the churches. Established churches almost always lose essential ecclesial freedoms and the strong commitment of their members. Established churches notoriously exhibit low rates of religious practice.[66] No less obviously, the church will not find its proper social niche in the economy. Churches are non-profit organizations. An exaggerated sense of a market metaphor for the voluntary church could drive the

63 T. H. Marshall, *Class, Citizenship and Social Development* (New York: Anchor Books, 1956).

64 Michael Walzer, *Spheres of Justice* (New York: Basic Books, 1983). See especially his first chapter on membership rights in a polity.

65 Judith Shklar, *American Citizenship* (Cambridge, Mass: Harvard University Press, 1991).

66 For the deleterious effects on church practice of established state churches see David Martin, *A General Theory of Secularization* (Oxford: Basic Blackwell, 1978).

church into an uneasy alliance with the wealthy, lead it to preach a debased gospel of wealth or to follow an organizational logic which undermines its central mission.

In a real sense, the churches were the original generators, at least in the Anglo-Saxon world, of civil society. It is their daughter. In England it came as the fruit of the dissenting reformers, in America as the result of the amazing proliferation of voluntary associations stemming from the voluntary church. Tocqueville called the American church, "the first of America's political institutions" because of the way it spawned paradenominational schools, welfare agencies, hospitals, moral reform societies. Moreover, the church taught its disciples, even when they were exercising a measure of self-interest, to look to a more altruistic communal good, to see their self-interest 'rightly-understood' as tying them to the fate of others. The bell, the churches knew and taught, tolls for me as well as thee. The church has, thus, rightly been called the godmother of the independent sector.[67]

Even today, the majority of America's volunteers, members of the small-group movement, donors to philanthropies, providers of charity stem from or direct their beneficence toward the churches.[68] Churches garner a higher degree of commitment than any other civil institution short of the state. No other organization in America can convoke as many people in any given week. No other voluntary organization gets as much money or time from its members and generates as much voluntary activity outside its own boundaries. None so accompanies its members from cradle to grave or pretends in the same ways to forge character and mold a self as a disciple. In Putnam's terms, the American churches represent a tremendous "social capital" for the whole of society.

Again and again, as an almost monotonous refrain, we heard in our interviews with the disciple-citizens in our six groups that they were in it (i.e., their citizen-activism) for the long pull. As the director for development of Bread for the World told us in one interview: "Art Simon made it a major point not to appeal exclusively to people's self interest. What is done is done for obedience to God regardless of results. This gives the Christian a 'leg-up' on the general population. We are in it for the long haul."

I do not think it was only by chance that the community-organizing groups in America turned to the churches as an essential anchor of their activity. Community organizers came to see that no other resource—not neighbor-

---

67   This is the metaphor used by Michael O'Neil, *The Third America*, 20.

68   For the evidence see Virginia Hodgkinson, Murray Weitzman, and Arthur Kirch, *From Belief to Commitment: The Activities and Finances of Religious Congregations in the United States: Findings from a National Survey* (Washington, D.C.: Independent Sector, 1988). Also Paul Schervich, Virginia Hodgkinson, and Margaret Gates, eds., *Care and Community in Modern Society* (San Francisco: Jossey-Bass Publishers, 1995).

hoods or other civic institutions—could rival the churches in providing the networks of solidarity and trust on which they depend in building their community organizations. Nor was it, I think, by sheer chance that the churches spawned or strongly supported the social movements in the 1980s whether in dissident Eastern Europe or in Latin America which aimed at building the new civil societies. I was struck when I read Francis Moore Lappe and Paul DuBois's study, *The Quickening of America*. Their book attempts to avoid joining the chorus of voices complaining about the decline of citizenship in America or to whine about what isn't working. They try to highlight groups which are working, citizen-education groups which are already making a difference in revitalizing citizenship. One cannot miss that just about every other group they lift up had a name such as Shelby County Interfaith, Joint Ministry Project, Valley Interfaith. Even many of the groups with more secular sounding names such as San Antonio's COPS (Communities Organized for Public Service) drew their constituencies principally through the churches.)[69]

Finally, it is probably no coincidence that when one reads resource-mobilization literature, churches or church members show up frequently as key actors in the peace, ecology, civil rights, and feminist movements. John Lofland, drawing on this resource mobilization perspective in sociology, has sketched for us the ebbs and flows of the American peace movement. Not only were four church-based peace organizations, for example, among the top ten largest groups in the heyday of the peace movement in the 1980s (as they were in the 1950s, 1930s, and the teens of this century) but in low-water periods of quiescent decline during this century they soldiered on as other more secular groups faded away. They became in each of the recurring cycles of peace mobilization throughout this century essential building resources for a later social peace mobilization movement when the political and social circumstances again became favorable.[70] They are in it, as we heard, for the long haul.

Much of the dramatic story of disciple-driven citizenship activism rarely gets told or we focus our attention almost uniquely on the Christian Right groups (perhaps because they are so new and so successful in large-scale mobilization), forgetting that more liberal groups such as Pax Christi, Bread for the World, or church-based community organizing not only hold their own in numbers and continue in operation but are, in some cases, actually expanding in numbers and activities. Again, we live in a time of globalization where, as Daniel Bell has famously noted, the nation-state is too large for many of our urgent problems and too small for many others. We need sociological carrier

69   Frances Moore Lappe and Paul Du Bois, *The Quickening of America* (San Francisco: Jossey-Bass Publishers, 1994).

70   John Lofland, *Polite Protesters: The American Peace Movement in the 1980's* (Syracuse, N.Y.: Syracuse University Press, 1993). See also Sam Marullo and John Lofland, eds., *Peace Action in the 1980's* (New Brunswick, N.J.: Rutgers University Press, 1990).

units which bear both the renewal of local citizenship and couple it with a global sense.

The churches seem pre-eminently suited to this task of keeping a global sensibility alive. In any event, most of the citizenship responses in our sample of interviews focused almost uniquely on a local and global sense of citizenship. Millard Fuller, the founder of Habitat for Humanity, captures this global motif in an interview he gave for our project: "I wear my citizenship in the United States very lightly because there is a citizenship greater than being a U.S. citizen. Jesus never had a U.S. passport. He was not a U.S. citizen and I think my citizenship in the kingdom is infinitely more important than my citizenship in the United States." Habitat translates these global sentiments into real practices and behaviors when it insists that every local American Habitat chapter tithe to help build houses for the poor in the Third World or when Habitat refuses to accept money which would exclude usage for Third World housing.

Public Religion That Is Modern

We need to heed Jose Casanova's voice in his award-winning study, *Public Religion in the Modern World*.[71] Casanova demonstrates that modern religion, when it accepts its niche in civil society, need not be privatized. Even more strongly, modern religion can be an indispensable carrier-vehicle for modern democratic movements of human rights for all or the defense of civil society. *Amnesty International*, after all, was founded out of religious motivation and finds in the churches its major source of information about human-rights abuses. Such public religion, to be sure, needs to acknowledge the rightful autonomy of the secular sphere, if it would be relevant in the modern world. But this does not mean that it has to accept the claims of these spheres to detach themselves completely from morality. Nor must it accept the relegation of religion and morality to the private spheres. By resisting the radical individualism that accompanies privatism, public religion insists on the links between private and public morality. In doing so, churches move from mere religious resistance to a more full-blown civic resistance, defending civil society and public input to policy discussions and decisions.

Casanova posits three conditions in which religion can be a legitimately public religion in and of modernity (as opposed to pre-modern collective effervescences, in protest against the project of modernity but longing for conditions of pre-modern *Gemeinschaft* which cannot, institutionally or morally, be sustained in the conditions of a modern differentiated economy and polity):

(1) When religion enters the public sphere to protect not only its own

---

71   Jose Casanova, *Public Religions in the Modern World* (Chicago: University of Chicago Press, 1994).

freedom of religion but all modern freedoms and rights, and the very right of a democratic civil society to exist against an absolutist, authoritarian state.

(2) When religion enters the public sphere to question and contest the *absolute* lawful autonomy of the secular spheres and their claims to be organized in accordance with principles of functional differentiation without regard to extraneous ethical or moral considerations.

(3) When religion enters the public sphere to protect the traditional life-world from administrative or juridical state penetration, and in the process opens up issues of norm and will formation to the public and collective self-reflection of modern discursive ethics.[72]

Casanova would restrict the activities of public religion entirely to the sector of civil society. I think he tends a bit toward an absolutism on this point. If we recall the discussion earlier about Cohen and Arato's distinction of four distinct spheres—polity or state, economy, political society, and civil society—we will recall that political society plays an essential mediating role vis-à-vis civil society and the state. Political and civil society, while distinct, at times shade into one another. This represents the principal controversial arena for public action by the churches. While an amalgam of church and partisan political party, on the one hand, seems contrary to modernity, not all church activity in the political sphere (e.g., non-partisan lobbying for the general interest) should be ruled out of court. In principle, there should be no objections to a public role of religion in civil society. Modernity has learned to separate church and state. In political society, the closer the political society is to the state apparatus (e.g., political parties) the more problematic public-church engagement. The closer political society is to civil society, the more legitimate church-public action in that domain. Clearly, an important distinction here is the necessity for the church to accept that public goods can be arrived at in democratic societies only by consensus and the free adherence of citizens, not be coercion or fiat.

Much has been written, especially by philosophers from the camp of liberalism, about the need for a religious gag-rule in public discourse. In the name of secular equality and democracy, this liberal philosophy for public life seems to suggest that the religiously motivated must leave their deepest selves, their strongest convictions and motivations, their cherished religious symbols and metaphors which provide the narrative structure to their lives and actions outside the room when they sit down at the table of public discussion in what has been called, 'the naked public square.' Such talk about the need for a decent silencing of all religious symbols in public is, of course, nonsense, more—it represents a species of intolerance, a refusal to recognize the legitimacy of the other and a form of secular oppressive domination. It is quite clear from our interviews that for the overwhelming majority of our

---

72   Casanova, *Public Religions in the Modern World*, 57–58.

disciple-citizens, discipleship trumps. It is the main reason they give when asked to provide an account of why they are involved in citizen activism. Almost universally they claim that, in hypothetical cases of a conflict between their citizenship and discipleship status, they would privilege their discipleship status. Yet equally universally they accept the pluralist nature of our society, the separation of church and state and the need to respect the dignity of those who disagree with them. Needless to say, not all faith-based politics show these admirable traits!

I give Casanova the last word since his remarks are humanely sensible and a good summary of an account of how a deprivatized faith can revitalize citizenship:

> Normative traditions constitute the very condition of possibility for ethical discourse and, fictional 'ideal speech situations' and 'original positions' notwithstanding, without normative traditions neither rational public debate nor discourse ethics is likely to take place. It seems self-evident that religious normative traditions have the same rights as any other normative tradition to enter the public sphere *so long as they play by the rules of open public debate*. Indeed, it is when other nonreligious traditions have failed, abandoned the public sphere, or abdicated their public role that religious traditions are likely to step in to fill the public vacuum. One after another, all the modern public institutions which at first tended to exercise some of the public functions traditionally performed by religious institutions abandoned their public normative roles: academic philosophy, the specialized social sciences, the universities, the press, politicians, intellectuals. Under such circumstances, one cannot but welcome the return of religion to the naked public square.[73]

---

73   Ibid., 205. Italics in the citation are mine to stress that this is, of course, for some church engagements in the public order a big if. Not all public religion—as Casanova reminds us—is compatible with modern, pluralistic, and free societies of open public discourse. Accepting the rules of modern discourse ethics seems one criteria to distinguish between kinds of public religion.

Politically Active Churches: Some Empirical Prolegomena to a Normative Approach

David Hollenbach, S.J.

The activity of religious communities in the political sphere has been the subject of much apprehension and debate in recent years. In the United States, the visibility of the so-called religious right has been of particular interest. This political involvement by conservative Christians leads to fears that public activism by religious communities inevitably tends to support right-wing politics. But several journals of opinion noted for their progressive orientations have recently harked back to religious involvement in the abolitionist, labor, and civil rights movements to propose a different scenario. They suggest that more public activity by religious communities, if it is of the kind they favor, can contribute to a politics more to their liking. For example, the *Washington Quarterly* featured an article entitled "Why We Need a Religious Left." *The Nation* offered an essay by a theologian on the relevance of "The Transcendent Dimension." Its subheading declared: "To Purge the Public Square of Religion Is to Cut the Values that Nourish Us."[1]

Such ambivalence toward political involvement by religious communities is also evident in discussions of the global picture. In a much noted article in *Foreign Affairs*, Samuel Huntington conjectured that the conflicts in the world politics of the emerging post-Cold War era will be driven by a clash of civilizations and cultures rather than of ideology or economics. Huntington noted that civilizations are communities distinguished from each other by "history, language, culture, tradition, and, most important, religion."[2] Huntington's diagnosis raises the specter of religious war on a global scale. But Huntington has also noted that one of the most visible religious forces in the domain of world politics, the Roman Catholic Church, has been the most effective source for the global advancement of democracy over the past several decades.[3] From 1974 to 1989, more than thirty countries in Europe, Asia, and Latin America have moved from authoritarianism to democracy. In most of

1   Amy Waldman, "Why We Need a Religious Left," *Washington Monthly*, December, 1995, 37–43; Harvey Cox, "The Transcendent Dimension," *Nation*, January 1, 1996, 20–23.

2   Samuel P. Huntington, "The Clash of Civilizations," *Foreign Affairs* 72 (Summer 1993): 22, 25.

3   For evidence of the strong alliance of Catholicism and democracy that has developed since the Second Vatican Council, see Huntington, "Religion and the Third Wave," *The National Interest* 24 (Summer 1991): 29–42. This article is based on Huntington, *The Third Wave: Democratization in the Late Twentieth Century*

these countries the majority of the population is Catholic, and Catholicism has shaped their cultures in important ways. From Portugal and Spain in the mid-1970s, to South America in the late 1970s and early 1980s, to the Philippines in the mid-1980s, to Poland and Hungary in the late 1980s, "Catholic societies were in the lead, and roughly three-quarters of the countries that transited to democracy between 1974 and 1989 were Catholic."[4]

These are confusing developments to those observers who have identified the modern and the secular. The so-called theory of secularization hypothesized that in modern societies religious belief would exert declining influence in the public sphere. The church-state issue would be more or less automatically solved by the withering away of the church, or at least the elimination of the church's presence in the public square. It has become apparent that this interpretation of the direction of the trends is at least questionable today. Gilles Kepel, of the *Centre d'études et de recherches internationales* in Paris, wrote a book on the re-emergence of religion as an important political factor that became a best-seller in France. Kepel is not entirely happy with these developments, as is evident from the book's title: *La Revanche de Dieu*, provocatively rendered in English as *The Revenge of God*.[5] Its best-seller status is a sign that the descendants of Voltaire are a bit worried that the "infamous thing" is not entirely *écrassé*. Kepel examines movements such as the Ayatollah Khomeini's revolution in Iran, the militant Zionism of the Gush Emunim in Israel, the highly politicized Catholic lay movement *Communione e Liberazione* in Italy, and the Moral Majority inspired by Protestant fundamentalism in the United States. I will suggest below that Kepel is mistaken in taking such movements as adequate representations of the public role of religion today. Nevertheless he points to the fact that the disappearance of religion from the political domain seems not to be working out the way the secularization hypothesis had predicted.

One of the results of these developments is that the proper role of religion in politics has become a much discussed topic among moral philosophers and political theorists. The strength of these fields is their careful analysis of important theoretical issues raised by the religion and politics issue. The recent work of John Rawls, for example, argues that public normative discourse in a pluralistic society must ultimately be accountable to the standards of what he calls "public reason."[6] This has led others to propose alternatives to the

---

(Norman, Okla.: University of Oklahoma Press, 1991).

4   Huntington, "Religion and the Third Wave," 30.

5   Gilles Kepel, *The Revenge of God: The Resurgence of Islam, Christianity and Judaism in the Modern World*, trans. Alan Braley (University Park: Pennsylvania State University Press, 1994). French original: *La Revanche de Dieu: Chrétiens, Juifs et Musulmans à la reconquète du monde* (Éditions du Seuil, 1991).

6   See John Rawls, *Political Liberalism* (New York: Columbia University Press, 1993), Lecture VI, "Public Reason Revisited." That I agree with this discussion is

constraints Rawls would place on the public role of religion by proposing alternative theories of rationality.[7] This has in turn stimulated a discussion of the meaning of rationality and of moral epistemology. Important as these discussions surely are, they are several steps removed from the conflicts and possibilities that arise when religious communities actually enter the public square. As Robin Lovin has observed, even when a theory of rationality provides some space for engagement between religious belief and political activity, few believers find this "authorizes them to do something that they would otherwise have refrained from doing." Thus these discussions in moral and political theory are often "curiously abstract and unrelated to the role that religious beliefs actually play in the thinking of many persons."[8]

I propose, therefore, to approach the question of the political activism of religious communities from an angle that is somewhat different from that adopted in recent moral and political theory. These theoretical discussions need to be linked to the historical situation we face today if they are to provide practical guidance. Thus I will take note of several empirical studies that have raised questions about the state of civic life in the United States today and that have made suggestions about the de facto contributions of religious communities to that civic life. Once some descriptive approaches to the religion/politics dynamic have been laid out perhaps we will be in a position to make more helpful prescriptive or normative judgments. Though the focus will be primarily on the United States, broader international aspects will occasionally be noted.

I. The Decline of Civic Participation

In a series of articles noted widely outside the academy, Robert Putnam has

important is evident from my participation in a recently published symposium on the question. See Paul J. Weithman, "Rawlsian Liberalism and the Privatization of Religion," responses by Timothy Jackson, "Love in a Liberal Society," David Hollenbach, "Public Reason/Private Religion?" and John Langan, "Overcoming the Divisiveness of Religion," *Journal of Religious Ethics* 22, no. 1 (Spring 1994): 3–51. Rawls has himself been rethinking the issue of religion in politics through refinements on his idea of public reason in an essay that is as-yet unpublished, "The Idea of Public Reason: Further Considerations."

7   See, for example, Kent Greenawalt, *Religious Convictions and Political Choice* (New York: Oxford University Press, 1988); Greenawalt, *Private Consciences and Public Reasons* (New York: Oxford University Press, 1995); Michael Perry, *Morality, Politics and Law: A Bicentennial Essay* (New York: Oxford University Press, 1988); Perry, *Love and Power: The Role of Religion and Morality in American Politics* (New York: Oxford University Press, 1991. See also the symposium on "The Role of Religion in Public Debate in a Liberal Society," *San Diego Law Review* 30 (1993), which includes essays by Greenawalt, Perry, Robert Audi, and myself.

8   Robin W. Lovin, "Perry, Naturalism, and Religion in Public," *Tulane Law Review* 63 (1989): 1518, 1523.

argued that the United States has been undergoing a notable decline in overall civic participation in recent decades. The United States has been experiencing a depletion of the "social capital" that is requisite for effective democracy. Putnam describes social capital as the "networks, norms, and trust . . . that enable participants [in social life] to act together more effectively to pursue shared objectives."[9] It includes a rich associational life in groups like the Elks Club, the League of Woman Voters, labor unions, churches, and even bowling leagues. In more classical terms, a high level of social capital is another way of speaking about the strength of civil society. Civil society is a complex web of human communities including families, neighborhoods, churches, labor unions, corporations, professional associations, credit unions, cooperatives, universities, and a host of other associations. Calling this network of associations "civic" implies that the domain of public life is broader than that directly under the control of state power.

Putnam cites extensive data to argue that the associational life of civil society in the United States is weakening today. For example: participation by Americans in religious services and church related groups has declined by about a sixth since the 1960s; membership in labor unions in the non-agricultural sector has dropped by more than half; participation in parent-teacher associations declined from 12 million in 1964 to 5 million in 1982 before recovering to 7 million in 1993; volunteer activity declined by about one-sixth between 1974 and 1989 (by 26 percent in the Boy Scouts, 61 percent in the Red Cross). Putnam illustrates the trend with an example that has caught the imagination of commentators: between 1980 and 1993 the number of Americans who went bowling increased by 10 percent while league bowling declined by 40 percent. This means that the social interaction and even occasional political conversations that occur among those who regularly bowl together has dropped. Thus Putnam has entitled one of his essays "Bowling Alone: America's Declining Social Capital." Bowling alone, Putnam suggests, is a whimsical symbol of a serious reality: the decline of the associational life needed to undergird and support democratic politics.[10]

Putnam's argument that strong associational life in civil society is essential to democracy is in harmony with the civic republican tradition in political

---

9   Robert Putnam, "Tuning In, Tuning Out: The Strange Disappearance of Social Capital in America," *PS: Political Science and Politics* 28, no. 4 (December 1995): 664–65. See also Putnam, *Making Democracy Work: Civic Traditions in Modern Italy* (Princeton, N.J.: Princeton University Press, 1993), "The Prosperous Community: Social Capital and Public Life," *The American Prospect* no. 13 (Spring 1993): 35–42), "Bowling Alone: America's Declining Social Capital," *Journal of Democracy* 6, no. 1 (January 1995): 65–78. Putnam's definition of social capital follows James Coleman. See Coleman, *Foundations of Social Theory* (Cambridge: Harvard University Press, 1990).

10   Putnam, "Bowling Alone," 69–70.

theory. It also coheres with the Roman Catholic tradition's stress on the principle of subsidiarity as one of the key normative bases of politics. According to this principle, civil society is the soil in which the seeds of human sociality grow. When communities are small or of intermediate size, they enable persons to come together in ways that can be vividly experienced. The bonds of communal solidarity formed in them in them enable persons to act together, empowering them to shape some of the contours of public life and its larger social institutions such as the state and the economy. Thus in a democratic society, government does not rule but rather serves the social "body" animated by the activity of these intermediate communities. Pope Pius XI formulated the principle of subsidiarity this way: Government "should, by its very nature, provide help [*subsidium*] to members of the body social, it should never destroy or absorb them."[11] Civil society is the primary locus in which human solidarity is realized. Its strength is essential to the success of participatory government. In Putnam's words, it is a prerequisite to "making democracy work."

Putnam's studies add a particularly helpful element to the ideas drawn from the civic republican and Catholic traditions in setting the context for discussions of the public role of religion. His argument is based on extensive empirical data and analysis. Before launching his recent work on American civic participation, Putnam conducted long-term empirical research in Italy to determine the factors influencing the success or failure of new institutions of decentralized regional governance that were launched there in 1970. Very briefly put, Putnam concluded that the new institutions of regional government were successful in encouraging strong democracy in those regions of Italy that possessed a richly developed life in civil society and did not succeed where the communities of civil society were weak. In Italy's northern regions the "horizontal civic bonds" that build social capital had long been "embodied in tower societies, guilds, mutual aid societies, cooperatives, unions, and even soccer clubs and literary societies."[12] Putnam found that both the state and the market worked to serve the needs of the people better in the north of Italy because of the presence of strong bonds of civic life resulting from the extra-governmental social solidarities he identified as present in northern regions. In the south of Italy, on the other hand, the new regional governmental institutions were considerably less effective and citizen satisfaction with them notably lower because the mutual bonds of civil society were less developed there. Analyzing the data on Italy's regions, Putnam observed that the stronger the civic context, the better the government and the more successful the economy. Appealing to a congenial example of Northern Italian civic life, he

---

11   Pope Pius XI, *Quadragesimo Anno* (Washington, D.C.: National Catholic Welfare Conference, 1942), no. 79.

12   Putnam, *Making Democracy Work*, 181.

observed that "The harmonies of a choral society illustrate how voluntary collaboration can create value that no individual, no matter how wealthy, no matter how wily, could produce alone. In the civic community associations proliferate, memberships overlap, and participation spills into multiple arenas of community life. The social contract that sustains such collaboration in the civic community is not legal but moral. The sanction for violating it is not penal, but exclusion from the network of solidarity and cooperation." Thus by induction from empirical study rather than deduction from moral or political theory, Putnam concluded that Tocqueville was right: Effective democratic government depends on civic virtue and the vigorous bonds of civil society that promote it.[13]

II. Religious Communities and Civic Participation

Putnam's study of the regions of Italy is relevant to many other parts of the world. His own more recent work is pursuing its relevance to the civic and political life of the United States; others are pursuing analogous lines of inquiry on the conditions needed to make democracy work in the nations of the former Soviet bloc. A major recent study by Sidney Verba, my colleague Kay Lehman Schlozman, and Henry Brady, *Voice and Equality: Civic Voluntarism in American Politics*, shows that this sort of empirical investigation of the dynamics of civic participation is very illuminating on the question of the public role of religion in the United States today. Verba, Schlozman, and Brady present the most comprehensive and detailed study of participation in political activity in the United States yet produced. It is based on a large-scale, two-stage survey of the way Americans are involved in politics and in various forms of voluntary activity, including church life. They define political activity broadly as "activity that is intended to or has the consequence of affecting, either directly or indirectly, government action."[14] This activity takes a number of forms: voting, working in election campaigns, contributing money to candidates and political causes, becoming active in local communities, contacting public officials, joining political parties or other political organizations, attending rallies, protests or demonstrations, serving on governing bodies like school or zoning boards. Verba, et al., go beyond the compilation and interpretation of data on who becomes involved in such political activities; they seek to explain why and how people do so. This leads them to detailed empirical investigation of the relation between political activity and the dynamics and structures of association in American civil society. They state the overall import of the study this way: "We show that both the motivation and the

13   Ibid., 182–83.
14   Sidney Verba, Kay Lehman Schlozman, and Henry Brady, *Voice and Equality: Civic Voluntarism in American Politics* (Cambridge: Harvard University Press, 1995), 9.

capacity to take part in politics have their roots in the fundamental non-political institutions with which individuals are associated during the course of their lives. The foundations of political involvement are laid early in life—in the family and in school. Later on, the institutional affiliations of adults—on the job, in non-political organizations, and in religious institutions—provide additional opportunities for the acquisition of politically relevant resources and a sense of psychological engagement with politics."[15] *Voice and Equality* thus strongly supports Putnam's argument.

Verba, Schlozman, and Brady have also made interesting discoveries about the role actually played by churches in American politics. One of the major findings of *Voice and Equality*, somewhat to the surprise of its authors,[16] is that religious institutions make a major contribution to political participation in the United States. In their analysis, three factors are at the basis of political involvement: the *motivation* to become politically active, the *capacity* to do so, and involvement with *networks of recruitment* through which requests for political activity are mediated.[17] The data lead them to the conclusion that all three of these factors are enhanced in the life of individual citizens who are actively involved in a church or other institutional religious community. That the factors of motivation and recruitment for political activity are present in religious communities is perhaps intuitively evident. Pastors preach about matters that touch the well-being of the polis; religious values orient those who hold them to pursue the realization of these values in the public domain. Churches can provide an institutional base for political mobilization, as has been evident across the ideological spectrum from the civil rights movement to anti-abortion campaigns. *Voice and Equality* provides a wealth of data that backs up such intuitions and that clarifies their import with illuminating analysis.[18]

But Verba, Schlozman, and Brady have reached an important finding that goes beyond what many would have suspected without benefit of this study. Active involvement in church life not only provides *motivation* and a context for *recruitment* for political activity; it also has a significant, measurable impact on the *capacity* of Americans to become politically involved. This capacity is dependent on the possession of certain resources, chiefly money, time, and civic skills. Verba, Schlozman, and Brady measured who has the civic skills needed for political activism by asking those surveyed whether during the past six months, in any setting whether political or otherwise, they had written

---

15 Ibid., 3–4.

16 Personal conversation with Kay Lehman Schlozman.

17 Verba, Schlozman, and Brady, *Voice and Equality*, 3.

18 See Ibid., chap. 5, esp. 145–49, and chap. 13 on church-based recruitment for political involvement; chap. 14 on motivation for engagement on specific issues, some of which are related to religious belief.

a letter, gone to a meeting where they took part in making decisions, planned or chaired a meeting, given a presentation or speech. The possession of skills needed for such activities is of course heavily dependent on family background, level of education, and the sort of job one holds. In other words, possession of such skills is significantly correlated with social-economic status. Since these skills are important in political activity, the higher one's social-economic status the more likely one is to become politically active. This has long been known to social scientists who study American political culture. But notably, *Voice and Equality* has also discovered that the acquisition of these skills is significantly correlated with active involvement in a church. The communal participation that takes place in churches helps people learn them. Further, churches enable Americans to develop these skills in a way that is independent of their social-economic status. When looked at nationally and across denominations, religious affiliation is not stratified by socio-economic status, race, ethnicity, or gender. Rather, opportunities for the development of skills relevant to political participation are accessible in a more equal way to those active in churches than in American society at large. Indeed most of the other factors that encourage political activism, such as a successful family of origin, a high level of education, and a high-paying job, converge with each other to produce unequal levels of political participation tied to unequal social-economic status. Church participation, on the other hand, provides a counterweight toward the side of more equality in political participation. Thus the authors reach a provocative conclusion about the United States: "The domain of equal access to opportunities to learn civic skills is the church."[19]

The implications of this finding for discussion of the role of religion in American politics are considerable. Putnam argues that civic participation is declining and that such a decline is traceable to the loss of the social capital of strong civic associations. Verba, Schlozman, and Brady find that political participation is sustained by participation in extra-political civic communities, and that the churches are among the most important of these communities. The percentage of Americans who are actively involved with religious communities is considerably higher in the United States than in many other developed democracies. Religion has a correspondingly more important influence in American politics. *Voice and Equality* concludes that churches play a compensatory role for the relative weakness of unions and political parties in the United States, another example of "American exceptionalism."[20] On the basis of these studies, therefore, one could conclude that churches play a key role in sustaining the civic involvement that is essential to the health of democracy. One could also conclude that civically strong and politically active churches help "make democracy work," to use Putnam's language. Indeed it

19   Ibid., 320.
20   Ibid., 519–21.

seems that churches play an especially key role in the political empowerment of those with lower social-economic status. Thus more church activism, not less, would seem called for if more active, more egalitarian representation in democratic politics is judged desirable.

Churches, of course, do not exist simply to encourage active participation in politics. As religious communities they have properly religious ends: worship of God; response to the deepest questions of human beings about the meaning of life, love, work, and death; the nurturing of moral values and virtues that enable people to live in accord with that meaning. Thus it would be a mistake to assess the vitality of religious communities solely in terms of their contribution to successful democratic political activity. Nonetheless, religious belief has consequences for the whole of human life, not only that part which occurs on Sunday morning. The Catholic Church, for example, stressed the impact of its properly religious mission on public life when the Second Vatican Council stated that "out of this religious mission itself comes a function, a light, and an energy which can serve to structure and consolidate the human community according to divine law."[21] So though churches are very different kinds of communities from bowling leagues, they can be expected to have considerable impact on social life. Indeed the fact that their distinctive identity addresses the meaning of the whole of human existence suggests that they will have social influence that ranges much more widely than communities with more narrowly defined purposes.

Thus Verba, Schlozman, and Brady are right when they note that religious institutions are not ideologically neutral venues for the development of politically relevant skills. Because of their distinctive identities and missions, churches have significant agendas of their own that influence the issues around which their members are motivated and recruited to become politically active. The range of these issues is large. Today they extend from advocacy for the poor to abortion, on both the pro-life and pro-choice sides of the debate. *Voice and Equality* suggests that the center of gravity of the religious agenda today is tipped toward more conservative social concerns. It also concludes that different churches have differing effects on the development of the civic skills needed for political activism, with membership in Protestant churches today more positively correlated with the development of these skills than is membership in the Catholic church.[22] I do not wish here to dispute these suggestions nor am I competent to do so. It would nevertheless be useful to remember that the involvement of churches in political life has ranged over a wide array of issues in the history of the United States, from abolition, to

---

21   Vatican Council II, *Gaudium et Spes (Pastoral Constitution on the Church in the Modern World)*, in Walter M. Abbott and Joseph Gallagher, eds., *The Documents of Vatican II* (New York: America Press, 1966), no. 42.

22   Verba, Schlozman, and Brady, *Voice and Equality*, 320–24, 520–21.

prohibition, to the civil rights movement, to opposition to the Vietnam War and the nuclear arms race. It is also relevant that different churches and segments within churches have played quite different roles in leading their members to civic engagement at different points in American history. For example, immigrant members of the Catholic Church were more heavily involved in the labor movement and urban politics in the first half of the twentieth century than their Protestant counterparts. The study by Verba, Schlozman, and Brady could therefore well be complemented by historical inquiry beyond its already ambitious scope.

Even taking these caveats into account, the work of Putnam and of Verba and his colleagues highlight aspects of the question of religious involvement in politics that are rarely attended to in contemporary academic debates on the subject. In light of these studies, does it really make sense to see the presence of religious communities in the public square as threats to the integrity of democratic political life? Given the correlation between religious and political participation analyzed in *Voice and Equality* does it not make more sense to direct our discussions to the *kind* of political engagement we wish to see churches encouraging rather than to whether churches should be encouraging such involvement at all? In light of Putnam's description of the overall decline of civic participation and its causes, churches seem to play a role that should be encouraged rather than discouraged. The center of the discussion ought to be how to achieve wise forms of political engagement by religious communities and their members.

III. What Kind of Public Religion?

Sociologist of religion José Casanova addresses this question by providing several alternative models for the public presence of religion in our time. Like Kepel he concludes that religious communities are playing significantly different roles in social life today than was predicted for them by theories that identified modernization with across-the-board secularization. Casanova distinguishes three possible meanings of secularization: (1) the *decline of religion* in the modern world, which will continue until it finally disappears; (2) the *privatization of religion*, i.e., the displacement of the quest for salvation and personal meaning to the subjective sphere of the self, a displacement that renders religion irrelevant to the institutional functioning of modern society; (3) the functional *differentiation of the role of religion* from other spheres of human activity, primarily the state, the economy, and science.[23]

Casanova argues persuasively that the first two meanings of secularization are contrary to fact. Looked at worldwide, religion is not declining. In the

---

23   José Casanova, *Public Religions in the Modern World* (Chicago: University of Chicago Press, 1994), chap. 1. This account neglects the theoretical richness of Casanova's account for purposes of simplicity in this context.

United States the level of religious belief among the populace has declined somewhat over the past few decades, but it remains notably higher than in earlier periods of American history. Casanova argues that the thesis of the decline of religion is largely based on the experience of modern Western Europe and is not generalizable to other parts of the world. I would add that it is probably not even useful in the Paris of today, where it seems more Muslims attend Mosque on Friday than Catholics attend church on Sunday.

Secularization understood as the privatization of religion is also a factually questionable generalization in light of the religious involvement in public affairs already noted. Whether it is desirable to propose it as a normative objective can be questioned as well. Kepel has argued that the conservative religious movements discussed in *The Revenge of God* arise from the fact that many persons experience a growing malaise about the fragmentation of their social milieu. As sociologists since Durkheim have observed, this fragmentation pushes life-sustaining structures of meaning out of the shared realm of public experience into private zones. All values, especially those rooted in religion, become personal preferences. This seems unsatisfactory to adherents of the conservative religious movements who "complain about the fragmentation of society, its 'anomie,' the absence of an overarching ideal worthy of their allegiance."[24] Such complaints have arisen among the better-educated segments of their societies, especially among those with technical expertise. The adherents of these movements are children of modernity who have rejected the secularist ideology often associated with modernization but who employ the technical fruits of modern instrumental rationality. "They see no contradiction between their mastery of science and technology and their acceptance of a faith not bounded by the tenets of [technical] reason."[25] This later characteristic makes both the resurgence in the Islamic world and the new Christian right in the United States so effective in advocating their agendas through the electronic media and by other technological means. The pressure to treat religion as a purely private affair may thus be a source rather than a cure for the emergence of fundamentalist religion as a political force. If fundamentalism is normatively objectionable, as I hold it to be, normative recommendations that religion be kept private will be counterproductive.

One normative proposal for keeping religion private sometimes suggested today distinguishes spirituality from institutionalized religion. If modernity fragments social existence and acts as a solvent on meanings that provide purpose in life, perhaps the renewal of personal spiritual experience can knit up the raveled sleeve of society without the divisiveness that often accompanies institutional religious commitment. Once again, however, the empirical data suggest otherwise. Sociologist Robert Wuthnow's survey-based research

---

24 Kepel, *Revenge of God*, 4.

25 Ibid., 192.

has shown that, in the United States, people's concern with "spirituality" translates most readily into active civic engagement when this concern is lived out in the context of an organized religious community. When religion or spirituality is understood as a purely private affair between an individual and his or her god, without the mediation of a institutional religious community with a public presence in society, it has little effect on the level of civic voluntarism.[26] In particular, Wuthnow interprets survey data to suggest that religious inclinations have little or no influence on voluntary activity aimed at helping the needy unless one is involved in an organized religious community. When a religious person is involved in an organized church, however, higher levels of piety correlate with higher levels of sustained effort to respond to the needs of the poor and disadvantaged. This suggests that the *kind* of religion one practices is linked with both the level of one's civic involvement and form that involvement will take. In Wuthnow's view, the spread of individualistic religious styles that separate spirituality from institutional religious commitment are therefore likely to have a dampening effect on levels of civic voluntarism.[27] He also suggests that when individualistic religion does lead to political activism it is less likely to be the sort of activism concerned with the plight of the poor and the disadvantaged. This may in part explain why televangelism is linked with conservative politics in the United States today.[28] Praying alone, or in front of a television set, may be as apt an indicator of the decline of social capital in the United States as is bowling alone.[29] If one is seeking to strengthen civic life in a democracy, encouragement of secularization as the privatization of religion does not appear to be a fitting normative objective.

Casanova's third meaning of secularization—the differentiation of religion from the other spheres of public life such as the state—looks more promising however. Casanova fully supports the modern Western achievements of respect for religious and personal freedom. Thus he argues that any public role for religious communities must avoid a quest for hegemonic control of social, intellectual, and political life by religion. This raises the questions which I take to be central in a consideration of the contribution of religion to civic and political life today. Is it possible for religion to provide a sense of ultimate

---

26   Robert Wuthnow, *Acts of Compassion: Caring for Others and Helping Ourselves* (Princeton, N.J.: Princeton University Press, 1991), 156.

27   Ibid., 156.

28   See Jeffrey K. Hadden, "Religious Broadcasting and the Mobilization of the New Christian Right," *Journal for the Scientific Study of Religion* 26 (1987): 1–24.

29   Putnam's most recent writing hypothesizes that television is the prime suspect in his effort to identify the causes of declining civic participation in the U.S. today. See his "Tuning In, Tuning Out: The Strange Disappearance of Social Capital in America," esp. 677–81.

meaning and salvation that includes the meaning and hope we seek in political, economic and intellectual activity? Can this happen without religious truth claims becoming legitimations of political authoritarianism and intellectual obscurantism? If this cannot be done, religious efforts to identify and pursue the public rather than the private good will amount to attempts not only to question the sufficiency of modernity but to negate its achievements.

In other places I have outlined philosophical and theological arguments on how this task might be pursued.[30] Here I will stay within this essay's purpose of suggesting ways that some discussions of the question by social scientists may lend plausibility to those normative proposals. Casanova in particular has addressed the issue as a social analyst in a way that is particularly helpful. He argues that religious communities can play legitimate public roles in pluralist societies that value freedom in three ways. The first is by entering the public sphere to protect not only the freedom of religion of the church itself but in support of all modern freedoms and rights for believers and nonbelievers alike. Casanova cites the role of the Catholic Church in the process of democratization in Spain, Poland, and Brazil as illustrations of such a role. The second is by entering the public sphere "to question and contest the absolute lawful autonomy of the secular spheres and their claims to be organized . . . without regard to extraneous ethical or moral considerations." The United States Catholic Bishops' Pastoral Letters on strategic nuclear arms policy and on economic justice are cited as examples. The third is when a religious community enters public contestation "to protect the traditional life-world from administrative or juridical state penetration, and in the process opens up issues . . . to the public and collective self-reflection of modern discursive ethics." He cites the roles of the so-called Moral Majority and the Catholic moral stand on abortion and the right to life as examples, though I would add

---

30   See Hollenbach, "Religion, Morality, and Politics," *Theological Studies* 49 (1988): 68–89; "Religion and Political Life," *Theological Studies* 52 (1991): 87–106; "Fundamental Theology and the Christian Moral Life," in Leo J. O'Donovan and T. Howland Sanks, eds., *Faithful Witness: Foundations of Theology for Today's Church* (New York: Crossroad, 1989) 167–84; "Afterword: A Community of Freedom," in R. Bruce Douglass and D. Hollenbach, eds. *Catholicism and Liberalism: Contributions to American Public Philosophy*, (Cambridge University Press, 1994) 323–43; "Virtue, the Common Good, and Democracy," in Amitai Etzioni, ed., *New Communitarian Thinking: Persons, Virtues, Institutions, and Communities* (Charlottesville and London: University of Virginia Press, 1994) 143–53; "Contexts of the Political Role of Religion: Civil Society and Culture," *San Diego Law Review*" 30 (1994): 879–901; "Public Reason/Private Religion? A Response to Paul J. Weithman," *Journal of Religious Ethics* 22, no. 1 (1994): 39–46; "Freedom and Truth: Religious Liberty as Immunity and Empowerment," in *John Courtney Murray and the Growth of Tradition*, ed. J. Leon Hooper and Todd Whitmore (Kansas City, Mo.: Sheed and Ward, 1996), 129–48.

that these examples seem to indicate more of his aspiration for what the abortion debate could be like than what has in fact transpired in it.[31]

Casanova, in other words, is arguing for an active role of religion in public life on the level of the discourse that occurs in civil society rather than through religious control of the state. Religion can contribute to public life when it relies on civil discourse about the meaning and hope for our common existence rather than on the imposition of such meanings and hopes through the power of the state, the administrative bureaucracy, or the market. Such a proposal is based both on analysis of various possible public roles of religion provided by sociologists of religion today and on a normative vision of the importance of civil society as both the sphere of meaning-generation and as a crucial check on the growing power of states, administrative bureaucracies, and markets. It is a theory that has learned not only from the model of the Western revolutions in America and France but also from more recent revolutions in Eastern Europe where the ancien régime was avowedly secularist, even atheist, and from struggles in Latin America, where liberation from economic and authoritarian-political forms of oppression has been underway. In both Eastern Europe and Latin America (as well as in the Philippines, Korea, and South Africa) the public role of religion has in significant measure been pursued in ways that exemplify all three of Casanova's potential roles.

Such a role for activist churches is fully compatible with respect for religious freedom. Indeed it demands it. It rejects what Seyla Benhabib has called "integrationist communitarianism"—the effort to overcome social fragmentation, individualism, and alienation by reorganizing all of social life around a single integrating value scheme that denies or ignores the reality of pluralism.[32] When a religious vision and value orientation are reduced to a political agenda for the whole of public life, with no institutional space left for critique of that religious vision, suspicion of hegemonic intent is quite justified. In the Catholic community this is known as "integralism." It stresses the *unity* of religion, politics, the sciences, the economy, and the whole gamut of human endeavor. Considered positively, it manifests an instinct to see all things human as potential mediators of the divine presence and grace. This is an instinct rooted in the nature of religious belief as an all encompassing worldview through which believers enter into relationship with the God who is creator and lord of all that is. Negatively, however, it becomes perverse when this unity is interpreted to mean that all knowledge can be reduced to theology or that all social institutions ought to be extensions of the church. In the words of the eminent theologian Karl Rahner, it leads to a way of thinking that simply assumes that "human life can be unambiguously mapped out and manipu-

---

31   Casanova, *Public Religions*, 57–58.

32   Seyla Benhabib, *Situating the Self: Gender, Community and Postmodernism in Contemporary Ethics* (New York: Routledge, 1992), 77.

lated in accord with certain universal principles proclaimed by the church and watched over by her in the manner in which they are developed and applied."[33] This integralist or hegemonic approach was firmly rejected by the Catholic Church at the Second Vatican Council, which affirmed both the civil right to religious freedom for all persons as well as a legitimate autonomy of secular intellectual disciplines.[34]

Respect for religious freedom, however, does not require either the withering away of the church or the privatization of religion. Religious traditions and communities are among the principal bearers of the cultural sources for our understanding of the human good. They can evoke not only private self-understanding but public vision as well. Both believers and unbelievers alike have reason to risk considering what contribution religious traditions might make to our understanding of the public good. For a society to try to exclude such visions of the good life from public simply because they are identified with religion would be to impoverish itself both intellectually and culturally. This would deprive society of one of its most important resources for a more publicly shared self-understanding. Religious communities make perhaps their most important contribution to political life through this contribution to the formation of culture. If they seek to make this contribution through a dialogue of mutual listening and speaking with others in civil society, it will be fully congruent with the life of a free society.

Our options, therefore, are not restricted to self-assertion of group power by religious communities or the privatization of religion. Many of the discussions of the role of religion in public life today are driven by the fear that religion is fundamentally uncivil and that its presence in public life is a threat to liberty. Whether it be Kepel's suggestion that Khomeini and Falwell are paradigmatic of the public role of religion today or John Rawls's frequent suggestion that the wars of religion in the sixteenth and seventeenth centuries are the relevant historical memory, fear of religion as a public force shapes much of the discussion. On the other side of the argument are those who invoke figures like Abraham Lincoln, Martin Luther King, and Archbishop Oscar Romero of San Salvador to hold out more hopeful models. For such figures, religious convictions played a formative role in the contributions they made to freedom, equality, and democracy. These contributions were possible because they sought to make them in a way that was governed by the conditions necessary for all genuine conversation and mutual inquiry: pursuit of the truth and respect for the other in an atmosphere of freedom. Such

---

33 Karl Rahner, "Theological Reflections on the Problem of Secularization," *Theological Investigations*, vol. 10 (New York: Herder and Herder, 1973), 322.

34 See Vatican Council II, *Dignitatis Humanae (Declaration on Religious Freedom)*, no. 2, and *Gaudium et Spes* ("Pastoral Constitution on the Church in the Modern World"), no. 36, in Abbott and Gallagher, eds., *The Documents of Vatican II*.

conditions, rather than neatly drawn lines or high walls of separation, should determine the proper role of activist religious communities in a pluralistic and democratic society today.

Thus the analysis of the compatibility of public activism by churches with respect for religious freedom will be largely shaped by whether its guiding assumption is fear of abuse or hope for positive contributions by religious communities. As Robin Lovin puts it, do we conceive the relation of the religious and the political in terms of "the discourse to which we aspire" or of "the distortions that we fear"?[35] In this essay I have attempted to lay out a few considerations drawn from social analysis that make it plausible to aspire to positive contributions by the churches to public life. I have not here discussed the ways that religious belief and full respect for the religious liberty of all persons are compatible. A compelling case has been and must continue to be made for such compatibility. Those churches and religious communities that have fully internalized this synthesis of religion and the values of liberty are positioned to make a contribution to democracy that can help overcome the threats to it identified by Putnam. In my judgment, there can be little doubt that democracy in the United States is today in need of considerable help. My hope is that this essay might suggest ways that activist churches might contribute to "making democracy work."

---

35   Lovin, "Perry, Naturalism and Religion in Public," 1539.

Index

Editor's Note: Where a subject is mentioned in the text and in a footnote on the same page, I have not included the note as a separate entry. Page references for footnotes are to the pages of the accompanying text.

Abbott, Walter M., 305 n.34
Abolition, 4, 30, 152, 167, 214, 253, 291, 300
Abortion, 18, 32, 56, 60, 65, 67 n.43, 71, 119, 141–42, 148–51, 154, 210, 219, 222, 297, 299, 303–4
Abraham, 51 n.20, 52 n.21
Absolutism, 4, 258
Abu Bakar Siddiq v. A.B. Siddiq (Bangladesh), 116 n.68
Ackerman, Bruce, 53 n.23, 246 n.73
Adams, Robert M., 151 n.41, 156–58, 251
Adoption, 116, 125
Afghanistan, 117–18
African Methodist Episcopal Church, 267
Agape, 194, 201 n.26, 202, 206, 212 n.46
Agarwal, Bina, 114 n.65
Agudah, Justice, 115 n.66
Akbar, 104
Alberuni, 104
Alinsky, Saul, 266
Allah, 93, 104, 120
Alperovitz, Gar, 273
Amnesty International, 288
Anarchism, 144, 277
Andolsen, Barbara Hilkert, 202 n.27
Anti-Semitism, 127 n.96, 133, 158, 213
Antony, Louise, 229 n.28
Apartheid, 100, 167
Appleby, Scott, 1 n.2
Aquinas, St. Thomas, 54, 184,, 206–14, 245 n.72
Aquino, Corazon, 281
Arab Women's Solidarity Association, 112
Arato, Andrew, 27 n.47, 165 n.2, 167 n.4, 274 n.27, 275, 278, 289
Arendt, Hannah, 26, 254–61
Aristotle 55 n.24, 228 n.27, 256
Assembly rights, 40, 93, 99 n.22, 112, 127, 242. *See also* Human rights.

Attorney General v. Unity Dow (Botswana), 115 n.66
Audi, Robert, 3, 4, 13–15, 18, 22, 26, 29–32, 34–35, 39 n.2, 49 n.15, 53 n.23, 82, 139–45, 147 n.34, 153, 156 n.59, 160 n.67, 200 n.25, 205 n.32, 210 n.43, 246–47, 250, 293 n.7
Augustine, 220, 229, 238, 261
Authoritarianism, 291
Autonomy, 38, 53, 59, 67, 202, 210, 225, 237, 240

Bahá'í, 121
Bai, Metha, 105, 107, 110, 117 n.72
Baier, Annette, 188
Baird, Robert, 96 n.10
Bangladesh, 94, 98 n.18, 104, 105, 106, 108–11, 113–14, 116–17, 120, 122, 125
    Constitution of, 108
Bangladesh Rural Advancement Committee, 93–94, 136
Bano, Shah, 95, 96 n.10, 104 n.32, 116, 122, 125
Barnes, Fred, 84 n.21
Barth, Karl, 200
Basu, Kaushik, 96 n.10
Bauer, Gary, 267
Bayless, Judge, 130 n.102
Beatty, Maria, 233 n.40
Beauchamp, Thomas, 199 n.23
Becker, Mary, 100 n.23
Beckley, Harlan, 212 n.46
Beg, Mrs. Tara Ali, 117 n.71
Beijing Conference on the Status of Women, 99
Belgium, 259
Bell, Daniel, 287
Benhabib, Seyla, 304
Bentham, Jeremy, 237
Berger, Peter, 274 n.27
Berlin, Isaiah, 21 n.39, 219 n.4
Beschle, Donald L., 82 n.19

Bianchi, Eugene, 282 n.58
Bibi, Safia, 94
Blaine, James, 227 n.23
Bloom, Leopold, 127
Bob Jones University v. United States, 130
Bork, Robert, 84
Bosnia, 183
Botswana, 115, 126
Bourke, Vernon, 206 n.34
Bowers v. Hardwick (United States), 89
    n.34. *See also* Homosexuality.
Bowling, 294, 302
Boyte, Harry, 268, 270
Bradley, Gerald V., 64 n.39, 87 n.30
Bradwell v. Illinois (United States), 110
Brady, Henry, 29, 296–300
Braley, Alan, 292 n.5
Branch Davidians, 183
Brandenburg v. Ohio (United States), 131
    n.103
Brazil, 303
Bread for the World, 266, 287
Brennan, William, 84–85
Brinkley, Alan, 4 n.10
Brown, Peter, 262
Buckley, William, 272
Burger, Warren, 89
Burke, Tom, 266
Burkina Faso, 117
Burr, Aaron, 226 n.23
Bush, George, 272
Byron, (George Gordon), 186
Byron, Michael, 160 n.67

Cairo Conference on World Population,
    119
Caesar, 211
Cajetan, Thomas Cardinal, 260
Calvin, John, 200
Campbellites, 200
Canada, 126
Carter, Jimmy, 264
Carter, Stephen, 1 n.1, 53 n.23, 59 n.32,
    66 n.42, 73 n.50, 78, 80 n.11, 84–86,
    138–39, 177, 248 n.80
Casanova, José, 288–90, 300–304
Casey, Helen, 266
Caste, 100–105
Catholicism, 27, 30, 67 n.43, 78, 119,
    128, 200, 291 n.3, 292, 295
Catholic Church, 130–31, 141, 235 n.44,
    260, 282 n.58, 291, 299–300, 305

Chagla, M. C., 124, 127
Chandrachud, Chief Justice, 95
Chen, Martha, 93, 94 n.4, 105 n.36–38,
    107, 110–12, 114 n.65, 117 n.72, 118,
    134 n.108, 137 n.112
Chicoine v. Chicoine (United States), 81–
    83, 90
Childress, James, 199 n.23
China, People's Republic of, 95, 98 n.18,
    104, 105 n.36, 106, 110, 112, 117
Christian Environmental Council, 180
Christianity, 25, 46, 48–49, 54, 68, 89,
    100, 104, 122 n.85, 159 n.66, 160, 179,
    183–84, 211, 213, 256, 264, 267
Chulalongkorn University, 129 n.99
*Church of Jesus Christ of Latter-Day
    Saints v. United States*, 89 n.33
Churches, 14, 29, 31, 36, 38, 63–70, 167
    n.4, 178, 265–67, 282 n.58, 285–90,
    294, 297–300, 304, 306
Cioffi, Ron, 266
Citizenship, 3, 7, 11–13, 28–29, 34, 42–
    47, 63-69, 74, 137, 141, 144, 146, 160,
    264, 269, 278, 284–85
City of Milwaukee v. Wilson, 81 n.12
Civic democracy, 27–33, 36
Civic friendship, 5, 33–34, 151, 249
Civic republicanism, 10 n.13, 28 n.51,
    198, 294–95
Civic virtue, 2, 14–15, 26–33, 43, 48–54,
    60, 62–63, 71, 74–75, 296
Civil rights, 4, 30, 32, 152, 167, 253, 280–
    81, 287, 292, 297, 300
Civil society, 28–33, 36, 67 n.43, 145
    n.24, 264, 267–90, 294–96, 304–5. *See
    also* Secondary associations.
Civility, 4, 6–7, 12, 19, 22, 26–27, 31, 33–
    36, 147–52, 159, 172 n.8, 180, 182,
    197, 211, 215–16
Cleveland, Harlan, 89
Cleveland v. United States, 89 n.32
Clinton, Bill, 83–84, 87
Cochin Christian Succession Act (In-
    dia), 114
Cohen, Jean, 27 n.47, 165 n.2, 167 n.4,
    274 n.27, 275, 278, 289
Cohen, Joshua, 29 n.54, 36 n.59, 61 n.37
Coleman, James, 294 n.9
Coleman, John, 16, 27–36, 277 n.39, 282
    n.58
Communio e Liberazione, 292
Confucius, 95

Confucianism, 95, 105
Conscience, liberty of. *See* Human rights; Religious liberty.
Conscientious objection, 40 n.5, 41
Conscription, 48
Constant, Benjamin, 218
Contraception, 17, 118–19, 125, 134, 219
Convention on the Elimination of All Forms of Discrimination Against Women, 98, 102, 114–15, 126, 133
Cook, Rebecca, 95 n.5, 102 n.26
Coomaraswamy, Radhika, 95 n.5, 106 n.41 and 43
Columbia University, 110 n.54
Cox, Harvey, 291 n.1
Creationism, 57
Crocker, D., 101 n.25
Crombie, Frederick, 206 n.33
Crozier, Michael, 271–72
Cuba, 117
Culler, Jonathan, 78
Culture of Disbelief. See Carter, Stephen.

Dahl, Robert, 10 n.13
Das, Veena, 96 n.10
Daly, Lois, 202 n.27
Darwin, Charles, 170
De Marneffe, Peter, 150 n.38
Decalogue, 43–44, 45 n.11, 51 n.19
Declaration of Independence, 73 n.51, 218, 249 n.83, 258
Delaney, C. F., 160 n.67
Denmark, 113
Deontology, 187
Descartes, Rene, 257
Dewey, John, 59 n.33, 242 n.61
DeYoung, Rebecca Konyndyk, 37 n.60
Divorce, 81–83, 100, 112, 115, 125, 128, 267
Dobson, James, 267
Domestic violence, 107
Donaldson, James, 206 n.33
Douglas, William O., 89–90
Douglass, R. Bruce, 34 n.58, 303 n.30
Draupadi, 103
Drewery, Benjamin, 260 n.16
Drèze, J., 103 n.27, 105 n.35, 106 n.44, 107 n.45, 117 n.73, 117 n.75, 118 n.77
DuBois, Paul, 287
Dugger, Cecilia W., 136 n.111
Dulles, Avery, 239 n.49
Durkheim, Emile, 301

Dutt, Madhusudhan, 134 n.107
Dworkin, Ronald, 10, 88, 218, 241

Education rights, 117–19, 126–27
Egypt, 109 n.53, 112, 114
El Salvador, 66 n.42
Elshtain, Jean Bethke, 16, 26, 64 n.39, 261 n.19, 270, 273, 274 n.28, 281
Engineer, Asghar Ali, 96 n.10, 125
England, 286
Enlightenment, 4, 77, 177, 182, 185, 205, 208, 242 n.61
Entanglement, 41
Epstein, Richard, 10 n.13
Eritrea, 109 n.53
Establishment Clause, 82 n.19, 87, 129, 160, 165. *See also* United States, Constitution of.
Estlund, David, 10 n.13, 13 n.28
Ethiopia, 109 n.53
Ethnicity, 183
Etzioni, Amitai, 303 n.30
Evans, Peter, 270 n.19
Evans, Sarah, 270
Evans v. Romer (United States), 130 n.102

Fallibilism, 47, 155
Falwell, Jerry 305
Family law, 100, 107, 109, 115, 122. *See also* Adoption; Bano, Shah; *Chicoine v. Chicoine*; Divorce; Hindu Adoptions and Maintenance Act; Hindu Guardianship and Minority Act; Hindu Marriage Act; Indian Adoption Bill; Inheritance rights; and Personal Law for Muslims Act.
Family Research Council, 267
Fatwah, 112, 131
Faux, Jeff, 273 n.25
Federal Shariat Court (Pakistan), 44
Feinberg, Joel, 219 n.4, 224–25
Feinsilber, Mike, 271 n.21
Female genital mutilation, 17, 107, 109–10, 133, 135–36
Fichte, J. G., 245
Finland, 113
Finnis, John, 245 n.72
Fish, Stanley, 232 n.37
Flannery, Austin, O.P., 7 n.11
Focus on the Family, 267
Forey, M., 121 n.84
Foucault, Michel, 82, 281

Foundationalism, 19, 77, 170, 189, 192, 199, 208
France, 113, 301, 304
Free Exercise Clause, 129 n.101. *See also* United States, Constitution of.
Freeman, Marsha, 111 n.59, 115 n.66
Freud, Sigmund, 194, 236
Friday, Nancy, 234
Frug, Gerald, 64 n.39
Fuller, Millard, 264, 265 n.4, 288
Fundamentalism, 1, 67 n.43, 89, 103–4, 155, 259 n.12, 292, 301

Gallagher, Joseph, 305 n.34
Galston, William, 34 n.58, 195
Gambia, 109 n.53
Gandhi, Mahatma, 103
Gandhi, Rajiv, 96, 106, 125
Garcia, Jorge, 16, 23, 25–26, 34
Gardner, J., 121 n.84
Gates, Margaret, 286 n.68
Gauthier, David, 9 n.12
Genocide, 183
Germany, 113 n.64, 133, 167, 259
Gewirth, Alan, 184
Glover, Jonathan, 101 n.25, 119n,81
Goa, 114
Goodmann, Len, 52 n.22, 75 n.53
Goerner, H. C., 212 n.45
Goldfarb, Jeffrey, 271
Golding, Martin, 160 n.67
Gore, Albert, 82–83, 87–88
Gowans, Christopher W., 191 n.10
Graham, Gordon, 73 n.50
Grant, Ulysses, 226 n.23
Grasso, Kenneth L., 64 n.39
Gray, John, 9 n.12
Great Britain, 113 n.64, 121–22, 133
Greenawalt, Kent, 16, 51 n.19, 53 n.23, 73 n.49, 74 n.52, 75 n.53, 78 n.8, 80, 83–87, 91–92, 143–44, 154, 293 n.7,
Grisez, Germain, 245 n.72
Gustafson, James, 75 n.53
Gutmann, Amy, 247 n.76
Guyana, 113, 117

Habermas, Jürgen, 22 n.40, 61 n.37, 151 n.39, 218, 247 n.79, 268, 283
Habitat for Humanity, 264–65, 288
Hadden, Jeffrey, 302 n.28
Halim, Asma Mohamed Abdel, 112 n.61
Hamlin, Alan, 29 n.54

Hampton, Jean, 61 n.37, 150 n.38, 160 n.67
Hart, Gary, 226 n.23
Harvard University, 100
Hasan, Zoya, 125
Hauerwas, Stanley, 178 n.11, 182
Havel, Vaclav, 269, 272
Hegel, G.W.F., 192
Henderson, Justice, 81–84, 87–88, 90
Herbert of Cherbury, 182
Herman, Barbara, 24 n.41, 229
Herod, 211
Hill, Anita, 91
Hindu Adoptions and Maintenance Act (India), 116
Hindu Guardianship and Minority Act (India), 116 n.69
Hindu Marriage Act (India), 97, 108
Hinduism, 97, 103, 105
Hobbes, Thomas, 256
Hodgkinson, Virginia, 286 n.68
Hoffman et al. v. Officer of the Western Wall (Israel), 97 n.17
Hollenbach, David, 16, 27–33, 35–36, 67 n.43, 292 n.6, 295 n.7
Holocaust, 183
Homer, 185
Homosexuality, 67 n.43, 81–83, 89, 219, 226 n.23, 239
Hooper, J. Leon, s.j., 303 n.30
Hossain, Sara, 108 n.51, 116 n.68
Human rights, 17, 39 n.3, 93–94, 98–99, 101, 102, 112 n.61, 113, 120–21, 124, 126, 133–34, 187, 222, 224, 227, 245. *See also* Universal Declaration of Human Rights.
Hume, David, 199
Hunt, Robert P., 64 n.39
Huntington, Samuel, 292
Hussain, Chowdry Hyder, 124
Hutcheson, Francis, 194
Hutter, Reinhard, 260 n.17

Idleman, Scott C., 80 n.11, 81
Immigration and Naturalization Service (United States), 136
Incarnation, 207, 209, 214, 257
India, 95, 98 n.18, 103, 104–6, 108–9, 11–14, 116–19, 122–24, 127–28, 134, 136
    Constitution of, 95, 96 n.12, 122, 123–25
    Parliament of, 97, 106, 127

Supreme Court of, 95, 108, 125–26
Indian Adoption Bill, 116
Indian Council for Child Welfare, 116
Indian Succession Act, 114
Individualism, 182. *See also* Autonomy.
Infallibility, 58
Infanticide, 104
Inheritance rights, 114
Internal Revenue Service (United States), 130
Iran, 97, 98 n.18, 103–7, 110–11, 113–14, 117–18, 121, 292
Isaac, 51 n.20
Islam, 68, 94, 103 n.31, 104, 105, 108–10, 112, 119, 122 n.85
    Islamic Law, 95, 97, 107, 111, 114–16, 125
    Islamic Personal Law, 95
Ismail, Mohammed, 123 n.86
Israel, 97, 100, 113, 119, 122, 125–26, 128, 132 n.104, 292
    Supreme Court of, 97
Italy, 208, 292, 295–96

Jackson, Timothy, 16, 23–25, 26, 32, 34, 75 n.53, 187 n.6, 205 n.32, 212 n.46, 213 n.47, 292 n.6
Jacobs, Jonathan, 72 n.47
Jaising, Indira, 107 n.47
Jamaica, 113
James, William, 260
Japan, 113 n.64
Jay, Sara, 272 n.24
Jefferson, Thomas, 138, 165
Jerusalem, 97, 118, 126
Jesus, 24–25, 42–43, 44 n.8, 45 n.11, 54, 69, 82, 182, 201, 203, 207, 209, 237, 240, 244, 256, 288
John of Salisbury, 255
John the Evangelist, 203 n.29, 260
John Paul II, Pope, 25, 98–99, 101, 134, 239–46, 285. *See also* Wojtyla, Karol.
Jonestown, 183
Jordan, Jeff, 160 n.67
Joyce, James, 127
Judaism, 25, 46, 48–49, 68, 95 n.6, 97, 100, 104
Judicial review, 126

Kabir, 104
Kama Sutra, 103
Kant, Immanuel, 6–7, 10–11, 24, 51 n.20,

59, 185, 193, 211, 216, 221, 229, 237, 239, 250
Kanwar, Roop, 106, 131
Kelly, George Armstrong, 259 n.11
Kelsay, John, 135 n.109
Kennedy, J.B., 160 n.67
Kepel, Gilles, 292, 300, 305
Kerala, 114
Khomeini, the Ayatollah, 131 n.103, 292, 305
Khory, Kavita, 96 n.10, 104 n.32
Kiernan, Barney, 127 n.96
King, Martin Luther, 152, 204 n.30, 205, 214, 305
King, Rodney, 267
Kirch, Arthur, 286 n.68
Koran, 116
Korea, 113 n.64, 304
Kourany, Janet, 160 n.67
Kraut, Richard, 160 n.67
Kymlicka, Will, 126–28, 282 n.58

Langan, John, S.J., 9 n.12, 292 n.6
Lappe, Francis Moore, 287
Larmore, Charles, 3, 10, 158 n.65, 188 n.9, 196 n.16, 201 n.26
Leland, John, 211 n.44
Lemon v. Kurtzmann (United States), 41 n.6
Levinson, Sanford, 15–16, 18, 76 n.1, 78 n.7, 84 n.23, 156
Lewis, James, 267 n.8
Lewis, Stephanie, 160 n.67
Li, Xiarong, 105 n.36
Lincoln, Abraham, 120 n.82, 305
Literacy, 117–18
Locke, John, 19, 163–64, 168–70, 218
Lofland, John, 287
Lovin, Robin, 293, 306
Luke the Evangelist, 25 n.43, 203
Lukes, Steven, 264 n.2
Luther, Martin, 256, 260–61

Machiavelli, Niccolò, 194
MacIntyre, Alasdair, 37 n.60, 160 n.67
Madonna, 182
Mahmood, Tahir, 96 n.10, 96 n.12, 116–17, 123 n.86, 124 n.88, 125, 136
Mainwaring, Scott, 270
Mali, 109 n.53
Mansfield, John H., 96 n.10, 96 n.11
Mara, Gerald, 34 n.58

Marcos, Ferdinand, 281
Marcuse, Herbert, 236
Marilley, Suzanne 160 n.67
Marital rape, 17, 99, 107–8, 120, 133
Marshall, John, 86
Marshall, T.H., 294–95
Martin, David, 285 n.66
Marty, Martin, 1 n.2
Marullo, Sam, 287 n.70
Matthew the Evangelist, 24 n.42, 69, 203 n.29, 205 n.32
Mayer, Ann Elizabeth, 111 n.60, 112 nn.62–63
Mazumdar, Vina, 119 n.81
McCann, Hugh, 75 n.53
MacFarquhar, Larissa, 234 n.43
McGary, Howard, 218 n.1
McInerny, Ralph, 64 n.39
McNeal, Patricia, 266 n.7
Meeker, Kevin, 160 n.67
Metz, John Baptiste, 268
Michnik, Adam, 268
Mill, John Stuart, 73 n.51
Miller, Eugene, 199 n.23
Miller, Fred D., Jr., 188 n.9
Mimaya, Lawrence, 267 n.8
Misogyny, 103–4
Mirhosseini, Akram, 97 n.15, 110 nn.55–56, 118 n.78
Model Penal Code, 131–32
Modernity, 182, 257, 263, 275, 283, 289, 301, 303
Moghadam, Valentine, 105 n.36, 118 n.76
Mohammed, 109 n.52
Moore, G.E., 224 n.18
Moral dilemmas, 190–91, 193, 205
Moral Majority, 292, 303
Moses, 43, 45 n.11, 69
Mother Theresa, 62
Mothersill, Mary, 160 n.67
Murphy, Frank, 89
Murphy, Mark, 37 n.60
Murray, John Courtney, S.J., 11, 27, 134, 136, 303 n.30
Muslim Women's Act, 96
Mutahari, the Ayatollah, 110
Mutual respect, 4–5, 8, 12, 18, 22, 34, 75

Nagel, Thomas, 10, 25, 77–79, 188, 220–39, 241–44, 252
Nasrin, Taslima, 112

Nationalism, 21 n.39, 22, 166–67, 177–78, 180, 183, 276–77
Natural law, 54, 78, 210
Natural theology, 43, 58 n.30
Nazis, 64, 93, 133, 158 n.65, 159 n.66, 210 n.43
Nehru, Jawaharlal, 103 n.29
Nelly Zaman v. Ghiyasuddin, (Bangladesh) 108 n.51
Netanyahu, Benzion 183 n.1
Netherlands, 57 n.29, 113, 143
Neuhaus, Richard John, 232 n.37, 274 n.27
Neutrality, 39, 40–42, 64–70, 71, 74–75, 165–66, 177, 179, 246
New School for Social Research, 274 n.27
Nicaragua, 113
Nietzche, Friedrich, 185, 194, 229 n.29, 249 n.83
Nixon, Richard M. 226 n.23
Norman, Waynew, 282 n.58
Norway, 113
Norwood v. Harrison (United States), 130
Nozick, Robert, 184 n.3, 197 n.19
Nussbaum, Martha, 16–18, 101 n.25, 105 n.35, 119 n.81, 120 n.83, 121 n.84, 160 n.67, 191 n.10

O'Connor, David, 160 n.67
O'Donnell, Guillermo, 270 n.19
O'Donovan, Leo, S.J., 303 n.30
O'Keefe, Georgia, 244 n.69
O'Mahoney, Joseph, 84–85
O'Neil, Michael, 272 n.24, 286 n.67
Origen, 184, 206–13
Other minds, problem of, 257
Outka, Gene, 157 n.60

Pacific Institute for Community Organizing, 265
Pacifism, 153, 251
Pakistan, 94, 98 n.18, 104, 106, 107, 113–14, 117, 121, 122 n.85
Participation, 14–15, 26–33, 48, 93, 112–13, 139, 146, 154, 218, 222, 242, 258, 266, 282 n.58, 293–300
Pascal, Blaise, 82
Paul the Apostle, 182, 195, 202, 203 n.29
Paul, Ellen Frankel, 188 n.9
Paul, Jeffrey, 188 n.9
Pax Christi, 266, 279 n.49, 287

Pelagianism, 205
Perfectionist liberalism, 183–84, 195–99,
    201 n.26, 208–9
Perot, Ross, 274
Perry, Michael, 18, 61 n.37, 75 n.53, 76
    n.1, 79, 145 n.23, 154–58, 160 n.67,
    293 n.7, 306 n.35
Perry, Ralph Barton, 219 n.4
Personal Law for Muslims Act (Sudan),
    111, 115
Peters, Julie, 97 n.15
Pettit, Philip, 29 n.54
Philippines, 304
Pius XI, Pope, 295
Plato, 185, 217, 256
Pluralism, 4–5, 7, 18, 33, 41, 48, 155,
    182–83, 188–95, 200–13, 246, 248. *See
    also* Religious pluralism.
Pluralistic democracy, 9, 10 n.13, 29
Poggi, Gianfranco, 282
Pohl, Rinaldo Galindo, 97 n.16
Poland, 268, 303
Political capital, 34, 36. *See also* Social
    capital.
Polyandry, 103, 115
Polygamy, 89–90, 97, 115
Pontius Pilate, 209
Popenoe, David, 230 n.31
Portuguese Civil Code (Goa), 114
Posner, Richard, 137 n.113
Postmodernism, 182, 185, 205, 208, 213
Privatization of religion, 1–3, 5, 21–23,
    35, 139, 238, 288, 300–302. *See also*
    Secularization.
Public forum (including political
    sphere; public square), 8–9, 13, 22–
    23, 33, 35, 38–75 *passim.*, 80, 139, 146,
    152, 154, 157, 159, 162–63, 166, 177–
    79, 212–17, 246–52, 289–92, 303
Putnam, Robert, 29, 271, 275, 282, 283–
    84, 286, 293–96, 298–300, 302 n.29,
    306

Quinn, Philip, 16, 18–19, 21 n.38, 23, 26,
    32, 34, 55 n.25, 75 n.53, 138 n.1, 205
    n.32, 210 n.42, 246, 248 n.81
Quinn, Warren, 222

Racism, 68, 158, 204 n.30, 222
Rahner, Karl, 304–5
Ram, 104
Ramseyer, Mark, 137 n.112

Rawls, John, 3, 4, 9, 10 n.13, 11–13, 15–
    24, 27, 32-6, 37 n.60, 47 n.12, 53 n.23,
    61 n.37, 73 n.50, 77, 79, 93 n.2, 98–99,
    100 n.24, 101, 119, 120, 134, 136, 145–
    54, 160 n.67, 164, 167, 168, 170–77,
    179, 180 n.12, 183, 187, 195 n.14, 196–
    99, 206, 209–17, 218 n.3, 242 n.61,
    247–50, 253–54, 292–93, 305
Raz, Joseph, 77, 79
Reagan, Ronald, 66 n.42
Reeder, John P., Jr., 157 n.60
Reflective equilibrium, 21, 46. *See also*
    Theo-ethical equilibrium,
Reformation, 5, 26
Reich, Wilhelm, 236
Reinders, Hans, 160 n.67
Relativism, 182, 207, 213, 223
Religious authority, 26, 43, 67 n.43, 74,
    79, 139, 141, 153, 260
Religious experience, 43–44, 74, 301
Religious liberty, 6, 17, 25, 38–40, 68, 93–
    94, 98, 99 n.22, 113–14, 121, 123, 125,
    130–31, 140, 241-3, 285, 302, 305–6
Religious obligation, 42–48
Religious pluralism, 1, 6–8, 25, 182, 184
Religious Right, 1, 159–60, 292
Religious toleration, 6–7, 11–12, 15, 33,
    104, 165
Reproductive rights, 118–19. *See also*
    Abortion; Contraception.
Reston, James, 76
Reuther, Rosemary, 282 n.58
Reyes-Ortiz, Judy, 266
Reynolds v. United States, 90
Richards, David A. J., 3, 30 n.55, 78, 168
    n.5, 227 n.25, 242 n.62
Richardson, Henry, 34 n.58
Roberts, Alexander, 206 n.33
Rodes, Robert, 160 n.67
Roe v. Wade (United States), 142. *See also*
    Abortion.
Rogers, Joel, 36 n.59
Roman Catholic Church. *see* Catholic
    Church.
Romero, Oscar, 305
Roosevelt, Franklin D., 219, 221
Rorty, Richard, 3–4, 24, 77, 138–39, 160
    n.67, 179, 184, 187 n.6
Rosen, Charles, 229 n.29, 234 n.43
Rousseau, Jean-Jacques, 6, 10, 278
Roy, Mary, 114, 126
Rupp, E.G., 260 n.16

Rushdie, Salman, 112, 131 n.103
Ryan, Alan, 242 n.61

Sade, the Marquis de, 229 n.29, 233—34
Safire, William, 268
Saheb, Pocker, 123 n.86
Sandel, Michael, 242 n.61
Sanks, T. Howland, 303 n.30
Santurri, Edmund, 191 n.10, 202 n.28
T. Sareetha v. T. Venkata Subhaiah (India),
    108
Satha-Anand, Suwanna, 129 n.99
Sati, 106, 132
Saudi Arabia, 98 n.18, 100, 111–13, 117,
    127 n.93
Schervich, Paul, 286 n.68
Schmitter, Philippe, 270 n.19
Scholzmann, Kay Lehman, 29, 296–300
Scott, Diane, 265 n.4
Seaver, Richard, 229 n.29, 233 n.38
Secondary associations, 3, 26, 28–30, 36.
    See also Civil society.
Secularization, 3, 23, 285 n.66, 292, 300–
    303, 305 n.33. *See also* Privatization
    of religion.
Seidman, L. M., 131 n.103
Seligman, Adam, 279 n.48
Selznick, Philip, 275 n.29
Sen, Amartya, 96 n.10, 96, nn.12–13, 103
    n.27–29, 104 n.33, 105 n.35, 106 n.39–
    44, 107 n.45, 117 n.73 and 75, 118
    n.77, 119 n.79, 123 n.87, 134 n.107,
    136, 137 n.112
Sen, Kshiti Mohan, 104 n.34
Seneca, 205
Separation of church and state, 39, 42,
    63–70, 74, 121–22, 152, 165–66, 176,
    285, 289–90
Sesardic, Nevan, 160 n.67
Shakespeare, William, 134
Shalev, Carmel, 97 n.17
Shariat Act (India), 96 n.10
Shattuck, Roger, 229 n.29
Sherbert v. Warner (United States), 129
    n.101
Sherry, Suzanna, 78
Shklar, Judith, 184, 285
Sima, Vern, 56 n.27
Simon, Arthur, 266 n.6, 286
Simon, Paul, 266 n.6
Singer, Irving, 185 n.5

Singh, Kirti, 96 n.10, 97 n.14, 108 nn.49–
    50, 116 n.69
Slavery, 86 n.28, 89. *See also* Abolition.
Smith, Adam, 194, 208
Smolin, David M., 155
Social capital, 27, 29, 32, 283, 294–95.
    See also Political capital.
Solomon, David, 13 n.28, 37 n.60
Solum, Lawrence, 72 n.47, 156 n.59
Somalia, 109 n.53
Sorabji, Cornelia, 111, 118
South Africa, 100, 113, 136, 167, 304
Spain, 93, 303
Speech, freedom of, 93, 218, 226, 242.
    See also Human rights.
Stackhouse, Max, 183 n.2
State of Bomba v. Narasu Appa (India),
    123
Steiner, George, 199
Stepan, Alfred, 270 n.19
Sterba, James, 249 n.84
Stewart, Potter, 129 n.101
Stone, Geoffrey, 100 n.23, 131 n.103
Stout, Jeffrey, 143 n.18, 257
Strauss, David, 137 n.112
Stump, Eleonore, 160 n.67
Subrahmanyam, Sanjay, 96 n.10
Subsidiarity, 212, 295
Sudan, 98 n.18, 109 n.53, 110 n.54, 111,
    112 n.61, 114–15, 117, 121
Sunstein, Cass, 10 n.13, 21 n.37, 28 n.51,
    119 n.80, 131 n.103, 132 n.105, 132
    n.112
Supervenience, 50–51
Sweden, 113

Tagore, Rabindranath, 104 n.34
Taxation, 65, 267
Taylor, Charles, 194
Ten Commandments. *See* Decalogue.
Thailand, 128
Theism, 42 n.7, 49, 53 n.22, 54, 72 n.47
Theo-ethical equilibrium, 14, 52–54, 62–
    63, 71–72
"Theology of the hammer," 264. *See also*
    Habitat for Humanity.
Theonomy, 240
Thomas, Clarence, 84, 90–91
Thompson, Dennis, 247 n.76
Tinker, Irene, 106 n.39
Tocqueville, Alexis de, 27, 258–59, 271–
    72, 282, 286

Togo, 136
Tolerance, 182. *See also* Religious liberty.
Tomka, Miklos, 277 n.39
Torah, 97
Toubia, Nahid, 109 nn.52–53, 110 n.54
Travancore Christian Act (India), 114, 126
Trinidad and Tobago, 113
Trobriand Islanders, 190
Trust, 15, 29, 33, 269, 271–72, 282–83
Tushnet, Mark, 131 n.103
Twiss, Sumner B., 135 n.109

Unitarianism 59 n.33
United Nations, 98, 134, 217, 241
United States, 25–26, 77 ff., 98 n.18, 99, 102, 113 n.64, 119, 126, 128 n.97, 133, 144, 153, 159–60, 163, 171, 177, 208, 212, 217, 254, 268, 271–72, 283, 286, 296–300, 306
   Constitution of, 16, 85, 87–88, 99, 113, 133, 160, 165, 180 n.13
   Supreme Court of, 79, 84–85, 90–92, 129 nn.100–101, 130, 131 n.103, 215
United States v. Seger, 129 n.100
Universal Declaration of Human Rights, 98–99
University of Notre Dame, 131, 182
University of Southern California, 182
Utilitarianism, 187, 193

Van Roojen, Mark, 75 n.53
Van Wyk, Robert, 73 n.50
Vatican II, 7 n.11, 291 n.3, 299, 305
Verba, Sidney, 29, 296–300
Verma, Roop Rekha, 103 n.31, 105 n.36
Virginia v. Rosenberger (United States), 166 n.3
Virtue, 25–26, 54–55, 225. *See also* Civic virtue.
Voting, 10 n.13, 20, 28, 42, 48, 80, 146, 154, 172, 175–76, 218, 220 n.6, 283, 296
Voucher system, 41 n.6, 57

Wainhouse, Austryn, 229 n.29, 233 n.38
Wainwright, William, 200 n.25, 205 n.32
Waldman, Amy, 292 n.1
Waldron, Jeremy, 4 n.9, 156, 158, 199 n.22
Walters. Laura Sharper, 57 n.29
Walzer, Michael, 28 n.50, 185, 187, 194, 203, 206, 275–78, 285
Wars of Religion, 1, 3–4, 12, 144, 182, 305
Watkins, Michelle, 64 n.39
Weakness of will, 220, 251
Weithman, Paul J., 20 n.36, 68 n.44, 72 n.47, 75 n.53, 137 n.112, 160 n.67, 212 n.46, 214, 215 n.48, 218 n.1, 243 n.63, 246 n.23, 292 n.6, 303 n.30
Weitzman, Murray, 286 n.68
Welfare, 65, 67
Werpohowski, William, 202 n.28
Westerhoff, John H., 178 n.11
Whitmore, Todd David, 303 n.30
Wilde, Oscar, 275
Williams, Armstrong, 90
Willis, Jessica, 233 n.40
Wind, James, 267 n.8
Witt, Charlotte, 229 n.28
Witte, John, Jr., 183 n.2, 211 n.44
Wittgenstein, Ludwig, 60
Wojtyla, Karol, 239, 244, 248 n.80, 268. *See also* John Paul II, Pope.
Wolfe, Alan, 282
Wolfe, Christopher, 64 n.39
Wolin, Sheldon, 254
Wolper, Andrea, 97 n.15
Wolterstorff, Nicholas, 16, 19–23, 30, 32, 34–35, 75 n.53, 168 n.6, 246 n.73, 249 n.83
Wuthnow, Robert, 163, 265, 302

Yantra, Phra, 129
Young, Brigham, 89

Zina Ordinance (Pakistan), 94
Zionism, 292